Beyond the Creative Species

Beyond the Creative Species

Making Machines That Make Art and Music

Oliver Bown

The MIT Press
Cambridge, Massachusetts
London, England

© 2021 Massachusetts Institute of Technology

All rights reserved. No part of this book may be reproduced in any form by any electronic or mechanical means (including photocopying, recording, or information storage and retrieval) without permission in writing from the publisher.

This book was set in Stone Serif and Stone Sans by Westchester Publishing Services. Printed and bound in the United States of America.

Library of Congress Cataloging-in-Publication Data

Names: Bown, Ollie, author.
Title: Beyond the creative species : making machines that make art and music / Oliver Bown.
Description: Cambridge, Massachusetts : The MIT Press, [2021] | Includes bibliographical references and index.
Identifiers: LCCN 2020017931 | ISBN 9780262045018 (hardcover)
Subjects: LCSH: Technology and the arts. | Arts--Technological innovations.
Classification: LCC NX180.T4 B68 2021 | DDC 700.1/05--dc23
LC record available at https://lccn.loc.gov/2020017931

10 9 8 7 6 5 4 3 2 1

Contents

Preface   vii

I   Questions

    1   Inklings   3
    2   Coming to Terms with Creative Machines   43

II   Humans

    3   Creativity and Culture   73
    4   Artistic Behavior   111

III   Machines

    5   Creative Algorithms   157
    6   Putting Computational Creativity to Work   215

IV   Impacts

    7   Making Creative Systems Effective   269
    8   Speculative Futures   295

Notes   323
References   365
Index   391

Preface

This book is about the practice, the technology, and the deeper implications of the automation of creative tasks in artistic domains. It was written primarily to provide a broad introduction to the field—which is in fact really a cluster of different fields that come together to inform this fascinating topic. It is aimed first and foremost at professionals working in creative industries who want to understand how their field might be influenced by technological advances in the automation of cognitive tasks, some part of which involves cutting through the noise we find today around the impact of AI, whichever the area. As such it is also aimed more generally at anyone interested in learning more about this area of exciting and rapid development. This bringing together of different fields, from AI, design, social theory, the psychology of creativity, creative practice research, and elsewhere, also gives the book a secondary function, to collate the breadth of relevant ideas and their interconnections in a way that may be useful for experts in any specific one of these subdisciplines. It may be especially useful for engineers and data scientists unfamiliar with work in social, psychological, and creative domains, perhaps offering some common language and reference points that can be used to work across the richly multidisciplinary communities that must come together to work in this field.

As such, this book is unashamedly jack-of-all-trades-master-of-none. Most importantly, it is only partly about the technology and what it can do. To narrow the topic to just this question would be hopelessly lacking in context; every engineer respects the importance of understanding a problem clearly before you can solve it. The question of how to make convincing or effective creative algorithmic systems is a core theme. But to answer this question merely from the perspective of algorithms, or even combining algorithms and cognitive science, is insufficient. I am certainly not the first person to stress in this context that human creative artistic activities are not only social in important ways but *primarily* social. This is probably the majority view. But exactly how creative practice is best viewed through a social lens remains more than a little bit challenging. To understand in any depth what people are doing (and why) when they create, and hence understand what the technical challenges are, is at least as vexing as those technical challenges themselves. This book aims to provide informed discussion across this spectrum of topics and may seem to do so sometimes at the expense of depth or coherence. There is no subject covered in this book that couldn't have been given more time and detail. The book's reviewers were thorough in pointing out omissions of work that they themselves considered important in their respective fields of specialist interest. I addressed some of these omissions, but I did not labor each subject exhaustively where I felt that the underlying idea had been covered.

Having thought about this subject for many years, situated in different university departments and talking with people from very different walks of life, I feel certain that covering such broad ground can be done equally well from a wide number of starting points and, for each starting point, looking in many different directions. There is no obvious order of events, and my choice of structure is undoubtedly grounded in various biases and niches of interest I have accumulated from researching computational creativity in those contexts I have encountered it, from anthropology to the science of artificial life, to music psychology, design, and creative practice research. For practical reasons, this book has a broad arc, starting and ending in more accessible and broad discussion, while digging deeper into academic depth toward the middle of the book. Its progression through the psychology of creativity, social creativity, the arts, algorithms, design, evaluation, and social impacts follows the narrative that I feel is most relevant but is certainly not the only possibility.

I have also tried not to become trapped by the shackles of one academic filter bubble over another, so wherever possible—and it has not always been easy—I've tried to talk in plain language and maintain some skepticism about the limits of respective fields. I'd rather write something that jumps position and risks consistency than to write something too deeply entrenched in a certain framework. At the same time, I'm liberal in drawing in diverse theoretical ideas that may not be always be very well supported by evidence, and I hope that this liberty is understood as a way of getting ideas on the table, not as a naive, unfiltered acceptance of any particular body of theory. Likewise, this book may appear to omit my own view and have no overt thesis. This is largely by design; I try to speak through others as much as possible, and I don't believe a subject as sprawling as this can be easily tamed by any one overarching thesis. But the choice and ordering of material is mine and outlines a thesis of sorts.

These considerations can be summed up in four principles that I followed for writing this book: what you leave out can be as important as what you include; order knowledge to help others; speak through other people; work in manageable units.

It is worth commenting on the timing of writing of this book. When I pitched the concept in 2016 to MIT Press there were no full single-authored books in this field and even as recently as then, there was some question as to whether people would be much interested in, or take seriously, the idea of AI-automated creative production as anything more than speculative. The small International Conference on Computational Creativity was, in my view, the only real place to be showing work in this area, and progress wasn't occurring at lightning pace. To my simultaneous delight and horror, as I set out to write the book in 2017, and in the subsequent two years getting distracted and delayed by grant writing, teaching, children, and creative projects, the subject exploded in a big way in the wake of the deep learning revolution, with this book still sitting in draft status. Google were making music generation tools, mainstream artists were using machine learning to compose albums, ML-generated paintings were being sold for large sums at auction, and the number of academic conferences and journals and other public forums hosting special sessions on AI and creativity had multiplied many times. My social media feeds brimmed with a stream of articles asking with tedious repetition whether "an AI" might be the next Bach or Picasso, and every day a new world-first in AI art or music was announced. I was happy for (if a little overwhelmed by) the constant feed of new material to reference, but also a little anxious that this ship was sailing far more rapidly than I could keep up with.

At the time of writing, the burst of interest seems to have plateaued, causing me to reflect once again on the hype-cycle that a field such as this regularly passes through, as I discuss in chapter 1. There is no doubt that with such a fast-moving subject the material in this book will need refreshing frequently, but it is also hopefully possible to recognize the continuity of many themes, tracing back to earlier work in the field. On the one hand, we are already inhabitants of the fantasy world of someone else's future, where machines routinely perform magic; our worldview has already changed significantly with respect to our relationship to AI and the computational built environment as we adapt to it. On the other hand, machines remain brittle and glaringly incapable except in the most structured of contexts. The primary takeaway for me, becoming another principle for this book, is to avoid committing to predictions! Another useful piece of advice, from a colleague with several books under her belt, is that everyone who writes a book on a subject will write a different book that appeals to a different audience, so not to worry about getting in there first, and to focus on clearly and patiently communicating the themes I've developed in my work over several years.

I wish to acknowledge my potential biases. Some of the academic fields related to this topic are historically male dominated, and consequently the literature and history of the field are too. This book reflects that history, but I acknowledge my potential complicity in reinforcing a biased view of the field. The contemporary field has a greater gender diversity but still has far to go. In writing this book, I have been inspired by the work of many women, including Anna Jordanous, Anna Kantosalo, Kate Compton, Gillan Smith, Amy Hoover, and Alice Eldridge, and by the significant work of creativity researchers such as Margaret Boden and Teresa Amabile and social researchers Georgina Born, Genevieve Bell, Kate Crawford, and Lucy Suchman. The book is also grounded in a predominantly European and North American community of research and practice, and may not evenly represent the world's contributions to this field.

Writing this book was made possible first and foremost by the work of the computational creativity research community, whose work you will find discussed throughout. This includes several people whom I've had the pleasure of collaborating with, and who have taught me much in the process: Geraint Wiggins, Alice Eldridge, Jon McCormack, Tim Blackwell, Arne Eigenfeldt, Philippe Pasquier, Andrew Brown, Kaz Grace, Alan Dorin, Rob Saunders, and Petra Gemeinboeck. An extra special thanks goes to Dan Ventura for more detailed feedback and ideas, and to my partner Alana George not only for putting up with the emotional roller coaster of such a big project but for some very practical formatting and document management support in its final stages. My faculty management generously supported the sabbatical break to work intensively on the first draft on the manuscript and strategically dangled carrots in wait of the final publication. During that sabbatical break I had the opportunity to visit some of the most interesting people in the field in their home environments: Douglas Eck, Jesse Engel, Bill Hsu, Andy Elmsley, Pierre Barreau, Sebastian Risi, Michael Casey, Bob Sturm, Paul Brown, Georgina Born, Alan Blackwell, Julian Togelius, and Amy Hoover. In no particular order, I'd also like to extend my thanks to the following people for, variously, their engaging conversation, ideas, and collaborations: Sam Britton, Dan Wilson, Estelle Hoen, Margaret Boden, Benjamin Carey, Aengus Martin, Craig Vear, Lian Loke, Christian Guckelsberger, Christopher Redgate, François Houle, Petros Vrellis, Palle Dahlstedt, Lindsay Kelley, Roger Mills, Linda Candy, Caleb Kelly, Deb Turnbull, Dan McKinlay, Matt Yee-King, Prue Gibson, Anna Munster, Keir Winesmith, Toby Walsh, Caroline Pegram, Justin Shave, Charlton Hill, the Sydney Google Creative Lab team, Liam Bray, Steffan Ianigro, Sam Gillespie, Angelo Fraietta, and my family. I also thank Chloe McFadden for some help with the final proofs.

Needless to say, without MIT Press the book wouldn't have received such extensive reach, and I thank Doug Sery and Noah Springer for their ongoing support and patient responses, as well as the book's copyeditor, Lunaea Weatherstone, and Melody Negron at Westchester Publishing Services.

This book is dedicated to my fantastic dad, Bruce—who always encouraged me to pursue my interests and who declared that this is the first academic thing I've written that he can make sense of—and to the memory of Harold Cohen, an innovator and a most thoughtful individual.

I Questions

1 Inklings

A machine is a small part of the physical universe that has been arranged, after some thought by humans or animals, in such a way that when certain initial conditions are set up (by humans or animals) the deterministic laws of nature set to it that that small part of the physical universe automatically evolves in a way that humans or animals think is useful.
—Emanuel Derman[1]

What's a machine?—Till further notice, it is any system that operates according to the causal laws of physics. And what are we?
—Stevan Harnad[2]

Visions of Machines That Make Art

Intelligent machines that behave in various ways like humans are a critical ingredient of any vision of the future, increasingly so as our social media feeds become filled with robots that can play table tennis or cause financial crashes. In some of these visions, they are nearly indistinguishable from humans, as in the "replicants" of the movie *Blade Runner*, who only fail to pass as real humans under subtle emotional and biometric analyses. Sometimes they have glaring but specific differences, as with *Star Trek*'s android character, Data, who, besides his robotic eyes, seems human enough and yet almost as if from a different culture that doesn't get some of the nuances of our behavior; he thinks we're a bit odd, as we do him. Artificial intelligence (AI) characters in popular culture abound, each used to explore a different manifestation of machine intelligence and its relation to human intelligence, from *2001*'s HAL to Marvin the Paranoid Android in *A Hitchhiker's Guide to the Galaxy*. A common theme, as in those first two examples, is that there is something about humans that would be very hard to replicate, not so much to do with the domains of logic, memory, reasoning, and calculation, but to do with emotion and our appreciation of beauty, wit, the sublime, and the various forms of art that we engage with. This is the stuff of interpersonal relations, culture, individual conscious experience, and, some would say, souls.

Increasingly we recognize these speculations as bearing on a very real transformation taking place around us today. Machines are getting smarter, and as they do we tend to benchmark their progress against human behavior. At the same time, we come to see that the possible manifestations of machine intelligence are far more diverse than dictated by a mere likeness to humans. Spam filters and timetable schedulers are not particularly profound algorithms, but they are nevertheless very smart; they can perform cognitively challenging tasks with autonomy of a sort. It is hard to tell quite how these miscellaneous intelligences relate to ours. In mainstream media, machines have been described, often with a fair dose of metaphorical license, as dreaming, imagining, having new ideas, and working things out.[3] But even when there is a clear semblance to human intelligence—as in neural networks, which are inspired by our own biological brains and achieve human-level competence at object recognition and other tasks—the context in which these algorithms operate is so different from ours that it is hard to see the big picture. What do they "know" and what can they really do "on their own"?

This inspires excitement and terror. *"Let's make all humans redundant, brilliant! Has everybody really lost their soul?!"* exclaims an anonymous reader of the UK's *Daily Mail* newspaper, in response to an article about a neural network[4] that has been trained to generate folk melodies—a fairly commonplace approach to the automated generation of music based on machine learning and big data. It is a familiar reaction, alluding to the impact of such work on both meaningful employment and the wider meaning of life. The system's co-creator, Bob Sturm, meanwhile, is actually quite well known for writing papers that stress the *lack* of understanding such a big-data approach has, compared to what we humans do when we create music. For Sturm, such systems are like the fabled Clever Hans, "a real horse that was claimed to be capable of doing arithmetic and other feats of abstract thought" but that turned out to have learned some much simpler cognitive tricks in order to create this illusion.[5]

Many pages have been written about this coming age of machine intelligence, including the automation of jobs, the dangers of killer robots, and the singularity—a hypothesized time when machine intelligence exceeds human intelligence and thus accelerates further innovation in machine intelligence. This book is about a seemingly more niche topic—the idea of making machines that are artistically competent, productive, and even creative—and yet one that is no less important in the story of the rise and potential impact of AI. For some, art is a profound part of human behavior that could be portrayed as the ultimate hurdle in the creation of artificial humanlike intelligence. Even if it is not seen to be the most sophisticated of human behaviors, it is still suitably mysterious and has a great deal to do with that other final frontier, emotion. Those stereotypical sci-fi robots who can do everything humans can do but lack that indistinguishable humanness typified by a sense of awe, or some such phenomenologically grounded sensation, set out a kind of grand challenge to AI researchers. Will AI always be out of reach of this goal?

That is the grander theme of this book: how is AI taking on this challenge, what might the results look like, and what will this tell us about ourselves and our love of art? But "machines that make art and music" can refer to much more down-to-earth stuff as well. The creative industries are no less susceptible to small incremental advances in automation than areas like manufacturing and piloting aircraft. The speedup, if not the full automation, of creative tasks by technological means is nothing new. Just as "virtual" software instruments have streamlined the production of film music by replacing entire orchestras, driven by massive cost savings (sometimes at the expense of quality), we see many areas where applied AI might transform creative work without the need to invoke *Blade Runner*'s replicants. Given a moment's thought, it can be seen that such a gradualist creep toward automating creative tasks is no less impactful and deserves equally rich analysis.

Consider two views of the rise of machine-generated music. In Ray Kurzweil's grand vision of the forward march of AI, written in 1999,[6] he predicts that by 2019 it would be routine for algorithmic musicians to take to the stage to perform with live musicians, and it wouldn't be long before celebrated machine artists were autonomously producing reputable work, possibly exceeding the quality of human artists. (In the same book he predicts the simulation of the human brain to be complete by 2099.) This is a vision of machines that would be perceived as the originators of creative work, far removed from our present notion of machines as tools in the hands of a human creator. They would fall short of human intelligence but would be *like* humans, fitting existing human roles such as musician and artist.

More modestly, but with equal impact, a couple of years earlier the composer and producer Brian Eno reflected on his experiments with computer generated music in the liner notes to a highly celebrated album. Eno asks whether, in the future, audiences might come to treat ever-changing compositions as the norm. "You mean you used to listen to exactly the same thing over and over again?" he imagines his grandchildren asking.[7] Eno envisioned a world in which the music would come out of your headphones "generatively," meaning that rather than being fixed in form, musical patterns would be generated on the fly according to an algorithm. Many others since (and some before) have explored the idea of listening to music that is dynamically generated based on where you are, who you are, what you are doing, or just to introduce new variants to a compositional theme, as performing musicians routinely do. Recent excitement around the impacts of AI have seen renewed interest in this vision. High-profile tech investor Vinod Khosla, for example, has claimed that we will stop listening to precomposed music altogether, preferring instead algorithmically generated music that responds to our mood.[8] Unlike Kurzweil's, this vision is more in keeping with a view of human creators using computers as smart tools. Such generative variation can be done in the simplest of ways: the random function on any standard CD player enabled albums of tiny fragments that could be reconfigured randomly in a new order, the most basic of generative processes spurring new ways to think about uniqueness and variation in the listening experience. The artist Eluvium is one to have recently continued this tradition into the world of Spotify, with his album *Shuffle Drones*, which he invites you to play in a random order to produce a new listening experience.

Of these two views, Kurzweil's vision would seem to be a good deal further off the mark. We are beginning to see an increasing number of systems that at least *claim* some form of autonomous musical and artistic competency, but they are far from common and do not come near the level of sophistication his prophecy would appear to require. That said, how far off we are is a subject of some debate. One recent appraisal, far more positive than mine, is that "the state of the art in mechatronics and computation is such that we can now begin to speak comfortably of the machine as artist."[9]

Both Kurzweil's and Eno's visions are *socio*technological, depending not only on some technological foundations but on adoption by listeners and creators (or metacreators, those people who author the systems that do the creation). Kurzweil's prediction is more squarely focused on the capability of the technology, but this prediction is not just about whether machines could in principle create art, but whether, and how, a culture would emerge that embraces these metacreated artifacts. This in turn depends on the specifics of the technology, which itself progresses in part according to how much demand there is for it, a cycle of feedback we will also need to take into account.

Eno's prediction is more overtly cultural, since he was already working with generative tools at the time, proclaiming that "now, there are three alternatives: live music, recorded music, and generative music."[10] The cultural question is, what will this technology do to music listening culture? But even for Eno, as for Kurzweil, technological unknowns still play a part in how this path unfolds. Eno was able to make beautiful *ambient* music with the generative systems he had to hand, but we would still struggle today to use a machine to generate a good variant on a Talking Heads or Roxy Music tune, let alone compose an original work in that style. Some styles of music are harder to create with generative means than others. The cultural and the technological play off each other intensively. Indeed, subgenres of *algorithmic* music have long existed that don't really try to recreate existing musical styles, instead exploring the creative nature of the medium, just as synthesizers, jukeboxes, and powerful PAs have changed the nature of music in their own ways.

Between the cultural and the technological, we also have that question of the *interface*. *How* should the inheritors of Eno's vision compose their generative music, and *how* should their audiences consume it? If there's no compelling process to adopt—more compelling than picking up a guitar and playing it—then adoption of such technology may be a nonstarter, even if the technology is robust and there is a cultural demand. After making generative music myself with code, with all its bugs and opacity and uncertainty, I'm sometimes very glad to go back to making "normal" music—that is, for me at least, arranging sounds on a timeline—where I can control what is going to happen next. These are questions of human-computer interaction (HCI), interaction design (IxD), and user experience (UX) design, which may at first sight seem to have little bearing on the real hard challenges of automation but can turn out to be pivotal in many situations.

Such questions have become consolidated into a field of inquiry called computational creativity. This is the name given to the study of the automation of creative tasks by machines.[11] If its interdisciplinarity hasn't already hit you, then consider that we've just skimmed fleetingly past algorithms, cognition, psychology, creative practice, theories of art, anthropology, philosophy, and human-computer interaction, and there are more disciplines to add to complete the picture, such as complex systems and evolutionary biology. Computational creativity is about machines that play some role in the creation of art or other creative outcomes. For the moment, I take the gross liberty of using "art" here as a shorthand or placeholder for the production of a wide variety of cultural artifacts: visual art, music, stories, poems, jokes, games, furniture designs, and so on.[12] There will be some wrangling to come about where the boundary lies around this vague cluster of activities and what the correct terminology is, as well as where neighboring activities such as science, innovation and scholarship fit in.

For now, take these prototypes, some of them already discussed above, as a guide to what the subject matter is: a robot who appreciates and can discuss fine art; a machine that can sit in on bass with an improvising jazz band, playing standards with flair; a generative algorithm that can be "composed" (or instructed) to produce variations on a style of art or music; or an architectural modeling program that fills out odd corners of a building in a baroque style of the designer's choosing.

Amilcar Cardoso, Tony Veale, and Geraint Wiggins, three leaders in the field of computational creativity, put it that "the study of creativity in AI is not new, but it is unusual."[13] The interdisciplinary nature of this topic introduces several extraordinary challenges, but its foundation in a computational practice has the fantastic advantage that you can actually test out your ideas by building something:

> Researchers ... come [to conferences] ... with laptops primed to give demos of what their systems can do, ready to show off features that have been added since their papers were first accepted. No abstract insight can compare with the ability to show a real creative system in full flow.[14]

In this chapter, I provide a cursory sketch of the work going on in this field and the wider perception of it, followed by a summary of the challenges and questions faced by those who aspire to automate aspects of creativity. This begins with a portrait of some early work in the field, followed by a wider look at how its practice has progressed. This sketch will show some of the ways in which computational creativity is progressing rapidly in certain areas but also illuminate some of the confusing hype surrounding the field, which muddies the waters.

The central message of this book is that understanding this field requires understanding what computationally creative algorithms are actually doing but also developing a strong, multidisciplinary understanding of the domain of creative artistic activity itself, in order to properly frame and evaluate the goals and achievements of computational creativity. This will show that some of the hype around this field is valid and some is misguided, but sometimes in a way that is not expected. It is perhaps less of a problem to make the bold claim that a computational system created an artwork or composed a piece of music all by itself than it is to attach to such activities grandiose mystique or to misrepresent exactly what that task entailed in its proper context. Such activities can be seen, on the one hand, as nothing more than mundane acts of arranging pixels on a screen or notes in a timeline. To create novel configurations that conform to expectations of a particular style can sometimes be a trivial task, and I will argue, indeed, that of course computers can do this and do so very well. On the other hand, these forms of production can, and should, also be seen as deeply social activities that are grounded in identities, group membership, and social competition, which have material outcomes for human beings. To arrange pixels or notes *in such a way* as to achieve individual social goals, as humans do through processes deeply ingrained in our biology and culture, is a different matter altogether, one that cannot be achieved merely by training a neural network to generate patterns, *even if those resulting patterns may pass as something a human would have made*. The analysis I offer is one in which artistic creativity is understood as occurring in the networked interaction *between* multiple people and objects, not *within* individual humans, and where value must be seen as an emergent property of this interactive process, not bound to individual goals and expectations. Many commentators have argued that it is the social nature of artistic activity that makes it difficult for computational systems to be employed in this space in any simple way. Exactly what is social about artistic activity, why we do it and care so much about it, is an important part of this book's analysis.

Artistically creative machines, in this analysis, will be reframed as modules that perform aspects of tasks otherwise performed by humans, perhaps in complex combinations that achieve impressive feats. They already occupy a no-man's-land of creative agency, changing the nature of creative production, not grounded in the same needs and goals as humans, yet creatively productive nonetheless.

Early Pioneers and World Firsts

The Low-Hanging Fruit

Between the conception of this book and the moment the first words were written, one of the pioneers of computational creativity passed away. Harold Cohen had become a successful visual artist in London by the time, at the age of 40 (in 1968), he set off to California to join the Visual Arts Department at the University of California, San Diego. Here he created AARON, arguably the world's first generative art system and arguably still one of the best. Cohen worked on AARON and *with* AARON for the rest of his life. I met him in 2009 at the Dagstuhl Symposium on Computers and Creativity, and at the age of 81 he was still enthusiastically reporting on new developments in his work. AARON was what we call a classic rule-based system. It performed no learning, it did not evolve or develop in any way except when Cohen tinkered with its code, nor did it perform any evaluation of its output (although this was always a fascination of Cohen's). All it did was generate paintings according to a series of rules of composition that Cohen had programmed, first rendered to the screen and then sometimes physically painted to canvas using a robotic mechanism. Furthermore, Cohen was often involved in curating the output, selecting some works and rejecting others. Despite these various reasons that might lead us to determine a lack of creativity in this description of AARON, the works were deemed impressive, Cohen himself reported being regularly surprised by the system's output, and both the public and expert response was general enthusiasm about the possibilities it evidenced. It was significant work and generated a great deal of excitement about the potential of machines to act creatively or artistically.

Cohen died the most celebrated and written-about computational creativity practitioner of his time, and he seems set to remain so for some time to come. He was a hero of Ray Kurzweil's, and his work was also discussed extensively by the philosopher of cognitive science, AI, and creativity Margaret Boden. He was also a competent commentator and theorist himself, and in today's academic language we would describe him as an exemplary practice-based researcher in the field, reflecting and commenting on his practice, and developing his own conceptual and theoretical framework to work with.[15]

It is historically significant that Cohen was already an accomplished artist, who made the leap from this platform into the world of computer science. Firstly, in the production of rule-based systems, the most important thing you need is an expert's knowledge of the activity in question to turn into rules. Although Cohen's initial vision was of a more general artistically intelligent system,[16] he arrived at an approach to AARON that embodied a complementary dualism. He was engaged on the one hand in understanding, by transcribing in code, his own painting practice. Formalizing a task in the strict language of computer code offers new insights into that activity and is a form of knowledge creation in its own right. In tandem with this, on the other hand, Cohen was interested in the more general technical achievement of building machines that could create original artworks. As many others have found, this fascination with a machine that makes art is as much about understanding oneself as an artist as about understanding machines. The former acts as a complement to the latter, for Cohen not only because it was the means for technical success but because it offered him a very different formulation of what he was achieving, one that was much less about the nature of mind and more about the simple goal of understanding the creative domain of painting. This began to feed into a picture of the place of the computer in his work, framed as a philosophical question. Here, for example, he foregrounds a conceptual ambiguity that arises whenever computers-as-tools start behaving like active agents:

> If a photographer takes a picture, we do not say that the picture has been made by the camera. If, on the other hand, a man writes a chess-playing program for a computer, and then loses to it, we do not consider it unreasonable to say that he has been beaten by the computer. Both the camera and the computer may be regarded as tools, but it is clear that the range of functions of the computer is of a different order to that of the camera.[17]

The second reason that Cohen's artistic background is important is much more pragmatic. He knew the art world and was already widely exhibited. He was in a good position to ensure that his work with AARON should make it into art galleries and receive the attention of critics and the public. This has proven to be a recurring theme in computational creativity, where some of the more successful work has taken place "in the wild," leading to questions about how the rigor of the research lab can engage with the cultural contexts in which such work has meaning.

Two other celebrated artist-programmers followed very similar paths in the wake of Cohen. Both musicians, David Cope and George Lewis were, like Cohen, already recognized talents in their respective genres before embarking on (very different) studies of musical computational intelligence. Lewis's Voyager system can be seen as the jazz-improvising equivalent of AARON's painting, handcrafted from Lewis's formal and intuitive musical experience without doing any learning or self-modifying or performing any sort of reflection. Although an improvising system, Voyager does have one responsibility that AARON is free of: it must "listen" and respond dynamically to other musicians.

As a jazz and improvised music lover, I delight at watching Voyager in action.[18] Even knowing what Voyager is doing under the hood, knowing that its algorithms are conceptually relatively simple, watching it in action interacting with other improvising musicians still creates a sense of awe. There is a richness of output and a seeming conversation going on between musician and machine. Voyager appears to develop musical themes in interesting and appropriate ways and to respond meaningfully to performers. Like Cohen, Lewis has nurtured a kind of co-creative relationship with the system as part of his lifelong creative practice. It is a relationship that is very one-sided, that makes significant creative progress only when the human hacks away at the code, but a relationship in which the machine can act as a prolific mass-producer beyond the capacity of the artist, and in its own small way act as a fruitful originator of ideas.

David Cope's work developed throughout the 1980s and 1990s and, like Cohen, was situated in California's innovation-rich culture. He too used his compositional insight to develop an expert system for the automated generation of music[19]—sheet music this time, for performance by orchestral musicians—and with a focus on style imitation. He worked with a corpus of machine-readable annotations of music by various composers in order to extract these composers' melodic "signatures." He also created generative grammars by hand that captured higher-level aspects of their style, guided by his own musicological framework based loosely on a well-known theory of music called Schenkerian analysis. Thus while Cope followed the same trend as Cohen and Lewis of a co-creative relationship with his own software construct—hacking away, guided largely by expert intuition, reflecting, curating, tweaking—his work also took on a more musicological slant by aspiring to imitate great composers.

Possibly for this reason, Cope took on a slightly more confrontational role in the early philosophical discussion of art-making machines. Because his work was concerned with style imitation, it was positioned to pose the tricky philosophical provocation, for the first time, that a machine might create works of great composers as if they were still alive today. This was unsurprisingly not a palatable concept to many scholars and lovers of classical music. In addition to suggesting that computers could create music, an already challenging idea, Cope's work could be read as suggesting that we could in effect bottle the essence of Bach and Beethoven. He also tended toward statements that heightened the provocative nature of his work:

> Much of what happens in the universe results from recombination. The recombination of atoms, for instance, produces new molecules. ... Music is no different. The recombinations of pitches and durations represent the basic building blocks of music. Recombination of larger groupings of pitches and durations, I believe, form the basis for musical composition and help establish the essence of both personal and cultural musical styles.[20]

For some of his musicologically expert critics, such statements have read as oversimplification, and the limits of the system's style-imitation were more visible to them than for general audiences, who were on the whole not expert enough to tell the difference between the system's imitations and their original counterparts. Cope's presentation of his work was also more dramatic overall. He tells the story of the creation of Emmy (the name derives from the more formal acronym EMI—experiments in musical intelligence) as one arising from a writer's block. In the dramatic prose of one journalist:

> In 1980, Cope was commissioned to write an opera. At the time, he and his wife, Mary ... were supporting four children, and they'd quickly spent the commission money on household essentials like food and clothes. But no matter what he tried, the right notes just wouldn't come. He felt he'd lost all ability to make aesthetic judgments. Terrified and desperate, Cope turned to computers.[21]

Accounts vary on how much of a role Cope and Emmy both played in the creation, curation, and manipulation of the resulting works. With the objective merely of breaking his writer's block, there was no need for the system to compose complete works, only to generate workable material for Cope to play with; this is definitely how it was used in early works. At other times, the system is presented as one that operates autonomously in the creation of complete works, and Cope has produced a body of five thousand pieces composed by Emmy, quite the proof that his block was overcome.

In addition, various altercations with reviewers, record labels, and other "gatekeepers" led Cope to claim that there was a strong subconscious bias in people against the idea of computers being able to create meaningful music.[22] He became a champion for the view of AI optimists like Kurzweil that what people think is the preserve of a human soul, too profound to be ever explained, is in fact perfectly modelable. He argued that people were prone to significantly overemphasize the mystery of music and reject Emmy's work outright on essentialist grounds.

Another voice in this early conversation, Douglas Hofstadter, wrote the following in his earliest and most famous book, *Gödel, Escher, Bach*:

> **Question**: Will a computer program ever write beautiful music?
>
> **Speculation**: Yes, but not soon. Music is a language of emotions, and until programs have emotions as complex as ours, there is no way a program will ever write anything beautiful. There can be "forgeries"—shallow imitations of the syntax of earlier music—but despite what one might think at first, there is much more to musical expression than can be captured in syntactical rules.[23]

But Hofstadter later claims that Cope's work made him question this view. "And what do I make of it now? Well, I am not quite sure," he mused, explaining his surprise as he examined Cope's creations and started to concede that mere syntactical rules might go further than he had initially imagined.[24]

It is fair to say, without any cause to dismiss their contribution and the brilliance of their work, that early figures like Cohen, Cope, and Lewis were at the right place at the right time to pluck the low-hanging fruit of computational creativity, looking at the new world of personal computers through the lens of their artistic expertise and asking a simple question: can I formalize some of my creative production, or that of others, in algorithms? In a certain light, the answer was a resounding yes; algorithms were producing novel outputs, and audiences were engaging.[25] But on closer inspection, these systems posed more questions than they answered, and the ways in which they were lacking began to outweigh their accomplishments. These initial experiments became the platform for further questions and considerable technical problems. Kurzweil, ever the optimist, saw systems such as AARON and Emmy as evidence of his vision of proliferating autonomous computer artists. But hindsight hasn't been so kind. Looking at where

Kurzweil predicted the evolution of the technology would be at this stage, we do not seem *that* much closer to building systems that have the ability to do things like iteratively evaluate what they are doing, let alone the full trappings of a culturally embedded social artist.

This is a familiar story in technology. Over the past few years virtual reality (VR) has been enjoying a second wave. I remember seeing the first incarnation as a teenager, a VR game with enormous head-mounted displays and jagged-line graphics, at the Trocadero Centre in London in the 1990s. The hype was ecstatic, but the VR bandwagon was not going anywhere. The technology just was not good enough to create that rich immersive experience that makes VR worth caring about. It took twenty years to be revived, during which time processors, graphics, and sensor technologies got cheaper, smaller, and more reliable, with more established ecosystems of creators and creative tools to jump into action when the market was ready. This process of expectation-based boom and bust in technology is widely documented and has been neatly expressed by the "hype cycle," a model of technological maturity that predicts a period of initial hype, followed by a depression, a regrouping around more realistic technological expectations, and then a steady maturation of a workable technology. The hype cycle, developed by research firm Gartner, describes how some "killer demo" of a technology's potential can create overexcitement and overinvestment in a field that still has a long way to go toward a practical product.

It is not really appropriate to locate computational creativity itself on this cycle, because it is a mélange of different technologies with different objectives, but there is nevertheless some sense that the field as a whole experienced its initial hype phase in these early days. The doors were pushed ajar in the late twentieth century to offer glimpses of a new world of possibilities, but we are still grappling with challenges spanning the technical, the methodological, the social, and not least the reaction to it in our culture. Now computational creativity is experiencing a second burst of activity driven by new advances in machine learning, which will be discussed at length in this book.

It is worth noting too that a similar such lull occurred in the wider field of AI research, dubbed "the AI winter," an era of relative doubt about AI's prospects, accompanied by reduced funding, at least in the US. AI chronicler Pamela McCorduck comments that "all sciences move in rhythms, thriving, then lying fallow (or simply assimilating what has gone before), then growing once again. In the 1990s, shoots of green broke through the wintry AI soil."[26] Now the tables are turned. AI is booming, and funding is currently doubling every two years.[27] It has also become a buzzword in business, and the mystique of having a business that uses AI has all but vanished.[28]

It is also important not to understate the achievements of earlier work, in spite of its shortcomings. As highlighted by Stanford University's latest report into the state of AI's progress and its future, "Ironically, AI suffers the perennial fate of losing claim to its acquisitions, which eventually and inevitably get pulled inside the frontier, a repeating pattern known as the 'AI effect' or the 'odd paradox.'"[29] From a common definition of intelligence as "that quality that enables an entity to function appropriately and with foresight in its environment," we tend to perennially redraw the line between the unintelligent machines of the past and the intelligent machines of the future. In fact, the Stanford authors reason, "The difference between an arithmetic calculator and a human brain is not one of kind but of scale, speed, degree of autonomy and generality."[30]

A similar view is warranted with the domains of creative and artistic production. Those early arguments about whether machines can be creative, charged with significance by the appearance of work by early experimenters, paved the way for a more fragmented and piecemeal view of the emergence of machines that make art, in which hybrid systems comprising human and nonhuman entities, intelligent and autonomous to differing degrees, participate in creation. This is how we now witness the current state of progress. A diverse offering of computational creativity systems corresponds to an almost equally diverse number of strategies for bringing human and machine together in creative partnerships, or automating one but not another part of a larger creative process. Some strategies are inspired by human cognition, others apply proven but not biologically or human inspired brute-force methods from computer science. Some have clear commercial objectives while others are the work of practicing digital artists. The current wave of AI-powered creative systems is undeniably exciting but still has much to prove to warrant the more optimistic visions of the future.

The World Firsts and the Public Imagination

With this excitement in mind, it is worth considering how computational creativity has been handled in wider public dissemination, most importantly in the media, with its understandable hunger for AI breakthroughs.

Here the question of which is the first computational system to generate original art or music "on its own" gets constantly revised and revisited, and has been prone to much loose interpretation. Consider music systems. Two clear pioneers were Lejaren Hiller and Leonard Issacson.[31] Their *Illiac Suite*, created in 1957,[32] used a variety of now common generative music techniques, including Markov models. Perhaps this was indeed the world's first automated music composition system, but many other popular candidates serenade media attention for a place among the world firsts. These include Cope's EMI work in the 1980s[33] and Stephen Thaler's 2007[34] pairing of his Creativity Machine with a human composer to create an album that was "95 percent to 98 percent computer generated"[35] spanning multiple styles. There is the Iamus system, which in 2010 was described as creating "the first fragment of professional contemporary classical music ever composed by a computer in its own style."[36] François Pachet's team at Sony Computer Science Labs[37] used their Flow Machines system in 2016 to create a pop song derived from statistical models of previous popular works (one article asks, is this the world's first "good" robot album?).[38] In 2016, *Beyond the Fence*,[39] billed as the world's first computer-generated musical, was presented to audiences in London's West End. Like Thaler's album, the latter project married human professionals in various fields of musical theater production, including directorial oversight, with researchers working with their various generative systems across scenario development, plot, music, and lyrics. In 2017, a company called Aiva presented a music composition system that claims to be the first to have been registered as a composer with SACEM, France's creative rights organization. Another service, Endel, which generates "bespoke soundscapes" with specific mood objectives, has signed the first-ever record deal[40] with Warner Music. But was it the first? According to a recent survey paper,[41] in 2000 Universal Music worked with generative music label J13 Records to release computer-generated dance tracks that the authors claim were successful in dance clubs, but without telling anyone they were computer generated.

Similar stories play out in other domains. In visual art, contemporaries of Cohen such as Freider Nake, Paul Brown, and Ernest Edmonds branched out in different directions, but each in their own way explored the capacity of machines to produce things autonomously. Evolutionary methods were a major source of activity in computer-generated visual art and animation in the 1990s with the work of artists like Karl Sims, William Latham, and

Jon McCormack, and later artists such as Scott Draves. As with music, style imitation is also prevalent in visual art. This has taken a little longer to develop, as painting lacks an obvious or at least readily available equivalent symbolic layer to the notes of a music score. But recent work like The Next Rembrandt[42] project has drawn public attention and driven further debate about what constitutes style and originality.

Looking to language generation we find an even more crowded field, with its obvious rich application potential and centrality to AI. It can also be seen as a greatly fragmented area in which generative world firsts abound across the board; subdisciplines investigate the generation of stories and narratives, jokes, poems, interactive conversations, and metaphors. One of many high-profile projects that recently made the news for its obvious implications for creative employment was McCann Japan's AI system for the creative direction of television commercials.[43] In a blind test comparison between human- and machine-generated commercials, the human-made commercial narrowly won.

Generative applications in other domains such as games, 3D design and architecture, installation art, and, not least, cooking frequently claim new achievements in their respective areas. In architecture, in particular, the nature of the problems and the scale and structure of the industry have underscored the serious development of commercial applications such as the use of evolutionary computing that are starting to tangibly transform the industry.

The frenzy of world firsts seems to be abating slightly. We are gradually transitioning into a world where the use of AI in art production has a more everyday feel. When Holly Herndon produced an album that used an AI choir to augment her singing, also acting as a creative compositional support tool, the story still generated much attention but presented itself as a focused and considered rationale for using AI as an expressive tool, not the usual world first story.[44]

The public imagination is easily captivated by stories of computational creativity innovation, and reporting such events can be a source of confusion and hype, glossing over the hard detail to present a simplistic but inspiring narrative. Some of the main potential forms of misrepresentation are worth noting. In some cases, the narrative tends to favor the intent of the creator over any scrutiny over the nuts and bolts of the system's working in practice. According to an article in *Pop Matters* reporting on

Stephen Thaler's musical work, "Thaler has *taught* his computers to learn and improve themselves" (my emphasis).[45] This sounds remarkable, but it could refer to any of the known techniques in machine learning that bear none of the anthropomorphic qualities implied in this phrasing. Similarly, in the piece on David Cope quoted earlier:

> Cope wrestled with the problem [of making his Bach imitations more convincing] for months, almost giving up several times. And then one day, on the way to the drug store, Cope remembered that Bach wasn't a machine—once in a while, he broke his rules for the sake of aesthetics. The program didn't break any rules; Cope hadn't asked it to.[46]

In other cases, indirect markers of success are offered as proxies for evaluation of the system. According to Philip Ball in the *Guardian*, the composition system Iamus has created "the first music composed by computer considered good enough for top-class musicians to play."[47] But the same top-class musicians who played Iamus's composition are also prone to play the sometimes purposefully random or mechanical works of composers like John Cage and Conlon Nancarrow, so despite the kudos, it is hard to interpret the value of this claim to fame.[48]

Elsewhere, readers are invited to see for themselves how good the system's outputs are. The *Guardian* article on Iamus asked readers to take a Turing test[49] requiring them to try to tell from several compositions which were human composed and which were produced by Iamus. This is a form of evaluation that looks more promising on the surface, but it is not as infallible as it may seem. If done well this can be a great source of insight. But it can easily be done in a way that neglects sensible controls or is even purposefully deceptive, such as when only a small number of outputs from the system are hand-selected. The judge may not really gain a good sense of what the system is up to and what human creative input went into the results.

It is only a partial truth that any of the systems discussed above were firsts in their field, if at all; such narratives of invention, compelling though they are, can be better at muddying the waters than offering insight into what has been achieved. The tasks to which these various creative systems are put are fragmented and often incomparable. Teasing apart what the system did on its own—its creative autonomy—from its human programmers or the source data it was fed is no small feat. It requires you to pin down carefully what the creative task in question actually looks like and undertake a forensic examination to unpack what the system actually does. In each one of the cases described above, some human contribution to the creative output is necessarily present—at the very least someone had a hand in programming the system—and this is a considerable source of ambiguity, just as it was for Harold Cohen's work with AARON. Culturally grounded expectations and norms guide how we approach originality in different domains, and our critical faculties are not necessarily well primed for processing this new world of artistic creation by human-machine hybrids.

Nevertheless, there is considerable momentum behind the idea that the creative capacity of machines is on the rise. Glenn W. Smith and Frederic Fol Leymarie,[50] the latter a successful maker of robotic art systems, suggest that all of the following bear witness to the newly—*already*—established role of machines as creative producers:

1. The kinetic or robotic art works whose movement and/or behavior has become so sophisticated that we are entitled to regard them as performance artists in their own right.
2. The algorithmic studio assistants set loose to embellish computer-mediated graphic or sculptural works of art, and which work is then output via large-format ink-jet printer or additive manufacturing system, or as video.
3. The autonomous and cleverly designed painting robots which, drawing upon the emergent properties of minimally intelligent systems, are nonetheless able to create striking abstract works.
4. The far more computationally intensive anthropomorphic robots able to create sensitive and imaginative portraits of their human subjects, or engage in other forms of graphic virtuosity.
5. The purely computational/AI systems which qualify themselves as aesthetically competent entities, if not actual artists, by their ability to predict the style, period, and/or author of existing works of graphic art.
6. The purely computational/AI systems capable of isolating and capturing the style of a given work of graphic art and applying it in an aesthetically pleasing manner to an arbitrary image.
7. The purely computational/AI systems capable of generating striking imagery based on otherwise mundane or even random visual input fields.[51]

It is worth considering a real system in a little more detail to help put this in context. The Continuator[52] is a system for music improvisation developed in the early 2000s by François Pachet, now director of the Spotify Creator Technology Research Lab after being director of Sony's Computer Science

Laboratory in Paris. It uses a popular time-series modeling technique called Markov modeling, which learns the probabilities of temporal events happening in a given dataset of time-series data, given some knowledge about the preceding events. In Western tonal music, for example, a G might have a high chance of being followed by a C, more so than being followed by a C-sharp. After being exposed to enough example music, a Markov model will learn to encode these note transition probabilities. Sequences of two, three, or more notes (second, third, and higher-order Markov models) can be used to help nail down more precise expectations of what is going to come next, the previous N notes being used to make a prediction about what the next note should be. This technique has been used in music generation extensively, and the Continuator is one of the most well-known examples of a real-time generative music system that uses this technique. Something that makes the Continuator interesting is that it is deployed in a real-time performance context of call-and-response. A live musician plays a couple of bars of music and then stops. This signals to the Continuator that it is its turn to take over, and it applies the Markov model, trained on what it has just heard, to generate a continuation to the performance. Over time, as this call-and-response continues, the system continues to add the recorded input to its model, learning the style of the musician it is performing with, and playing with him or her in that same style. This has been described as "mirroring" the player's style. Continuation is now a common paradigm of music generation. A more recent example, the MuseNet system, made by OpenAI,[53] performs continuations using a predictive neural network model. A user can specify a training dataset and a musical seed to feed into the network for it to continue. This model is more sophisticated in that it can work with multiple instruments, outputting a single, multi-instrument sequence.

Loose anthropomorphization, appeals to fame, and blind tests of the system's output all carry potential sources of misrepresentation of what the Continuator is capable of. (There is no insinuation whatsoever here that the Continuator's authors are guilty of this! Quite the opposite—the papers describing the Continuator are transparent and frank.) Statements such as the Continuator feels the groove, understands the music, or thinks ahead would be examples of unwarranted anthropomorphism; recall Bob Sturm's earlier appeal to look out for Clever Hans, "the horse inside."[54] That

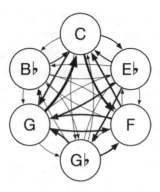

Figure 1.1
Example of a simple musical Markov model. Each node represents a musical note and each arrow represents a potential transition between notes. Thicker arrows have a greater probability of occurring. To run the model, select a starting point, then follow a path of arrows, with greater likelihood of following thicker arrows than thinner ones. Image credit: Oliver Bown.

the Continuator, like AARON, Voyager, and Emmy, is a success, sharing the stage with various musicians, needs to be understood in the context of people's excitement at working with this technology. Success can be a self-fulfilling prophecy. In my experience working with improvising musicians, they are adept at bringing out the best of such systems and making them look good. Meanwhile, blind tests can conceal false impressions of a contextual and representational nature. In principle, a Markov model might generate verbatim copies of what it has previously heard, or short of that, something that would at least be considered plagiarized. Indeed, in certain contexts, such as when there has been very little data to train on, and the Markov model is of a high order (i.e., long sequences of notes are used to make future predictions) this copycat behavior can even be quite likely. A potential misrepresentation then could occur in a blind listening test in which a musician was effectively playing call-and-response with previous recordings of himself or herself.

The only real resolution to such potential misrepresentations is to dig deeper, taking them to be an occupational hazard to be mitigated as best as possible (again, Pachet and his team do this well).[55] For this, computational creativity researchers are increasingly drawing on methods from design, ethnography, and practice-based research, which emphasize detailed descriptions of the context of evaluation and a holistic view. Make no mistake, the Continuator is a successful system because it works very well, not just because people willingly attribute anthropomorphic qualities to it. It is a novel tool with original affordances, able to create immersive, engaging experiences and stimulate new creative ideas—both qualities that are increasingly formalized as goals in computational creativity. Likewise, more recent deep learning systems such as MuseNet[56] clearly learn aspects of musical structure. As promised, they can *model* musical styles very well, and this is powerful, transformative technology.

One thing that is clear about historic and current systems is that they are not social beings in any sense. Even if we have systems that perform impressive feats of intelligence with respect to musical or visual content, and may even, as Smith and Leymarie state, understand the properties of styles, periods, and specific artists, they are tools that are operated by human social agents rather than agents in their own right operating via the means of social interaction. In the same *Arts* special issue as Smith and Leymarie's article, Aaron Hertzmann asks bluntly, "Can computers create art?" His answer, which is comparable in ways to this book's analysis (elaborated on greatly in chapter 4), is that artistic behavior is primarily social, and so machines that make images (and ditto with sounds) are not machines that make art until they become social beings:

> Why do we create and consume art? I argue that art is primarily a social behavior: art is about communication and displays between people. For example, people often speak of art as being about personal expression, which is an act of communication.[57]

Hertzmann elaborates, however, that we do seem inclined to happily attribute artistic creativity to machines where they have the potential to exhibit specific properties of human artists (by "we," creators of computationally creative systems are particularly implicated). A common trick then is to "identify some attributes of human artists, and then hypothesize that AIs with these attributes will be considered artists."[58]

Thus from where we stand, computational creativity may be seen to be producing increasingly sophisticated systems that can generate artistic content using a diversity of AI techniques, as well as developing methods for embedding these systems into human creative workflow and experiences. At the same time, these systems' behaviors still sit a million miles from human behavior, much less the complex embedding into a sociocultural environment that we all experience as humans. They can be seen floating within a vast unexplored chasm which separates on the one hand simple tools and instruments and on the other hand human intelligence. It is because we are in this unexplored conceptual territory that AI is subject to confusion about where exactly in this chasm it sits. What can we do and what is yet to be explored? As we will see, as much work is needed to better define the problems of computational creativity as to solve them, and these two aspects of the field are in constant interdependent flux.

The Computational Creativity Frontier

How can programs be made to generate artistic output? What does a computer need to do to make a pun, write a poem, compose a piece of music, or paint a painting? Psychologists and cognitive scientists have developed models of human creative thought—discussed in the following chapter—so one view of a computationally creative algorithm is that it should specifically implement some or all aspects of such a model. But this is an ambitious goal that needs to be broken down into more immediate objectives. While we have good abstract models of creativity, real computational creativity systems have to work with real data and produce real outputs, so a challenge lies in connecting various levels of abstraction together. Proficiency in creative tasks involves specific capacities such as the ability to learn representations, evaluate outputs, and generate outputs. More pragmatically, then, it is common to start with this question reversed—what existing algorithmic methods can be adapted to creative tasks?—before we think about the big issues of human creative thought.

Algorithmic methods for creativity are often divided into a few broad categories based on where the system's knowledge comes from (see, for example, Todd and Werner, 1999).[59] Cohen described his system AARON as an excellent colorist, and Lewis's Voyager is clearly adept at navigating jazz scales and rhythms. We have already seen that these systems only gained this domain expertise because their makers hand-coded their own artistic expertise into them. Generally we describe such systems as rule-based systems; you write the rules and the system executes them. If you write rules that apply coloring principles, then and only then the system embodies knowledge of coloring.

Hand-coding intelligence into computers has its obvious limitations, but it clearly served these projects well, as well as in other areas of applied AI, in a field known as expert systems. Such systems can be relatively easy to understand and manipulate, and a lone artist without extensive training in computer science can go far with such an approach.

Another way for a system to embody knowledge is to learn from its environment. In machine learning (ML), currently the most successful and well-known domain of machine intelligence, the system learns from training data. Whereas Voyager knows its jazz scales from tables or hand-coded rules, ML-based music systems such as the Continuator or Aiva instead derive some form of knowledge of musical scales and other musical information by analyzing examples of existing music. This analysis might take place in terms of probabilities or network connections or some other encoding of the knowledge, and it might entail learning in real time or offline from a database. In such systems, scales might not constitute explicit knowledge. We may not be able to open up the system and see C-majors and D-minors, whereas if we looked under the hood of Voyager we would see these structures represented explicitly in the code.

There are several different approaches to machine learning. *Supervised learning* involves training a system on a database that contains both inputs and the outputs expected of the system. In a standard computer vision classification task, digital bitmap images might make up the inputs, and the expected outputs will consist of tags describing the things in the images. The training of the system is based on the idea that for any input we feed into the system, we can compare its output to the output we would expect to see, determining a measure of the system's error. Training involves making many tiny adjustments to the system's structure, each time reducing the error slightly, until the system converges on a good overall model.

In *reinforcement learning*, rather than specifying expected outputs, we simply tell the system whether what it did was good or bad. You could train a robot to find its way across a room by telling it how well it did overall, without specifying exactly where it should go. In data-driven or *unsupervised learning*, meanwhile, there is no expected output at all. Instead, the system discovers structural properties of the data. Learning to distinguish between different phonemes, sets of which differ from language to language, can be done simply through repeated exposure to these sounds in natural language, since in natural speech they fall into clearly distinct clusters which a listener can learn.

A different set of approaches is based around the algorithms of search and optimization. The most popular algorithms here are inspired by evolutionary theory, particularly the idea that evolution in nature is able to drive the optimization of specific traits within species. Evolutionary strategies use trial and error to solve problems, and so they take the form of a *blind* search for a solution, key to which is the ability to measure the "fitness" of competing solutions.[60] A pool of solutions is first generated at random and each solution is tested, then fitter solutions from the pool are successively copied and transformed at random, in the hope that some of these transformations will result in fitter solutions still. Transformation can include simple random mutations to the solutions, or the random combination of two solutions in the hope of obtaining the best of both (which happens in sexual recombination in nature). As the population of solutions evolves, the main challenge in evolutionary computing is to get the search to spread out widely across the space of all possible solutions to make sure that the space is properly explored, but then also converge on the areas of greatest potential to find the most optimal solution.

Taking such a blind search approach invokes the possibility that the system could come up with solutions that we didn't know about, even though we clearly understood the problem that was trying to be solved. The case of NASA's evolution-designed antenna[61] illustrates this well and is one of the earliest examples—and perhaps one of the best—of a computer coming up with a design that no human was able to think up.

As well as thinking about systems in terms of where their knowledge comes from, we can also think about systems in terms of their properties as generators of output. We saw above that once a Markov model has learned the probability of different notes occurring following a sequence of preceding notes, then it can make an informed prediction about what note should come next. We can therefore run a generative Markov model to feed back on itself, starting with a given note or sequence of notes, and then using its predictions to iteratively generate new notes. Neural networks take many different forms, not all of which are conducive to generation. We can set up recurrent neural networks to perform basically the same task as the Markov model, predicting events and therefore feeding back on themselves to generate unlimited strings of output. Image-generating networks learn

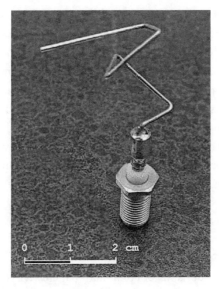

Figure 1.2
A radio antenna design optimized by an evolutionary algorithm. The algorithm tries a population of different designs, testing their performance in simulation and selecting those more successful for future "breeding." Over time, designs improve. Image credit: NASA (public domain).

to output entire bitmap images that possess structural similarities to the images they have been trained on. In other cases source images are iteratively modified. In the deep dream approach, the network iteratively modifies a given image to gradually improve its confidence that it can see certain objects in the image.

These various algorithmic domains do not necessarily play well together or lend themselves to the specific demands of creative tasks. Better machine learning, bigger and better datasets, better representational formats for images, music, language, and so on, will feed advances in computational creativity, but the challenge remains to adapt and put such systems together in innovative ways that satisfy creative goals.

The unique engineering challenges involved in creating successful systems come along with another challenge that is unique to computational creativity: how to demonstrate which systems are the most successful and why. Here the interdisciplinary complexity of the field is most pronounced. We've seen some of these challenges manifest in the earlier discussion of media representations of computational creativity. Creative tasks don't often offer up neat quantitative measures. One problem is that we want, above all, to make systems that are autonomous—capable of acting on their own—but they are never entirely autonomous: we feed them rules and inspiring examples, operate their parameters, and filter their outputs. It can be hard to know exactly where the system ends and its human creators and operators begin.

There is also a commonly noted distinction between two tiers of computational creativity capability, which guides an understanding of applied systems. This is between systems that support generation but without the ability to perform evaluation, and systems that are capable of performing an iterative cycle of generation and evaluation in a way that is similar to human creative search.

Basic Generative Systems

Aside from the grander aims of computational creativity—machines acting in ways that we would recognize as creative—there is a plethora of ways in which algorithms have begun to be used to automate the more manageable subtask of generation, without automating the critical evaluation that human creators perform when producing creative outputs. The techniques and systems described above, applied to simple creative tasks, all fall into this category.

This is prevalent in *generative art*, including generative music as mentioned earlier. A widely used definition of generative art is given by Philip Galanter:

> Generative art refers to any art practice where the artist creates a process, such as a set of natural language rules, a computer program, a machine, or other procedural invention, which is then set into motion with some degree of autonomy contributing to or resulting in a completed work of art.[62]

Galanter's appeal to autonomy leaves a wide scope for how minor or major the system's role might be in this process. As we have already seen in the case of AARON, despite the system performing no humanlike reflection, learning, or complex concept formation, there is still reason to attribute it a sliver of creative autonomy in the context of a human-computer co-creative process. These systems do after all determine aspects of the final creative product that the human co-creator leaves to them. Generatively produced art is now a decades-old tradition, with large and active communities of practice, university courses, dedicated creative tools, and a gradual but certain creep into mainstream creative practice.

A system, like those of Cohen or Cope, may generate original outputs using any of the techniques just introduced, without exhibiting the full gamut of human creative intelligence. Even incredibly sophisticated machine learning techniques enact a basic generation process, without reflection or evaluation, and yet still autonomously derive and apply a sort of structural understanding of the aesthetic domain in question. The simplest examples of generative systems can be found in rule-based generative methods. When I teach generative art to undergraduate students in media arts and design, one of the core concepts I cover is parametric systems, where a set of parameters is used to control how some process executes to produce an output. Parameters are simply values, usually real numbers, that define some feature of a system. In a computer game, gravity might be one example of parameter; turn up gravity and things fall more quickly. Consider what parameters might define the form of a computer-generated mountainscape in a game: perhaps visible qualities such as bumpiness, overall variation, and maximum steepness. Parametric methods are common in procedural content generation (PCG), the name given to the on-the-fly production of digital content, typically for computer games or movies, where the quantity of the content needed is large and repetitive enough to warrant automation, or where the context may necessitate automated generation, as in infinite-world games where it is not possible to precompose the material.

Spirographs give us a precomputational example of what a parametric generative system looks like. This 1960s children's drawing toy consists of a series of plastic shapes such as ovals and circles with geared edges and pen holes. In the hands of an adept child, these interact to prescribe beautiful mathematical patterns. The simplest form of spirograph consists of an inner circular disc which rolls around inside an outer circular cavity, and we may consider the parameters of this simple generative system to include the diameter of each of the two circles, as well as the distance of the pen from the center of the inner circle. Thus we have a set of three numerical parameters describing the "space" of all possible two-circle spirographs.

Now think of this set of three parameters as a three-dimensional space, with each parameter corresponding to a dimension in the space. Each point in the space corresponds to a certain spirograph configuration and thus a specific spirograph pattern. Spirograph space is a relatively easy space to grasp. We intuitively know that it won't produce pictures of people and motor cars, only lumpy, layered, semiregular circular patterns. While the underlying parameters define a space, we can also think of spirographs in terms of another space, defined by observable properties of the resulting images, such as degree of rotational symmetry or overall diameter. These properties, unlike the parameters, are *derived properties*. It is important to note that parameters and properties are not the same, and that there is a great deal of freedom involved in choosing what parameters and properties are used and looked at in generative systems.

There are a few ways we might use our spirograph space as a generative tool. We could just use it to generate variation: all spirographs are quite nice looking after all—we are in a relatively unadventurous, low-risk space of aesthetic possibilities. For example, we might just want to create a generative desktop image that keeps mixing up its content. The artist Paul Brown, a contemporary of Harold Cohen, whose work we will look at in chapter 5, has a body of work spanning several decades that explores dynamic, ever-changing artworks based on simple parametric systems. Or we might want to assign distinct spirograph badges to players in a game. MIT's Media Lab did something similar with their logo in 2011, specifying a simple parameterized geometric pattern for which the parameters were adjusted at random to produce multiple variations.

We can also engage in a more goal-oriented search of the spirograph space, with a more or less clearly conceived target pattern in mind. We could try to find the spirograph pattern that most clearly resembled a poppy or the Mercedes-Benz logo. As a variation of this, we might want to automatically search not for specific properties but simply for *novelty*, perhaps as a way to find surprising spirographs we'd not seen before, or perhaps as a more sophisticated way to generate variations that had the property of being clearly distinguishable from others.

Parameterizing digital objects also provides a way for an act of creation to be split across multiple individuals—one or more people who make the parametric system, and one or more people who use the parametric system to make a real instance of an output of that system. Kate Compton, an artist and developer working in games and interactive media, suggests the name "casual creator" for the kinds of objects that result.[63]

> A casual creator is an interactive system (often software) that encourages the fast, confident, and pleasurable exploration of a possibility space, resulting in

the creation or discovery of surprising new artifacts that bring feelings of pride, ownership, and creativity to the users that make them.[64]

The generative artifacts perhaps don't automate creation on their own but do shift the social relations between human creators to one in which a coder can program a casual creator, which others can then use as simple creative playgrounds to produce final outputs.

More complex parametric systems might warrant far more detailed search. An example is the complex 3D morphologies created by generative artist Andy Lomas.[65] Lomas's morphologies are created through simulations of growth processes that largely resemble natural organic structures. These growth processes are defined by large sets of parameters that have the potential to offer spaces of possible forms far too vast to be fully explored by machines, let alone through a manual process by a human artist.

Another type of simple generative process takes its inspiration from complex systems science and artificial life, and looks at how simple agents interact to produce sophisticated structures. Dutch duo Driessens and Verstappen are exemplary artists filling this new creative niche, working across a wide range of media to extend studies of form to a generative domain. Their landmark work *E-volver* takes the form of an ever-changing generative

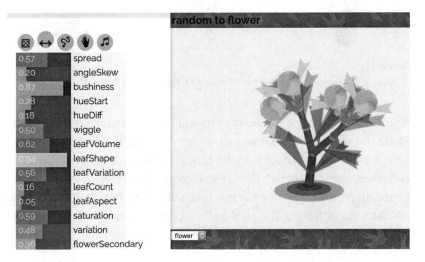

Figure 1.3
One of Kate Compton's casual creator systems, a parametrically controlled plant designer. Image credit: Kate Compton.

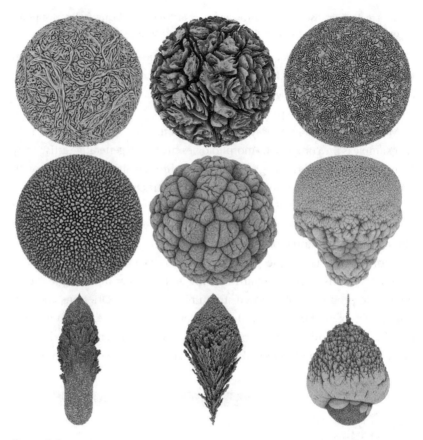

Figure 1.4
A series of 3D organic forms evolved by Andy Lomas. Image credit: Andy Lomas.

texture, an instance of a generative art technique sometimes known informally and somewhat unglamorously as ant-drawing. Simple computational agents trawl the surface of a digital canvas following biologically inspired behaviors, sensing different pixel colors around themselves, and responding by moving or manipulating the pixels like small insects or bacteria feeding on nutrients or leaving chemical trails. As the program runs, rich abstract color textures resembling mold, rock surfaces, terrains, and weather patterns gradually come and go.

Generative art theorist Mitchell Whitelaw points out that in such artistic contexts the means can be as important as the end.[66] Even when processes such as these seem focused squarely on the aesthetic properties of the output, there is still a "system story," laden with meaning, underlying the algorithms and their perception by an audience. In *E-volver*, the visual coherence of the resulting images, afforded by the ant-drawing algorithm iterating gradually over the pixel landscapes, also doubles up in offering a conceptual coherence: the story of local interactions resulting in emergent structure, of the complex interplay between the actions of different agents, of the feedback cycle of influence between an agent and its environment, and the way nature can create complexity through simplicity. This story permeates both the creation and perception of the work.

Related to generative art and computational creativity, but with a slightly different slant is creative AI.[67] This refers more generally to the use of AI in creative work but without necessarily focusing on the role of the system as a creative agent. For example, a search for images of cats might use intelligent computer vision trained to recognize cats. If we used those images to automatically generate a collage, this would be a tenuous example of computational creativity but a safe example of creative AI. Here the system uses advanced AI techniques but under the creative operation of a human artist. Once again, the sophistication of the technique is not necessarily a direct indicator of how much creative agency the system embodies.

Generative art, PCG, and creative AI are quite rapidly making their way into creative practice and commercial products, and transforming how we think about creative production. They have immediate industrial applications and already-established artist's legacies such as that of Cohen.

In this applied area, practical goals and questions of usability and interaction design come to the fore. In the world of generative systems, there are many interesting questions that interaction designers have to consider when designing effective interfaces that may be less common in other domains. How do users manage the potential complexity of behavior of a generative system? How do you make them aware of the range of possibilities afforded by it? How do you provide control over opaque algorithms such as Markov models, neural networks, or genetic algorithms, or even represent these systems visually to users? At what level, if any, does the user need to know how to program in order to configure or control the generative system, or is it possible to come up with intuitive forms of graphical control?

Figure 1.5
The *E-volver* generative artwork by Erwin Driessens and Maria Verstappen. Top left: The interaction context showing how people can selectively breed designs. Other panels: A range of agent behaviors. Image credit: Driessens and Verstappen.

In addition, creative movements, constantly responding to the potential of new technologies, adapt such technologies in ways that inevitably reinterpret their function. For example, the glitch aesthetic that has grown up with digital technology, which transforms errors and damage into creative materials, applies in a potent way to creative AI tools. Many artists working with creative AI have purposefully or inadvertently gravitated toward the most inane or obviously erroneous outputs of AI systems, in part, one might assume, because of the poetic imagery of the hacked and malfunctioning robot performing pale imitations of real human intelligence. Here is an example of song lyric generation discussed in an MIT *Technology Review* article:

> come on, uh
> you remember the voice of the widow
> i love the girl of the age
> i have a regard for the whole
> i have no doubt of the kind
> i am sitting in the corner of the mantelpiece

This example did not itself purposely aim for banal lyrics, but it illustrates the resulting glitch, the comedy of its aesthetic being what inspired a news article to be written about it.[68]

Beyond Mere Generation

Everything that I have just described has become known to computational creativity researchers, somewhat in jest, as *mere generation*. A disparaging term intended lightheartedly, this directs focus toward a higher ambition—to build creative systems that not only generate outputs according to rules, learned structures, or prespecified objectives, but that we actually judge as creative ourselves. We could equally call these "lowly" and "lofty" forms of computational creativity, respectively. Lowly computational creativity employs algorithmic processes as tools in the generation of new forms. But as human creators with our grounded goals and motivations, and our ability to shift viewpoints and reframe problems, to understand and interpret and to subjectively declare likes and dislikes, we invariably stand apart from such systems. Some or all of these things may be needed to advance the objectives of lofty computational creativity.

Of these, the element most prominently discussed among computational creativity researchers is that step of evaluation, whereby a system not only generates possible artifacts but applies judgment over their quality. Evaluation in computational creativity is not reducible to the identification of functional objective criteria where some measurable feature is optimized. (Although we do find many examples of functional optimization related to computational creativity. An example of this is in parametric building design, where we might aim to optimize the sunlight exposure a certain apartment has, a task that can be performed automatically and precisely given a good model of the building.) These readily calculable features are not unimportant in creative practice, but unless you are an extreme functionalist you will find them lacking when it comes to a completed picture of human aesthetic appreciation—the kind of evaluation that takes place when we choose a sweater in a shop, select which music to listen to, or compare views on early and late Stanley Kubrick movies. Any system that could meaningfully apply such judgment would be qualitatively different from the kinds of generators discussed earlier and would be humanlike in a way that has not been well explored in computational systems. This is the wide open territory of computational creativity, and even the language for discussing such a goal is not well developed. Those engaged in this pursuit acknowledge that to do so with a real depth of understanding of human creative concerns, such as the multiple levels of meaning we might immediately recognize in a work of visual art, is, to quote Cardoso, Veale, and Wiggins again, "so far beyond the current abilities of AI systems that it is almost painful to contemplate how we might ever reach this level of creative generation."[69]

But in the spirit of computational creativity, where "no abstract insight can compare with the ability to show a real creative system in full flow,"[70] there is no harm in trying. Consider this playful experiment in making such an evaluative agent by computational creativity researcher Dan Ventura: PIERRE, "a system for culinary creation, which, given access to existing recipes, learns to produce new crockpot recipes."[71] PIERRE has access to an online database of recipes along with the ratings of those recipes by real people. Some expert knowledge is applied to this database so that ingredients are structured according to groups and with the similarities between ingredients also modeled. PIERRE then trains a neural network on this data, the goal of which is to successfully predict the rankings of given ingredient combinations. The network is a first crude approximation of an evaluative system, a model of people's taste. PIERRE then searches for new recipe combinations and tries each one out on its evaluation system. Using evolutionary optimization, it finds combinations for which the evaluator scores highly.

If you care to try PIERRE's "Scrumptious Broth with Bean," which includes coconut milk, halloumi, green tea, evaporated milk, sherry, and baking cocoa among its ingredients, you can refer to the original paper, in which the recipe is given in full.[72] I for one am quite sure I won't like it. I question PIERRE's taste. I don't think such a monstrosity has really passed his virtual gullet (but it has passed Dan's, who assures me it is actually quite good). Nevertheless, PIERRE offers an instance of the basic architecture of a nontrivial computationally creative system, where some form of human evaluation is modeled and applied as a selection routine in a generative task.

But closing the loop between generation and evaluation is not the end point of computationally creative systems. Human reflexivity involves being able to generate not only new possible outputs but also new methods, goals, and conceptualizations. Pablo Gervás, a computational creativity researcher working primarily in poetry generation, proposes a general schema that "could be applied to most processes of artefact generation, including those carried out by humans," which includes not only a basic form of search among a set of possible artifacts but also some degree of modification of both the methods and the objectives of the system:

1. **Procedure selection**: selection of constructive procedure
2. **Ingredient selection**: selection of ingredients to use
3. **Lower bound definition**: establishment of candidate rejection criteria
4. **Upper bound definition**: establishment of candidate success criteria
5. **Construction**: application of the procedure that resulted from 1 to the ingredients that resulted from 2
6. **Selection**: application of results of 3 and 4 to results of 5
7. **Reflection**: reflection upon the accumulated results with a view to refining steps 1 to 4[73]

Such candidate architectures, loosely formed, provide a roadmap for the creation of powerful computationally creative systems. Imagine a future PIERRE that modifies its evaluative neural network to better predict human preferences, restructures its ingredients database based on newly discovered relations, and adds new constraints to its criteria for success. Could such a system cause genuine culinary delight?

Recognizing Differing Goals: Avoiding the Methodological Malaise
Computational creativity builds on studies of creativity to achieve the goal of building creative machines. But unlike creativity research, it is harder to pin down exactly what motivates computational creativity and what constitutes successful outcomes. For example, as well as building systems for creative applications, computational creativity offers in return a new

methodology for studying creativity itself: simulating and testing the effects of hypothesized computational processes.

Marcus Pearce, David Meredith, and Geraint Wiggins,[74] talking of the automation of music composition, identify four distinct motivations for researchers working in this area. In algorithmic composition, composers use computational processes to compose music in new ways. In the design of compositional tools, music technologists create tools that can be used by others (or themselves) to support composition. In the computational modeling of musical styles, researchers examine musicological questions concerning musical style and structure. And in the computational modeling of music cognition, psychologists attempt to understand how we engage in musical perception and thought.

Pearce, Meredith, and Wiggins claim that a "methodological malaise" has led to an all too easy conflation of these different motivations. An academic composer developing their own algorithmic composition software, for example, may encounter methodological tension between their own compositional aims and the study of the functional design of their software. If their software involves models of musical style, they may also wish to make musicological claims derived from their system's output. Pearce, Meredith, and Wiggins appeal for clarity about how these different goals necessitate different approaches to achieving those goals, in particular different approaches to grounding their results in evidence. This attention to academic methodologies, connecting the right methods to the right types of questions and claims, has been an important part of the process of forging this new multidisciplinary field of research. Although many still fall foul of the methodological malaise, computational creativity now has a mature and thorough body of exemplary research literature (evaluation methods are discussed in more depth in chapter 7).

If this book does nothing else I hope it will encourage readers to be critical of claims in the media about the achievements of computational creativity, and question where computational creativity is useful and meaningful. In particular, claims about the capacity of an algorithm to produce something of a certain nature requires a strong and convincing framework with which to describe the nature of the thing being produced. How else can we judge the claim? As we will see in chapter 4, something can achieve the status of being classified as an artwork in a wide number of ways: one example is anything that an art gallery chooses to put on its walls; another is anything produced with the intention of being art; another is anything that is perceived as beautiful by an observer. All are potentially valid, but none may be definitive. Each definition also comes with problems when translated into a machine context, not least because most definitions of art *presuppose* that it has been made by a socially situated human. If being placed in a gallery or possessing visual harmony is a sufficient condition, then it becomes an unremarkable triviality that a computer *can* create art, but such a framework renders the result unexciting. If demonstrating that the machine had intention, then, by contrast, the task is very hard if not intractable. It is essential to avoid misalignment between the aims of any given computational creativity project and its measurement.

A Sociotechnological Perspective

This chapter has offered a rapid sketch of a field of activity that looks set to radically influence creative production in coming years, as the seemingly inevitable advance of computational intelligence continues. While this book advocates critically challenging some of the claims made about AI and creativity—the endless world firsts and simplified claims that computers have developed the necessary cognitive tools to occupy the status of artists—I do believe, nevertheless, that advanced computationally creative systems will start to have significant impact in this area soon. At least in certain domains, they will have a rapid and profound impact on creative practice, with benefits and costs to different people. This in turn will challenge conceptions of what it means for humans to be creative and artistic, to be the dominant creative force in the universe.

In order to sift through and sort the claims and discussions around machines performing cultural work, a strongly interdisciplinary approach is needed. We need to understand what algorithms can actually do, and then we need to relate those capacities and affordances to what people actually do in creative artistic domains and why they do these things. Any approach must tread carefully between the essentialist trap of assigning some mystical quality to humans that is unattainable by machines, and similar simplifications of human cultural activity that make artistic machines a triviality while misrepresenting the depth of cultural behavior.

For this reason, this book takes what might seem an unreasonably long detour—for a book about technology—into discussions of human creativity, art, and cultural behavior in its own right, in which I focus particularly on the social nature of human behavior, based on the reasonable assumption that artistic behavior is largely if not fundamentally social in nature. The goal is a sociotechnological analysis which I claim has the best chance of avoiding the pitfalls of simplification and essentialism, but also of coming up with a perspective on human artistic behavior that is truly capable of integrating machine behaviors without reducing them to "mere tools" or getting stuck trying to analyze them in human terms when they are so fundamentally different.

In the next chapter, I look at some of the historical discussion concerned with the very notion of machines being creative. One dimension of this discussion is the well-rehearsed debate around the Lovelace objection, the question raised by Ada Lovelace about whether machines, programmed by humans, could possibly originate anything. As a philosophical objection this will be quickly rejected; we have a good understanding of how simple mechanical processes can originate things, and arguably, we need look no further than the nonhuman "algorithm" of natural selection to see this at play. Far more attention is given instead in this chapter to the nature of creative thought and its generalization in algorithmic terms, but seeding a discussion in subsequent chapters of creativity taking on different properties when viewed in more distributed contexts.

2 Coming to Terms with Creative Machines

> We can see no a priori objection to the gradual development of a mechanical life, though that life shall be so different from ours that it is only by a severe discipline that we can think of it as life at all.
> —Samuel Butler[1]

> Words do not express thoughts very well. They always become a little different immediately after they are expressed, a little distorted, a little foolish.
> —Herman Hesse[2]

> The formal study of creativity ... [may reach] ... the stage of advancement which botany reached when Linnaeus organized flora into phyla and into classes.
> —Mel Rhodes[3]

How Can Creativity Be Computational?

While artists like Cohen, Lewis, and Cope were reflexively tinkering with their machines, a great body of research and commentary has risen up on the nature of human creativity. This spans myriad academic areas, from developmental and evolutionary psychology to organization science, management, and philosophy. As a subject of study, creativity became a topic of serious focus in the nineteenth century and one of great social importance in the twentieth. In the twenty-first century, it is a veritable juggernaut of debate and research, reshaping our cities, governments, and corporations.

As a concept, creativity has historically been something of a moving target and one that is still very much in motion. According to Raymond Williams,[4] the terminology of creativity evolved through and in the wake of the Enlightenment. Deriving from the Latin *creō*, meaning "to make," the earliest uses of the verb "to create" referred exclusively to the divine creation that was the domain of God, setting the tone for its later designation in the activities of mortal humans: a special form of making that was profound and fundamental rather than mundane. Gradually, forms of artistic practice, beginning with poetry, became designated as sharing this godlike capacity to bring new forms into being, and for a good length of time creativity was exclusively associated with the arts among human endeavors. A persevering association between art and divine creation, through this use of words, suited some of the prevailing conceptions of art during this time, embodying a connection to the sacred.[5]

In the nineteenth and twentieth centuries, along with the rise of atheism, the theory of evolution, and the science of psychology, the concept of creativity came to incorporate a wider set of activities, including scientific discovery, design, and the problem-solving of the everyday bricoleur. The modern sense of the term is most prominently associated with a "power of mind,"[6] a psychological rather than metaphysical concept, and is less and less limited to any specific domain of activity; *accounting* can be creative. However, as many commentators have observed, the term gets applied inconsistently to different entities. It can denote a process, or a property of the products of such processes, as well as applying to the collective capacity of a group rather than an individual.[7]

Although creativity may have shed its theological origins, it has carried the original contrast with its ontological cousin, "to make," into the twenty-first century. Making is mundane whereas creativity is extraordinary. Under the microscope these activities may seem hard to distinguish. Yet the latter maintains the higher status of association with a powerful metaphysical trick, not only restructuring existing matter, but, godlike, bringing new essences into the world. Making means making the same thing as everybody else. Creating involves differentiation. It also carries with it the baggage of its historically exclusive association with art. In some circumstances we talk of the "creative industries" as an economic category containing art, music, graphic design, film, and so on, and designate certain workers as creatives. This designation has broadened over time. Recent formal analyses of this sector, such as the work of Richard Florida on the creative class,[8] correspond to a contemporary sense of creativity as including science, engineering, and research, conflicting with the more specific sense of creative as referring strictly to art-oriented cultural production. (How exactly we distinguish art-type activities from other activities is a topic for chapter 4.)

Creativity is one of several slippery concepts found in this book. Scientists and engineers can find themselves pining for rigorous, operationalizable definitions that help precisely pin down, measure, categorize, and manage a subject of study. Precision of language, and more formal representations of concepts as in code or mathematics, are powerful tools, but concepts in the wild don't necessarily obey these requirements of precision, as the brief history above highlights. "Ask most people the question 'what is creativity?' and you are more likely to elicit an anecdote, an aphorism, or a metaphor than you are a literal definition," note Cardoso, Veale, and Wiggins.[9] For Wiggins, "'creativity' is ill-defined, but we do tend to know it when we see it; [but] … 'creativity' as a word is overloaded, and is usable in distinctly different and confusing ways."[10]

In fact, established understanding of how we process concepts such as creativity as mental representations shows that a definitional formulation is generally inadequate.[11] Concepts work in practice as effective tools for understanding our world, and communicating that understanding with others, by using one or more prototypes as markers against which we seek a "family resemblance."[12] According to this view of how concepts work in the wild, a concept fans out from a small number of things that definitely fit the concept, toward a wider number of things that lie at the concept's periphery and may or may not fit, as the context demands. As Gregory Murphy illustrates:

> You might have an idea of the prototypical dog, for example, that is average-sized, dark in color, has medium-length fur, has a pointed nose and floppy ears, is a family pet, barks at strangers, drools unpleasantly, and has other common features of dogs. Yet, this prototype may be something that you have never specifically seen—it is just your abstraction of what dogs are most often like. Other dogs vary in their similarity to this prototype, and so they differ in their typicality. Miniature hairless dogs are not very similar to the prototype, and they are considered atypical; … if you saw a thing with four legs but a very elongated body, no hair, and whiskers, you might think that it was somewhat similar to a dog, but not similar enough to actually be a dog. However, this is the point at which different people might disagree, and you might change your mind.[13]

According to this body of theory, typicality is a smoothly varying quantity. At concept boundaries, like the one described above, we are slower to categorize and more prone to change our minds. We also determine category membership by appealing to nonmembership of other categories. So by extension to creativity, if something exhibits properties of imitation, then it is less likely to be seen as creative. We associate creativity with a number of qualities including novelty, aesthetic value, surprise, non-obviousness, insight, individuality, problem solving, reconceptualizing problems (seeing things differently), and divergent thinking. These are elements that might be used to typify instances of creativity. Similarly, creativity has been described as an "essentially contested concept,"[14] one that by its nature evades being pinned down.

The essentially contested nature of creativity makes it appropriate to appeal to a know-it-when-you-see-it definition of creativity, which is how computational creativity researchers have tended to approach the definition of their core subject of study. Wiggins defines computational creativity as "the study and support, through computational means and methods, of behaviour exhibited by natural and artificial systems, which would be deemed creative if exhibited by humans."[15] But reassuringly, although the concept of creativity may be ambiguous, studies into people's judgment of creativity by Teresa Amabile have shown that a robust consensus can be reached in these judgments. That is, within specific domains of creative practice, people tend to agree on what constitutes creativity. This is particularly true of domain experts, who can even agree well on the perceived creativity of an artifact, despite not agreeing on whether they like the artifact or whether it is technically good (a 0.77 correlation among experts in judgments of creativity compared to a 0.52 correlation for liking).[16] Thus despite the necessary subjectivity of creative evaluation, we can, under the right circumstances, reliably use human evaluation as a means to establish when something or someone is creative.[17]

Such issues draw attention to the disciplinary differences of approaches that are bound to arise amid any study of creativity. In an article entitled "Soft Sciences Are Often Harder than Hard Sciences," Jared Diamond describes how some "areas are given the highly flattering name of hard science, because they use the firm evidence that controlled experiments and highly accurate measurements can provide," whereas "soft sciences, as they're pejoratively termed, are more difficult to study for obvious reasons. ... You can't start ... and stop [experiments] whenever you choose. You can't control all the variables; perhaps you can't control any variable. You may even find it hard to decide what a variable is."[18] In such fields, it is less of an issue to bypass the precise definitions of terms, and the family-resemblance view of concepts supports such a stance. A family-resemblance view transforms the task of dealing with concepts like creativity (and art, which we come to later) from one that is constantly confounded to one that is stable.

The concept of creativity comes with its own set of unmistakable prototypes that readers will share. Our prototypes of creativity might derive from famous individual figures, artifacts, and acts of creation—the *Mona Lisa*, Einstein's relativity, Madonna, Mozart, the iPhone—or from personal examples of individual creativity, such as those involving the developmental progress of one's own children. Every parent has an example of recognizing creativity in their children, even if their child is *actually* doing exactly what we would expect them to do at that stage in their development.

As these examples illustrate, creativity is additionally confused by the different objects of focus the term might be applied to. As early as 1961, Mel Rhodes catalogued how overlapping strands of research into creativity had begun to appear and were causing confusion. He termed these strands person, product, process, and press (the meaning of the last term is not that obvious; it refers to the relationship between human beings and their environment). "Each strand has unique identity academically, but only in unity do the four strands operate functionally. It is this very fact of synthesis that causes fog in talk about creativity and this may be the basis for the semblance of a 'cult.'"[19]

Novelty, Value, and the Rest

What are the properties that guide our judgment about whether something conforms to our prototypical expectations of creativity? Two dimensions that are almost universally agreed to be part of the reckoning of creativity are *novelty* and *value*, and a third, more contested, candidate is *surprise*, or *non-obviousness*. Novelty doesn't warrant much scrutiny at this stage, except to warn against the assumption that there is anything objective about measuring the novelty of something. Any measure of similarity or dissimilarity between two things always assumes a frame of reference, and different frames of reference will produce different measures of similarity between entities. A wine connoisseur will have greater capacity for distinction than a novice and would be more attuned to the discovery of a novel wine. But this aside, it would be safe to argue that identicality is strictly mutually exclusive to creativity; novelty is a nonnegotiable criterion for creativity.[20]

Value is the source of more conceptual trouble. It is, like novelty, also subjective, defined relative to a person or group, situated in a given context. Value, like creativity, may also be seen to represent a cluster of concepts with differences in the contexts in which they are applied. For example, Amabile defines creative results using the cluster of terms "appropriate, useful, correct, or valuable,"[21] and other creativity researchers have also tended to diffuse the focus on value alone with a similar set of related adjectives.

As I will argue, value makes sense from a psychological perspective where creative individuals work toward creative goals. But it becomes a more elusive quality in the distributed view of creativity that I present in the following chapters, which is irreducible to individual psychological creativity. At a social level, we see a creative process which has more in common with biological evolution, unfolding blindly. While the creations of an inventor or artist have value to that creator or to the people around them, there is nobody or no thing that derives value from the creations made by an evolutionary process. Yes, the elephant's trunk is certainly useful to the elephant, but it was not created because the elephant's ancestors needed trunks. Whatever process did create the trunk wasn't *directly* driven by the value of the trunk.

Surprise or non-obviousness is occasionally also included in discussions of creativity, and this usually depends on the application domain in which the discussion is being held. For example, two theorists I will discuss in the following sections include these terms. Dean Simonton refers to the US patent-office definition of a patentable invention as including the criterion of non-obviousness,[22] and Margaret Boden includes surprise in some (but not all) of her influential discussions of creativity.[23] We can consider either of these to be a component in a list of elements that define prototypical creativity. The term "compelling" has also been used in a similar way.[24] In some ways, surprise, non-obviousness, and compellingness are linking concepts that overlap with both novelty and value. For example, in science, something can't be *obvious* and *novel* at the same time, whereas in humor, something may gain *value* from its *non-obviousness*.

Creative Thought
Psychological research on creativity is concerned with the processes taking place in people's minds when they create. A starting point for such inquiry lies in the reflexive accounts of celebrated creative individuals.

Mathematicians and scientists such as Poincaré, Einstein, and Kekulé have provided well-known autobiographical accounts of their thought processes that offer a starting point for formalizing aspects of creativity. The French mathematician Henri Poincaré, for example, observed:

> Often when one works at a hard question, nothing good is accomplished at the first attack. Then one takes a rest, longer or shorter, and sits down anew to the work. During the first half-hour, as before, nothing is found, and then all of a sudden the decisive idea presents itself to the mind. It might be said that the conscious work has been more fruitful because it has been interrupted and the rest has given back to the mind its force and freshness.[25]

The idea that human creativity might come about through different stages or layers of cognitive processing became formulated in theory as researchers turned their attention to explaining these accounts. One of the earliest such formulations is Graham Wallas's four-stage model of the creative process,[26] developed in the 1920s. The stages Wallas identifies are those of *preparation, incubation, illumination,* and *verification.* According to Wallas's model, a problem is defined and elaborated upon in the preparation stage. The incubation stage is then manifest as a kind of passive mulling over of the problem, leading to a moment of illumination, which can then be more formally and logically verified. The middle stages of incubation and illumination are understood as involving subconscious mental activities, during which candidate solutions and combinations of ideas are processed. The beginning and end stages involve more conscious processes, where the problem is framed and the solutions are examined.

What happens during incubation and how these incubated ideas present themselves in the form of illumination have subsequently become two prominent areas of inquiry in the psychology of creativity. It is a fascinating prospect (especially from the point of view of computational creativity) that the creative mind does its magic out of sight of our conscious awareness, like a separate machine that we feed creative tasks to. But it is a view that tallies well with the majority of intuitive and anecdotal accounts of creative inspiration. Like Poincaré, you may be familiar with the experience of suddenly encountering a solution to a problem at an unlikely moment, or having a great idea come to you and not being able to trace where it sprung from. More exotically, the chemist Kekulé recounts moments of dreamy reverie underpinning his discoveries.[27] In one case he daydreams of snakes biting their own tails, suddenly realizing that this vision provides the solution to his problem of the structure of benzene; the molecules form rings.[28] Poincaré's accounts also allude to these dreamlike states of mind: "Ideas rose in crowds; I felt them collide until pairs interlocked, so to speak, making a stable combination."[29]

Attempts to develop concepts to explain what is going on under the surface of our conscious awareness have been in no short supply. Arthur Koestler, a journalist who turned to popular science, writing extensively on creativity, elaborated on the illumination stage, identifying different forms of emotional response grounded in surprise and aesthetic experience. For Koestler, responses to striking new ideas could take the form of aesthetic pleasure (AH), a "eureka" moment (AHA), or amusement (HAHA).[30] Koestler was also one of many proponents of the idea that, as the earlier quote from Poincaré suggests, the key process of idea formation involves the combination of previous ideas. He called this process *bisociation*. More recently, and relatedly, Gilles Fauconnier and Mark Turner have proposed that *conceptual blending* is a fundamental tool of human cognition, possibly a critical step in humankind's evolutionary psychology.[31] A conceptual blend brings together two inputs to create a blended concept or mental space, which, importantly, can then be used to think in new ways, a kind of mental simulation or thought experiment. In Fauconnier's words, "Conceptual blending is a basic mental operation that leads to new meaning, global insight, and conceptual compressions useful for memory and manipulation of otherwise diffuse ranges of meaning."[32] Others have described the emergence of new ideas in a way more akin to the incubation of organisms. From a psychoanalytic perspective, Silvano Arieti[33] proposes the *endocept*, a concept in its early stage of formulation, as in the incubation period. By contrast, an *exocept* takes a mature form that can be properly expressed. The creative mind, then, is an incubator for exocepts.

Closely associated with these hypothesized phases of incubation and illumination is the idea that creative cognition involves exploratory search. Amabile distinguishes creativity from other forms of problem solving as involving heuristic rather than algorithmic processes, the latter being "those for which the path to the solution is clear and straightforward."[34] For example, solving a long-division problem using the method of long division taught to you at school is formulaic (and easily programmed into a computer), whereas coming up with that long-division method itself is not; there is no obvious formula for doing so and no certainty about the outcome.

Correspondingly, the incubation phase has become understood as the process of broadly scanning and processing the world of possibilities in order to bring up candidate solutions, which are then evaluated, preempting illumination. Thus a dominant theme in the study of creativity resulting from this view has been the study of how people successfully engage in thinking that fans out to include unlikely or apparently unrelated ideas, which are needed if one is to escape the straightforward path' and come up with novel solutions.

The issue is illustrated by a well-known experiment called the candle problem.[35] This involves a task in which a person is given a candle, a box of tacks, and a book of matches. The participant is asked to mount the candle onto a pinboard on the wall and then light it, using only the items provided. However, an additional criterion is that the candle must not drip wax onto the ground. Tacking the candle straight to the wall would not work. The solution instead is as follows: empty the box of tacks, tack the box to the wall so that it forms a shelf, place the candle in the shelf and light it.

The solution is obvious in hindsight. However, one of the ingredients of this solution is neatly hidden: many people do not immediately recognize that the box containing the tacks is itself an available resource, assuming it only to be there to hold the tacks, a phenomenon known as *functional fixedness*; the presumed function of the box blocks it from being seen as a shelf. The speed at which people arrive at this solution therefore depends critically on how quickly they overcome this misrepresentation of the box in their formulation of the problem. Experiments have shown how this response factor can be directly influenced through the problem representation: if you present the box and tacks separately, participants solve the problem more quickly. You can even speed up the solution time simply by saying "a box and some tacks" instead of "a box of tacks."

Thus when the environment is not kind enough to reveal the components necessary in solving a problem, we must employ heuristic strategies to help us search for them, epitomized in the now clichéd notion of *thinking outside the box*. Psychologists of creativity have subsequently been interested in what enables us to reformulate problems and broaden our search for solutions. The Torrance test,[36] designed to examine an individual's natural capacity for such *divergent thinking*, requires participants to list as many possible answers as they can to questions such as "What can a brick be used for?" You might start with boring answers such as "building a wall," or "propping a door open," and end up with ideas further removed from traditional expectations, such as "to draw right angles." Respondents' answers are then evaluated according to four criteria:

- *Fluency* The total number of interpretable, meaningful, and relevant ideas generated in response to the stimulus.
- *Flexibility* The number of different categories of relevant responses.
- *Originality* The statistical rarity of the responses.
- *Elaboration* The amount of detail in the responses.

While such tests may tell us something about individuals' natural propensities for divergent thinking, we can also employ more overt strategies to support creativity. Mathematicians are known to learn heuristic abstractions to help solve problems,[37] and organizational strategies such as brainstorming encourage teams to work together to expand a space of possible solutions by actively withholding judgment and encouraging weirder ideas.[38]

A more general theoretical formulation of exploratory search in creativity is offered by Dean Simonton, who draws on Donald Campbell's 1960s theory of blind variation and selective retention (BVSR). Simonton defines blind variation as any stage in the creative process where possibilities not immediately to hand are examined for their fit. Given two possibilities, X and Y, if X is more likely to be encountered than Y, but Y is more valuable than X, then, he contends, the discovery of Y as the preferred solution must be arrived at in a blind manner, not a sequential one. Wherever problems have this structure, blind variation will necessarily play a part in the solution. As "problems become more ill-defined, not only must the person rely increasingly on weak heuristic methods that do not promise a proper solution, but it also becomes ever less evident what are the best heuristic methods to try out first. ... The creator may have no other option than to generate-and-test all available heuristic methods without any assurance that even one option will actually work."[39]

Simonton warns against the perception that this view reduces creative cognition to mere random trial and error, firstly on the basis that blindness should not be considered synonymous with randomness. A blind search can be highly systematic; to make the point, Simonton uses the example of a radar sweeping in a circular search pattern. The radar searches blindly, meaning that it spins around ready to encounter objects rather than actively homing in on them, but its rotation is systematic and makes for a sensible heuristic (visit each compass direction equally often at equal intervals). It is not random. Secondly, Simonton emphasizes that in real creative cognition blind search is integrated with other strategies and needn't be considered the primary strategy. "Problem solvers will endeavor to use algorithmic methods whenever doable, but frequently they will have to fall back on a more heuristic search through the various possibilities." He goes further to say that "ideational variations in creativity and discovery take place along a continuum from wholly sighted to entirely blind." He posits that blind variation may be integrated in different ways among creative processes such as mental association and behavioral tinkering. This includes a distinction between internal blind variation, as in the ideation discussed above, and external blind variation, for which he studies Picasso's initial sketches for the painting *Guernica* as an example. In the analysis of Picasso's sketches, the blindness of the search is evidenced in a series of progressions and regressions that do not clearly progress toward the ultimate end point.[40]

In real life, the problems we encounter are situated in different specifics and present opportunities for the use of creative thinking intertwined with other strategies. Real-world "candle problems" present themselves to us in different ways; sometimes the box is hidden, at other times it is in plain sight.

In Robert Sternberg's investment theory of creativity,[41] which I discuss in more detail in the following chapter, "Creativity requires a confluence of six distinct but interrelated resources: intellectual abilities, knowledge, styles of thinking, personality, motivation, and environment." Among intellectual abilities, he includes divergent thinking, but also adds "the analytic skill to recognize which of one's ideas are worth pursuing and which are not, and the practical-contextual skill to know how to persuade others of—to sell other people on—the value of one's ideas." In personality, he includes attitude to risk. In motivation, the focus is on the value of intrinsic over extrinsic forms of motivation, a topic studied closely by Amabile and also central to Mihaly Csikszentmihalyi's concept of flow, a particular state of mind that occurs when one is deeply engaged in a task. Further research on the candle problem showed how much the context in which we encounter the problem matters: counterintuitively, those who are paid rewards to complete the problem do so more slowly than those who are not. Thus pressure to complete a task can hinder exploratory search, supporting the intuitive notion that creativity requires a certain state of mind and a certain freedom.

The preceding passages frame creativity largely in terms of problem solving, and while such topics may be of importance to mathematicians, scientists, and people trying to pin candles to walls, it is not quite so obvious what this has to do with making art and music. But this core idea of creativity as involving a blind search applies to artists equally. Creation of any kind involves something analogous to setting and solving problems. For example, "problem finding" is a key concept in the psychological study of art and design.[42] Indeed, Simonton suggests that "artists are truly creative, whereas scientists merely make discoveries. ... If Michelangelo had never been born, there would be something else painted on the [Sistine] chapel's ceiling, but if Newton had never been born, someone else would have come across the universal law of gravitation."[43] This theme will be picked up in depth in chapter 4.

With this overview of the study of creative psychology in mind, we can begin to look at how such themes have been tackled from a computational perspective.

Algorithmic Creativity: Searching through Spaces

Margaret Boden, a philosopher of cognitive science, is most widely known as driving creativity theory in the direction of computing and automation in her 1990 book *The Creative Mind*.[44] One of Boden's core themes is the idea that creativity occurs in a set of *conceptual spaces*, abstract spaces of ideas held by individuals or shared among groups of people. She posits that in our interactions with such conceptual spaces we exhibit fundamentally different forms of creativity.

The simplest form of creativity is *exploratory creativity*, whereby we search through a conceptual space, finding new variants on a concept. This may sound relatively formulaic, and therefore not fully satisfying the heuristic nature of creative search, but this depends on what exactly is involved; the exploration may still require smart search heuristics and evaluation. Another of Boden's creativity types is *combinatorial creativity*, which involves combining concepts together, similar to the way Koestler talks about bisociation. Lastly, Boden proposes that a more sophisticated form of creativity called *transformational creativity* involves actually changing the conceptual spaces themselves, so that new possibilities become available that weren't previously. In very simple terms, this might be understood as the difference between a musician working in a standard traditional jazz idiom and a musician innovating a new style, such as bebop or free jazz. Or it could describe the new conceptual spaces introduced by Einstein to replace Newtonian physics.

Boden's combinatorial, exploratory, and transformational forms of creativity describe different modes of human creation with respect to an existing stock of ideas but also suggest models of the different ways in which a computer might do the same. We might explicitly set out to build combinatorial, exploratory, and transformational creativity systems. But while combinatorial and exploratory creativity appear to offer reasonable designs for a computational system, transformational creativity seems problematic, leading some to think of this as a holy grail. Part of the problem lies in the fact that conceptual spaces are not dealt with formally by Boden, and so the idea of exploring them or transforming them remains too abstract to be meaningfully interpreted.

This has been addressed to some extent by Geraint Wiggins, who uses a formal framework, the creative systems framework, to explore Boden's ideas in finer detail.[45] Wiggins defines a conceptual space (C) in terms of a set of constraints or rules (R) applied to a universe (U) of all possibilities. He then defines the search of that space using a given strategy T. Importantly, for Wiggins's formulation, it is essential to recognize that while we can define a conceptual space, C (for example, the conceptual space of jazz music), we do not have direct and unrestrained access to this space but must search for things in it. While the space in some way *contains* all of jazz music, and we may understand the rules of jazz (or criteria for determining if something is jazz or not) in some capacity, we do not hold all of jazz music in our heads!

Any search strategy T searches the universe U, to find things in the space C. If we sit at a piano to compose a piece of jazz, our process of searching for possibilities is by no means limited to things that conform to jazz rules. We might come across all kinds of things that sound nothing like jazz during our search. Generally, we combine the search strategy T and the rule set R in some way, so that we keep our search constrained to the jazz space, but a critical distinction introduced by Wiggins is this separation between R and T. In addition to R, which constrains the area we're looking in, we also apply some kind of evaluation, distinguishing good from bad, whether inside or outside of the space defined by R. We might find good jazz music, or something that we think of as good, that doesn't conform to expectations about jazz.

Wiggins's formulation leads to slightly different conclusions to Boden, or at least to many of the most common interpretations of Boden's approach. The distinction between the definition of a conceptual space (C, defined by rules R applied to U) and the method for searching it (T) means that searching within the conceptual space might still be hard, requiring a search among possible alternative Ts. "It is perfectly possible," Wiggins claims, "for an exploratorily creative system to generate real novelty (because it can produce results which are unpredictable) and in some circumstances for those results to be valued, even if it works by brute enumeration."[46] Likewise, the transformation of the conceptual space C by a change in the rules R needn't be as revolutionary as the notion of transformational creativity evokes. Transforming R needn't be any more sophisticated an activity than searching through C. Wiggins proposes instead that transformation of the underlying basis for how the rules are described might be considered a more radical form of transformational creativity. Wiggins therefore suggests that transformational creativity is "exploratory creativity at the metalevel." Instead of an exploration through a conceptual space, it is an exploration through different possible conceptual spaces.

But what are conceptual spaces really? The answer remains vague, although a body of work is beginning to grow up around studying conceptual spaces in cognitive science, and tantalizingly is starting to intersect with work in AI systems. Peter Gärdenfors[47] defines them simply as geometric spaces that are made up of "a collection of one or more quality dimensions," where quality dimensions "represent various 'qualities' of objects." For Gärdenfors, the critical thing about conceptual spaces is that they define perceptions of similarity between objects: "For instance, we can meaningfully claim that the taste of a walnut is closer to the taste of a hazelnut than to the taste of popcorn in the same way as we can say that the color orange is closer to yellow than to blue."

For example, much research has gone into the perception of musical pitches, and we know (as much from the underlying acoustic principles as anything else) that certain notes are closely related to each other harmonically (they sound well together and in some sense sound more similar). Octaves (middle C and the C above) or fifths (middle C and the G above) are harmonically closer than semitones (middle C and the C-sharp above), even though the semitone is closer when you look at it on a piano keyboard or a guitar's frets. Thus when we represent pitches in a conceptual space, we may want to represent them in a way that places the more harmonically related notes closer together, *not* how they are represented on a piano keyboard. There are various multidimensional representations that researchers have developed to do this, sometimes in the shape of a spring or a spiral, although we are not sure if there is such a thing as a definitive conceptual space for pitches.

We find corroboration from other fields for Wiggins's approach of defining creative domains in terms of sets of constraints. The psychologist of artistic creativity Patricia Stokes proposes a hierarchy of constraints with which creative practitioners navigate their work: "Constraints facilitate problem solving by directing and limiting search for solutions. Thus, they come in pairs. In creative problem solving, one constraint precludes (or limits search among) low-variability, tried-and-true responses. The other simultaneously promotes (or directs search among) high-variability, novel responses."[48]

At the top of Stokes's hierarchy lies a set of *goal* constraints, which are involved in defining different domains of artistic practice: "Goal constraints are overall criteria. Accepted by a domain, they become stylistic conventions, answers to questions like 'is this a Fauve painting?'"[49] Stokes's view is that individuals choose to adopt these constraints upon entry into a domain of creative work. An individual then develops a series of additional, more individually specific personal constraints as part of their practice, which help them solve the problem of producing quality work according to the goal constraints and quality criteria. These include source constraints, the choice of stylistic elements; task constraints, the materials and methods you use; and subject constraints, the choice of subject content.

This model offers a way of thinking about what might be considered a transformational event (in Boden's sense). For Stokes, "as a new style develops, its goal criterion will be specified, albeit gradually."[50] Her study of individual painters shows how they adopt goal constraints, which are generally then treated as fixed, and then apply and manipulate other chosen constraints in their solution. The emphasis here is on the fact that only sporadically do painters revisit their goal constraints. But when they do, transformation occurs, in the sense that Boden intended, even if, as Wiggins notes, this transformation need not be particularly earth-shattering (though it may be).

In this way, we begin to perceive a complex of relations between individual creative practitioners and the domains of creativity activity that they navigate. Individuals are trained in their arts but by necessity engage in generally applicable creative search strategies—at different levels, over their lifetimes and each time they sit down to create—that have parallels with creative work in science, design, and engineering.

From Algorithmic Thinking about Creativity to Implementing Creativity in Machines

The Evolution of Thinking on Machine Creativity

Parallel to research into humans' unique creative capacity, a more abstract discussion of mechanized creativity reaches back into the nineteenth century and beyond. Two important strands feed into this discussion. The first is the idea that animals and other organisms are themselves essentially types of machines, extended to humans if we are content that humans are merely a type of animal. The hearts, lungs, and limbs of animals are easily understood as machinelike elements, with the pumps, engines, and pistons of the industrial revolution inspiring some confidence that what we find in nature, we can also build. Brains and nervous systems have been less palatable as a subject for automation and held out against subjugation to a materialist perspective far longer, although the makers of playful automata, mechanical instruments, and weaving looms were providing food for thought about thinking machines long before the arrival of the computer. (We can follow this thread as far back as ancient Egypt, where Hero of Alexandria made mechanical theatrics, including simple autonomous vehicles.) It is now becoming increasingly hard to maintain a nonmaterialist perspective in the face of discoveries in neuroscience and developments in AI and bionics. As a materialist perspective has gained ground, its proponents have contended that there can no longer be seen any a priori reason to believe that machines can't be built to have capabilities comparable to brains. This is nothing like saying "brains are computers," which has the added and needless complication of having to define what a computer is. It also does not follow that thinking machines will necessarily resemble brains in their style of behavior—we might already anticipate that they will be less forgetful and delusional.

The second strand of thinking concerns the idea that simple mechanical processes can readily create novel forms, thus *be creative*. In particular, this is what Darwin's algorithm of evolution by natural selection has been shown to do. Human creative minds are, after all, its creative product, or as the cybernetician William Ross Ashby put it, "The brain is merely Nature's latest means of self-preservation."[51] This strand has expanded into theories of ever-growing complexity, emergence, and self-organization, as well as more or less palatable applications of Darwinism to domains beyond biology, including culture. This seems to present a parallel, less orthodox perspective for computational creativity theory because it has little or nothing to do with the creativity of the thinking human with goals and motivations.

Straddling both of these strands is the emergence of the social sciences, and in particular the idea of social or cultural systems as coherent entities in their own right, that shape individual people's views, goals, and behaviors and have their own dynamics that are irreducible to individual human actions. At the turn of the twentieth century, Emile Durkheim[52] used this principle of irreducibility to help establish the foundations of contemporary social science, proposing that just as the principles of physics do not provide the necessary tools to study chemistry, neither does psychology suffice to study societies, which should be understood as occupying their own stratum of scientific rules and logic.

Contemporaries of Darwin were quick to apply his theories to the evolution of the social and technological world, involving both of these strands tightly intertwined. Documented by George Dyson in detail in his book *Darwin among the Machines*, the maverick thinker and sometimes antagonist of Darwin Samuel Butler presents a vision that reads like a precursor to the prophecies of Kurzweil:

> [Is] the animal phase to be the last which life on this globe is to assume? Or shall we conceive that we are living in the first faint dawning of a new one? Of a life which in another ten or twenty million years shall be to us as we to the vegetable? What has been may be again, and although we grant that hardly any mistake would be more puerile than to individualise and animalise the at present existing machines—or to endow them with human sympathies, yet we can see no a priori objection to the gradual development of a mechanical life, though that life shall be so different from ours that it is only by a severe discipline that we can think of it as life at all.[53]

As computers proper emerged, a vision of thinking machines came clearer into focus. With Jacquard's weaving loom, which could be fed different weave patterns encoded into punched cards, came a tangible instantiation to support the notion of the programmable machine. Soon after, Charles

Babbage's work on the difference engine and analytical engine gave the world its first real glimpse of the idea of a machine that could perform a diverse range of "thinking" tasks. Babbage's collaborator Ada Lovelace, who was instrumental in recognizing this potential, sparked a debate central to AI by considering the proposition that "the Analytical Engine has no pretensions to originate anything. It can do whatever we know how to order it to perform."[54]

Now known as the Lovelace objection, this was most notably contested many years later by the pioneer of modern computing Alan Turing in his famous paper "Computing, Machinery and Intelligence," in which he also introduced the test that bears his name.[55] Turing's paper ostensibly sets out to argue that computers, with the right algorithms, are in principle capable of humanlike intelligence, with all of its creativity, wit, and awe thrown in.

Against the Lovelace objection, Turing's response combines the dual strands of emerging thought about machine creativity: that brains are not fundamentally different entities from machines, and that simple mechanistic processes can be creative. He first responds to the idea that machines can't produce anything new by drawing a parallel conclusion regarding humans, making what is essentially an argument from the perspective of social creativity. "Who can be certain," he says, "that 'original work' that he has done was not simply the growth of the seed planted in him by teaching, or the effect of following well-known general principles."[56]

As well as his more famous work on thinking machines, Turing was also a major contributor to our second theme, discovering the creative power of simple mechanical processes. Also bearing his name are Turing patterns, sophisticated spatial structures that he modeled mathematically, produced by simple local chemical interactions playing out on a surface. We see these patterns produced chemically in the striped markings on a tiger or zebra, and in the distribution of grasses over a terrain. In Turing's time, the marriage of a mechanistic Darwinian view of the biological world with creative engineering and design was emerging into a research agenda in its own right. Known as cybernetics, the field was defined by one of its founders, Norbert Wiener, as the "scientific study of control and communication in the animal and the machine."[57] While control and communication were more typically associated with animal behavior, Turing's chemical models were among many instances of work that set out foundational research questions in what we now call artificial life. How does information propagate around a distributed system in such a way as to produce coordinated high-level effects, and what role does each element play in the creation? Notions such as self-organization and emergence followed and began to feed into a wider appreciation that creativity could be seen as a general phenomenon, not one limited to human thought, and not least in the relationship between human social systems and human individuals.

This line of thinking was on the cusp of entering the mainstream as Turing wrote in "Computing, Machinery and Intelligence." Darwin's *Origin of Species*[58] had not yet been published at the time of Lovelace's objection, but it carries a clear message about the idea of simple, unintelligent—let alone unintentional—processes being able to originate things. Here was a process through which the complexity and sophistication of natural structures had seemingly progressed with a consistent and stable direction, just as the Second Law of Thermodynamics runs the other way, breaking down order. By Turing's time, this far-flung notion of mechanical creativity would have started to have become more palatable to the person in the street, though perhaps not as much as to the pioneering computer scientist.

The argument is now well rehearsed and has been honed by Stevan Harnad, who classifies the objection as one of several "granny objections" to the potential for machine intelligence: "The correct reply is that (1) all causal systems are describable by formal rules (this is the equivalent of the Church/Turing Thesis), including ourselves; (2) we know from complexity theory as well as statistical mechanics that the fact that a system's performance is governed by rules does not mean we can predict everything it does; (3) it is not clear that anyone or anything has 'originated' anything new since the Big Bang."[59]

Harnad also offers a more pithy version of this argument: "What's a machine?—Till further notice, it is any system that operates according to the causal laws of physics. And what are we?"[60]

Turing goes on to investigate a more specific instance of the Lovelace objection, that machines can't do anything that would surprise us. To this his response is more impressionistic: "Machines take me by surprise with great frequency. This is largely because I do not do sufficient calculation to decide what to expect them to do, or rather because, although I do a calculation, I do it in a hurried, slipshod fashion, taking risks."

In recent work on evaluating computational creativity, Selmer Bringsjord, Paul Bello, and David Ferruci[61] take exception to this second line of argument. They view the characterization of the observer's misunderstanding or of programming error as being an instance of "surprising output" as a straw man, to which they argue that being surprising is not a sufficient condition for originating something. They give an example: imagine a malfunctioning robot in a Toyota Camry factory sticks a spare tire to the rear bumper of a car. The designers see this and are inspired to develop a new design, blending a sedan with a sports utility vehicle. This, the authors argue, is the kind of situation Turing is thinking of as an example where the machine could be argued to originate something, by virtue of producing a surprising outcome that would not otherwise have been produced. But, they continue, this is not the machine's originality, and besides it is a trivial case. In chapter 3, I will return to this example to make the case that while Bringsjord et al.'s analysis seems entirely reasonable, this distinction between their view and Turing's is of critical importance. In their dismissal of the creativity of the errant robot, they place too much weight on the individual and their intentions, and require that the robot is either a fully blown creative agent or is not. A distributed view of creativity would allow, instead, to understand robot error as having creative capacity as part of a larger system.

Bringsjord et al. propose what they claim is a more useful formulation of the Lovelace objection in the form of a "Lovelace test" for computational creativity. To pass the test, the computer must produce an output that is not a fluke (it is repeatable) and cannot be explained by the programmer (or someone equivalent) "by appeal to [the system's] architecture, knowledge-base and core-functions." Their appeal to explainability is commensurate with Simonton's appeal to include non-obviousness as a required trait for creativity.

With this in mind, it is interesting to return to the question of public perceptions of machine creativity, as discussed in chapter 1. Computational creativity researchers Martin Mumford and Dan Ventura[62] have more recently surveyed people's perceptions about how creative computers might one day become, and asked their respondents to suggest what evidence would make them feel the computer was being creative. Their results suggest that the demonstration of *autonomy* by the computer, showing that it did what it did independent of the programmer, is a fundamental concern, especially to those who are more skeptical of computers' creative potential. They do not specifically identify Bringsjord et al.'s criterion of unexplainability, however, and the specification of what might actually constitute autonomy in the terms of the respondents remains an open problem. Mumford and Ventura's study also indicates that in 2015 people were generally quite willing to accept the possibility of machine creativity, whether this is because they had witnessed firsthand the steady surge of progress in machine intelligence, or because we have come to appreciate a much more mechanical, social, or distributed view of what creativity is.[63]

The Imitation Game

Mention of Alan Turing in the context of creativity wouldn't be complete without reference to Turing's own imitation game, which in some sense stands aside from these discussions of human and machine potential.

In his version of the imitation game,[64] based on a popular parlor game, two people and one computer communicate only via written text, rendered on a screen. One human, the judge, has the task of telling which of their correspondents is the human and which is the computer. Both the human candidate and the computer program are hidden from the judge. Both must convince the judge that they are the true human, through written correspondence only. If the judge cannot reliably identify the true human, then the computer has passed the test.

Turing's test has come to mean many things for many people. For several key commentators, it was never intended as anything more than a thought experiment aimed at leveling our underlying assumptions and highlighting the fallibility of privileging human intelligence without good cause, to dispel the idea that there is anything more to human thought than that which we can observe empirically. It does so simply by illustrating what empirical evidence of intelligence would look like. If the machine *appears to* appreciate the beauty of a sonnet, or to come up with something original and non-obvious, and through repeated testing seems no less capable of doing so than a human, then what reason would remain for denying the system intelligence? We should certainly suspect some kind of trickery, and vow to keep testing. Indeed we should maintain a cynical stance, since nowadays systems are being built explicitly to try and score well on the test, as we will see below. But that is the point: the Turing test admits as much scrutiny as we care to give it. In Robert French's words, "Turing's central claim is that there would be no reason to deny intelligence to a machine that could flawlessly imitate a human's unrestricted conversation."[65]

Another way to think of Turing's test is as a kind of operational definition of intelligence—*that which can be observed*, as opposed to a tautological and essentialist view in which being human is a prerequisite of having human-like intelligence. As we have seen, computational approaches to creativity appeal to the same basic reasoning. The Turing test certainly does offer an operational definition of intelligence, but several critics, Blay Whitby, in particular, have argued that such a view has been counterproductive to AI research: "Much AI work has been distracted by a view of intelligence as a holistic phenomenon, demonstrated only by human beings, and only to be studied by the direct imitation of human beings."[66] Whitby argues that aiming for human intelligence in this holistic way is of little use if we do not have good theories of intelligence that can be explained in terms that do not appeal to humans. He grounds this point in an analogy with the invention of flying machines: "Direct imitation of natural flight proved a relatively fruitless avenue of research. … Working aircraft were developed by achieving greater understanding of the principles of aerodynamics."[67]

More vexing to such critics is the emergence of a high-profile obsession among certain communities with winning the Turing test. In 2014, in one of several regular annual Turing tests, a chatbot named Eugene Goostman, taking the persona of a thirteen-year-old boy, caused a third of its judges to guess that it was a human. In doing so, it purportedly passed some variant of the test, and some consequently declared 2014 a landmark year for AI. As more pessimistic commentators were quick to point out, this exercise only served to highlight the potential fickleness of specific implementations of the test. Consider a short transcript of one of the interrogations by a judge of Eugene:

Judge: what is your gender

Eugene: I'm a young boy, if you care to know. And not very ugly, by the way!

Judge: what are you aware of at this moment

Eugene: I would rather not talk about it if you don't mind. Could you tell me what are you? I mean your profession.

Judge: how old are you

Eugene: I'm a little boy 13 years old.

Judge: what are your qualifications

Eugene: My qualifications? I'm not gonna tell you. Oooh. Anything else?[68]

There is some reason to find Eugene's AI impressive. The system can hold an engaging conversation, even taking the upper hand in steering it, and there should be no doubt that the technical challenges involved in getting this smoothness of response are nontrivial. But as to whether conversations such as these should be considered informative enough to adjudicate on human-comparable intelligence is another matter. Consider AI veteran Marvin Minsky's disparaging response: "Ask the program if you can push a car with a string. And, if not, then, why not?"[69] Why, indeed, did the judge not ask this or some similar question? Such a question requires a model of the world and all of the concepts we use to represent it, as well as how those concepts might interact in unforeseen ways. *Can you carry water in your pocket? Should a former terrorist who has served time in prison be allowed a job as a security guard?* Any thirteen-year-old can make good work of the conceptual material involved therein, yet it is a devilishly hard challenge for AI. The judge only gets out what they put in, and they should certainly put questions such as these in if their goal is to pick out the nonhuman. It should not be hard to ask questions that would reveal a depth of understanding beyond Eugene's, who we might guess from the above would cockily shift topic rather than provide a convincing answer.

Make no mistake, AI is rapidly advancing in its ability to process complex linguistic operations, leading to advances in comprehension. For example, Radford et al. were able to show that a system trained to continue a word sequence, much like the musical continuation task discussed in chapter 1, also performed very well at answering trivia questions, since answering a question coherently *is* basically a continuation of the question sequence. This applied to other specific language tasks such as translation: ask the computer to "translate *bonjour* into English" and, again, the response "hello" is a natural continuation. The language sequences that this model creates demonstrate deep contextual awareness even though it is just a model of word prediction.

A longer continuation of a fictional story is provided by Radford et al. (see box "Text Generated Using the GPT-2 Language Model by OpenAI"). We can read this text and be impressed, without needing to be tricked. Indeed the authors are able to find many ways to ways to measure the performance of their system's output to provide rich detail.

Text Generated Using the GPT-2 Language Model by OpenAI

Context (human-written): In a shocking finding, scientists discovered a herd of unicorns living in a remote, previously unexplored valley in the Andes Mountains. Even more surprising to the researchers was the fact that the unicorns spoke perfect English.

System output (continuation): The scientists named the population after their distinctive horn, Ovid's Unicorn. These four-horned, silver-white unicorns were previously unknown to science.

Now, after almost two centuries, the mystery of what sparked this odd phenomenon is finally solved.

Dr. Jorge Pérez, an evolutionary biologist from the University of La Paz, and several companions were exploring the Andes Mountains when they found a small valley with no other animals or humans. Pérez noticed that the valley had what appeared to be a natural fountain, surrounded by two peaks of rock and silver snow.

Pérez and the others then ventured further into the valley. "By the time we reached the top of one peak, the water looked blue, with some crystals on top," said Pérez.

Pérez and his friends were astonished to see the unicorn herd. These creatures could be seen from the air without having to move too much to see them—they were so close they could touch their horns.

While examining these bizarre creatures the scientists discovered that the creatures also spoke some fairly regular English. Pérez stated, "We can see, for example, that they have a common ´ 'language,' something like a dialect or dialectic." Dr. Pérez believes that the unicorns may have originated in Argentina, where the animals were believed to be descendants of a lost race of people who lived there before the arrival of humans in those parts of South America.

While their origins are still unclear, some believe that perhaps the creatures were created when a human and a unicorn met each other in a time before human civilization. According to Pérez, "In South America, such incidents seem to be quite common." However, Pérez also pointed out that it is likely that the only way of knowing for sure if unicorns are indeed the descendants of a lost alien race is through DNA. "But they seem to be able to communicate in English quite well, which I believe is a sign of evolution, or at least a change in social organization," said the scientist.[70]

I agree with David Auerbach when he says:

> Turing was trying to establish a beachhead for conceiving of intelligence in a way that wasn't restricted to humans. Now that we can conceive of it, the question shifts not to whether a computer can trick people in one particular way, but to the vast varieties of ways in which it can display intelligence, human or not.[71]

Put simply, the value of such interaction tests is in the detailed analysis, not in the binary outcome of pass or fail, which if Eugene's example is anything to go by can be quite deceptive. Eugene should rightly have been celebrated for its achievement by highlighting its true capacities, such as the ability to engage in a playful linguistic interaction. This includes some sense of human personality, even perhaps some essence of social intelligence: the ability to tease or please or steer the interaction in a targeted manner. All that considered, the Turing test win is itself something of an aside, an arbitrary landmark.

What about an art Turing test? One of the most important and direct ways we can appraise any automated art-generation system is by asking people to evaluate its outputs, and it is natural that the Turing test comes to mind as a potential model for how to go about this. In the previous chapter I mentioned an example where the *Guardian* newspaper asked readers to take such a test for Iamus, a music-generation system, and try to guess which compositions were made by a real human and which by a computer. The pieces sound impressive, and it may be hard for a non-expert to make the distinction. Auerbach's response applies here perfectly well, and I could paraphrase it more succinctly as follows: the question is not "can it do it" but "what can it do?" Evaluations of *human-likeness* for individual musical pieces should be just one sort of data gathered about the system.

French also points out the problem of being able to create Turing test variants that, rather than being open conversations, take the form of "restricted domain" tests. Art-based tests would certainly fit this description. French draws attention to "the virtual impossibility of clearly defining what does and does not count as being part of a particular real-world domain."[72] I return to this discussion in chapter 7, which looks at methods for evaluating computationally creative systems and considers in greater detail some of the attempts to run blind tests on the output of computationally creative systems.

Generative and Adaptive Creativity

The central idea put forward in this chapter is that creativity often involves blind search to discover things that would not have been discovered via non-search-based processes, algorithmic processes that have a clear progression to an outcome. Humans possess exemplary cognitive abilities to deploy creative strategies, which are the main focus of study of creativity researchers and the main source of inspiration for computational creativity systems. A key part of that cognitive machinery is the performance of heuristic strategies, both consciously and subconsciously, along with cognitive capacities that support such a process, in particular the ability to incubate concepts subconsciously. However, although far less formulaic than so-called algorithmic processes—those such as long division where there is a clear path to the solution—there is no good reason to believe that a machine can't implement such processes, while humans can. This is seen as an essentialist view, exemplified by the Lovelace objection that Turing dismisses, giving a simple "yes" to the question "Can computers be creative?" While I think this answer is entirely satisfying, the question of the social dimension remains poorly addressed, and it is to this that we turn properly in the following chapter.

I conclude this chapter by drawing out a key distinction that I feel clarifies an area of persistent confusion. It is broadly true that we intentional humans set out to create things with goals and an evaluation framework, and our creative machinery is constructed in such a way as to seek out things that we perceive to have value. Yet this is also a problematic formulation: I wish to claim that in addition, much that is created, artistically and in other domains, demonstrates a significantly more complicated relation between the intention of the creator (or creators) and the outcome, and its respective value and impact. In this more complicated relation, things may be created by accident or are adapted in ways not previously foreseen (not part of the original creator's intention) and are vaunted and valued in ways that are determined by their cultural interpretation and also beyond the creator's relation to the work.

One way to approach this is to allow that in essence creativity means the creation of new things independently of how they are valued or what the intention of the creator was, if any. One reason for this is to be able to admit evolutionary processes into the canon of processes that we call creative, not simply to offer a more inclusive concept of creativity, but because it is also a relevant aspect of human creativity. When viewed at the collective cultural level, where movements emerge and great works of art are defined, human activity can be understood as much in terms of a blind evolutionary process that *emerges* out of individual action, as in terms of a directed intentional processes led by individuals. As mentioned in this chapter, key to avoiding tautological treatment of Darwinian processes, we must not view the creation of elephant trunks as being "in order to" benefit elephants, but as part of a process of emergence in which elephants and their trunks came about. This is also why it may be wrong to dismiss Bringsjord et al.'s errant robot in the car factory as a noncreative force, when seen as part of a wider distributed process.

A more universal view of creativity over different timescales and in different configurations might start from the central argument of many proponents of a social view of creativity: that the understanding of individual creative cognition must be complemented by an understanding of the social dynamics involved in the various forms of human creative production. Social factors *act* upon individuals as much as social phenomena result from individual actions. This is a different idea of creativity from that associated with the human cognitive capacity to be creative, rather than a competing hypothesis. On a universal epochal scale we witness value-free blind creation of form, equivalent to Darwinian evolution, if not identical in detail. While we can't talk about this in the same language as the psychology of human creativity—and simplistic metaphors should certainly be avoided—we can observe, with Simonton, that a form of blind variation and selective retention is common between them. In our daily lives, meanwhile, we witness value-laden purposeful creativity employing powerful dedicated neural circuitry that is unique to the human species. Now zoom in to the neural processes where concepts are being generated, and at some point we again see a system that is incubating or brainstorming, looking far and wide without being steered by the constraint of evaluation. Zoom back out, and at the social scale we see both purposeful creativity, as when teams of individuals come together with a common goal, and less purposeful creativity, as in the emergence of subcultures that arise from the work of individual actors with disparate goals but that have no overall purpose themselves.

In short, creative outcomes that are not directly grounded in goals and values can be found everywhere—interlaced with creativity that is grounded in value. In earlier work,[73] I have attempted to distinguish this as a different category of creativity, called *generative creativity* by association with the notion of a generative process. It blindly and mechanically generates new stuff, which comes about in a process of emergence. The more recognizably human creativity-with-value I have, by contrast, called *adaptive creativity*. In this form, there is always an agent for which the creative outcome serves a purpose. These categories were an attempt to help more clearly locate the former kind of emergent process in studies in computational creativity and, more generally, to explore different relationships between creativity and value, such as how an influential artist may have greater freedom to be nonconformant than a newcomer.

For the purpose of this book, I treat these terms as a useful way to probe this distinction, but not necessarily as an essential framework. Nevertheless, creativity might more productively be understood not as the production of novel and valuable things but as the *situated production of novelty*. Creative systems are by definition responsible for producing novel outcomes, but the way in which they do so can be understood through the way in which they are situated in a given context. In adaptively creative situations, the creative system is an agent, situated in a context in which it has motivations and tangible outcomes, and its creativity does produce things that can be said to have value. In generatively creative situations, these conditions may not be so apparent. The creative system may be a distributed process involving multiple competing agents with conflicting goals, or even a blind mechanical process that has no reason to its creative productivity. These ideas will continue through the following chapter, which further develops this socially oriented treatment of creativity.

II Humans

3 Creativity and Culture

The brain is merely Nature's latest means of self-preservation.
—W. Ross Ashby[1]

Everything is the way it is because it got that way.
—D'Arcy Thompson[2]

Our species is the only creative species, and it has only one creative instrument, the individual mind and spirit of man. Nothing was ever created by two men. There are no good collaborations, whether in music, in art, in poetry, in mathematics, in philosophy. Once the miracle of creation has taken place, the group can build and extend it, but the group never invents anything. The preciousness lies in the lonely mind of a man.
—John Steinbeck[3]

Variables external to the individual must be considered if one wishes to explain why, when, and from where new ideas or products arise and become established in a culture.
—Sami Abuhamdeh and Mihaly Csikszentmihalyi[4]

Not until Vespucci recognized that the so-called West Indies were part of an entirely different continent did Columbus's almost superhuman efforts get retrospectively revised as a "discovery." And if in the fullness of time it turns out that it was Erik the Red who really discovered America, that "discovery" will be as much a result of scholarship and politics as a result of Erik's travels.
—Mihaly Csikszentmihalyi[5]

From Individuals to Distributed Creative Systems

Creativity in Humans, Nature, and Machines

This book began with reference to a familiar vision of robots walking among us, perhaps indistinguishable from us, perhaps quirky reflections of ourselves. In such visions, it is simple but effective to treat the world as if there are two types of things: humans and other objects. Humanlike artificially intelligent robots make good material for fiction, conceived through the interaction between protagonists in the medium of language. In the narratives of films like *Ex Machina*, they pop into existence from the world of mundane objects in the hands of a lone genius. The glacial gradualism of technological advance is skipped over; it just doesn't make good movie material. Inevitably, however, the distinction between humanlike intelligence and simpler algorithms must reveal some kind of fuzziness at the boundary. Today's AI systems are largely (but not entirely) utilitarian tools with only restricted autonomy, but as AI gets more powerful, the gap between people and things is being gradually filled in with a spectrum of machines of varying degrees of intelligence and autonomy.

For many theorists of agency in the social sciences, this is a common and problematic dualism. Andrew Pickering, for example, refers to it as asymmetrical dualism, according to which "the world is a knowable machine, while ... humanity calls the shots as the only locus of genuine agency."[6] Pickering describes this as "the natural ontological attitude of modernity, the way we all tend to approach the world."[7] For the anthropologist of art Alfred Gell, according to this default perspective,

> whereas chains of physical/material cause-and-effect consist of "happenings" which can be explained by physical laws, which ultimately govern the universe as a whole, agents initiate "actions" which are "caused" by themselves, by their intentions, not by the physical laws of the cosmos.[8]

At the same time, the discussion in chapter 2 worked with the broad simplification that individual human agents perform creative acts in relative isolation, given that they have the cognitive machinery to create. An alternative perspective that will be explored in detail in this chapter is that individuals are always operating situated in networks of creative activity, making *contributions* to a process of creativity. That is, creativity really only happens at a super-individual level which cannot be reduced to individual cognition. While the cognitive machinery of individual brains is critical to this process, it is not the only ingredient, and anyway leads to effects that are only manifest and observable at the network level. Breaking the dualism of human-object relations is important to developing this framework and also in building unbiased models of creative processes that *admit* a creative role for machines, of all kinds, that fall short of humanlike cognition and social situatedness.

A social perspective on creativity is most notably associated with the work of Mihaly Csikszentmihalyi, in his call for researchers of creativity "to abandon the Ptolemaic view of creativity, in which the person is at the center of everything, for a more Copernican model in which the person is part of a system of mutual influences and information."[9] The result is a subtle shift from the question of how a given entity *is creative* to what role an entity plays in contribution to a larger creative process. Such a shift in stance allows for the study of social aspects of creativity, which as we will see are not insignificant. But it also means that nonhuman entities—including advanced AI systems, but also dumb algorithms, as well as everyday objects and materials—can more easily be treated as contributing to accounts of creative processes, without having to be understood as creative agents themselves.

This chapter proceeds through three sections. Firstly, I undertake this review of creative systems as collective phenomena. Secondly, I look specifically at how evolutionary thinking informs the understanding of creativity. Thirdly, I convert this into a useful set of concepts that helps us analyze different creativity scenarios, in particular locating artistic practices and movements among human creative activity.

Socially Situated Individuals

It is widely acknowledged that groups of people putting their heads together enhances the effect of creative search. Dean Simonton's studies of scientific creativity[10] reveal a pattern of distributed creative effort, looking at the relationship between quantity and quality of a researcher's output, which supports his blind variation approach to creativity. Simonton's data shows that increasing quantity increases the chance of producing a quality output but also increases the chance that the researcher produces junk. "It is significant," he says, "that those who publish the most highly cited works also publish the most ignored works, so that quality is a probabilistic consequence of quantity. In fact, the ratio of high-impact publications to total output—the 'hit' rate—is uncorrelated with total output. This has been called the *equal-odds* rule." This lends evidence to the view that, as far as individual creative success is concerned, chance is an important factor in the success of creative work; raising one's quantity of output is one of the most accessible strategies for increasing the chance of making a breakthrough, and increasing output becomes a genuine part of an overall creative strategy.[11] For Simonton, this means that the same strategy of blind variation and selective retention that works for an individual also works across a social group.

Over a large enough body of output, given an underlying stochastic process, the chance of quality output becomes increasingly certain. In Simonton's view the creative capacity of individuals is revealed over long rather than short time scales, and creative productivity would appear to be more deterministic at a population level than at an individual level. Note once again an important clarification: this does not mean that chance is the only factor. This argument has (almost) nothing to do with a million monkeys managing to write a good play; the researcher must be an expert in the field and must apply methods appropriately. The production of quantity must be production at a certain threshold of quality. In the sciences, peer review and other forms of quality control further feed into this, influencing the quantity of output in the first instance, setting basic checks and balances that are reliable enough to successfully constrain the blind search toward a sensible subset of candidates. Simonton's work tallies with Thomas Kuhn's[12] influential account of the scientific process. Scientific progress takes place, Kuhn argues, as a series of periods of normal science, punctuated by rare, high-impact scientific revolutions. Normal science tends to be more formulaic and may be less prone to chance effects on success. But the paradigm underlying the stable progress of normal science becomes strained by the increasing demands of explaining new data, necessitating revolution. As we will see, other domains of collective activity experience such cycles of stability and disruption.

Thus a socially situated perspective illustrates one very simple way in which creativity scales from individuals to groups. Simply put, the process of creative search that any individual engages in works perfectly well as a distributed process. Ten people searching for a solution to a problem will be more effective than one. One individual from the ten may independently find a winning solution, but it would be mistaken to infer in hindsight that the other nine people were redundant. That would be to ignore the stochastic nature of creative search. As well as distributing the process of generation, this introduces a hierarchy of levels at which evaluation is conducted. In Simonton's example of academic work, the individual researcher generates and evaluates outcomes, which are further iterated through the peer-review process, and then again are placed in the market of long-term collective evaluation, in which some work will sink and other work will swim. In Csikszentmihalyi's words, "It has been said that 99% of all new ideas are garbage, regardless of the domain or the status of the thinker. To sift out the good ideas from the bad, another system is needed."[13]

But except when faced with some imminent task in a restricted domain—say, extracting a dropped piece of clothing from behind a wardrobe with a coat hanger—being socially situated means, among other things, not only performing creative tasks but first of all making choices about which tasks to take on. Much of the research into the psychology of creativity therefore deals with a more holistic approach to the strategies involved in creative success. As Csikszentmihalyi puts it, "We cannot study creativity by isolating individuals and their works from the social and historical milieu in which their actions are carried out. This is because what we call creative is never the result of individual action alone."[14]

The study of individuals as problem seekers as well as problem solvers—choosing where they will situate themselves to perform creative work—leads to theories of creative individuals as situated in a broader social context, involving a wider set of strategies for getting by in a world where creativity is not only a way of solving imminent problems but a valuable social commodity. Robert Sternberg's investment theory of creativity,[15] for example, draws a parallel between the world of financial investment and creative work: creative individuals are those who "buy low and sell high" in the world of ideas. Some may choose to avoid the mainstream and go for the higher risk outside chances. In doing so they take on the risk of failure but also increase the possibility that they will hit upon a more radical, creatively explosive outcome with greater rewards.

The parallel with investors helpfully frames a fundamental relation between problem-solving capability and *chance*. In a hypothetical example by the "black swan" investor Nassim Taleb, related by *New Yorker* writer Malcolm Gladwell,[16] we are asked to imagine ten thousand investment managers winning and losing money on the markets. Imagine that each year, each investor wins or loses money completely by chance, with an even chance of winning or losing. Follow this thought experiment through for ten years (you could easily model this in an Excel spreadsheet); the statistics have it that nine of those investors will have made money every year in a row. While this might give the impression to an observer that these nine investors had some special competence not possessed by the others, this number is the consequence of a model in which all investors are equally skilled and knowledgeable, and winning is a completely chance event. Furthermore, it is possible in some circumstances that investors with higher risk strategies will come out richest. Someone will have become fantastically rich, far richer than could be possible by taking only the safe bets. The point of this thought experiment is to highlight how easy it is to miss the large number of people, employing *exactly the same strategy*, who are worse off than if they had played a safe game (this common misjudgment is known as *survivorship bias*, focusing only on those who have survived and thrived in some risky situation and ignoring those who haven't). By analogy, while we tend to assume that those who are more creatively successful must be more creatively capable, a situated view reveals an alternative possibility, with a greater emphasis on chance.

This is the backdrop to the problem of creative search for individuals, a reminder that there need not be as strong a correlation between success and capability as we might expect. With investors as with creative work, skill and strategy will nevertheless improve your chances. Investors have knowledge about what they are investing in, both specific to the field of expertise—understanding how IPOs work, say—and more generally in terms of approaching risk—understanding how to spread bets or how to manage long- and short-term investment strategies properly, the factor in which Taleb was particularly prescient.

And so with creative work, approaches to risk management and uncertainty in the world of creative ideas, combined with a certain domain-specific expertise, are dominant factors in understanding how individuals best set themselves up for creative success. In a similar way, David Perkins[17] compares the risk involved in creative work with that of gold diggers trawling the land for gold deposits. He dubs the conceptual spaces that we search for creative outcomes "Klondike spaces," after the gold rush of the Klondike region of the Yukon in Canada. The analogy works on several levels. Firstly, upon hearing about the gold of the Yukon the first step of the hopeful gold digger is to head to that region, rather than doubling down on their efforts to find gold in their own backyard. This is obvious but important, because any creative person starts by making several apparently very uncreative steps: choosing a field, getting to know the area, learning from others, trying to imitate their methods. Once on the gold fields, the problems of search begin proper. Now that you've traveled to an area known for gold, you'd hope that you would find it everywhere you dug, but at this finer resolution it turns out that gold in one place does not necessarily mean gold in an adjoining area. Perkins thus describes the features of creative problems through this metaphorical landscape: there is the "wilderness of possibilities," the simple fact that high-impact outcomes are rare; the "clueless plateau," the "lack of signs that point to the gold," even once you've found traces of gold already; the "narrow canyon of exploration," the fact that you are generally forced by practical constraints to restrict search to a specific local area, which may yield no results; and the "oasis of false promise," that it is overwhelmingly tempting to carry on looking in your current location.

Perkins builds this analogy with evidence from studying a variety of creative practitioners, where he witnesses the kinds of heuristic strategies that suggest this kind of terrain. Creatively successful people, his evidence shows, don't tend to work on just one thing but have a number of separate activities on the go, keeping each up in the air in the hope of a breakthrough. You could say they are spread betters, and following Sternberg's metaphor, they are gauging not only the chance of success but the impact: comparing hitting the jackpot on a wild outside chance with building a number of safe but small wins.

As with Wallas's four-stage model, this broader view of creative practice can be framed as a series of iterated phases of production and reflection, in which both the goal and the strategy are reviewed. Todd Lubart shows further how artists structure such processes around their specific relation to a given task. For example, they perform more exploratory association tasks after breaks when they are coming to their work cold, rather than performing evaluation tasks then.[18]

The evolutionary computing researchers Ken Stanley and Joel Lehman develop this argument from a computational perspective,[19] claiming that creative discovery can't follow a targeted approach. In a targeted approach, you think you have a good clue about what the solution to your problem

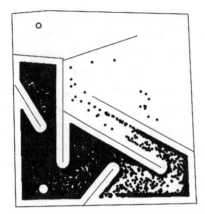 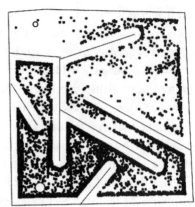

Figure 3.1
Lehman and Stanley's original demonstration of the effective power of novelty-based search, even for traditional goal-based search tasks. In both images, the large white dot (bottom left) is the starting point for an agent that is trying to find its way to the small white dot (top left) through the maze, within a given time limit. The black dots represent the final resting place of the agent in many different trials. In the left panel the agent search strategy was evolved using target-based evolutionary search: agents that got nearer the target were deemed fitter and more likely to seed future generations. However, the shape of the maze means that fitness might be rewarded for agents that are close to the target as the crow flies but not in reality. In the right panel, novelty search is used: fitness is rewarded to agents whose resting position is novel—that is, dissimilar to previous agents. The images show that the novelty search strategy is actually more effective at reaching the target. Image credit: Joel Lehman and Kenneth Stanley.

might be, and so you orient your efforts in that direction. They claim, instead, that even when searching for a specific solution to a specific problem, it is often more effective to conduct the search based on the novelty of solutions rather than on their suitability to the problem. Creative problems, in short, are like mazes, in which the path to the exit is almost never *actually* in the direction of the exit, and heading in that direction is at best no better than choosing any other direction and at worst counterproductive. That is by definition: we have never explored this territory before, so we could not possibly know its structure. This is one reason why a terrain metaphor is potentially misleading: in physical terrains you can generally (though not always) walk toward something and you'll get there.

A consequence of this tangled path to discovery is that the history of discovery is full of people solving problems they hadn't set out to solve.

And indeed it is common for innovation to work this way around: explore a space of possibilities, such as new materials or chemicals, and use your exploration to discover where applications lie. Designers and pharmaceutical companies engage in this kind of solution-first thinking quite systematically. The tale of the Post-It note is an example with mythical weight. Dr. Spencer Silver's goal was to make a new kind of strong glue. What he came up with was the Post-It note glue, which, despite his failure, he noted had interesting properties: it was low-stick, reusable, and pressure sensitive. For a long time, however, nobody could see a viable application. Silver's perseverance in seeking a "problem for his solution" eventually led to the collaboration with Arthur Fry in the development of the Post-It note.

It is amazing to think that something that is now so ubiquitous in offices and homes took longer than five years of puzzling to invent *after* the main technical challenge had been solved. In the field of design, where artistic and goal-directed technical factors play an equal role, such an approach to creativity is widely recognized and formalized in creative strategies. For example, in product design, one can approach concept ideation from a problem-first perspective, a scenario-first perspective, or a technology-first perspective. All are valid. In the latter two cases, we talk of "need finding."

Collective Creativity Is Greater Than the Sum of Its Parts

This already gives us good reason to understand human creativity primarily as a group process, but so conceived, this is still a view of group creativity occurring only as the sum of its individual parts, which are readily separable; in algorithmic terms this is parallelizable search. But there is good reason to believe that the creativity of human groups does not simply involve summing the creative efficacy of individual humans in a structured hierarchy. Groups structure creativity in various ways, leading to Csikszentmihalyi's appeal to correctly view creativity as a multi-actor dynamic process, and leading us to look at concepts of individual and collective agency.

In the simplest case, social processes can be seen to organize groups around specific goals, to which the creative power of distributed search can be applied. Consider, for illustration, the case of the solving of the problem of longitude, elegantly documented in Dava Sobel's popular history book *Longitude: The True Story of a Lone Genius Who Solved the Greatest Scientific Problem of His Time.*[20] John Harrison, a modest but highly skilled clockmaker, developed a series of clocks during his lifetime—throughout the eighteenth century—that made dramatic improvements to the accuracy of timekeepers overall and specifically in the face of adverse climatic conditions—changes in temperature, air pressure, and humidity. These improved clocks, which consisted of a large number of distinct innovations, meant that naval navigators could properly tell their location at sea, which had huge implications for the safety and efficiency of naval operations, and hence a staggering economic benefit and competitive advantage.

We can say with relative certainty that Harrison was a creative agent who transformed clock design with dramatic impact on the world. Yet even though in the book's subtitle Harrison is declared a lone genius, Sobel's account points to an alternative agency responsible for the achievement. The British government had in fact set up a prize for solving the problem of longitude. A tantalizing sum of money (£20,000) and a precise test were detailed in the award. As well as recognizing Harrison's agency, would it be equally fair to call the government a creative agent, establishing an intention (to solve longitude) and implementing a sort of meta-method (define the criteria for success and offer the reward)? The government's strategy was well adapted to the exploratory nature of creative discovery, exploiting a divergent search process, a little bit like the genetic algorithms we use today. Rather than betting on a solution (the problem was longitude—it was clear that better clocks could offer a winning solution but not the only possible solution), they displayed a purposeful ambivalence to what form the solution should take, focusing instead on devising the most accurate test of success, a strategy in keeping with the issues of creative problem-solving described above.[21] The government achieved its goal, demonstrating the efficacy of such a creative meta-method, now familiar in a range of market-minded devices at the heart of modern industry, such as patent law and crowdsourcing strategies. I will certainly not devote any time to laboring the argument over which was the true agent; the point is that they can both be seen to contribute to the creative outcome in their own right. But we can note some properties that distinguish these respective agents. Firstly, as mentioned, the British government was ambivalent to the form of the solution, whereas Harrison had all his eggs in one basket, so to speak. Secondly, the longitude prize exerted a force on individual actors, altering their choice of problem by incentivizing them. Along with his formidable intrinsic motivation, Harrison was further directed toward a specific task by the promise of the prize.

That different social configurations, such as governments that set prizes, embody different mechanisms of social creativity is lived out in today's cities, which compete to be powerhouses of creativity. For example, Charles Landry's influential book *The Creative City*[22] outlines how cities can be structured to stimulate knowledge transfer, serendipity, and evaluation, and urban planners talk of things like "serendipity management."[23] Richard Florida's work on the creative class[24] discusses how policies, such as those of increased inclusion, can support the nurturing of creative capacity. Fields like design thinking and organization science seek to untap the creativity of organized groups of individuals, pitching social creativity as greater than the sum of individual human creative acts, all because we can steer, stimulate, and structure individuals' behavior.

Although it is not without predecessors and peers, the work of Mihaly Csikszentmihalyi consolidated the social strand of creativity research. Csikszentmihalyi rejects the attribution of creativity strictly to specific individuals: "Where was Mendel's creativity? In his mind, in his experiments, or in the use his results were put to by later scientists? The answer, it seems to me, must be that it is to be found in all three."[25] In place, he outlines a systems-based view, the Domain Individual Field Interaction (DIFI) theory, comprising these three core elements. The domain is the area of activity in which the individual performs creative acts. Take abstract expressionist art, for example. The domain can be thought of as a passive repository of knowledge, concepts, and precedent work relating to the subject matter. The individual acts upon this domain, transforming it through some form of creative production. The field is the community surrounding that domain. This might involve other abstract expressionist artists or artists from the wider domain of visual art, critics, collectors, galleries, and the gallery-going public. The field's primary role in this conceptualization is to evaluate and select elements within the domain, but this is treated as equally active in the task of creation, and it may perform other roles as well.

Csikszentmihalyi's model frames specific networks of interaction: the individual must interact with the domain, becoming an expert in it before being able to thoroughly engage with it: "The information that will go into [an] idea existed long before the creative person arrived on the scene. It had been stored in the symbol system of the culture, in the customary practices, the language, the specific notation of the 'domain.'"[26] The field may influence the success of individuals and the acceptance of elements into the domain. An important part of the model is the collective effort that is involved in identifying and validating a discovery, regardless of who made it: "Not until Vespucci recognized that the so-called West Indies were part of an entirely different continent did Columbus's almost superhuman efforts get retrospectively revised as a 'discovery.' And if in the fullness of time it turns out that it was Erik the Red who really discovered America, that 'discovery' will be as much a result of scholarship and politics as a result of Erik's travels."[27] Historians of science have also illustrated how social evaluative interactions underlie those domains as well. Simon Schaffer presents an image of collective creativity that involves not only validation but also the mythologization of success:

> Much recent work on discovery and invention in the sciences demonstrates that retrospection and celebration play key roles in the production of discovery. Because discoveries acquire their status as the result of subsequent work with the relevant community, the "fetishism" of discovery is therefore the consequence of the whole process through which change is analyzed, debated, and assessed.[28]

He reiterates a view that "innovation is perhaps less a product of uniquely creative individual attitudes ... and more a matter of being pivotally situated during those comparatively brief passages of industrial history when the balance of collective choice can be tipped one way or another."[29] One example is Edison, a prolific and widely acclaimed inventor, who can be seen to manage, promote, and negotiate as much as cogitate on the design of electric devices, channeling the work of many people and placing himself historically. Kekulé is also discussed, and his famous reveries are shown to have a degree of social construction to them, a collective retelling of the story of the problem and its discovery. Schaffer's view is that "discovery is as much a judgmental process in culture as it is the intrinsic property of some isolated mind." But he also maintains that we should not be disparaging of any such mythologizing but rather remain open to its potential importance, a driver for individual action. In the creative arts, he draws on the work of Ernst Kris and Otto Kurz,[30] who witness a similar construction of "culture heroes," with a common narrative of nurtured genius.

The effect of Csikszentmihalyi's model is to diffuse the obsession with individual creativity and provide a way to take account of the nontrivial social effects beyond the sum of individual creative actions. In a similar way, studies of creativity in design have shown how in collaboration individuals adapt toward each other forming new collaborative units of creative productivity[31] that involve skills like negotiation, including both persuasion and the ability to remain open. These may be manifest in different individuals' personalities in complementary ways.

But this is a challenging proposition. Once we start to view creativity as something that happens in groups, some assumptions about what a creative agent is become complicated. What Csikszentmihalyi refers to as "the generative force of the field" is a different type of creativity from that of the individual, and in the next section I consider how this approach is part of a wider movement in the social sciences to truly confront the dualism mentioned at the beginning of this chapter. Such a distributed view has real consequences for how a creative computational system might be understood. In Csikszentmihalyi's model, not only must lone humans be understood as components in creative systems, rather than creative systems in their own rights, but they must also be understood as performing different roles within the larger creative system. Some roles may be minor, and not all roles require the sophisticated creative machinery required by the kinds of ideal creative systems imagined in what he calls the Ptolemaic view. As such, a computer program might be tasked with performing any one of these roles, and this needn't require advanced AI. The work of computational creativity practitioners like Cohen and Cope illustrated how farming out content generation to a machine can produce effective and surprising results, even if the system is being highly mechanistic. In other circumstances, such as in building analytics and other goal-directed design tasks, computers can be very good at making judgments by which to evaluate things.

Questioning Agency
Parallel to Csikszentmihalyi's model is a wider effort, crossing academic disciplines, to address the dualism that leaves us stuck with the idea that individual humans can exhibit genuine agency while other systems, including *collectives of individuals*, cannot. This mission of addressing asymmetrical dualism in the social sciences was introduced at the beginning of this chapter through the thoughts of Andrew Pickering and Alfred Gell. The basic gist of this movement is to rethink agency, the capacity for action in the

world, as something that can be manifest in more temporary and loosely bounded organizations such as classes, companies, movements, and so on.

When I discussed the British government just now as such an agent, it was relatively easy to picture this organization as if it were a single individual with a coherent goal. But a complete account of any social organization never just amounts to a group of people. Instead it must be fully understood through nonhuman elements that give it its capabilities—books, rooms, rules, maps, machines, and so on. There is also not likely to be a common goal among the people (and perhaps the objects); in Sobel's account of the longitude prize, the drama takes the form of numerous conflicts among entities both within and outside the body we have just identified as an agent.

Such questions have for some time now preoccupied social scientists and philosophers. Most famous of the proponents of a revision of the application of agency are the actor-network theorists. In a well-known passage,[32] actor-network theory figurehead Bruno Latour narrates the central concern of this movement through the example of the US gun control debate. "Guns kill people!" gun control advocates say, to their opponents' riposte, "People kill people, not guns." For Latour this is the false dichotomy between a materialist and a sociological account. Instead, Latour proposes that "a third agent emerges from a fission of the other two. ... Who, then, is the actor in my vignette? *Someone else* (a citizen-gun, a gun-citizen). ... It is neither people nor guns that kill. Responsibility for action must be shared."

Thus Latour sets up a resolution in the idea that the gun-citizen is a vague, temporary actor who is capable of actions (including forming realizable intentions) which are not accessible to either entity on its own. That is, networks of interacting entities temporarily merge to form sites of possible action, at which point the component entities are no longer the same as they were before. He calls such changes "translations." The resolution sounds like a sleight of hand: critics have complained that *it was only the person* who could have formed the intention, chosen to acquire the gun, pulled the trigger. And yet that person's path through life was in fact a constant interaction with a world of influences, changing course at every stage based on what is deemed possible, what is to hand. Latour's main contention, then, is that "the twin mistake of the materialists and the sociologists is to start with essences, those of subjects or those of objects," and that this is doomed to failure because "neither subject nor object (nor their goals) is fixed."

This analysis has proven particularly powerful in the discussion of the contemporary scientific method, where Latour's main work was focused, pointing to "a new actor ... inert bodies, incapable of will and bias, but capable of showing, signing, writing, and scribbling on laboratory instruments before trustworthy witnesses. These nonhumans, lacking souls but endowed with meaning, are even more reliable than ordinary mortals, to whom will is attributed but who lack the capacity to indicate phenomena in a reliable way. ... In case of doubt, humans are better off appealing to nonhumans."[33] This allows a framework in which both the actions of scientists and the action of the objects they study come together with a shared responsibility for scientific outcomes, something that a purely sociological account struggles with.

A consequence of this revised view of agency is to replace human intentions with real tangible outcomes as the fundamental marker of agency; everything that happens in the world is given equal attribution to an agency that caused it. If one building falls down because of an earthquake, while another is demolished by developers, it does not allow that in one case agency was involved whereas in the other case it was not.

In a similar vein, Lambros Malafouris investigates "material agency" through the description of a potter at a wheel, creating a pot from clay. The potter's hands are in a direct and dynamic interaction with the clay. What happens when you indulge in a detailed analysis of this interaction is that causality reduces to our physics-eye view, the view alluded to by Turing in his treatment of the Lovelace objection.[34] As the potter, wheel, and clay interact there is no way to describe the potter as originating the action. Neurons are firing, but they are being influenced by the visual and tactile senses, responding to the shape and behavior of the clay. There is no clear beginning to the process and we cannot identify the process of origination that is supposedly the possession of the potter and not the clay or the wheel. Malafouris concludes, "If human agency *is*, then material agency *is*, there is no way that human and material agency can be disentangled. Or else, *while agency and intentionality may not be properties of things, they are not properties of humans either: they are the properties of material engagement, that is, of the grey zone where brain, body and culture conflate.*" (original emphasis)[35]

This conclusion is drawn from zooming in very close to a specific act of embodied creation to reveal the impossibility of true origination. The same can occur by zooming right out to witness longer-term cultural effects. The potter may have intended to produce a pot of a certain style, but all of this may well be scripted (Latour's term) by the potter's cultural precedents and demands—even the intention came from elsewhere. The potter, with his motivations, norms, aesthetics, and cognitive equipment, is the product of millennia of cultural evolution and hundreds of thousands of years of human biological evolution, as well as the things that were said to him or that he saw on the news that morning.

This is a potted summary of a vast topic. Variations of this essential idea can be found cutting across many different strands of late twentieth- and early twenty-first-century thinking. Related thinking can be found in the extended-mind hypothesis of Andy Clark,[36] which views technological artifacts as *aspects* of our cognitive capability: from eyeglasses for improved perception to notepads that allow us to iterate visual ideas or offload information from short-term memory, to pocket calculators that perform other magical feats of cognition.

Likewise, in design it has proven fruitful to understand humans as users of objects in this way. Relevant strands of thought include distributed cognition and situated cognition, and a bundle of practices that have become known as third-wave human-computer interaction (HCI). Susanne Bødker notes in third-wave HCI an increased attention paid by designers to the "webs-of-technology" or "artefact ecosystems" in which human action takes place: "We never design single, monolithic devices or systems, but technology that must be seen and used in relation to many other devices, applications and systems. Webs-of-technology are used to describe ubiquitous interaction as a process of negotiation between the users and the technology, focussing on the availability of technology and interpretability of services."[37] It is understood that "users' shared capacities and experiences are not just based on individual acting and learning in the world; rather, they are bound to shared practices, joint activities, and so on. ... It is against this background that the relationship between the user and the artifact exists." Another design-focused anthropologist, Paul Dourish, argues in a similar way to Malafouris that "embodiment is not a property of systems, technologies, or artifacts; it is a property of interaction. ... In contrast to Cartesian approaches that separate mind from body and thought from action, embodied interaction emphasizes their duality."[38]

For designers, social theorists, and historians, the challenge of constructing a workable framework for describing and designing for systems that do not privilege human actors is a monumental task. Despite the huge body of theoretical work dedicated to this effort, only lightly touched on above, a clear and universally accepted picture is still lacking. I will draw two key points from the above summary.

The first is that it can be effective—and many would say it is essential—to view creativity as occurring through interaction, and for the agency responsible for any creative act to be defined by a shifting boundary, perhaps drawn around individuals, groups of individuals, individuals interacting with materials and machines, and so on.

In our daily lives, it is practical to think about humans as originators of things, or more generally as causes of external effects, to think of ourselves as fully autonomous agents. We affect the world in ways that we have generally planned. Even if you agree with Turing in principle, in your everyday life you don't give up claiming credit for coming up with a good idea or cracking a fine joke. Rightly so; as a system you are capable of behaviors that are irreducible to their lower-level components. Only in the sophisticated configuration that is *you* could that joke have come into the world.

But despite our prototypical tendency to point to ourselves, as well as to great individuals of art and science, as creative exemplars, we should always do so with caveats, scare quotes, and question marks. Likewise, asking if a computer program is creative will always require a situated view that takes into account that system's interaction with the world; the preferred question is whether and how any computer program *contributes* to creative outcomes.

The second point is that, as Latour frequently reiterates, as different entities collide in the formation of temporary agents, it is not only their capacities that change. Everything is in flux, including *goals*, which is the reason we can't just describe outcomes in terms of individual intention. This is important to the idea established in the previous chapter that a creative act is one in which something of value is created. The question that remains is, when we ascribe value to something we have to address the more complex problem of "valuable for whom or what agent?"

The Lovelace Objection Revisited

These ideas lend a new perspective on Lovelace's question of origination. In his response to Lovelace's objection, Turing's view bears a resemblance to Malafouris's challenge to human agency. He reminds us that in a classical view of systems, everything is at some low level just following a cold, hard path of determinism—just simple billiard balls smashing into each other and bouncing around, a causally uncomplicated state of affairs. To trace the cause of anything, run back the tape and see where the billiard balls went.[39] For Turing, as we have seen, the idea that we are originators of things is no less dubious than the idea that computers could one day be.

Somewhat harder to stomach, Turing also argues that machines routinely produce surprising behaviors, taking an indifferent attitude to whether such surprises are simply due to errors—accidents that result in behaviors that aren't there by design (being errors, you can say they aren't really there for any reason whatsoever). Bringsjord, Bello, and Ferrucci proposed one specific hypothetical example of such a machine error in their response to Turing, which was discussed briefly in the previous chapter.[40] They imagine that, due to a hardware error, a production-line robot sticks a spare tire on a car in the wrong place, and as a result a designer is inspired to produce a new car design based on what the machine has accidentally initiated. For Bringsjord, Bello, and Ferrucci, this is a clear-cut case of the machine *not* being creative: "Would we want to credit the malfunctioning robot with having *originated* a new auto?" they ask. "Of course not," they reply, but why not?

It is understandable to reject the errant robot's creativity a priori, being so dysfunctional in its genesis, but applying criticism derived from Latour, Malafouris, and company, we might question if this prejudges that one part of a holistic creative process is more important than another. From a standard perspective on creativity, the errant robot is not creative because it did not know what it was doing (and like Bringsjord and colleagues, applying our creativity prototype detectors, we would be inclined to agree). But on the other hand, there is no way of explaining the particular outcome that occurred without reference to the particular actions of the errant robot. Importantly, as Simonton says of artists like Michelangelo—*fundamentally creative in the sense that they make things that wouldn't have otherwise been made*—it may well be that had the errant robot not done what it did, such a car design would never have seen the light of day. Perhaps the new car design sparks a butterfly effect chain of radical change in the use of cars and the design of cities. Now, imagine that, so pleased are they with their accidental discovery, the designers decide that they need *more* errant robots, to stimulate more accidental discoveries. They build factories with random variations added to the production-line robots, which now routinely perform blind variation. Then we have what might look a bit like an act of Darwinian evolutionary creation: a "random mutation" in the robot causes its "genes" future success. As Csikszentmihalyi notes, since the full gamut of outcomes is not prespecified at the moment of such a potentially creative act, it will be necessary to revisit the attribution of creativity later on anyway.

This could be taken as a profound dilemma. But it is a tedious trap to be stuck in. There is no need to quibble over the creativity or not of an errant robot, only to recognize that multiple heterogeneous actors are involved in pretty much any creative process. To be clear, I certainly do not wish to claim that the robot is creative, only that it is a part of the temporary entity through which (and only through which) the new car design is created. Likewise, this is not a call to dismiss the power of human intelligence in the creativity of distributed creative systems. Human brains are systems that possess great creative capacity. Without them, airplanes and symphonies would not exist, and neither would the new car design. Instead, we need a different way to think about creativity, to construe it as an entirely distributed process.

Analyzing Interactions between People and Things: Functions and Affordances

This analysis leads to a somewhat negative stance in which default assumptions are broken down but little is left to grab on to. But as the product of this thinking, various concepts are available for describing the relationship between components within distributed creative systems in general and specifically, for us, in relation to their creativity.

Of greatest importance to these relational questions in human-artifact interaction is a cluster of concepts associated with the notion of *function*. The act of the errant machine discussed earlier was seen as creatively problematic because of its lack of any creative objective, whether designed or emergent. While the designer comes with a complex of function-oriented properties—goals, motivations, objectives, intentions—the errant robot is literally *malfunctioning*; it has not performed whatever function we might attribute to the robot by its design. It has not devised new goals or evolved new behaviors, it is simply broken. We find it nearly impossible to imagine that something under these circumstances could be an agent in the creative process, let alone the originator of anything, precisely because of this failure of function.

But on closer inspection we find that a rejection of creativity on the basis that it does not arise from a clear function would taint many acts of creation, above all in seemingly agentless processes such as emergence, evolution, or autopoiesis; these fulfil the concept of *generative creativity* that can work even when there is no objective or preemptive function. This is particularly relevant in creative arts where any discussion of the utility of the product is inevitably fuzzier than in contexts such as design and science, as I will discuss in the next chapter.

In discussing agency and interaction in different systems comprising humans, human-made artifacts, and even other natural biotic and abiotic elements, we have encountered several different types of functions. Biological agents exist and act in the context of an evolutionary logic. Often it is valuable to understand their actions and traits in terms of how they serve the survival of their genes, and this generally describes the function of biological traits. The predator has front-facing vision to focus in on its prey, whereas the prey has wraparound vision to keep an eye out for predators. Both are good for that particular species' particular niche and its associated needs.

Meanwhile, we can talk about human-made artifacts having functions ascribed to them by design (the hammer is for driving nails into surfaces) or by some creative appropriation (the hammer, by virtue of it being small and heavy, makes a good paperweight). Aristotle distinguished final and efficient causes—the purpose for something existing versus the immediate sequence of events leading to its existence. But final causes are problematic in the context of natural evolution: evolved things don't have purpose, as such, even though they appear to.[41] These are all functions, but it is valuable to distinguish them, as Dan Sperber does,[42] following Ruth Millikan, using the separate term *teleofunction*. Teleofunction refers to the kind of function we see in biologically evolved systems, a function that arose and serves only to continue its own existence. The function of a bird's wings is to fly, which has arisen and exists because of its success at continuing the phenomenon of flying birds (not "in order to" but by continuation of what it has done with success previously). Importantly, however, teleofunction can be found in artifacts and social practices too, which may arise because they are useful to us, but may equally arise not because we need or want them but because they *exploit us*. This is perhaps best known in the concept of the meme (this term is discussed below, but like Sperber I dislike the confusion this term brings).

Also, Sperber notes, we actually live among strange hybrids of biological and human-made, functional and teleofunctional artifacts. Sperber suggests examples of these such as seedless grapes; they are of biological origin but adapted through interaction with humans to exchange one biological teleofunction (seeds) with another (being tasty to humans), and henceforth reproduce through the human act of grafting. Other cultural phenomena can be broken down accordingly. They can also be analyzed in terms of who is being served in the functional interactions taking place. Compare the goals of a company that produces an unhealthy but addictive soft drink product and the goals of one of its customers. The drink and associated advertising materials form a nexus of artifacts that these agents interact with.

These various considerations begin to shape an effective toolkit for thinking about artifacts. From another direction, James Gibson's concept of affordances is a powerful tool for thinking about how the world around us might more specifically guide our actions. Although better known nowadays as a theory concerning artifacts, Gibson developed the theory of affordances to understand behavior in evolved ecological contexts. "The verb *to afford* is in the dictionary," Gibson explained in 1977, "the noun *affordance* is not. I have made it up. I mean by it something that refers both to the environment and the animal in a way that no existing term does. It implies the complementarity of the animal and the environment."[43] Affordances are the interactional relations of potential between an animal and its environment. A water bug can skate over the surface of water. A lion cannot. This of course influences how water bugs and lions approach a pool of water. To the water bug, water affords skating.

The concept of affordance is beautifully obvious! It is a marvel that the simple derivation of a noun from a verb could have had such a remarkable effect on our thinking to be considered one of the great intellectual contributions of the last century. Affordances help us deal with the most mundane and hidden of interactions. Gibson refers to the ground as "stand-on-able." Something's possible affordances can form a lengthy and perhaps very abstract list: "Air affords breathing, more exactly, respiration. It also affords unimpeded locomotion relative to the ground, which affords support. When illuminated and fog-free, it affords visual perception. It also affords the perception of vibratory events by means of sound fields and the perception of volatile sources by means of odor fields."[44]

What the theory of affordances does, as applied in design, is help to enmesh this two-way interaction between things and people, indeed between all types of entities. Gibson's world consists of complex layers of species interactions, negotiated through affordances and growing in complexity through evolution's exploitation of these affordances. Things get interesting when the complex cognitive abilities of one species actually become an affordance for another species (*bee eyesight affords attracting bees using visual stimuli, as performed by flowers*). This is interesting because it is not always the more cognitively sophisticated species that is doing the exploitation; cognitive complexity can be hijacked, which happens in many instances where a plant or fungus uses an insect or animal to spread its seeds or spores, or with any sort of biomimicry. These examples, where the manipulator is not a cognitive entity, while the manipulated entity is, provide another example of why we should admit a more fluid theory of agencies.

Likewise, in the world of human artifacts, many affordances are straightforward. A skateboard affords rolling down a hill. In the Gibsonian sense, this means it *can be done* (whether you recognize it or not—if you don't, it is simply a hidden affordance). Donald Norman's translation of the theory of affordances into the world of design[45] then poses issues of how we can manipulate and establish affordances in our built environment—not just what the affordances of something are but how you present the affordances of an object to a user in a way that improves usability. Many poorly designed things, Norman observed, fail for this reason—there is some deficiency in the *perceived* affordances.[46]

But there are also situations where an affordance needn't be perceived at all for the artifact to function. Consider the difference between two types of electric hand dryer: one is button operated while the other has a proximity sensor, which is designed to detect when something is placed under the dryer. These are near identical systems. The proximity sensor is a binary switch which is, from the point of view of the hand dryer's electrics, functionally identical to the button. But whereas in one case there is a button that affords pushing—you are clearly the agent operating the machine—in the other case there is a "smart" hand dryer that senses when a pair of hands is waiting to be dried. In the latter case, you are really just pushing an invisible button (everyone has experienced waving their hands around in front of such a device failing to activate it, wishing they could *perceive* the button). Indeed, the proximity sensing hand dryer is at the somewhat humble end of smart technologies. But the point remains that the way we conceive of the relationship between participants in this interaction can shift quite some way with only a subtle shift in the basic conditions.

The theory of affordances provides a low-level description of how our agency relations with artifacts exist as two-way exchanges. The affordance of a designed artifact is at once something that a user actively *chooses* to act upon and something that influences their behavior by indicating various action possibilities. Indeed, along with usability comes the broader concept of user experience. This might include seductive or manipulative features of an object's design that are not functionally beneficial to the user. In other cases, the affordances are put to the service of someone who is not the immediate user. Adding a heavy weight to a hotel room key is a well-known strategy for hotel managers to reduce the instance of lost keys (an example discussed by Latour). Thus, at a stretch, weighted hotel keys afford for the hotel staff "being left at reception," but they are a nuisance to the hotel's customers (though perhaps less of a nuisance than a hefty fine).

Affordances form a central pillar for Vlad Glăveanu, a contemporary proponent of an inclusive distributed approach to creativity grounded in social psychology. For Glăveanu, "creative phenomena cannot be properly understood and studied outside of their integrated and dynamic totality defined as a creativity complex."[47] Replacing Rhodes's four Ps of creativity—product, person, process, press—he offers his own five As—actor, audience, action, artifact, affordances—that constitute the units of analysis of a "molecular" perspective, with affordances providing the relational component. Glăveanu is at the same time keen to stress the forced nature of such a framework: "to analyse creative activity means, in essence, to engage in a form of 'violence' towards the lived experience of creators, to segment the wholeness of a creative experience into parts and units that might, in the end, be foreign to it."

For Latour, the interaction between the larger network structure and the individual is also seen as one in which more or less active or passive relations may play out. He uses the term *script* to refer to the way in which a situation may dictate what any individual might do at a given time. The individual can either stand under the script (be passive in the unfolding of events) or stand above the script (enact a form of agency, redirecting events).[48]

Alfred Gell[49] applies similar thinking about agency to cross-cultural art production, and in doing so offers what I think is a slightly more palatable terminology that aligns with a modern view of agency but offers a handle on the classical view at the same time. *Primary agents*, he says, are those "self-sufficient" agents that have all the stuff of intentions and cognitive power.[50] He also wryly refers to these as "pukka" agents—in other words, the real deal—satisfying the classical view of human agency. *Secondary agents*, then, are artifacts that don't really do anything on their own but can *act* as agents in various ways, meaning simply that they have an effect on their environment. They might act as delegates for the agency of their maker—as the weighted keys of the hotel management have an effect on the behavior of hotel guests. In Georgina Born's interpretation, "the artifact mediates and relays social relations across space and time."[51] But they could equally have effects that were not intended, when something takes on a *life of its own*, such as whenever something malfunctions.

Affordances, scripts, and secondary agency can all be seen as ways of capturing how individuals are subjugated under complex distributed creative systems, and how artifacts have the potential to play a part in that subjugation. Having worked through concepts of agency, autonomy, and function across different contexts, we have a better chance of breaking down and describing computational creativity systems without getting stuck in asymmetrical dualism: believing that human individuals form distinct and privileged sites of agency. The value of these terms is that they are not specific to computationally creative systems and so help establish a continuity. The breakdown of the binary distinction between humans-as-agents and artifacts-as-non-agents carries over to the *timeline* of emerging computationally creative systems,[52] which can instead be understood as systems that can perform in different ways in the formation of temporary distributed creative agencies. For example, we have already looked at the artist, Cohen, and the system, AARON, in terms of a coupled interaction that defines a new collaborative agency, mediated by the various affordances of the technology and the artistic domain, and involving a nontrivial set of interacting teleofunctions alongside more traditional imposed functions. None of these concepts really shifts our technical understanding of what AARON is doing under the hood, but they provide a more structured view of how the system, despite being "merely generative" and exploratory, feeds creative outcomes. The terminology now introduced means we can move beyond asking whether or not AARON (or an errant robot) is a creative agent and begin to build a rich profile of the system in terms of its relationship to agency and function.

Bringing this back to the distinction between generative and adaptive creativity, very many processes, consisting of different human and nonhuman elements, can perform generative creativity. Computational systems such as AARON are very easily accepted as performing creative functions insofar as they are understood as producers of constrained variations: generators of unscrutinized novelty operated by a human actor. Fewer systems have the more narrow properties of adaptive creativity. Humans can be seen as such systems, with the machinery not only to generate novelty but evaluate it and tailor this process of generation to specific needs. In the above I have started to outline how, while much of human creativity is adaptive creativity, there is also a lot of creativity that is generative and accordingly deserves to be evaluated by different criteria. Individual humans compose melodies and paint paintings, but they do not create movements or perform the work, on their own, of turning their artistic outputs into symbols of cultural significance. This is done by large groupings of people working in distributed and less coordinated ways. Such groupings in the world of art are largely less purposeful than the British government setting the longitude prize. They enact generative creativity because they do not act with such common, unified purpose; what comes out of them cannot be said to have been created with a pre-established objective or common value.

What Created the Creative Species? An Evolutionary View

This leads to a further detour to consider the generative, emergent, purposeless nature of this cultural level of activity, where cultural processes are understood not only in terms of human agents being adaptively creative but at the same time via the lens of Darwinian evolutionary theory, which is itself purely generative. Culture embodies different aspects of these distinct processes, and here I look toward the more mechanical, systems-based perspectives that fill out this framework.

The blind variation approach to creative search, discussed at the beginning of this chapter, and the notion of teleofunction encountered later, both relate unmistakably to Darwinian evolutionary theory.[53] Besides these associations, bringing Darwinian evolution into the discussion may seem like an arbitrary addition. But consider that Darwin's theory provides the link between two of the domains that have been central to the discussion of origination,[54] between blind mechanical physical processes and primary agents. It binds the deterministic view of the world, appealed to by Turing and others, to our everyday experience of intentions and will. In this sense it is a good way to frame the understanding of function necessitated by the previous discussion.

By Darwinian, do not think of the straw man caricature of a narrow adaptationist view, epitomized by the reduction of every biological trait to one adapted gene or another. Think instead of a rich and pluralist array of evolutionary phenomena, which has natural selection at its core, fleshed out by a vast array of other hypothesized evolutionary effects, including but not limited to: sexual selection, group selection, niche construction, the Red Queen effect, kin selection, ontogenetic and phylogenetic interaction, gene-culture coevolution, the Baldwin effect, genetic drift, symbiosis, and punctuated equilibrium. It should be accorded the generality found in the dictum attributed to D'Arcy Thompson that "everything is the way it is because it got that way."[55] Darwin's own research wasn't just about showing that natural selection worked as a mechanism, but constructing complex and very specific historical narratives to explain speciation events and adaptive pressures: could such and such a seed have floated on water or been carried by a bird in order to get from one island to another? His world involved many different interacting forces, with a great deal of happenstance in the emergence of evolutionary outcomes.

If creativity, like agency, should be defined by effects rather than presupposed intentions, then Darwinian evolution is a quintessentially creative force, and it is also one that our prototypical creativity detectors might grant creativity. It has generally been a challenge to reconcile evolutionary creativity with human creativity, because one is intentional and cognitive and the other is absolutely not. One is conceived of in terms of its value to us, while the other is seemingly value-ambiguous, and because the latter is simply more familiar (prototypical) than the former. The distributed creativity view developed in this chapter, by contrast, is inclusive of evolutionary emergence.

The theory of evolution by natural selection is based on a simple naturally occurring stochastic mechanical process that has three components: heredity, variation, and selective retention. To begin, we require replicators, structures that can copy themselves. The theory can't explain the emergence of replication, because it depends on its preexistence. But from the existence of simple replicating molecular structures, everything else follows: with replication comes heredity (the copy is similar to the source) as well as likely sources of variation (a simple copying error may introduce differences between the source and the copy). It then also follows that we will witness selective retention; with any accidental difference between two individuals, we may find that the difference enables one individual to have better chances of copying itself than the other. This fitter one's progeny will, by this definition, become more common and increase the occurrence of whatever trait led to the improved fitness. Furthermore, even the simplest replicating molecules consume some kind of locally finite resource, at least the raw chemical ingredients needed to construct them. When more or less successful individuals are forced to compete for these resources, the less successful individuals will be outcompeted, potentially to extinction. Thus from just the existence of self-replicating molecules, an extraordinary creative force arises, which Darwin used to explain nothing less than the origin of species.

The theory of natural selection emerged at a time when we were beginning to see the world as the product of quite radical interactions between micro- and macro-level processes. Darwin followed in the footsteps of Charles Lyell, whose seminal studies of geology[56] first portrayed the earth as a dynamic system, its volcanoes and earthquakes the signs of gradual processes that over time shaped mountains and seas. Likewise, Darwin's theory shows how the minute daily interactions of biological forms ultimately influence the forms themselves, given long enough.

An immediate consequence of an evolutionary perspective is that life on Earth is revealed to have followed a path of increasing complexity, marked by certain major innovations in the design of biological forms. John Maynard Smith and Eörs Szathmáry chart these innovations in a treatise on the "major transitions in evolution."[57] These include the transition from simple replicators to chromosomes, from asexual clones to sexual populations, from solitary individuals to colonies with nonreproductive castes, and the emergence of culture.

As with the success of individual species, each of these innovations was a winning design, definitively successful and never to be undone once discovered. We might add various other minor innovations such as skin, eyes, flight, and locomotion, that may have been lost at various moments to certain species but once introduced into the world have flourished and resisted eradication. But the major transitions are particularly special in that they each, in effect, change the rules of evolution. Sexual reproduction introduces the idea of a common gene pool and genetic recombination. This allows the diffusion of the best traits through an evolving population, making evolution more effective and adaptive, and also leading to completely new forms such as the baroque excesses of sexual display, principles of exogamy and endogamy, and complex social structures.

More recently, researchers in fields such as complexity science and artificial life have sought to understand more abstract principles by which blind processes may produce high complexity. Stuart Kauffman, most famously, has developed a general theory of the emergence of order,[58] based on studies of self-organizing systems, of which natural selection may be understood as a specific case. In parallel, the biologist-philosopher team of Humberto Maturana and Francisco Varela popularized the notion of an "autopoietic system," literally self-creating, which is defined and reinforced by the maintenance of an organization through a dynamic process.[59] Biological cells are exemplary autopoietic systems, involving a metabolic process that maintains a membrane, separating the cell from the outside world. By analogy, multicellular systems and other configurations such as social groups can be described in autopoietic terms, as was attempted by Niklas Luhmann in a detailed application of Maturana and Varela's work to the social sciences, particularly the domains of artistic production.[60] Autopoiesis not only describes the immediate maintenance of a system's structure but the long-term emergence of that organization through a process of structural coupling between elements. In the social domain, it provides a mechanism to think of something as being completely function-free yet complex and actively self-sustaining, sitting at the boundary between a process of emergence and one of formation by natural selection.

Cultural Evolution

Following the trend of increasing complexity, human culture rewrites the rules of evolution in yet another radical way. Culture is the product of human populations accumulating knowledge across individual boundaries. Any individual organism with the cognitive capacity to learn about its environment can accumulate knowledge. An animal will learn its territory, learn to recognize other animals, work out what is good or bad to eat and where to find it, and can also be creative, working out how to do things that it did not know how to do innately, like appropriating an object as a tool.

This body of knowledge is generally built up over a lifetime and lost when that animal dies. But it is not always lost; many species learn from each other in a variety of more or less sophisticated ways. A young bear first learns its way around a territory with the simple strategy "stay close to mother." This is an example of the vertical transmission of knowledge—vertical meaning that it follows the genetic transmission from parents to offspring. Social learning, here, is a crude blend combining a social factor without a learning component (stay close to mother), and a learning factor without a social component (build a map of the environment).

Such simple social learning can be horizontal or oblique as well—that is, from members of the population who are not our direct ancestors. Blue tits in Britain have been shown to learn from each other that they could peck into milk bottle tops to drink the milk. But, as with bear cubs, all it takes is for the tits to follow each other around and to randomly peck a lot at things around them. The learning still consists of an individual discovery; each individual blue tit, engaged in blind search, chances upon the milk bottle and discovers the reward. But this is all facilitated by the "teacher" bird who, by hanging around near milk bottles, constrains the blind search to set up the conditions for the learning event to occur. In this scenario, neither bird needs to have any intention to teach or to learn, nor even any kind of model of what the other bird is doing or thinking.

In humans, social learning has evolved into a dedicated and sophisticated set of cognitive capacities, including thinking about what another is thinking—their goals, intentions, and understanding of a situation; understanding another's actions in relation to our own; learning complex sequences, including making things; and of course the use of language and symbolic culture to create the ultimate tools of social transmission: shared environments of the mind. Social learning is a superb strategy for gaining knowledge. The useful knowledge that individuals work out for themselves is generally learned at a cost. Exploring a new territory or tasting strange foods involves taking risks that would be better avoided, and trial and error is, if nothing else, time consuming. So social learning makes sense for individuals; if you see someone else eating a strange food and not getting sick, then you have evidence that it is safe. These benefits, many have argued, provide a selection pressure that has driven the evolution of complex social learning machinery in humans.

Thinking about what someone else is thinking, known as applying a *theory of mind* (ToM), is one important ingredient for human social learning. The neurophysiological underpinnings of ToM include circuitry that connects seeing an action performed and performing that action oneself. The same circuits are active when you see someone grasping something, as when you grasp something. Such simple mechanisms are hypothesized to underlie the transition in humans toward collective modes of action, by enabling a form of shared cognition that ultimately underpins language and culture.

Along with the mechanisms that enable learning from other individuals come mechanisms for steering learning in the right direction. In a species that learns socially, a new demand arises: to sift through all of the people, and all of the things they do, and work out what is worth learning and what is not. A sensible starting point for this is to learn to do everything that our parents do. Vertical transmission, from parents to offspring, is a relatively safe bet because it perfectly tracks the genetic transfer of traits. If it works for your parents, then it will probably work for you, besides which, your parents are likely to be readily available and helpful, being interested in your success and willing to support your learning.

Unlike genetic inheritance, vertical cultural transmission speeds up the rate at which a given lineage can adapt, because it can add in the developments made through individual learning. This mirrors Lamarck's theory of evolution; Jean-Baptiste Lamarck, before Darwin, posited that evolving species could pass on learned traits to their offspring through biological reproduction. He was wrong when it comes to the genetic transmission mechanism, but this particular model of evolution still has a place in our wider understanding of evolutionary theory.[61]

Social learning can be even more powerful if the transfer of knowledge occurs horizontally or obliquely, not just vertically. For this, Robert Boyd and Peter Richerson[62] propose heuristics for the successful social learner, such as to focus on behaviors that are very common in the population. It is reasonable to assume that a common behavior is a successful behavior; if there are many people around adopting that behavior, then at worst it is not fatal, and at best, those people have adopted it because it improves their lot. This tendency to copy common behaviors is known as "frequency bias" and can be stated simply as the rule that the more common a trait is the more likely we will be to adopt it. Another strategy is to focus on learning primarily from successful individuals, whose success, we might presume, may be down to the success of their behaviors. This accords with the fact that celebrities are paid large sums of money to advertise products.

The powerful cognitive machinery of social learning enables culture and technology, which, like biological evolution, has a cumulative nature. Once an effective innovation has been made, its ability to reproduce, whether via biological reproduction or cultural transmission, means that it is likely to stick around. Each innovation also provides the basis for future innovations to be built upon it. Some innovations, like writing or telephones, even speed up and bolster the copying and accumulating processes itself.

This cumulative process has been described as a "ratchet" effect,[63] a ratchet being a device that allows movement in one direction but not the other. On this basis it seems reasonable to suggest that the human mechanisms underpinning social learning, not creative discovery, are the real powerhouse of human creativity, because they underlie the working of the ratchet. Without it, we would not accumulate knowledge, and each individual human life would consist of solving the same problems. By analogy with biological evolution, we see that as long as the ratchet is working, then even just random thrashing about will do to drive progress: every so often we advance a notch on the ratchet. Thus even human creativity may not actually require that there is a particularly powerful individual human capacity for creative thought.

This is not to say that cumulative culture is just another manifestation of Darwinian evolution. There are competing views of how cultural evolution or cultural replication relates to natural selection. For example, Richard Dawkins[64] proposed that if the gene is the unit of biological reproduction, then we could talk of an equivalent unit of cultural reproduction, for which he coined the term *meme*. While the term became popular for a while as an academic subject of study, others reject such terminology because there is no apparent need to talk in terms of units in the context of culture, and little more than confusion to be found in hypothesizing that some cultural thing akin to a gene actually exists and performs any such function. Why bias what the nature of cultural evolution might be with such a leading metaphor? Nevertheless, whether you use the term meme or some other framework for thinking about cultural evolution, the application of the ratchet effect concept to human culture is a common thread and has the essential features of a blind search process.

Some have suggested that biological and cultural evolution form a continuum of accumulating technologies. Kevin Kelly, for example, dubs the entire system the *Technium*,[65] and argues that its evolution toward increasing complexity is a far greater force than anything we may do to exert our will upon it.

For Brian Arthur, an economist responsible for the theory of increasing returns, technologies beget other technologies.[66] Specifically, "nature possesses many sets of phenomena. ... We can say that novel phenomena provide new technologies that uncover novel phenomena; or that novel technologies uncover new phenomena that lead to further technologies. Either way, the collectives of technology and of known phenomena advance in tandem."[67] As for Kelly, whose book on the subject is entitled *What Technology Wants*,[68] technological determinism supersedes human agency, and human ingenuity is merely a part of the mechanism by which this grand holistic process proceeds. As with Ashby's portrayal of the brain as just another technology invented by nature, this is the hardest of hard technological determinism. There are good cases against taking such a deterministic stance, but also strong evidence that we are set on a course of continuing complexification witnessed in the evolutionary major transitions.

Arthur observes that unlike in biological evolution, technology is capable of combinatorial evolution. Plants and animals can't hybridize, except within the limited scope of sexual reproduction operating within a species (and the tricky concept of horizontal gene transfer). But in technological combinatorial evolution, subsystems can be replaced and rearranged, and a solution from one domain can be brought to bear on another domain. This means that technological evolution experiences increasing returns: the more technology is out there, the more ways there are for elements to be recombined and lead to new innovations, and so the more quickly technology evolves.

Arthur also specifies four separate mechanisms of technological evolution:

Innovation consists in novel solutions being arrived at in standard engineering—the thousands of small advancements and fixes that cumulate to move practice forward. It consists in radically novel technologies being brought into being by the process of invention. It consists in these novel technologies developing by changing their internal parts or adding to them in the process of structural deepening. And it consists in whole bodies of technology emerging, building out over time, and creatively transforming the industries that encounter them.[69]

In short, if biological evolution is a powerful creative force, then cultural evolution combines this with additional power in the form of human agents' problem solving, planning, adopting, and so on. Nevertheless, these various technologically determinist views strictly place the power of emergence over that of planning and cognitive creative agency; essentially the same creative force found in nature, purely generative, is seen here to drive technological change, just with human brains as the conduit through which the emergence takes place. Artistic processes can be treated in the same way, with the individual subsumed by the system.

Niche Construction

The result of powerful social learning, Boyd and Richerson suggest, is a situation in which social learning is deployed so effectively, and thus adopted so extensively, that auxiliary and potentially adverse effects begin to arise. For example, if too many individuals focus too much effort on learning from others, then there is a risk that incorrect knowledge or dysfunctional behavior can filter into the population, especially if we are inclined to copy the most popular behaviors. More generally, human culture represents the most dramatic instance of a species constructing its own environment, both in terms of the alteration of the physical environment and also in the construction of a cultural "virtual" environment within which human concerns play out. In Richerson and Boyd's words, "We do seem to have cut our way to our extraordinary adaptive success dragging a canoe-load of junk behind us."[70]

Opportunities abound for risky positive feedback to occur in Boyd and Richerson's model: the frequency bias means that popular traits become yet more popular, whereas unpopular traits might struggle to get off the ground even if they are beneficial. The hypothesized preference to learn from successful people might mean that those people's status grows greater under the attention awarded them by prospective learners. Under such conditions, strategies for success might shift from innovating objectively useful behaviors to behaviors that have a greater chance of being acclaimed, useful or not.

A framework that helps us make sense of this is niche construction.[71] The concept of niche construction came from the idea that in order to understand the circular complexities of biological evolution fully we should pay equal attention to the process of individuals modifying their environments, as to the environment shaping organisms through natural selection. Unlike earlier theories of biological coevolution, niche construction pays greater attention to the adaptability and potential agency of abiotic elements, much like the distributed creative systems of human-artifact interaction discussed above.[72]

A canonical example is the effect of rainforests on their abiotic environment, creating clouds and drawing down the temperature. Such climatic effects can be seen to happen on a global scale, and indeed we know that the earth's temperature is lower than it would be if it had no life on it. The various species making up this environment both contribute to its creation and over evolutionary time continue adapting to the new conditions that are created. Other species also adapt to the newly constructed niche and might further drive the changing conditions for evolutionary adaptation. The result is commonly described by physicists as "far from equilibrium," a situation that is sustained not because everything has settled into its resting state but because a complex network of dynamic processes acts to maintain a far more complicated state.

Without involving the modification of the environment by species, niche construction theorists argue, an understanding of the evolution of those species is incomplete—they did not just adapt to a fixed environment, but instead coevolved along with their environments. As this idea has picked up, pitched by its proponents as the "neglected process in evolution," it can be seen everywhere. Nature is constantly creating new types of niche. Rainforests establish a canopy and thus a shaded mineral-rich environment under the canopy. The wood of trees uniquely defines the niche of the woodpecker, and so on. Rich ecosystem complexes form, in which species contribute to the niches of other species in an endlessly creative process.

Accordingly, the human case is niche construction on steroids, with an extensive reconfiguration of our physical environment—clothes, buildings, spectacles, submarines—and the creation of culturally constructed virtual realms of activity—religions, stories, law, morality, social roles—both seemingly subject to a long-term cumulative trend. Niche construction helps us think of these phenomena as coevolution between ourselves and our niches. For example, if we communicate via language, then selection pressures might involve being able to handle complex grammar, or having a loud voice, or being able to remember complex stories. If we wear clothes, then selection pressures might involve the fine motor skills required to manipulate materials in the fabrication of clothes, while the need to have warm body fur might become less important. If our lives are structured according to concepts of magic and religion, then selection pressures might be related to abilities to perform in certain ways that befit special roles: act piously, do magic, demonstrate leadership, remember names and life histories, or at least convince others of these abilities. Each of these selection pressures builds upon the constructed niche created by earlier biological or cultural evolution. In theories of the evolution of contemporary civilizations, subsistence agriculture established the conditions for cities to emerge. Spoken language established the conditions for written language to emerge, and so on.

Niche construction also provides a useful framework for thinking about the division of labor. Consider the activities that contemporary humans engage in: politicians, comedians, thieves, cooks, con artists, carers, priests, monks, musicians, and computational creativity researchers. Each of these can be seen as building upon layers of constructed niches and further creating niches for others—social media officers require courses on the latest trends in social media, for example, creating a niche for the social media educator or social media trend analyzer.

Creativity as the Situated Production of Novelty

This diversion into the cumulative creativity of natural distributed processes, in their biological, cultural, and technological guises, has taken us a long way from the prototypical view of the lone creative human. Definitions of creativity focused on the human actor, attached to novelty and value, don't tell us everything we need to know about creativity in these large-scale distributed contexts. Nature produces novelty, but there is no agency to which it has value; there is no intention underlying the creation of species. But this is also true of some long-term sociotechnical processes that may be viewed as autopoietic and not driven by a designer or long-term purpose. This can be seen most explicitly in Arthur's view of ideas and technologies recombining in new combinations.

Under a perspective that admits this distributed view of creativity, we can't strictly always say that creative processes produce things of value, only that they produce new things. This may be seen in the distinction between individual artistic creation that may largely be a product of some artist's intention, and an artistic movement that cannot be said to be the product of any one person but of a collective, emergent process, even if every work in the canon of that movement was the product of adaptive creativity. I may value certain styles of music, but I am myself the product of a process of coevolution with those styles, my value system being shaped over my lifetime and informed by a lineage of other music listeners before me. That is, the value of the style does not preexist the style itself. If listeners' value systems are not objective but contingent on myriad contextual factors that influence them (as we will see in the following chapter), then when viewed over a long enough time scale these listeners' tastes are as much the product of a creative process as the music they enjoy. Again, this may be best viewed by considering how human actors or other creative elements are situated in a broader system, both influencing and being influenced by it. The situatedness of different elements defines different frames with which we can view different forms of creative process.

We have now gone long enough without specifically considering artistic behavior. In the following chapter, the above ideas are developed in their application to this domain of activity. The result is a multifaceted view of artistic creativity, with particular focus on the sociocultural and its emergent nature, held up by forms of evolutionary feedback. At last, in chapter 5 we arrive at a discussion of the existing algorithmic methods being used in computational creativity.

4   Artistic Behavior

It is self-evident that nothing concerning art is self-evident.
—Adorno[1]

A work of art is useless as a flower is useless. A flower blossoms for its own joy. We gain a moment of joy by looking at it. That is all that is to be said about our relations to flowers.
—Oscar Wilde[2]

Nothing is more necessary than the unnecessary.
—*Life Is Beautiful*[3]

Art and Human Psychology

We shift our focus now specifically to artistic behavior. The last chapter's discussion of agency and function provides a framework for understanding creativity as an aspect of art practice, including what the underlying cultural and biological evolutionary foundations of art may be, how artistic creativity is distributed, and how function plays into this distribution. This ultimately leads to a better understanding of how creative art production and evaluation may be analyzed as sites of automation.

The term *art* is another bundle of concepts that will not be easily pinned down, and here it will be used in a particularly inclusive way to describe a myriad of activities including but not limited to visual art, music, decorative art, aspects of design, poetry, storytelling, fashion, and so on. Such a cluster can also be referred to as "cultural production." It is a given that bundling all of these activities together will gloss over the many critical differences between these areas. While taking this liberty I will keep check of when this is being done and whether it is acceptable in each instance. The differences themselves will be of particular importance in this chapter, since a key concept is that each domain has distinct properties.

As we have experienced with creativity, the diverse and changeable concept of art eschews a strict categorical definition. One option is to take a family-resemblance approach. Each of us has a sense of what art is, based on a set of properties that may be more or less aligned with those concepts of other people. We may admit things to be art based on their association with the model we maintain of the concept "art." For example, Berys Gaut[4] provides the following list of family-resemblance features, emphasizing that his approach does not require that all criteria are satisfied by all artworks:

1. Possessing positive aesthetic properties
2. Being expressive of emotion
3. Being intellectually challenging
4. Being formally complex and coherent
5. Having the capacity to convey complex meanings
6. Exhibiting an individual point of view
7. Being original
8. Being an artifact or performance which is the product of a high degree of skill
9. Belonging to an established artistic form
10. Being the product of an intention to make a work of art[5]

Thus it may be that we have prototypical works of art—painting, music, poetry, film, and so on—that satisfy all of these things unambiguously, and are the things our minds naturally go to when asked to think of art, but we experience many other things that we tend to categorize or perceive as artistic in some less definitive way. This may include "bad" art or art that we don't like; such work satisfies criterion 10 and perhaps other criteria such as 8 and 9, but not criterion 1, as judged subjectively. We would of course accept that bad art is still art, even if we cannot use criterion 1 to directly evaluate it as such.

As with creativity, the family-resemblance approach then also permits us to include things that we may treat as works of art despite our various reservations: a beautiful technical diagram; a natural rock formation; the

Mandelbrot set; the junk shrines of a compulsive hoarder; art made by animals trained to use paintbrushes or drumsticks. These are things that we see as having artistic value or connotations even though something is not quite right—the work has not been created for aesthetic pleasure, or is not in a recognized field of art, or does not even have a human origin. As with creativity, this approach also doesn't fix requirements on other problematic cases that tend to lead to absurdities. For example, although we generally require originality in art, it seems pointless to insist that a forgery—or worse, something trivially novel but ultimately derivative, a slavish imitation—is not itself a piece of art.

Most importantly, this approach to defining art is in keeping with the complex tapestry of contexts in which it appears in human behavior. We expect that many aspects of human behavior consist of intertwined and overlapping activities that are often caught between categories: art or not-art. This approach relieves us of the problem of art in anthropology. Cross-cultural studies suggest that all cultures possess behaviors *resembling* aspects of Western art, and yet do not necessarily share the same conceptualization of art possessed by Western societies.[6]

A family-resemblance approach stands in contrast to the idea that art is defined by what art institutions or experts declare it to be, although this is one of the listed criteria. As Alfred Gell[7] notes, this is hopelessly limited to our specific cultural context, but even worse, even within such a context this would mean a circular and fickle uncertainty about what was in and what wasn't, depending on the ebbs and flows of a dynamic art world. A family-resemblance approach relieves us of having to draw a boundary between the world of art and the rest of our lives, accepting that categories are porous and permeable. Notions such as that art is lived experience or life is art are more easily constructed across this boundary. For other art-related words in other cultures there could be other associative lists like the one above. What ties artistic behavior together across cultures is not necessarily the conception of art itself but a set of underlying cognitive traits and social dynamics that are associated with humans.

Item 1 in Gaut's list, nevertheless, may appear to many the most familiar and possibly the strongest determining factor in deciding what is and isn't art. We associate art with that stuff made by people that invokes a strong aesthetic reaction, and we know firsthand how powerful this reaction can be. The aesthetic impact of art, through awe, the sublime, or specific emotions, tends to make us endow it with sacredness, deeper meaning, and purpose. This demands sensitivity from fields such as computational creativity. Engineers promising to "solve"' art, or tame it, like the legacy of the Muzak company, easily become the focus of ridicule or contempt for overreach and simplification. Music frequently invokes such passion. For many, Confucius is right that "music produces a kind of pleasure which human nature cannot do without," it is the "universal language of mankind." This is usually mentioned with the implication that it can stimulate understanding between cultures, and music and art are commonly described as things that "make us human," notwithstanding the circularity of argument therein. To quote Robin Williams in the 2007 film *August Rush*, "You know what music is? God's little reminder that there's something else besides us in this universe, a harmonic connection between all living beings, everywhere, even the stars."

I would add one more element to Gaut's list. In many situations art is associated with an explicit rejection of other purpose, most notably manifest in the bohemian creed "l'art pour l'art," or "art for art's sake." For Oscar Wilde, "A work of art is useless as a flower is useless. A flower blossoms for its own joy. We gain a moment of joy by looking at it. That is all that is to be said about our relations to flowers."[8] Under certain circumstances things that serve some other purpose, such as a television commercial, are treated as lesser examples of art. This may be more than just a unique perspective from a particular romantic viewpoint; it crops up elsewhere and may have a more universal quality grounded in evolutionary theories of display.

The philosopher of art Denis Dutton,[9] for example, looks at common properties of what he calls high art, forming a "conspicuous consumption" view in which art: involves the use of expensive materials; is time consuming to create, either directly or via the accumulation of skill; is remote from any possible use; is intellectually challenging; and is possibly fleeting.

Following the structure of chapter 3, I will work through a number of considerations of human artistic behavior beginning with a narrow view of the individual and expanding outward to incorporate aspects of social behavior. In these sections, I interleave work from psychology, social science, creative practice, and evolutionary theory. As this review navigates topics that are at times disputed, conflicting, speculative, or weakly formulated, it does not work toward any sort of unified theory. The result, instead, is a set of sketches of human artistic behavior at different scales and in different contexts, grounded in the framework developed so far. The purpose of this is to provide a set of potentialities that any analysis of computational creativity practice can benefit from taking into account.

Evolutionary Explanations

In discussing art and psychology, it is useful to specifically consider the question of evolutionary psychology: how and why, if at all, we might have evolved specific psychological traits. An evolutionary perspective bridges the gap between the mechanical world of physical causality and the intentions and goals of lived human experience. It allows for functions and teleofunctions to be well grounded and nonmystical. Work in evolutionary psychology is often speculative and hard to support by experimental evidence: brains do not fossilize in useful ways, and archaeological artifacts give only very indirect clues as to how we thought and behaved, let alone how those thoughts and behaviors were manifest in genes. Nevertheless, a look at the spectrum of possible evolutionary psychology factors bearing on our understanding of art provides a useful grounding for the most fundamental questions of what art is and why we engage with it.

There are five broad classes of evolutionary narrative relating to human artistic behavior. The first four are concerned with human cognitive traits, while the last takes a cultural or biocultural evolutionary perspective.

Consequentialist theories posit that artistic behavior itself does not have any evolutionary value or functional origin but instead arises from a cocktail of other adaptations that cause us to gain pleasure from certain configurations. Steven Pinker[10] has most famously made this case for music, which he contrasts with language—a cognitive capacity clearly evolved with an adaptive function. His now notorious cheesecake analogy makes the point very well. Does cheesecake have an adaptive function? he asks. Quite evidently not, because cheesecake itself did not exist in the era of our most recent adaptive development. A taste for sugar and fat, however, quite clearly do. Cheesecake should rightly be understood as a human innovation that exploits these traits and others besides to create a supercharged stimulus. Music likewise. This argument has Occam's razor on its side.

Cognitivist theories appeal to the intellectual and aesthetic stimulation associated with artistic behavior, and posit that we engage in forms of artistic behavior in order to serve some form of either cognitive development, reasoning, or exploration and discovery. For example, one evolutionary explanation for our love of storytelling is as a tool that enables us to think through social scenarios.[11] Other possible explanatory scenarios include ways to structure thought, ways to scaffold the learning of language, and forms of pretend play that enable an exploration of physics, patterns, social relations, and so on.

Cohesionist theories look at ways that creative domains may function to bind individuals together into cohesive social groups. Particularly in music, evidence from anthropology and social psychology supports some sort of group fitness effect.[12] This has been posited as a reason we are expert entrainers (we have an ability to hold a beat, sharing temporal experience with each other). Our ability to act collectively in time and in tune has been compared to the chorusing of wolves[13] and a psychological effect of boundary loss has been posited,[14] whereby we literally lose a sense of self in the process of singing together.

Cohesionist theories are considered problematic because they are potentially *group-selectionist*. On its face, Darwinian evolution explains the selection of fit *individuals* well, but not of fit groups; adaptations that are beneficial to groups of individuals must be robust in the face of freeloading individuals. This is the wider problem of the evolution of altruism.[15] If singing music in a group stimulates more pro-group behavior in individuals, then the fittest individuals would be those who could fake the cohesive behavior without wasting effort in contributing—in other words, they are evolutionary tricksters or freeloaders. But this selfish-gene objection is not unsurpassable. Theoretical solutions for group selection do exist, and models of gene-culture interaction such as those of Boyd and Richerson[16] and the niche construction theorists[17] also suggest possible conditions in which pro-cohesion selection pressures can emerge.

A common approach to solving the problem of altruistic behaviors is by appeal to inclusive fitness,[18] or kin selection: the principle that any behavior that benefits one's closest kin is also likely benefiting one's genes and can therefore be selected for. Models that take into account population structure show that altruism caused by inclusive fitness can expand to apply to large populations.[19] This fits with another strand of cohesionist thinking around music, that posits primitive musical behaviors—basic gestures and the ability to rhythmically entrain—as essential to the development of intersubjectivity, and hence language and sociality, in caregiver-infant interactions. Dissanayake,[20] for example, develops a multifaceted theory that brings together the development of intersubjectivity in earliest childhood with the role of art, broadly conceived as a cultural act of *making special*, in constructing markers and loci for the development of group identity.

Competitivist theories posit scenarios in which artistic behavior might form the basis for interindividual competition. The most commonly explored instance of this is in sexual selection, typically with the male members of any species (who tend to invest less in their offspring due to the uncertainty and reduced physical cost of fatherhood) competing to attract females to mate with. Sexual selection may take the form of an unconstrained runaway train of coevolution toward bizarre and arbitrary aesthetic features, but many theorists believe that it will always be bound by the logic of *honest signaling* or the *handicap principle*,[21] according to which displays have evolved to be indicators of "good genes." Various evolutionary psychologists, most outspoken among them Geoffrey Miller,[22] have argued that baroque and apparently functionless social behavior in humans—music, art, storytelling, anything with the potential to show off one's skill in the construction of complex and elegant forms—is likely to be sexually selected behavior. Whereas for Pinker the apparent uselessness of art and music is because it actually serves no function, for Miller this apparent uselessness, coupled with the great time invested in it, is the signature of sexual selection and honest signaling theory: showing off through exuberance.

However, in humans there is good reason to believe that competition in creative (and other) domains is not only manifest in the attraction of mates. Late night dance floor exertions might have a more blatant connection to sexual display, but some of Miller's anecdotal themes (serenading at balconies, the promiscuity of male stars like Jimi Hendrix, and so on) are more tenuous. Looking at rich and famous musicians is confounding exactly because they are rich and famous. As others such as Paul Bloom[23] have noted, in the rich cultural context of humans a more general *social selection theory* is just as powerful at explaining the emergence of human artistic behavior. It is just as effective to attract a business partner with a display of creativity or aesthetic sophistication (and hence gain financial success with which to attract a mate) than it is to directly attract a mate.

Another body of competitivist theory includes social brain and Machiavellian intelligence hypotheses,[24] which posit that the evolution of human intelligence has largely been driven by selection pressures for social intelligence such as the ability to deceive, manipulate, and form stable alliances with others. This can invoke a runaway evolutionary process, with humans living in larger groups and consequently having greater incentives, and needing more sophisticated methods, for social intelligence.

Emergentist theories take a different tack from the other four. Rather than focus on how the human cognitive machinery underlying art has come about, they look at domains of art practice as complex systems that may be self-generating. Thus, rather than there being an identifiable external cause underlying these domains (musical skill indicates good genes, aesthetic pleasure arises from solving perception problems, and so on), the system as a whole is emergent. Luhmann,[25] for example, looked at cultural systems of art production and consumption as *autopoietic* systems, sustaining themselves through a metabolic process. A human being might be enculturated into an aesthetic cultural system, compete for success in that system, and then act to reinforce that system, much as in the social dynamics of a cult.

It can also be seen how learned or culturally emergent behaviors can drive further biological evolution. This effect, known as the Baldwin effect after its initial identification by James Baldwin, has been demonstrated in various species, most famously in humans in the case of the evolution of lactose tolerance in subpopulations of humans. This is closely related to the theory of niche construction discussed in chapter 3.

These five bodies of theory are diverse and piecemeal. Anyone looking at the biological foundations of human artistic behavior should reasonably expect that it is not a simple whole with a simple explanation, but a complex assemblage constructed from multiple evolutionary pathways. Claims to identify a simple origin story for art are likely to be suspect.

The Innate and the Universal

No matter how seductive the approach has been to computer scientists, it has long been untenable to uphold a strict theory of universal beauty, in which some set of measurable properties of an aesthetic artifact tells us how any human observer might form an aesthetic response to it. A growing body of work in psychology points to the extreme plasticity of the human brain, dismissing the wishful thinking that aesthetic objects can be understood simply in terms of universal features such as symmetry, complexity, and harmonic ratios. At the same time, it is equally problematic to think of brains as blank slates shaped only by lived experience. The plasticity of brains comes from powerful, genetically evolved learning capacities which have specific properties. Even if our brains were perfect blank slates (whatever that could possibly mean), the lived experiences of humans have many universal features: horizons, sun and stars, gravity, visual depth, the harmonics of resonant bodies, the blues and greens of nature, the feeling of water, animal behaviors, faces and bodies, sex and sexes, laughter and tears. Whatever the extent to which we are shaped by our genes or our environments, humans across the world and across millennia have much that is common in their behavior, and nontrivial perceptual universals do abound in human behavior: our recognition of facial expressions, the prosody of speech and the sounds we make to babies, the low-level mechanics of visual and sonic object perception, the tendency to perceive metrical structure in rhythmic patterns, and so on.

There are also various widely agreed upon aspects of the brain's overall structure. One is that the brain can be divided into two distinct thinking systems.[26] The first system is instinctive, subconscious, and designed for rapid response in critical situations. This system is known as the fast system or *System 1*. The second system is conscious, more general purpose, and analytical, dealing with problems that have not been encountered before and need to be thought through. This is known as the slow system or *System 2*. Several theories of aesthetic response, as discussed below, depend on this architecture, often explaining aesthetic phenomena in terms of interactions between Systems 1 and 2.[27] Another widely agreed upon architectural aspect is that myriad low-level neural processing components, such as for edge detection in visual processing, coexist and interact. Each of these individual elements and the overall architecture of such elements may be more or less fixed across cultures and individuals. In visual information processing, this model, sometimes known as the pandemonium model, has been used to explain how we manage to perceive objects regardless of their orientation, by abstracting the component elements of objects from the visual field and reconstituting them as higher-level concepts.

But what can we say about universal aspects of aesthetic perception? Are there things that all humans find beautiful, regardless of their lived experience? In classical theories of universal beauty, beauty is understood via the mathematical properties of an aesthetic object. Candidate properties include symmetry, various measures relating to complexity including fractal dimension, frequency distributions, and information content, and the existence of various significant ratios such as the golden ratio and the square root of five. Historically, researchers have come at these principles less from a grounding in psychology than from a preexisting belief in a mathematical basis for universal beauty. This is confounded by a potential cultural circularity: the fact that classical examples that are revered as great works have to greater or lesser extents been consciously created according to these mathematical principles.

George Birkhoff's influential 1933 work presented an early effort to develop an empirical study of aesthetics. Birkhoff explains:

> The typical aesthetic experience may be regarded as compounded of three successive phases: (1) a preliminary effort of attention, which is necessary for the act of perception, and which increases in proportion to what we shall call the complexity (C) of the object; (2) the feeling of value or aesthetic measure (M) which rewards this effort; and finally (3) a realization that the object is characterized by a certain harmony, a symmetry, or order (O), more or less concealed, which seems necessary to the aesthetic effect.[28]

For Birkhoff, the relation between M, C, and O is the surprisingly simple equation $M=O/C$. He explains this by analogy to a return on investment in business. "In each business there is involved a certain investment i and a certain annual profit p. The ratio p/i ... is regarded as the economic measure of success." For Birkhoff, the challenge for an artist is to make order out of complexity, as the businessman strives to make profits out of investment.

More recently, studies of complexity have been the focus of psychological research. Alex Forsythe and colleagues demonstrate a relationship between measures of human judgments of beauty and the visual complexity of images. The latter is measured by how compressible the images are, with GIF compression providing the most effective correlation with human judgments.[29] Their results support the theory of psychologist Daniel Berlyne[30] that there is an aesthetic preference for a sweet spot of complexity; we like things that are not too simple, not too complex.

Similar results have been obtained in music. Richard Voss and John Clarke[31] examined the structure of audio signals in music as well as language. They found that these signals exhibited a consistent pattern of complexity, described by the distribution of frequencies within the signal, which exhibit a 1/f law, which states that the presence of any frequency is inversely proportional to the frequency itself. This distribution is also known as pink noise, as compared to a flat distribution, where all frequencies are equally present (white noise), and a $1/f^2$ distribution (brown noise). Intuitively, a sequence exhibiting white noise will be too unpredictable to be enjoyable, whereas a brown noise sequence will be too predictable to be enjoyable. Voss and Clarke's results do not apply directly to the sound spectra themselves but to derived aspects of the signal: the power and the approximated overall frequency. It is the variation in these signals that exhibits the $1/f$ property. Voss and Clarke then generated musical sequences with these various distributions and showed that the $1/f$ sequences were considered the most pleasing. Bill Manaris and colleagues have similarly examined this law applied to note sequences in symbolic representations of music.[32]

Studies of complexity appeal to our perceptual ability to make sense of the world. I will continue this discussion below in the context of a more adaptive variant of the types of aesthetic theory just outlined. Meanwhile, other candidate fundamentals of beauty have been looked at in terms of more specific potential evolutionary origins. One example is the importance of facial and bodily symmetry in indicating fitness. Symmetry in body and face morphology can be an indicator of health or good genes and is believed to be a good predictor of perceived attractiveness for this reason.[33]

Reflectional symmetry of static images is only one form of symmetry. Other researchers have shown symmetry of dance moves to be attractive cross-culturally.[34] In both cases, it should be added that human faces and human bodies likely form a specific, cognitively, innately encoded category. We are far more sensitive to human bodies and faces than to other objects, with dedicated capacities for recognizing facial expressions, remembering hundreds or thousands of distinct individuals, and modeling and empathizing with bodily actions. So we might expect that a preference for symmetry falls into a class of specific body-related cognitive functions, rather than generalizing to other object forms.[35]

Others have attempted to identify biologically evolved universals at higher composite levels. The landscape preference hypothesis posits that we find certain kinds of landscape scenes aesthetically appealing because they represent suitable landscapes for habitation.[36] Preferable features, it posits, include open spaces with clustered trees, the presence of water, a vantage on the horizon, animals, and some degree of diversity or moderate complexity.[37] The supporting evidence suggests that the landscape preference is more strongly felt in children but is slowly overridden by learned preferences.[38] Such thinking stems from the late twentieth century turn in evolutionary psychology, pushing back against a view of the mind as a blank slate that gains its structure and knowledge through learning, to one in which the mind has multiple dedicated evolved subunits, sometimes described as analogous to a penknife. According to such a view, something as specific as a landscape preference might plausibly have evolved in some corner of the brain. Appeal to other examples of innate responses to visually encoded forms support the basic premise: "The system that identifies snake-ness in the visual array, coupled to fear-releasing circuits, is an adaptation that lowered deaths due to venomous snake bites among our ancestors."[39]

John Tooby and Leda Cosmides, chief proponents of this penknife view of the evolved brain, in which many such specific adaptive behaviors can be identified, have other such adaptive examples that apply to high-level phenomena. They offer our pleasure response to fiction as another candidate.[40] Stories provide a platform for exploring imaginary social scenarios, they argue, and so we have evolved a pleasure for hearing and telling stories. Essentially, narrative engagement helps us experiment with potentially real future scenarios just as the pretend play of the young of many species helps prepare them for fight and flight tactics. It is a form of social practice. As with the landscape theory, some compelling evidence is provided, but so far we have little idea how such preferences might be encoded cognitively.

More generally, Tooby and Cosmides appeal to nonconsequentalist approaches to explaining artistic behavior: "Almost all of the phenomena that are central to the humanities are puzzling anomalies from an evolutionary perspective. Chief among these are the human attraction to fictional experience (in all media and genres) and other products of the imagination ... involvement in the imaginative arts appears to be an intrinsically rewarding activity, without apparent utilitarian payoff."[41]

The strong adaptationism of evolutionary psychologists like Tooby and Codmides is commonly criticized as being *overly* adaptationist. Anti-adaptationist arguments, most notably those of Stephen Gould and Richard Lewontin, point out that many behaviors are unlikely to have direct biologically adapted origins and really do not warrant them.[42] They may instead be what Gould and Lewontin call *spandrels*,[43] stemming from an adaptive origin that does not directly relate to the behavior in question. Partly, this is an appeal to Occam's razor, but it is also simply a critique on the plausibility of certain attempts at evolutionary origin seeking. The phrase "just-so stories," named after Rudyard Kipling's famous short stories, is the pejorative term used to describe such speculative evolutionary storytelling. For reasons of programmatic simplicity, the lower-level the adaptive trait, the more plausible it is in evolutionary terms. An innate preference for simple harmonic ratios is more plausible than an explicitly encoded preference for complex symphonies or composite landscape scenes.

Consider, in the case of a landscape preference, what a good job conscious thought does of habitat selection, at least in modern humans.[44] "There's water, that's good! And there are trees, also good! But I'm not sure about that bear." Could such thought be subjugated to some subconscious urge that drives you blindly toward a preferred landscape? From an informational point of view it is hard to grasp the task of encoding such preference in a way that bypasses conscious categorical thought and goes straight into a pleasure response. Nevertheless, we do find ourselves rapt by certain landscapes and natural scenes in a way that does indeed appear to bypass conceptual or conscious thought, a phenomenon that warrants some explanation.

This brings us back to the Pinkerian perspective, where we identify low-level components contributing to aesthetic responses, whatever their evolutionary origins, but don't expect to find coherent evolutionary adaptations at higher levels. For example, we might like horizons to be horizontal because we like to be upright but not because they form part of a safe environment.

The Pinkerian view of music as a set of cultural technologies built to exploit existing pleasure responses leads us to look at how the basic work of making sense of our world provokes these pleasure responses. In auditory perception, it is widely recognized that we have a series of innate perceptual capacities, such as for clustering sounds according to common origins (streaming and source separation), tracking beats, and recognizing pitch intervals. Some of these capacities have fairly uncontroversial evolutionary adaptive origins based in making sense of the world. Source separation for example, is essential to our ability to analyze auditory scenes. We see this most clearly in the "cocktail party effect," the ability to train our attention on one voice in a room, amid a babble of people talking. Music often plays with such effects, mixing timbres and their movement through time in such a way as to construct complex auditory scenes where sonic objects merge and separate. Here Pinker's analogy is at its strongest: chefs and composers alike weave together known responses in original ways.

We also know that naturally occurring sounds have common structural properties.[45] When you hit a hollow tree or pluck a guitar string, the sound has a percussive initial phase, also known as the transient phase, which is characterized by a high noise content for a short duration—you've just excited a physical system and thrown it into a chaotic frenzy. After this transient phase the remainder of the sound is defined by resonance: a regular oscillation (hence non-noisy, with a clear tone) that emerges out of the energetic movement of the initial impact, which gradually loses energy and dissipates.

Another way to make sound is to scrape something or blow air across it. In both cases you get a noisy, grainy sound caused by myriad tiny interactions (imagine dragging something through gravel or wind blowing through trees causing leaves to move). In some cases (blowing across a bottle or scraping a string with a bow) the system also feeds back on itself so that those myriad tiny interactions coordinate to stimulate the natural resonances within the system they inhabit, and hence, again, create more regular, less noisy, sounds—tones such as those of a flute.

Furthermore, when sound-making objects do resonate they tend to do so with signature spectral properties. Stably oscillating objects produce sets of harmonically related frequencies. A harmonic frequency relation is simply one where the ratio between frequencies is simple, such as 1:2 (octave) or 2:3 (perfect fifth). Harmonically related frequencies reinforce each other, so it is natural that this should be the product of a resonating process. Some metal objects like bells, gamelans, and steel drums have more complex spectral signatures, as the material allows multiple resonances to co-occur, but strings, tubes, and vocal cords generally resonate with clear harmonic structures that define the *timbre* of the sound.

It is therefore a fairly uncontroversial suggestion that our auditory system may be specifically adapted to decoding these properties of naturally occurring sound, recognizing individual auditory events as percussive-resonant sequences, and grouping frequencies based on their harmonic relatedness. Note that *because* these types of sound reliably occur in nature, it is equally plausible that we exploit the environment to learn them, as that we are born with readymade perceptual systems that are already prepared for such an environment. A clear distinction between what *exactly* is encoded in genes and what is learned from the environment is not necessarily obvious. It has also been suggested that language and music mimic these properties because they are so well established in our perceptual system. Indeed, in speech we identify fricative (scraping), plosive (percussive), and sonorant (resonant) elements, but given that language and song also use natural physical actions to make sound, it is somewhat unremarkable that our vocal systems also display such characteristics.

A slightly more mysterious aspect of our auditory perception is the ability to track beats, known sometimes as entrainment. Specifically, if I start clapping at regular intervals, you will be able to clap along, even if I gently speed up or slow down. If I stop, you will be able to continue at the tempo I have established. I can join back in, you can lead the tempo changes, and so on.[46] Other animals cannot do this, at least nowhere near as well as we can. Many can synchronize cyclical behaviors but not in the adaptive, tempo-invariant, predictive way that we do. This ability is constrained to a specific speed range; try to follow a beat at intervals smaller than 100ms or larger than 2s and you will not manage to successfully predict the time of the next beat, but keeping within this range you have an innate capacity to keep time.[47]

Compared to our auditory event detection, the environment doesn't offer such obvious reasons why we might have developed this entrainment ability. Many ideas have been suggested, drawing on pretty much anything that creates a regular beat: heartbeats and walking are example candidates that have been appealed to in evolutionary theories. One theory has it that we needed to time our vocal communication with our cadence, for better audibility. Social factors are also compelling sources of explanation. Even if it has hitchhiked on the perception of natural sounds, vocal communication in various species seems to have occupied, or it is perhaps better to say forged, a novel acoustic niche in which to operate. A body of theory revolves around the basic mechanisms of developing the type of intersubjective engagement that is the foundation for language learning.[48] Studies of mother-infant interaction have claimed to identify rhythmic engagement between the participants.[49] Another idea is that rhythmic entrainment establishes a sense of boundary loss among individuals in a group, enforcing group cohesion: we unite by sounding and moving in time.[50] However, a Pinkerian explanation is equally possible here: perhaps we simply evolved the ability to manage timed sequences very well, for example in learning to make tools, or perhaps we simply have the general intelligence necessary to learn this skill and find it compelling.

As we move to higher levels of structure, appeal to environmental factors becomes harder. Theories such as the group theoretic work of Gerald Balzano in music propose an aesthetic preference for kinds of minimally complex structures.[51] Balzano's particular focus was on the structure of diatonic scales in Western music, noting the way in which these scales form near-symmetric subsets of a larger set (the major scale is a subset of the chromatic scale and is asymmetrically distributed—think of the arrangement of black and white keys on a piano keyboard). Balzano argues for a general principle of form that can be manifest in different ways in different cultures. For example, while diatonic groups are prevalent in Western music, similar patterns exist in rhythmic manifestations in certain non-Western cultures.

Balzano's work resembles a form of structuralism, the late twentieth-century movement that viewed our brains as inclined toward certain structuring relations, which might be manifest in different ways in different cultural contexts. The leading structuralist anthropologist Claude Lévi-Strauss mapped the categorical relations expressed in South American myths as they varied from place to place, identifying a common structure around which a series of well-formed variations exists.[52] According to this view, we have preexisting mental structures that are filled by some culturally or environmentally specific content. This is just one way of combining notions of fixed universal and fluid learned aspects of perception.

Increasingly, however, a *Hebbian* paradigm of neural learning is proving dominant, in which we view the interaction between evolutionary and developmental components of neural circuitry as one in which the process of learning shapes the neural structure.[53] The theories described in the following sections continue this theme, supporting a richer sense of cultural and environmental adaptivity.

Adaptive Perspectives and Behaviors

A more complex and more plausible view of aesthetics focuses less on universals and more on the adaptive capacity of the mind. Accordingly, the universal aspects of our cognition are the learning mechanisms sitting under the surface rather than the specific perceptual and evaluative systems. Human cultures are, after all, highly adaptive to their environmental or historically contingent circumstances, and yet cultural and individual variations are constrained in some way by these fixed structures of the mind. This is a theme continued in modern psychology. With respect to the aesthetic foundations of visual art, Vilayanur Ramachandran and William Hirstein propose ten psychological principles.[54] Each relates to evolutionarily and psychologically plausible properties of our visual system and appeals to the pleasure we obtain in the process of learning about and making sense of the world, much in the way that Pinker describes music as auditory cheesecake. The principles are: peak shift, perceptual grouping and binding, contrast, isolation, perceptual problem solving, symmetry, abhorrence of coincidence/generic viewpoint, repetition, rhythm and orderliness, balance, and metaphor.

I will not discuss each in detail, but consider some general properties. The elements in this list are more or less context dependent, combining a universal psychological principle with a cultural environmental context which dictates the specifics of the aesthetic response. For example, they explain the peak shift principle as follows:

> If a rat is taught to discriminate a square from a rectangle (of say, 3:2 aspect ratio) and rewarded for the rectangle, it will soon learn to respond more frequently to the rectangle. Paradoxically, however, the rat's response to a rectangle that is even longer and skinnier (say, of aspect ratio 4:1) is even greater than it was to the original prototype on which it was trained.[55]

This is how they apply the concept to art:

> Consider the way in which a skilled cartoonist produces a caricature of a famous face, say Nixon's. What he does (unconsciously) is to take the average of all faces, subtract the average from Nixon's face (to get the difference between Nixon's face and all others) and then amplify the differences to produce a caricature.[56]

The peak shift principle offers an explanation for why we don't just learn to like what we know, but are driven toward certain types of new and surprising forms. It makes for a good explanation for the extremes that emerging genres strive to achieve. Apply the same process as the caricaturist to a subgenre of, say, heavy metal, and you have a candidate explanation for why that subgenre pushes out at the extremes so readily, as in thrash or doom metal. It suggests a form of categorical learning: the rat hasn't just learned a shape but a concept, which itself defines a space of unexplored possibilities. The peak shift principle could be thought of as an example of where our ability to learn patterns is imperfect (the rat is not trained to generalize), but nevertheless drives aesthetic choice and a desire for certain forms of novelty.

Theories such as Balzano's and Ramachandran and Hirstein's form a bridge between preferences for simple mathematical qualities such as symmetry or fractal dimension, and a more adaptive concept of aesthetic preference based on the ability to model one's environment adaptively. The latter types of theory are often constructed in the language of information and complexity, although we find parallels in the work of Csikszentmihalyi and specifically his theory of *flow*.[57] Csikszentmihalyi's starting point for the concept of flow is that we find pleasure in things that support our learning about the world, and those things that best support our learning strike a balance between two extremes: they are neither too easy or common, nor too hard or unrecognizable. Pleasure in performing tasks comes when the tasks are neither boring nor overly challenging. Boredom is the expression of the desire to experience new things and thus learn. When we achieve what he calls a flow state, caused by an optimum balance of task difficulty, we become intensely immersed in what we are doing to the point of being lost in the task and losing sense of time. We can see how complexity-based theories of aesthetics such as Balzano's model of tonal structure, serving to provide a platform for engaging tonal puzzles, might satisfy Csikszentmihalyi's principle: aesthetic structures that are not too radically complex but not tediously simple either.

Peak shift and flow relate to a more general response profile that is familiar in psychology and relevant to creativity, where novelty and pleasure are related by an inverted-U curve, named after Wilhelm Wundt: the Wundt curve.[58] The Wundt curve underlies a model of curiosity and scaffolded learning about the world. The basic idea is that we are stimulated by new things (perceptual experiences), as part of an adaptive tendency for curiosity; it is good to learn new things about the world. Specifically, we are interested by things that are neither too familiar nor too unusual.

It is clear why familiar things don't tell us anything new about the world, but less clear what the problem is with things that are too unfamiliar. The proposed answer is that they are too hard for us to deal with. Learning about the world has to be done in small steps: some things just don't make sense until we have the framework to make sense of them.

Such phenomena illustrate ways in which cognitive strategies for learning about the world and sense-making might lead to culturally or individually determined aesthetic preferences. I discussed in the previous chapter how copying behaviors enable cultural transmission and hence cultural evolution. These learning phenomena show how cultural artifacts might be driven to change in a runaway evolutionary process. Given a motivation to learn about the world, then, we set the scene for cultural artifacts to undergo constant modification in response to a need for novel stimuli.

Daniel Berlyne was one of the first to formalize notions of boredom and curiosity. He defines human "epistemic curiosity" as "a drive reducible by knowledge-rehearsal."[59] In Berlyne's experimental research, he shows that absolute complexity of images combine with the degree of novelty to determine the "hedonic" response of individuals. More complex images become *more* pleasurable with greater exposure to them, due to familiarization, while less complex images become *less* pleasurable, due to boredom.[60] In more recent work the information theoretic dimension of such a line of research has come to the fore. For machine learning scientist Jürgen Schmidhuber,[61] the same idea of finding beauty in optimally complex learning material is presented as the need to get a good rate of *information compression*. To understand this we first note that learning about the environment necessarily involves data compression. Learning the underlying principles of form, rather than, say, keeping a complete log of every scene ever to pass in front of us, is essential if we are to efficiently remember things, let alone form a generalized understanding of the world. For example, when a child begins to learn language they first learn the set of phonemes of their native language (which differ between languages, dialects, and accents and hence must be learned), and this forms a discrete symbol set upon which the language is built. This is a form of data compression that mediates between the sound spectra we hear and the words and sentences we understand. If you later learn a distant language, like an English person learning Chinese, you need to add new phonemes to your palette, thus rearranging this compressed mental representation, and this may be a taxing process. Until you do so, you cannot correctly distinguish certain sounds in that language; they are inaudible to you. It is important to note that such learning can be done to some extent in an unsupervised manner, meaning that you just need to experience the world in order to learn this structure; you don't need to be told what the right classification is. Through repeated exposure we begin to notice more detail.

Thus according to this view we are constantly attempting to compress the data arriving via our perception of the world. A new musical melody would be understood in terms of the abstract representations derived from previous experience of melodies, and everything is jiggled around to fit this new melody into the model. For both Berlyne and Schmidhuber, then, in different ways, the idea is that our success at information compression is a source of pleasure; we seek experiences that help us make better sense of the world. Just as with flow, something too familiar or simple is boring and unstimulating, but so is something too unusual or complex. More generally, these theories offer some form of explanation of curiosity.[62]

Relatedly, in David Huron's research into the evolutionary psychology of music, he takes a "neural Darwinism" approach, according to which the mind is constantly trying out candidate perceptual strategies to see which ones perform best, thus cultural factors can strongly influence the way we learn to perceive the world. According to a neural Darwinist view of music perception:

1. There are competing mental representations of sound.
2. Representations are shaped by exposure to the environment.
3. Representations are differentially favored depending on their predictive success.[63]

As an example, Huron considers the development of absolute pitch versus relative pitch in individuals. Absolute pitch perception is a skill that enables someone to recognize a musical pitch without previously being primed with a reference pitch. Most people perceive pitch relatively (also known as intervallic perception); we are able to perceive intervals between pitches, even if we don't know what those pitches are. A trained musician who does not possess absolute pitch will typically prime themselves with a reference pitch, after which they can deduce further pitches based on their relative distance to the reference pitch, for a short period of time. According to a neural Darwinist view, our brains are equipped to adopt either of these ways of perceiving pitch, based on which works out best in our own lived experience of the world, but at some point we adapt to using one or the other and this aspect of our perception becomes more or less locked in.

Huron argues that this selection is made based on what works best in our given environment. Absolute pitch can be a useful skill for professional musicians, whereas it can also be a burden and is largely unnecessary. When singing happy birthday at a party, it is fine just to lock in on whatever key emerges among the singers and to use intervals from there on. Huron's evidence is that absolute pitch emerges under specific social circumstances, in particular in societies where there is an established standard tuning. It is learned very early on, at a time when the brain might be wiring in these kinds of perceptual strategies. Supporting this, tests show that absolute pitch performance is correlated to the exposure to specific pitches; someone with absolute pitch will identify more common pitches more quickly than less common pitches.

In these models, a set of cultural conditions might shape how our perception of the world forms. This is broadly consistent with the idea of forming successful "compressed" models of the world. Huron's central thesis is that these cognitive functions are there because we are forever trying to limit the unexpected, to model the world in such a way as never to be surprised. However, he argues, surprises themselves can be pleasurable exactly because they feed this learning function, through the interplay between our fast (System 1) and slow (System 2) cognition systems. System 2 appraises and feeds back into the System 1 response, and where contradictions occur, we are stimulated via a mechanism dubbed *contrastive valence*.

Putting all of this together, Huron proposes the imagination-tension-prediction-reaction-appraisal (ITPRA) model, designed to explain how aspects of musical experience are stimulating. The ITPRA theory takes into account five stages in the response to temporal sequences of auditory stimuli:

- I—*imagining* different outcomes, forming anticipation
- T—as anticipated event approaches, *tension* builds
- P—*prediction* response—feeling evoked in response to success of prediction
- R—At the same time as P, a fast *reaction* response (System 1)
- A—a slower *appraisal* response (System 2)

Such a model of perception again offers a framework in which new culturally determined experiences might dictate new neural perceptual frameworks, completely novel conceptual spaces, constructed on top of a fixed, high-level architecture, accounted for by sound evolutionary theory. The basic mechanism for musical pleasure is hardwired, but the ways in which different learned aspects of music are used to stimulate this system may vary considerably.

Geraint Wiggins and Jamie Forth[64] offer a computational model broadly related to Huron's ideas and drawing on a model of central cognitive information processing called the global workspace theory. The global workspace theory defines a top-level cognitive architecture in which a central cognitive system associated with conscious awareness interacts with a large number of simple, domain-specific subconscious systems, competing for attention. Specifically, in their Information Dynamics of Thinking (IDyOT) model, the focus is again on temporal sequences relevant to music and also language, and the submodules considered are Markovian processes that attempt to predict what will happen next in a given situation. When certain conditions are met, any one of these submodules might trigger the attention of the global workspace.

Such multiple hypothesis models are appealing for a number of reasons, not least that they offer a neural correlate to the incubation-illumination model of creative cognition. More generally, they offer a plausible neural model of the relation between conscious and subconscious cognitive processes (whether or not this strictly corresponds to fast System 1 and slow System 2 thinking). They can also plausibly support a neural Darwinism approach, helping explain *how* the brain manages to adapt to cultural specifics. Lastly, they correspond well with studies of music perception. For example, it is understood that our ability to track beats is associated with the way that we perceive metrical structure in music: not as a single temporal representation but as an array of harmonically related sensitivities to different tempi. One theory of metrical perception is that an array of coupled resonant oscillators interact to form a structured temporal representation.[65]

Wiggins and Forth's model is also generative as well as perceptual. In the absence of stimuli, the submodules "freewheel." This is a natural thing for a sequential model to do if it is allowed to feed back on itself, making predictions based on its own previous sequence of predictions. So the same system that is used to anticipate events in the world can also operate as a natural generator of imagined events. Just as these models present themselves to the global workspace in the course of perceiving the world, they can also do so in the course of idle thought, leading to what Wiggins and Forth describe as "spontaneous creativity."

In the IDyOT model, the condition for submodules to attract attention from the global workspace is that of high information content. When a submodule produces high information content, this alerts the central system. Such high information content shares the same properties of things we find as aesthetically pleasing according to models such as the Wundt curve: not already known, but not so unusual as to be treated as noise.

In summary, an important set of theories explaining aesthetic perception focus on the sophisticated mechanisms we employ for modeling and making predictions about the world, that variously hypothesize:

- Mechanisms for compressing and organizing information into efficient representations that help us make predictions;
- Mechanisms that *stimulate* us to seek experiences that drive efficient representations;
- A number of low-level, domain-specific neural processing structures ranging from more hardwired systems to more data-driven neurally plastic systems, possibly competing to be adopted based on performance;
- A central system associated with conscious awareness, that interacts with myriad subsystems, for which the high-level architecture is fixed;
- Certain subsystems that as well as being involved in perception can also be set to freewheel, causing imagination.

This model is not mutually exclusive to the idea of additional dedicated modules evolved to perform specific functions. Thus a very broad view of how genes dictate the shape of the brain is that certain global architectural features are hardwired—the very lowest-level features (how neurons grow, fire, and adapt) at least are definitely hardwired—and in addition certain domain-specific submodules may be hardwired, or at least set up so as to be very likely to form in certain ways given normal stimuli.

Acting in Webs of Significance

We now have a psychological sketch, albeit painted in a broad brush, that complements the themes developed in chapter 3 to fill out an image of humans acting as art-making or art-experiencing agents. Such models of perception provide a solid grounding for understanding how it can be possible for different individuals to develop different views of the world, to be motivated to explore new experiences, and also to spontaneously imagine and generate new things. Accordingly, individuals learn by building models of their world, and are intrinsically motivated to do so, through a distributed process that is compatible with the essential properties of individual creative thought. Given that much of what stimulates us, that is, much of what we spend our time trying to model, is cultural—produced by other humans—rather than from the biological world, then the possibility of runaway cumulative culture developed in chapter 3 follows relatively easily. Inhabiting a world of tonal music, for example, means developing perceptual models of tonal music to which we are attuned.

Even if the underlying psychological mechanisms are grounded in the simplest evolutionary context—that of learning about one's physical environment—this is sufficient for explaining open-ended cultural evolution. New concepts or patterns that arise in the realm of culture, absent in our physical environments, have the potential to form and evolve through cultural processes. This fits into consequentialist and cognitivist evolutionary frameworks. We have seen some cohesionist and competitivist evolutionary explanations, involving more complex selective pressures grounded in social behavior, that provide even richer models of runaway cultural or biocultural evolution. Although considering the impact of such theories on how we perceive human culture is tantalizing, they remain relatively speculative.

Either way, the anthropologist Clifford Geertz's celebrated maxim holds true that "man is an animal suspended in webs of significance he himself has spun."[66] Cultural systems can be autopoietic: generating themselves and maintaining their structure through the feedback of individual human action. Peter Berger and Thomas Luckmann's *The Social Construction of Reality*,[67] first published in 1966, successfully characterized this capacity for social systems to create their own contexts for future interactions. We might update this to a more snappy computational analogy proffered by some theorists, that the conceptual materials that occupy our cultural lives define a sort of *virtual reality*—much more immersive than the contemporary technology of the same name—that runs on the hardware of highly plastic human brains. This virtual world is the most spectacular of constructed niches, in fact a tapestry of interlocking niches. Because individual success is predominantly determined by social interactions, we accept these niches as the contexts in which we must act. The strategies of modern humans getting by are sociocultural strategies: do well at school, make desirable goods, bet on the right horse, learn a language, dress smart, get noticed.

Art may be far from an innocent bystander in this tapestry of social concerns, playing many different roles in culturally constructed niches and their social dynamics. That our taste in art, music, and jokes is sculpted by a process of learning about the world establishes the foundations for the diversity or artistic groups and domains but is only part of the story.

Individual and group identity is central to the development of this theme. More than simply being something that we learn to like, forms of art are things that we use to define ourselves, whether actively or subconsciously. The sociologist Pierre Bourdieu played an important role in introducing several useful terms and ideas to this area. He refers to *cultural goods* as these objects of exchange and identity formation, which as with my use of "art" can refer to practices and artifacts ranging from high art and music to tattoos and hairstyles. Bourdieu's empirical focus in his study of taste was on class identity, and one of his most important contributions is the idea that taste and its associated expertise in cultural fields become indicators of our class membership. We may not be expert composers, artists, or poets, but we become expert consumers, connoisseurs, of these fields, knowing and appreciating the finer detail:

> Taste classifies, and it classifies the classifier. Social subjects, classified by their classifications, distinguish themselves by the distinctions they make, between the beautiful and the ugly, the distinguished and the vulgar, in which their position in the objective classifications is expressed or betrayed.[68]

Two related cultural phenomena form the basis for Bourdieu's analysis: cultural competencies and cultural capital. *Cultural competencies* are those fine-tuned abilities that display depth of immersion in a field of practice. Competencies, Bourdieu argues, are not simply consciously and explicitly established through education but are established in "total, early, imperceptible learning, performed within the family from the earliest days of life." This acquisition must occur early on, and over a long duration, adding a cost that cannot be faked. This imperceptibly acquired cultural identity that is not easily faked or shaken off, Bourdieu terms *habitus*: "What are grasped through indicators such as educational level or social origin or, more precisely, in the structure of the relationship between them, are also different modes of production of the cultivated habitus, which engender differences not only in the competences acquired but also in the manner of applying them."[69]

For Bourdieu, *cultural capital* is that which is possessed by virtue of a lifelong enculturation giving access to this immersive learned experience (capital is "accumulated labor"). Bourdieu's analysis goes further, distinguishing between the types of cultural capital that can be acquired through education (educational capital), showing that education can provide *some* access to the more mainstream domains such as fine art or classical music by individuals who do not have access to such domains though family background. "Nothing more clearly affirms one's 'class,' nothing more infallibly classifies, than tastes in music."[70]

For Bourdieu, taste as a set of deeply felt preferences and interests is intimately tied up with competence in a field. Simply liking something is both an aspect of the underlying mechanism and a surface quality of the more functionally pivotal phenomenon of indicating competence in that area. Being able to reel off names of relevant artists and their various interconnections and histories, being able to recognize works of a given artist despite only subtle differences between them and others in their field, using the correct descriptive language and so on, these can be seen both a consequence of and a driver for love of a certain domain. Bourdieu elaborates on how such learned qualities can perform a critical function in a system of cultural economics (Bourdieu believed in a "general science of the economy of practices"—that is, economics applying elsewhere besides where money is found).

> The initial accumulation of cultural capital, the precondition for the fast, easy accumulation of every kind of useful cultural capital, starts at the outset, without delay, without wasted time, only for the offspring of families endowed with strong cultural capital; in this case, the accumulation period covers the whole period of socialization. It follows that the transmission of cultural capital is no doubt the best hidden form of hereditary transmission of capital, and it therefore receives proportionately greater weight in the system of reproduction strategies, as the direct, visible forms of transmission tend to be more strongly censored and controlled.[71]

As is evidenced from these quotes, Bourdieu's view of the cultural world, as Georgina Born outlines in a detailed analysis, centers around "competitive position-taking [by] … actors engaged in cultural production."[72] Born emphasizes Bourdieu's key contribution is this notion of the "field of cultural production" as a spatial domain in which human competition is played out: "The field … is a structured space of possible positions and trajectories, a social topology constituted through the competitive yet complementary position-taking of rival actors."[73] Born also notes the potential issues with cultural production being understood only as a struggle between classes. Bourdieu was perhaps too caught up with specific issues of French class dominance and maintenance, that drove and was in turn maintained by the "unequal distribution of cultural capital." A more generalized interpretation of Bourdieu's theory based on diverse forms of dynamic and competition may be more palatable.[74]

In a more recent critique of Bourdieu, Antoine Hennion questions the idea that "taste is conceived only as a passive social game, largely ignorant about itself." He instead elevates taste to "a form of presence in the world." Hennion examines the activities of amateurs who, with limited resources of cultural capital, still exhibit the capability to construct themselves through various relations with cultural material. Consider how this amateur record collector behaves toward his records:

> Before putting them away he used to leave many new records in the bottom right-hand corner of his bookcase—until the day he had the idea of transforming this disorder into the basis of a system for arranging his records. From then on he let them move upwards to the left, depending on the last time he had listened to them. This is a typical invention of an amateur: his record library gradually changed into a reflection of his tastes. The amateur triumphed over the musicologist: his taste, not the history of music, governs his system of classification.[75]

Hennion also emphasizes how interaction between individuals around taste exhibit aspects of cohesion and competition. Taste influences social relations and vice versa:

> The amateur's constitution of his taste and the practical methods used to develop it are based upon the recurrent presence of a mediator, an initiator. The example set by a recognized amateur is crucial here, like when an older opera fan corrects the prejudices of a younger one who still despises Bellini or Auber: "Wait a little; you'll see what you'll think of them later"; or when a techno amateur shrugs at seeing his young mate's records and lets him hear "the right thing," far from all this "commercial" stuff. There is no taste as long as one is alone, facing objects; no amateur knows from the outset how to appreciate good things, or simply what he likes. Taste starts with the comparison with others' tastes.[76]

Cultural competency also has a more overt manifestation, obviously, in the skills of those actively involved in, or seeking to be involved in, creative production. There is no doubt that skill, whether by nature or nurture, is critical to artistic success, above and beyond *mere* taste. But again, there may be more non-obvious connections between skill, labor, display, and the form that creative production takes. Philip Auslander, for example, suggests that individual musicians aim to overtly *display* their skill in various ways, and thus musical styles are not neutral but may be designed to draw attention to this skill accordingly. Such display might need to be exaggerated in order to communicate skill to audiences who, unlike other musicians, may not be expertly able to identify skill otherwise: "What counts, ultimately, is audience perception, not actual degree of difficulty."[77]

Although the tantalizing potential for Bourdieu's and others' thinking to be examined as a hypothesis of evolutionary psychology, this avenue seems not to have been explored in any depth. In the language of evolutionary theory, such cultural competency, like one's accent, would be recognized as an honest signal of one's background, hard or impossible to fake, because the finer details would be detected by anyone who was truly from that background. In my earlier classification, such a Bourdieuian evolutionary theory would be seen as competitivist,[78] bearing similarities to sexual selection theory, but importantly, operating at the level of a culturally constructed niche that has little (but not nothing) to do directly with the attraction of a mate. We have seen previously how evolutionary explanations of social functions are complicated by the selfish gene principle. For an evolutionary explanation to make sense it has to apply to the inclusive fitness of the genes. Costly signaling theory states that in order for musical or any other art preference, capacity, or knowledge to work as an identity marker it has to be hard to fake. It has to be an honest indicator of your inclusion of that group, something that can only be acquired under certain circumstances: over a long period of time, from an early age, or with privileged access to the right people. The logic goes that you spend your time in one group, and this time is marked by the identity markers that you acquire—certain tastes, styles, ways of doing things, and knowledge. It is not easy to enter another group and fake one's identity.

This can apply to highly salient things like accents, dialects, gestures, and walks, which are acquired in a contagious, subconscious manner. It also seems to fit the profile of fashion items like clothing and music (Hennion's critique aside): they are complex and fast changing, requiring one to keep up with what's going on. Also, insofar as class is concerned (though the same may be said of other types of social group), any competitive process (for Bourdieu it is the struggle between classes) also comes with a complementary cohesionist component, requiring some degree of cooperation between members of the group. In the wider picture, as selfish gene theory would predict, the system also involves power struggles between individuals or families, *within* classes, which constantly dictate what cultural traits are considered desirable indicators. Thus in Bourdieu's words "cultural (or linguistic) competence … is acquired in relation to a particular field functioning both as a source of inculcation and as a market."[79]

Developing a more general social psychology of music, David Hargreaves and Adrian North list cognitive, emotional, and social functions for music.[80] Social functions are split among self-identity, interpersonal relationships, and mood. Their research supports the central claim that we use music (and the same might go for fashion and other forms of art) to mark identity and to detect other people's identity. Their work demonstrates how, in doing so, it serves both a group cohesion function and its converse, the marking of individuals as others. "Musical preference acts as a 'badge of identity' during adolescence."[81] Respondents to surveys indicated significant perceived correlations between perceived musical taste and the perception of traits in others, such as the importance of physical attractiveness, an interest in deeper meaning, feminist views, vanity, and hedonism. Relative musical taste also elicited consistent responses to questions like "Would you make fun of that person?" and "Will they be successful later in life?" leading North and Hargreaves to note that "the effects of musical preference on the person's social standing seem to be associated with the extent to which the style in question was prestigious in the eyes of the participants." North and Hargreaves frame these effects as part of a wider pattern of in-group/out-group behaviors extending beyond music but interacting with musical taste. Subcultural distinctions can be subtle. In one study, North and Hargreaves compare attitudes to indie pop and chart pop, which are sonically very similar and closely related. Indie pop "is intended to be more difficult to comprehend, often requiring the listener to be more active in determining its underlying meaning ... and previous empirical research has established that these two styles elicit quantitatively different aesthetic responses from adolescents."[82] In a separate study, music was also identified as being *explicitly* used by people to create certain impressions with others.[83]

Other studies have implied that aspects of music taste, in particular the breadth of music taste, corresponds to personality traits.[84] Those with wider music tastes were seen to be more confident and having a stronger sense of self, but the causality underlying this correlation is not identified. The frenzied engagement we have with music in our early teens and late twenties plays into Hargreaves and North's model of musical identity formation.

More recently, in collaboration with Emery Schubert, North and Hargreaves have developed a theory that connects these social findings with neuroscientific models of associative memory. In this theory, associations are formed between musical style and perceptions of groups. Musical preference, in turn, is both influenced by and influences perceptions of identity. The "influenced by" part is particularly important. At some level we may strategically (albeit subconsciously) manipulate what we should like, but also our group membership will simply dictate what music we are exposed to. Schubert, Hargreaves, and North propose that these associations are formed in lived experience: "When playing music at a campfire with friends for the first time, the network of associations with the environment (the campfire and atmosphere), the friends and the music will form new networks which represent the cooccurrence of the music and social context, and thus future experiences involving any or all of these components can lead to a large amount of activation spreading through the network at a subsequent activation involving any or all of those components (the campfire, the friends and/or the music)."[85] They also appeal to a widely studied potential for the contagion of mood ("emotional contagion") that would further support the ability for music to become an associative marker for positive and negative social experiences.

Schubert, Hargreaves, and North's theory is identified with prototype theory: people will like the most prototypical music that they hear, "that is, music that sounds most similar to their existing mental representations of musical styles and pieces."[86]

Theories of in-group and out-group associations have also been applied to the *creation* of artistic material, with an even greater overhead required to become an expert producer, as well as connoisseur. Edward Hagen and Gregory Bryant propose an evolutionary theory of music and dance as a "coalition signaling system," by which a group would use performance to signal their coalition strength and hence coordinated fighting ability to other groups. This, they propose, would be done through the development of complex dances that required skill and coordination and could not be learned easily. Thus a complex coordinated group dance would be an honest indicator of how long that group had spent together and how much time they had devoted to practice, at the same time as indicating individual traits like fitness and coordination. Again this would have both an internal cohesive component (the investment of time literally representing an investment in that group over another), an external competitive component (the use of cohesion to signal group strength), and would also be subject to internal competition (those individuals most capable of enacting the complex sequences would achieve greater success within the group).

Rhythm, in this context, could be seen as a structuring primitive that facilitated learning and coordination, upon which layers of rhythmic and melodic complexity could be built. It defines a space in which an exploration of complexity can better take place, just as the discrete units that make up language do. According to such theories, music's complexity and diversity actually play a role in its social function. Hagen and Bryant's theory would require that dances are complex and original so that they are harder to learn and couldn't be transposed from one group to another. A similar expectation might exist in the context of Bourdieu's theory.

Kathryn Coe's ancestress hypothesis[87] takes a different but related stance, looking at the use of identity markers over long-term multigeneration lineages, applied to early evolutionary scenarios. She proposes that decorative designs and other cultural goods come to become associated with family groups, passed through lineages that lead back to specific ancestresses. Thus being born into a group immediately implies being born into an existing cultural identity, and the symbolic and decorative material that identifies the group is laden with the logic of group membership. "Mothers used art forms to anchor themselves and their kin to the father and his kin, and to promote the survival and reproductive success of kin and descendants. Individuals who abided by this strategy, accompanied by its strict codes of cooperation, left more descendants than did individuals who did not."[88]

In this case, again, we must consider not only one's attention to, and preference for, certain things over others as being driven through exposure effects but also being driven by identity and association—taste driven not only by immersion in a culture but by specific allegiances. If cultural competencies are so critical to getting by in culturally constructed niches, then rather than aesthetic preferences being influenced only by exposure to stimuli they should also be influenced by social factors that are external to the content itself. Whether you like something or not might depend on who made it, what has been said about it, or what other associations are made with it. This can include strategic or functional development of preferences based on social influences. Several experimental studies make the point.

Firstly, a bias has been observed toward preferring things that others prefer in general. In a famous study, Matthew Salganik, Peter Dodds, and Duncan Watts,[89] for example, looked at people's evaluations of pieces of music via an online evaluation task. They compared one scenario in which people rated pieces of music based purely on the content, with another scenario in which people were shown the current average preference ratings for each piece by other people in the study. They found that people were strongly influenced by these ratings in the latter scenario, tending to align their judgment with the consensus. This results in a process of amplification in the second scenario. They observe that a piece of music still needs to have certain qualities to get liked in the first place, but once it becomes identified as a popular track, the positive feedback begins, and new evaluations are more likely to fall into line with the consensus. This means that once again luck plays a significant role in the success outcomes of creative work, this time amplified. It is a familiar idea that a talented artist just didn't quite make it because the buzz around their work just wasn't there, or similarly, that a widely praised artist was not essentially more talented than their peers but managed to capitalize on their luck and get the best out of their chances. An interesting aside is that algorithms have this same problem or can confound it by reinforcing this winner-takes-all effect. In automated recommendation systems, it is common to make recommendations based on popularity, and so new creators struggle to get a foothold, and unrecognized genius remains unrecognized. This is known as the "cold start" problem in recommender systems.

This idea is bluntly illustrated by a notorious experiment in which the acclaimed violinist Joshua Bell busked on the New York subway, dressed casually, performing repertoire that he performs frequently to sell-out audiences. According to a video of the episode, only one passerby paid any particular attention to his performance, and it turned out that person had seen him play the night before and recognized him. As the evolutionary psychologist Paul Bloom notes, "This experiment provides a dramatic illustration of how context matters when people appreciate a performance. … It is a clever demonstration, but perhaps not surprising. Everyone knows that the value of a painting shoots up if it is discovered to be by a famous artist, and plummets if it is discovered to be a fake. … Origins matter."[90] This phenomenon is a manifestation of Boyd and Richerson's frequency bias discussed in chapter 3, where we look to the surrounding population to make decisions about what we should be paying attention to.

Building on this is the idea that the prestige of an artist can in some cases be the more pivotal factor in the evaluation of a work than the content of the work itself. Again, we can appreciate from anecdotal experiences that this may be the case. A famous artist might produce something seemingly monstrous and flawed, but our attention is already drawn because they are a person of interest, the work cannot simply be ignored or cast off, and there is much space for us to grow to like it. Questions such as "What is the significance or deeper meaning of the work?" or "Why has that artist chosen this subject?" might obscure the cruder and forever problematic question, "Is it good?" which would be thrown more easily at the wannabe beginner.

Bloom and colleagues[91] have studied a range of scenarios that attempt to isolate exactly where people derive value in the judgment of work, with a particular focus on those confounding factors that lie beyond the material properties of the work. One manifestation of this research is the question of why we think authenticity or originality is important in art. For Bloom, while our pleasure response is partly grounded in crude biological functional systems—the love of sugar, sex, or building a good model of the environment—it is always also heavily influenced by higher-level conceptual thought that is grounded in sociocultural concerns. His pithy contribution to the debate over what makes humans unique, then, is that *we like Tabasco sauce*. That is, we have the capability to like (or learn to like) things that we shouldn't like, things such as spices that on first experience cause us pain. According to Bloom's framework, the love of authenticity is a simple manifestation of the desire to convene with the *essence* of the artist, just as we seek autographs or pay to see our heroes in the flesh. An authentic painting has been physically touched by the artist, and although there may be no DNA trace worth hunting for, this is still meaningful to us.

It is a bizarre suggestion that we would care so deeply about such forms of essentialism, and it is unclear why we should. But Bloom's thesis of essentialism is applied convincingly to myriad cases: "Even a pleasure such as the satisfaction of hunger is affected by concerns about essence and history, moral purity and moral defilement. There is always a depth to pleasure." In each case that Bloom considers, we seem capable of reconfiguring our pleasure response, either on the fly (as with Salganik and colleagues' experiment, where additional information influences the evaluation there and then) or as our taste develops over time.

Bloom's essentialism hypothesis, as applied across different areas of pleasure, has a great depth of application. In one sense it fits well with those theories above such as Huron's and Schmidhuber's, where the pleasure response is associated with the task of building a good model of our environment. Essences in this sense are simply a manifestation of our categorical and formal understanding of the world. They inhabit the linguistic conceptual and symbolically grounded end of the spectrum, away from lower-level qualities like harmonic content or structural complexity, all of which come together to form a holistic and multidimensional relation to cultural goods. When we think about things or people, we structure them according to various essential concepts that we believe them to be attached to. This can be as simple as tracking a single object while distinguishing it from other objects or seeing it undergoing transformations, something so intuitive that we might not notice that this requires an underlying mechanism. Bloom explains:[92]

> We can think about cherries as individual things. You can easily imagine a pair of cherries in a box, each soft, moist, red and tart, but you know there are two of them, not one. And this is not because we are merely sensitive to the magnitude of the properties—anyone can tell the difference between two small cherries and one big one. You can easily track an individual even if its properties are unstable, as when a caterpillar turns into a butterfly, or a frog into a prince ... And if one takes a cherry, paints it green, injects it with salt, and freezes it solid, it now has none of the standard properties ... but it doesn't *disappear*; the individual lives on even though its properties have changed.[93]

Bloom's essentialism can also be understood as serving a role as part of a system of social function. These essential entities that guide our model of the world and our subsequent behavior are generally about social relations. According to Bloom's thesis, basic pleasure functions such as a love of sugar collide, clashing and combining, with these more socially functional factors guiding pleasure. The contrast between these drives resemble the extremes of Maslow's hierarchy of needs, with physiological and safety needs at the bottom of the hierarchy and esteem and self-actualization needs at the top of the hierarchy.

Bloom's essentialism thesis is particularly pertinent when directly applied to people, roles, and relations. People have roles, status, and other values attached to them that influence how we locate them in the virtual constructions of culture. Shamans, priests, poets, and lawyers all have invisible properties attributed to them that affect how we interact with them, according to more or less formal rules.

It is timely to reiterate the plea at the beginning of this chapter to avoid thinking of art as something that fits a neat definition, is neatly bounded from the rest of life, or deserves a neat explanation. In all of the above scenarios there is an inescapable layering of contributing factors that is not easily reduced to a single simple narrative. For Pinker, musical pleasure is a crafted hodgepodge that satisfies different evolutionary pleasure circuits. For Bloom, conflicts emerge between different forms of value, between levels in Maslow's hierarchy of needs, in the formation of taste. For Huron, fast and slow thinking systems feed back on each other to trigger different sorts of pleasure response to the satisfaction or breaking of expectations. Similarly, musicologist and evolutionary thinker Ian Cross identifies different levels upon which we interpret music: "The very low-pitched semitonal ostinato overlaid by a non-tonally related horn call at the outset of the film *Jaws*, overlaid on an otherwise fairly innocuous underwater scene, signifies to the listener/viewer that something big and unseen is out there in the water (only big things can produce low-frequency sounds) and that it may well be hunting (horn calls, in western culture, are conventionally interpreted in terms of hunting topics)—hence fear and perhaps terror may be wholly appropriate, and fairly universal, responses."[94] Here the literal size of the bass and the reference of the hunting horn invite a universal association and a culturally learned one, respectively. But for Cross, music is also successful in its social functions because of its great ambiguity of meaning.

Artistic Behavior as a Network Phenomenon

In chapter 3, I followed a path from thinking about social creativity as the sum of individual creative acts combining stochastically, to thinking about structured social processes supporting creativity, such as the constructive mythologizing described by Schaffer, or the design of urban environments to support serendipity and combinatorial creativity proposed by Landry.

Similarly, this chapter set off thinking about the effects of social learning on the formation of individual taste, looking at several social functions and strategies associated with taste, implicated in the structure of groups, to move on to looking at more substantial collective phenomena under two broad headings: generational effects, and network effects. When we think about styles, taste, genres or any other term to describe the qualities of creative artifacts, although the material in question may be intangible, loosely bounded, and ephemeral, it is safe to say that cultural production appears in clusters. Such groupings and their changes correspond to groupings and changes in the distributed creative systems of people and things, and vice versa.

These clusters of cultural practice can exhibit both adaptive and generative creativity depending on how concentrated each temporary grouping is on a common goal, or how conflicting individual objectives are. It is important to emphasize the generative dimension here: aesthetic movements needn't have purpose in and of themselves, but may be both the emergent results of large numbers of individuals who do have purpose, and the evolving context in which they must form goals, tastes, and actions.

One cultural dynamic scenario touched on already is a generational cycle. Given the hypothesized identity dynamics of individual life cycles, as discussed above with reference to Hargreaves and North's work on youth music cultures, it would be natural to witness cyclical effects. Hargreaves and North argue that individuals acquire musical taste at a key receptive age and carry that taste through their lives. Correspondingly, the coming and going of genre movements are not the result of entire populations shifting taste but of a rolling turnover of individuals arriving, acquiring taste, and carrying it through their individual lives. A genre might form amid the creative energy of a new youth movement, take shape, and evolve through stages as its key proponents mature.[95] Like oscillatory physical processes—water waves, drops forming on a tap, the circular movement of a lava lamp—feedback effects can transform a gradual evolution into something more bumpy or explosive, with visible oscillations emerging from the substrate of human action.

Martindale[96] offers one such cyclical model in which genres of creative artifacts follow a common life cycle, taking an evolutionary perspective. Central to Martindale's theory is the idea of habituation, which we have encountered in various forms above. The crux of habituation is that we do not sustain interest in things that we are used to. Martindale asks what effect habituation has on the long-term progression of a creative domain. In Martindale's terms, the arousal potential of stimuli is reduced over time, and we should expect that changes are made that sustain this arousal potential, else through habituation the desired impact of an artform would be rendered ineffective. An initial proposal is to simply increase the stimulus intensity, but Martindale rejects this on the basis that cannot be increased indefinitely. Instead, creative production takes the form of a sequence of inspiration and elaboration. Inspiration is associated with primary-process thought, which is "free-associative, concrete, 'irrational,' and autistic," whereas elaboration is associated with secondary-process thought, which is "abstract, logical, and reality-oriented."[97] Martindale proposes "regression" as a core concept of the evolution of artforms, which involve the development toward more primary-process thinking:

Novel ideas could emerge in two ways from the inspiration-elaboration process: holding the amount of elaboration constant, deeper regression (movement toward primary process thought) should lead to more free-associative thought and therefore increase the probability of original or remote combinations of mental elements. In other words, to produce a more novel idea one could regress to a more primary process level. Holding degree of regression constant, decreasing the amount of elaboration should lead to statements that are original by virtue of being nonsensical or nonsyntactic in varying degrees.

He goes on to hypothesize that regression is the core basis for transformation, but that it arrives eventually at an unsustainable extreme, at which point a radical stylistic change takes place:

> Across the time that a given style is in effect, we should expect works of art to have content that becomes increasingly more and more dreamlike, unrealistic, and bizarre. … Eventually, a turning point to this movement toward primary process thought during inspiration will be reached. At that time, increases in novelty would be much more profitably attained by decreasing level of elaboration—by loosening the stylistic rules governing the production of art works—than by attempts at deeper regression.[98]

Specifically, Martindale predicts that properties such as novelty, complexity, and variability should increase monotonically over time, while "measures of primary process content should exhibit cycles of increasing and decreasing density of [elements] indicative of regressive thought."[99] Other results of studies conducted by Martindale[100] suggest that the tendency to habituate varies among people, with more creative people habituating more slowly than less creative people, leading him to conclude that the desire for novelty is stronger than boredom as a creative driving force.

This thesis sets up a situation where the timing of genre revolutions matters—the drip on a tap needs to build before it will drop. Related to this is the question of who leads the revolution. Pioneering incumbents or unencumbered novices? If the latter, then individuals bidding to enter a field may find themselves well aligned with a rare window of opportunity to be part of a revolution; timing is everything.

More generally, those entering the field at different times might find a spectrum of strategies on offer. Are you one of the complexifiers who wants to push an old genre into new domains of richness, or a minimalist who wants to carve out a new space? The specific time and place at which an individual enters this cultural battleground matters, and this enriches our view of the formation of taste and individual objectives.

Likewise, the various frequency-dependent effects we have encountered can amplify and thus help define genres. Individuals entering a field don't branch out at random into new territory but engage with a well-established genre and reinforce its existence. But what happens at the point of revolution, where there is no bandwagon to jump onto? Is the emerging genre predetermined, the logical next step that is on the tip of everyone's tongue, or is there a conceptual vacuum that is filled opportunistically? There is some evidence for either, and the story is probably one of a combination of more or less deterministic factors, where certain overall pressures do preference some movements over others. For example, Nia et al.[101] argue that the historical evolution of violin designs toward louder and louder violins—achieved by optimizing among other things the shape of the sound holes cut into the violin body—exhibited a BVSR pattern, with different European violin workshops being differentially selected for success based on loudness. Loud violins have simple evolutionary advantages, and even if some tastes prefer other qualities, the power to bring larger numbers of people together in larger auditoria, to sound impressive, or literally to outcompete other instruments would all be factors that might drive this evolution *despite* people's preferences.

The same is true of recent history's notorious radio wars. Mix and mastering engineers can employ a range of techniques to get their tracks to sound louder than others, and they may do so for the success of the track *despite* their taste. Indeed, a number of these techniques degrade the quality of the music, not least by limiting its dynamic range. These examples may seem peripheral to the *real* creation of music but are just as relevant forms of creation and greatly influence the context in which music is made.

All artistic revolutions or gradualist transformations might be given such a narrative, but as with evolutionary theory, just-so stories can also be a seductive trap, and historical contingency, chance, and the potential arbitrariness of cultural goods may also play significant roles. Against a backdrop of relative technological and social determinism, the idea that the arts enable a more turbulent happenstance path through history, one that is even dictated by the free will of individual human agents, is a picture that resonates well for many people.

Using big data analytics, more recent studies have attempted to formalize the relational interactions between members of a field by studying network properties. We can trawl online databases to discover not only the properties and success of cultural artifacts but the networks of relations that connect the producers of these artifacts. Gino Cattani and Simone Ferriani[102] use social network analysis to be able to determine the "position" of individual creators in a field. For any given social network we can define a centrality property and its converse: peripherality. Social movers and shakers are central nodes in social networks. Peripheral individuals have less influence.

In network analysis, there are various ways to define centrality, but a common one is to measure, for each node in the network, what the average distance is to all other nodes (the distance is measured as the shortest number of connections one has to follow to get to that node). The node with the shortest average distance to all other nodes is considered the most central, while the node with the longest average distance to all other nodes is the most peripheral. If a network looked like a spiderweb, then the node at the physical center of the web would also be the most central node, and those around the outside would be considered the most peripheral. Social networks rarely look like spiderwebs, more like fur balls. If a network were fully connected, with every node connected directly to every other node, it would reveal no difference between nodes, and there would be no structure to speak of.

Naturally occurring social networks lie somewhere between spiderwebs and fully connected networks. They are typified by a "scale-free" topology, where a small number of nodes have a large number of connections, and most nodes have a small number of connections (such networks also have a fractal nature). For example, a town mayor or innkeeper has daily interactions with a lot of people, is known about, and exerts influence in various ways, whereas the town's factory workers interact with a small number of people and have little influence.

Cattani and Ferriani's[103] analysis of the IMDB movie database attempts to discover how the creativity of individuals and teams within the film industry relates to their position in the social network (defined as the set of connections between individuals based on their collaborative history). Specifically, in exactly the same way that the Wundt curve dictates a peak of interest between things that are too familiar and things that are too unusual, the hypothesis that is considered is that a peak of creativity is found among individuals or teams who are placed neither too centrally (the old guard, the incumbents) nor too peripherally (the young Turks, the insurgents). Creativity is measured here in terms of markers of prestige such as awards, also automatically gleaned from the database, rather than total sales or popularity. Cattani and Ferriani find some evidence for this hypothesized relationship by demonstrating that the relationship between centrality and creativity, so measured, follows an inverted-U relationship, which resembles the Wundt curve.

In a following study, they show that in fact there are significant differences between different communities involved in the evaluation of creativity with respect to network position. Whereas peers rate the creativity of *central* figures most highly, critics are much more willing to rate members of the *periphery* more highly. In this work, Cattani and Ferriani closely associate their thinking with Bourdieu, indicative of a general resurgence of interest in this approach to creative domains, in their words "a rich and vibrant tradition building on Bourdieu's pioneering insights treats cultural producers as engaged in an ongoing struggle to secure notoriety, prestige, and esteem from colleagues."[104] In particular the focus on an individual's *position* within a social network enables a truly situated study of creative individuals' goals, which can connect these goals with global effects.

> Because … judgments produce prestige hierarchies and affect field evolution, cultural fields are in a constant state of struggle between established and emerging actors who compete for symbolic distinction based on subjective rules of merit, and the vested interests and social objectives these rules embody. While incumbents work to defend and reproduce their views and impose consensus, challengers try to "break the silence of the doxa and call into question the unproblematic, taken-for-granted world of the dominant groups."[105]

More generally, this ties their work to oppositional models that pit an establishment against a wider population of outsiders. An interesting additional force influencing this dynamic is the establishment acting to lock in certain aesthetic criteria, defining a genre. For example, this could be seen as the main guiding process in Coe's model of ancestral groups competing for identity markers. Other big-data studies have contributed to this fleshing out of a model of creative competition. Noah Askin and Michael Mauskapf[106] study the success of pop songs and show that successful songs must differentiate themselves from the field; overly typical songs are less likely to succeed. They propose that "the pressures toward conformity and differentiation act in concert."[107]

This analysis does not say anything of the generational relations between individuals, but it is reasonable to assume that in general the more central players will have been around longer, establishing their centrality, while the peripheral players will be newcomers, trying to develop their connections. We can therefore imagine ways in which cyclic processes such as that identified by Martindale track the life histories of individual people.

Summary: Shifting Dimensions and Emergent Niches

The material in this chapter does not aim to offer a complete and coherent theory of artistic behavior. I have set out to gather together the most relevant theoretical strands on offer, which are diverse and may not always be entirely compatible, and present them in a way that helps frame how the algorithmic automation of creative processes can fit into human creative domains. Good models of what humans are doing when they are engaged in artistic creation or experience are important if we are to understand what algorithms can do well, where they fit into human networks of creativity, and how they need to be designed to interact with people.

These strands are disparate and interspersed with speculation, and no commitment has been made here to argue for any one theory or another, or to particularly defend any of these various theses. But there is a common theme throughout: human artistic behavior lives within a complex web of social motivations and interactions, and any model of human artistic behavior is complete only insofar as it is capable of modeling any actor's embedded relationship with this social context.

Nevertheless, the following features of these disparate theories can now be condensed into a loose framework for thinking about artistic behavior and its hybrid, networked agency.

1. The cognitive mechanisms we use to build an adaptive model of the world and form predictions about the future—evolved largely in the service of nonsocial learning—form a critical part of the understanding of aesthetic behavior. A picture is emerging of a structured high-level cognitive architecture and a series of low-level components that adapt in response to experiences, as well as a reward system that stimulates us to engage in certain experiences over others. There are numerous,

competing evolutionary explanations for artistic competencies, but the majority of mechanisms are best described as consequentialist, having nothing to do with art as functional behavior in itself, but rather positing artistic behaviors as emerging simply because preexisting cognitive structures motivate them.

2. Meanwhile, a speculative *functional* role for aspects of artistic behavior, grounded in the dynamics of group identity and cohesion, is supported by evidence from various sources. The passively attained habitus of individuals, immersed in a given cultural background, is coherent with an honest-signaling model of competitive evolution. Artistic behavior can be seen to serve the manifestation of groups in various ways, setting up the conditions for competition between groups, cohesion within groups, and also additional competition *within* groups, possibly taking a nested hierarchical and diffuse structure (groups within groups, and overlapping groups). This view potentially *subsumes* the go-to sexual selection theory of artistic behavior with a more comprehensive social selection model. It has roughly the same basic properties and implies at least one similar outcome: that individuals are in part attracted to one another based on tastes and competencies, as markers of identity.

3. Certain factors underlying aesthetic preference and artistic competencies *may* have other more specific evolved functions, such as the dedicated evolution of preferences for landscapes or stories or the ability to track beats and metrical patterns. If these theories happen to be validated in the future, they are still very likely to be isolated traits that do not explain artistic behavior in any depth. A possible exception, however, is that musical competencies, in particular rhythmic perception, may have evolved in a protolinguistic stage associated with the social function discussed in the previous point.

4. Artistic evaluation is necessarily multidimensional and dynamic. Interaction with any aesthetic object cannot be simplified to a single preference measure or given set of features. New information, including hidden (possibly in Bloom's *essentialist* sense) attributes of an object such as its provenance or popularity, can affect how we perceive it. As part of our learning about the world, we encounter radically new ways to think about things, from learning the rules of counterpoint to understanding the social relations that underlie the production of dance music remixes.

5. Bringing together the high plasticity of social learners, the functionality of artistic behavior with respect to group identity, and the related in-group and between-group dynamic factors causes certain social network and generational effects, such as cyclical patterns and roles assumed by individuals according to their location in social networks.

Bringing this all together with the concepts developed in chapter 3, we can characterize the relationship between creative activity and the creative domains themselves as a form of ongoing cultural niche construction: fluid and ecosystemic. A child is raised into a certain cultural environment, their plastic brain learning associations between styles and cultural artifacts and group identities. They may become a competitive agent in this creative landscape, seeking to successfully innovate and make their mark, if not as a cultural producer then as an active consumer who communicates and interacts with others through cultural consumption. Depending on their context—their specific social background, abilities, and timing—they may go mainstream or be radical, with various risks and payoffs associated with different strategies. They may seek alliances, perhaps in the form of artistic movements. All the while, their brains and the brains of those around them are adapting through ongoing exposure to aesthetic, cultural material. New associations are being formed, and their worldview might evolve rapidly through a cycle of feedback, interacting in a tight clique. The occupants of a subcultural niche will have trained themselves in a different pool of aesthetic data to the mainstream, drawn further into this constructed niche of domain specificity by pattern-hungry minds. Not only will this influence their judgment, but it will actually enable them to perceive things that others may not perceive, nuances and markers of value that only the trained can properly identify.

Specifically, something that was never before a factor of any great importance might suddenly become the new axis along which difference is perceived: the amount of swing, say, in a guitar lick, or the linearity of the unfolding of a film's narrative. This something may not be obvious to people, but that makes it all the more effective as a marker of identity, in the way that Bourdieu implied. For this reason, aesthetic evolution can be open-ended and constantly creative and radical.

Howard Becker's[108] sociological analysis of various art worlds outlines many examples of how such dynamics play out. Becker's emphasis is on the practical and the contextual minutiae that sustain forms of activity in an art world. He notes that certain Western art music movements are often highly obscure and certainly have little mainstream appeal. Instead, they rely on the specific subcommunities of music and art students for whom obscure experimentation is essential creative nutrition. Even more pragmatically, when describing how art must be made for art galleries and art gallery culture, it must, at the very least, fit through the gallery door.

This impressionistic sketch of the social dynamics of creative domains may not be particularly detailed or concrete, but it should suffice as a sketch that is easy enough to hold in the back of one's mind as we now move on to consider what is happening in the world of computationally creative algorithms.

III Machines

5   Creative Algorithms

The idea becomes a machine that makes the art.
—Sol LeWitt[1]

Switching to talking about algorithms involves a sharp break from the previous discussion. We set aside, for the moment, thinking about psychology, social science, art and creativity studies and consider what it is that we can do with computers and how this is being used to achieve the goals of computational creativity. The study of algorithms belongs to what Herbert Simon described as *The Sciences of the Artificial*,[2] where we do not study the world as it is, *out there*, but study our own built environment and the process of building that environment, which we can do in an interactive, probing manner through the production of new designs and inventions. In Simon's words, "engineering, medicine, business, architecture, and painting are concerned not with the necessary but with the contingent—not with how things are but with how they might be—in short, with design." I begin this chapter by returning to a theme from chapter 1, the essential distinction between processes of generation and evaluation in creativity, which will help frame the relations between algorithms in the construction of artificially creative systems.

Generators and Evaluators

From the first chapter, a natural if somewhat simplistic categorization of algorithms relevant to computational creativity is between those algorithms that generate, without necessarily being able to evaluate, and those algorithms that evaluate without necessarily being able to generate.[3] I will adopt these as very coarse process categories that appear in some guise in all creative processes and manifest in the numerous configurations discussed so far. Generators include any algorithmic process that outputs an artifact, including part artifacts, incomplete artifacts, and abstract concepts (such as instructions for how to make an artifact). Evaluators include anything that takes as its input an artifact or concept (an image, some audio, a block of text, some description or representation of an idea) and tells us something about that artifact or concept. As argued in the previous chapter, this does not simply reduce to questions of how *good* something is or how much pleasure or value it brings. Evaluation, even if this usage abuses the word somewhat, is treated here as any form of cognitive response to something, such as whether it is typical of a style or what associations it invokes. Inevitably there are some algorithms that involve aspects of both generation and evaluation, in which the distinction between them is less clear, and others that may not do either in any particularly clear way. Nevertheless, the distinction between generators and evaluators will be useful to structure our understanding of *the way in which* a given algorithm performs creatively.

As much of the discussion in the preceding chapters has emphasized, a combination of generation and evaluation tasks is key to creative processes, and there are diverse configurations by which a creative system might integrate generation and evaluation components. Generating and evaluating happen at myriad stages and levels—the dancer practicing in the mirror or the individual artist producing experimental sketches in a private exploratory search (even experimenting with visual ideas in their own head), teams brainstorming ideas, or communities of practice self-organizing to filter out and exalt creative talent from a pool. Likewise, computationally creative systems can involve many different configurations of generation and evaluation processes, and, importantly, hybrid human-computer *co-creative* systems can attribute different responsibilities for generation and evaluation to different human and computational agents.

This chapter is largely about what types of algorithm are currently available for either purpose, how they work and what their basic properties are. It covers a number of examples of creative work in the areas discussed, although many other examples are discussed in the following chapter. The discussion attempts to be reasonably exhaustive, while being readable for a general, nontechnical audience.[4] Putting these algorithms together into hybrid computationally creative systems will also be a focus of some discussion.

On Domain Specificity and General Architectures

One thing that will be immediately apparent in the ensuing discussion is that the real algorithms employed in computational creativity (as opposed to those abstract principles—learning, optimization, and so on—underlying the algorithms) tend to be relatively domain-specific. Pixel-based image processing and generation, drawing, text processing, symbolic music generation, audio processing, concept generation—each of these areas of creative activity may be associated with families of well-suited algorithms. Symbolic music generation may be more associated with recurrent neural networks whereas image generation may be associated with feed-forward convolutional neural networks, and although these have similarities and they certainly have general principles, they also have subtly different affordances that pull in different directions. Simulations of ant behaviors have been used in generative visual art in ways that would have no meaning translated to poetry. "Conceptual blending" is a technique very closely (but by no means exclusively) associated with text-based computational creativity. In computational creativity, as elsewhere, we find specialized communities of practice, as in the musical metacreation community, whose domain specialism might hinder their interaction with other communities. Computational creativity researchers grapple with the low-level idiosyncrasies of these algorithms applied in these specific domains, and innovation in one domain may not carry easily across domains; a visual artist might glaze over when it comes to the intricacies of representing musical meter to a machine learning algorithms.

Meanwhile, there is some cautious conviction that "there does exist some core abstraction or creativity 'algorithm' that can be applied to any domain"[5] (the caveat following this quote: "with suitable domain-specific augmentation, of course"). In chapter 1, I discussed Gervás's basic procedure for artifact generation. The natural starting point for this, as pursued by Ventura and Gervás, among others, is to schematize and possibly generalize a model of what a human practitioner does. Ventura proposes that an *abstract* creative system would include general properties such as "background knowledge, an ability to learn, intentionality, an ability to conceptualize, a sense of aesthetic,"[6] arranged in a bounded agent that allows iteration of creative output both internally and through interaction with the outside world. This book has advocated for a much more general conception of what a creative system might look like. In particular, knowledge of working practices and forms of creative inspiration in different domains, as discussed in chapter 4, suggest quite different configurations of process and practice, especially when expanding one's view from single-agent to multi-agent systems and examining the cultural mechanisms at play. At the psychological level, Wiggins and Forth's IDyOT model,[7] for example, suggests a process of musical inspiration whereby predictive neural circuits are "idling" and occasionally suggesting musical ideas, "spontaneous creativity." While Wiggins and Forth do suggest that this mechanism may have a more general applicability, its functioning as outlined in the model is specific to temporal phenomena such as music and possibly language. That this may apply to, say, a painter working in a representational genre may be conceivable but is certainly not a given. At the multi-agent level, the creative process is informed by cultural norms and social configurations, the creativity of new turns of phrase in a language operating very differently from the creative production of professional artists, for example. Thus again there is some doubt as to whether a general creativity algorithm is a useful concept.

In my view, a design patterns approach is well suited to this problem. Design patterns, as first developed by Christopher Alexander in the field of architectural design[8] and subsequently widely employed in the software engineering world,[9] describe powerful and reusable design abstractions that can be applied in many different circumstances. The algorithms described in this chapter suggest possible design patterns with more or less domain specificity, but it is uncommon for an algorithm to be ready-adapted to work across diverse media without modification. The most basic of design patterns associated with the features of creativity discussed so far, even simpler than Ventura's proposed algorithm, is the *generate-and-test* pattern, whereby a single generative process outputs artifacts that are evaluated by a single test process. Yet a number of the algorithms discussed below conform to an even simpler model; lacking an evaluation component, they are characterized by a *structure-and-generate* pattern, *structuring* here meaning either *training* in the machine-learning sense or *designing by hand* in the rule-based systems approach. The clear but constrained creative potential of such algorithms raise questions about how a more complete creative process is then established, given that the system itself performs no evaluation. The short answer is that the system is still creatively powerful but is of limited autonomy, requiring another system—or a human user—to evaluate and then manipulate the system or its output. I will make the claim therefore that the reduced scope of such algorithms does not invalidate their creative potential by any means, as long as we correctly identify what the algorithm is and isn't responsible for in the overall process. This will be a key topic in chapter 6. Evaluative systems that combined a generation stage and an evaluation stage, feeding back on the generation stage, could also constitute more complex design patterns than *generate-and-test*. We will see other distinct methods in this chapter, such as interactive genetic algorithms, that could form the basis for other patterns.

Another pattern that is somewhat specific to computational creativity is *conceptual blending* (mentioned in chapter 2 as a psychological theory), the idea of bringing together two concepts or elements to create a new concept or element. We can do this easily with words. Take the concepts of boat and house and ask what would happen if you merged them. What would a boathouse or a houseboat look like? We know the answer to this because they exist (note two different answers, both coherent and real), but we can also do this creatively with new blends. Conceptual blends can be visual: pick any two animals and set yourself the task of drawing a hybrid. They might form the basis of a joke or the plot scenario for a play as Colton and his team's *What If Machine* did; it came up with the scenario: "What if a wounded soldier had to learn to understand a child in order to find true love?"[10] A conceptual blending system has to understand—at least have some handle on—the things it is blending, and possibly to analyze the possible interpretations of the resulting blend. If instead of house and boat, I say sofa and computer, I might rapidly conclude that there isn't much value in the idea of a sofa-computer or a computer-sofa as a future product, but who knows? The creativity may come in the radical interpretation of such a strange combination.

The Algorithms of Computational Creativity

Broadly, the technologies of computational creativity are bound to closely follow innovation in computer science, particularly AI. The major forms of algorithms in AI, from learning to reasoning to search and optimization, have evolved gradually over the past half century, and major innovations leading to radical new algorithmic techniques are few and far between. The march of progress for fields such as neural networks and evolutionary computing is mostly slow and steady, with thousands of academic papers reporting minor improvements and variations on well-known algorithms each year, punctuated occasionally by a breakthrough. Improvements in computing and information infrastructure, including the accumulation of big data and growth of machine-readable material, equally drive steady advancement of the field, with occasional moments of radical transformation such as in the compilation of significant datasets or web services. While computational creativity does have its own areas of specialist algorithmic focus—those mentioned such as conceptual blending, and others coming up, such as interactive genetic algorithms, novelty search, curious agents, and specific computational models of creative thought—these are by no means strictly limited to computational creativity applications and will also be found in some form or other in other areas of AI. It is also worth noting as an aside that some areas of computer science and AI are also implicitly or indirectly creativity-focused. Hannu Toivonen and Oskar Gross point out that the field of data mining is defined as the "discovery of novel and useful information"[11] and as such is arguably a creative application. Meanwhile, computational creativity frequently draws from every niche of the vast canon of AI techniques and algorithms, such as deep learning neural networks, Markov models, genetic algorithms, Bayesian learning, and self-organizing maps. In short it is critical to the understanding of applied computational creativity to recognize that it is both limited by and driven by what current algorithms in AI happen to be capable of.

One of the most prominent areas in which AI technologies indirectly influence computational creativity is machine perception, largely focused around machine vision, machine listening, and natural language processing. Being key to a vast number of critical and lucrative application areas—robotics and autonomous vehicles, surveillance, augmented reality, voice interaction, and "Internet of Things" applications like automated agriculture, logistics and physiological tracking—it enjoys a huge groundswell of effort. Computational creativity benefits from foundational machine perception technologies, enabling things like the recognition of objects in a scene or the extraction of a piece of music from the noise of background sound, the correct identification of the notes that make up a chord or the instrumentation used, and so on. These provide new starting points upon which researchers can build generative and self-evaluating systems. For example, existing interactive music systems often take a stream of audio as a real-time input and perform some kind of pitch, event onset, or timbre detection in order to gain a symbolic representation of that audio stream, a nontrivial task that has taken years to achieve human-comparable performance in, still with some way to go. This affords forms of interaction and computation that raise the level of cognitive sophistication of the systems being built, but it is still primitive—real-time beat induction (clapping along in time to a piece of music), for example, is still hard for computers to do as well as the average human in *all* cases.

As discussed in chapter 1, a useful way to think about algorithms in computational creativity is to think about where the knowledge comes from that goes into these algorithms' behaviors. The cutting edge systems we have that can perform human-comparable perception tasks, such as being able to visually distinguish dogs from cats, are largely based on machine learning. Such a system's knowledge (about what dogs and cats look like) comes from being trained on existing data (existing images of dogs and cats) often but not always annotated with the knowledge that is required (the images are labeled with "dog" or "cat"). Other systems might have knowledge programmed into them, or the knowledge might be emergent, in the case where the system has worked something out through trial and error experimentation or automated reasoning.

The roboticist Rodney Brooks made several pleas to the AI community to understand intelligence as occurring as much in physical interactions as in symbol manipulations—elegantly expressed in the title of Brooks's celebrated essay "Elephants Don't Play Chess"[12]—and it is in this "nouvelle" AI spirit that *knowledge* is understood. It might be manifest in an innate fear of spiders, in factual knowledge such as that Paris is the capital of France or that a red light means don't cross the road, or even in muscle memory or manifest in physical designs (corkscrews embody knowledge about bottles and corks).

Rule-Based, Learning, and Evolutionary Systems

One standard categorization of algorithms relevant to computational creativity is to divide them between rule-based, learning, and evolutionary approaches. Although this classification is in some ways dissatisfying—it is imperfect and incomplete—it serves to group major areas of activity in AI fairly well. There are other areas that don't fit easily into these categories, such as approaches that are specifically focused on linguistic reasoning. There are also countless hybrid systems, those that mix together different algorithmic components from these categories, and those that naturally straddle different categories. In computational creativity it is common to find hybrid systems, as it is usually necessary to mix various components together to get to the point of having a system that can perform some type of meaningful generation. In the following sections, I will give overviews of rule-based, learning, and evolutionary methods, before moving on to discuss hybrid systems and social models.

Rules

Rule-based approaches describe computational systems in which the behavior of the system is dictated by explicit rules written by a programmer. Since programming languages are systems for entering rules that dictate the operation of a running program, and this is the principal entry point for creating computer programs, it is natural that rule-based systems comprise the bulk of generative systems and constitute the most elementary variety. Cohen's AARON embodied a rule-based approach. AARON had no input data or training set. It was never exposed to artworks that it could learn about. It had no information or means of acquiring information about whether any given painting had value. It performed no reasoning that could result in new knowledge. All that AARON "knew" was explicitly hand-coded into it by its programmer; everything that AARON knew, Cohen knew, and he knew that it knew it. We can certainly say that AARON embodied some aspects of a painter's knowledge: Cohen's knowledge encoded in algorithms. As above, this is a structure-and-generate model where Cohen, as coder, performed the structuring and set AARON to do the generation. Any feedback loop of evaluation occurred over the entire holistic system, with Cohen making updates to the code. There is a related area in computer science called expert systems, whereby expert knowledge is encoded by programmers into running programs that can then take the place of the expert.

Other computational artists of this pioneer era from the 1960s were likewise engaged with exploring the creative potential of the computational medium, developing artworks based on sets of rules where the artwork could generate variation on its own, within the space of variables that the artists had defined. The thing that drove the variation might be systematic, or random, or interactively driven from an external input. In Paul Brown's work, a common theme is the use of tiling patterns to create many variations of common forms, exploring the combinatorial power of simple systems (Brown uses cellular automata rules to dictate the rotations of tiles). In these tiling programs, each of a series of tiles can rotate through several positions; there are four different orientations for square tiles. As the tiles rotate, the patterns drawn on them combine to result in the construction of new shapes. In this constrained design space, the resulting forms are more predictable than Cohen's, but the basic architecture is the same: a system of rules resulting in forms that the artist has metacomposed, but not specified.

All running computer programs have a *state*, referring to the current values of all the stuff in the working memory of the program (this includes the program itself, which can change while it is running). In the example of

Figure 5.1
Paul Brown's artworks involve the automatic recombination of elements using algorithmic processes. The design of modular elements that afford recombination to create rich and complex structures is an important part of this art. Here the work is rendered as a series of cards that a person can tile manually. In digital form, the cards arrangement is often managed by procedural or evolutionary rules. Image credit: Paul Brown.

Brown's tiling patterns, the salient component of the system state is the set of rotational positions of the tiles, with each different set of positions corresponding to a unique resulting image. We can separate a program between those state elements that can be modified by the program itself, and those that are set once by the programmer at the start of the program. For example, Brown's program updates the tiles' rotational states itself, but there will be many other fixed variables contained in the program, such as the speed at which the tiles update, the number of tiles, or factors that affect the patterning on the tiles. Any of these things could easily be updated from within the program if the programmer so desires or could be defined as a control in a graphical user interface. Generative artists working with code can hand successive levels of decision-making over to automated processes within their programs, while holding other aspects of the design in their control.

It is therefore natural for programmers to conceptualize systems in terms of a set of control parameters that dictate a space of possible outcomes, as we saw in chapter 1. A parametric design is simply one in which some aspect of the design can be controlled by one or more parameters, usually continuous numerical variables. A building could comprise a series of stacked floors each of which is a variant on the same underlying geometric object, an irregular hexagon, say. At successive floors, the hexagon could be parametrically altered. In that case the hexagon could be defined simply by the coordinates of its six corners, in which case it would have twelve numeric parameters (the x and y positions for each of the six corners). Or it could be defined by more abstract metafeatures, such as how squashed it is or how much its points were clustered at one end. In practice, there is an art to neatly parameterizing forms so that the search space defined by the resulting set of parameters is *good for searching*.

Certain forms are parameterized in common ways, based on successful mathematical formulations. For example, while a straight line can be parameterized using its start and end points (four numbers), a curve needs further information to define its shape. Common curves such as parabolas and ellipses have well-known equations that define the curve with a minimal set of points, but these can be limited in their flexibility. A more flexible parameterization of curves comes in the form of a geometric structure known as a Bezier curve, which has become a widely used standard in computer graphics for the representation of arbitrary curved shapes. Bezier

Figure 5.2
An example of a parametric design exploring gradual variation in the positions of a hexagon's vertices. Image credit: Andrew Kudless, Andrew Payne (LIFT Architects).

curves are defined by control points at each end, and at anchor points along the length of the curve, which locate a point that the curve passes through but also the direction and intensity of the curvature around that control point. Bezier curves can therefore be used to create continuous lines with a high complexity using a smaller number of points than if you tried to do the same thing with straight line segments, and can produce complex shapes to a required degree of accuracy (the more accurate the modeling of the given shape, the more control points are needed to define the Bezier curve).

As with this example, part of the work of coming up with good parametric design systems lies in finding good ways to parameterize common forms. As Javier Monedero summarizes in a wide survey of parametric design in architecture, "Designers work in such systems at two levels: definition of schemata and constraints; and search within a schema collection for meaningful instances."[13] We can then think about what qualities make for a good parametric representation. These include expressive potential, compactness, robustness, and smoothness:

- *Expressive potential* The representation is capable of a wide diversity of outputs.
- *Compactness* The representation encodes resulting forms efficiently.
- *Robustness* The representation always results in a valid output.
- *Smoothness* Small variations in the representation result in small variations in the output.[14]

The expressive potential of a parameterization is probably of most immediate concern to anyone working with parametric systems. One may wish to find a general representation that has a great deal of potential for diversity or a very narrow representation that marks out a highly constrained space. For example, the creator of a parametric building design might specify a large number of factors by hand, which remain fixed, then choose to parameterize several elements of this design, and then search that parametric space. Like Brown and Cohen's artworks, the results will be unmistakably of a certain style, thanks to all of the hardwired design decisions, but nevertheless with possibly surprisingly diverse variation within that space. Parametric designs offer a simple technique to enable personalization or rapid variation-generating strategies that can be used in games, such as in the procedurally generated game *No Man's Sky*, or in the parametric planets and creatures that game artists like Kate Compton create.[15] As we saw in chapter 1, Compton introduced the term "casual creators" to describe these simple parametric systems that someone can casually tweak to make their own specific design without expert skill, simply through exploratory search or adjusting parameters.

In this way, parametric approaches enable a smooth transition from human-made design processes to a hybrid approach in which the machine might begin to make a creative contribution, or, simpler still, might just super-power the individual's ability to perform exploratory search. The transition is not that seamless, however; as Robert Aish and Robert Woodbury point out in the widely studied context of parametric architectural design, a parametric approach "increases complexity of both designer task and interface, as designers must model not only the artifact being designed, but a conceptual structure that guides variation."[16] I will turn to this question of automated search of parametric spaces under the topic of evolution, which will also help to contextualize why the properties of compactness, robustness, and smoothness are valuable. Meanwhile, more complicated compositional strategies enable parametric design that goes beyond styles that we tend to produce by hand—in other words, that are innately computational in style.

One area where this can be seen is in the *iterative* application of functions to create composite complexity. Think back to the spirograph discussed in chapter 2, which takes a circular path and draws it relative to a center point that is moving along another circular path. This produces complex patterns using only a small number of parameters. This is effectively a form of *modulation* or *pattern composition*, with one process modulating how another process plays out. A similar process goes into the sound synthesis methods called amplitude modulation and frequency modulation. In the latter, in the simplest case, the frequency of one oscillator, the carrier, is made to vary according to the output of another oscillator, the modulator, with three control parameters: carrier frequency, modulator frequency, and modulation depth. The effect of the modulation is to transform the carrier signal from a pure sine wave into a more complex waveform. The result is a wide timbral space of waveforms that can roughly simulate some natural sounds and also create many novel synthetic sounds. If such iterative processes are applied extensively, increasingly complex structures can be formed out of simple primitive elements. Moving from sound waves to musical notes, we find these modular iterative methods to be quite effective in producing music. For example, an abstract pitch contour, which just dictates whether and how steeply the pitch is going up or down, can be generated, mapped to a scale, transposed according to a chord sequence, and further manipulated by rhythmic transformations. George Lewis applied similar techniques in his Voyager software, resulting in rich diversity and musically coherent outputs.

The systematic application of such ideas can in principle enable practitioners to create arbitrarily complex structures and endless variation. The basic idea is one from complexity science: making lots of simple things interact with each other can lead to rich, complex forms. The challenge is how to control this complexity, to find its sweet spots amid large swathes of potentially bland or homogenous output. In cases such as Brown's, Cohen's, and Lewis's, the system design is manual, the conceptual space is relatively well understood, and the developer experiments iteratively, finding a space of possibilities that they are pleased with.

Taking this to higher and higher levels of complexity, and abstracting away from the artist's signature, has not proven easy. There seems to be a fundamental tradeoff for artists and designers here: greater complexity means a greater hindrance to manipulating objects with clear design objectives (in chapter 6 we will look at theories of human-computer interaction that attempt to frame such challenges). Nevertheless, we can take this idea of parameterizing systems to its logical conclusion, where entire complex programs are (more or less) parameterized, but in order to do so we must move from representations of systems not just in terms of fixed numbers of parameters, but as growable, often hierarchical structures. For example, a popular general approach to generative visual art is to construct a system for mapping from the x,y coordinates of any pixel in an image to the red, green, and blue (RGB) values of that pixel. Any one such equation would define a unique image. In a simple case, the red value might be proportional to $\sin(x+y)$, creating a diagonal pattern of wavy lines. We can construct arbitrarily complex equations using quite systematic strategies, such as adding $(\sin(a)+\sin(b))$ or nesting $(\sin(\sin(a)))$ equations iteratively. This kind of open-ended composition of procedural elements is part of a field known as generative grammars. Evolutionary artworks (I discuss evolution properly in a later section) such as those of Karl Sims or Penousal Machado show that these simple sequential transformation processes can generate richly structured images. Similar effects can be achieved via deformations of existing structures. This is particularly relevant in 3D design where deformation is a common approach to producing particular forms. Iterative geometric transformations are also common in generative design.

Rule-based systems fit a traditional conception of what computers do and how we program them. These are works that a lone artist can quite easily produce with a basic knowledge of mathematics, programming, and the graphics libraries required to render the work, but increasingly creative tools are emerging that simplify and speed up this compositional process, and generative capacity is being found increasingly in commercial software tools.

In music, the rule-based approach often has an even better fit to existing creative practice, since compositional styles are often dictated by rules applied to the discrete world of musical pitches and rhythms, whether these are explicitly or implicitly associated with styles.[17] Such rules may be of a statistical nature. An obvious example is that phrases often resolve on the root note of the scale they are played in. Another is that melodies often follow a statistical distribution in which small steps occur more frequently than bigger steps. Composers may easily formalize either an existing style or their own compositional strategies into rules that are explicitly coded in algorithms. Importantly, the expression of the rules depends on and can be greatly facilitated by the choice of representation of the music. For example, we could express Western music tones in terms of continuous frequencies (not very helpful) or discrete pitch classes (much more appropriate), but we can also think in terms of scale degree (the position of a note relative to the scale it is in) and other relative properties such as whether a note is "in chord" or "out of chord" given the current chord it is being set against.[18] These more structured representations allow more complex expressions of rules (such as resolution), although they may also constrain what kinds of music are well represented (for example, non-Western microtonal scales may not be expressible at all). It can also be possible to get a computer to extract rules from musical examples, as in the work of Man-Kwan Shan and Shih-Chuan Chiu[19] (this work is better suited to the section below on learning but is mentioned here because the learned rules are in a form that can also be expressed by a human).

Even if this is the mildest form of automated creativity, the resulting system generates novel patterns that the author may have never seen before and may be surprised by (but without usually finding the results inexplicable). The artist may iteratively adapt their code in response to what they see, just as Malafouris's potter couples his actions to the forming clay.

From the point of view of computational creativity, rule-based approaches seem relatively trivial. Here, Lovelace's objection seems to apply better than the other approaches we will look at; if the system's knowledge comes from the programmer's explicit knowledge, then it is hard to imagine the system doing things that were outside of the programmer's awareness. Cohen's system would fail Bringsjord et al.'s Lovelace test—which explicitly requires that the computer produces something the programmer can't explain. Cohen might have claimed to be surprised by the beauty or structure of some of AARON's output, but he could always apply his knowledge of the program to explain it. In the other categories below, learning and evolution, a programmer can conceivably program in forms of adaptation that might evolve beyond their knowledge. But in the rule-based case it is harder (but not impossible) to see how. And yet Conway's Game of Life (discussed below) and other complex generative processes like the Mandelbrot set produced outcomes that were so profound they had clever people working hard to explain their intricacies—although they would not satisfy the Lovelace test, because they just do one thing, the same thing every time. Thus it does still seem reasonable to believe that, whether through careful trial and error or careful calculation, one could manually construct systems of complex interaction that produced outcomes requiring detailed study to explain.

Creative Emergence
A creative manifestation of one of the core principles of complexity science—that simple elements can interact to beget richer more complex structures—consists of producing simple interactions between myriad small agents. Examples include flocking behaviors, cellular automata, and agent-ecosystem interaction models. Cellular automata include the remarkable Game of Life algorithm, in which through simple interactions between binary cells, nontrivial structures called gliders naturally emerge, "walking" like small naturally occurring creatures. If you configure the starting state of the Game of Life carefully, you can make other kinds of structures, like a glider gun, a structure that spits out gliders at regular intervals. Related to the Game of Life are more complex reaction-diffusion models that produce a range of behaviors resembling fluids, cellular patterns, and growth processes.

The gliders of the Game of Life, it is said, are *emergent*—that is, they come into being without someone explicitly putting them there, through the interactions that occur between lower-level elements. Artificial life and complexity science researchers talk about such elements inhabiting different metaphysical layers, just as biology, chemistry, and physics can be seen as strata of systems organization that sit on top of each other in layers. Gliders are admittedly very simple, but if they can just emerge like that from such a simple program as the Game of Life, then there is hope that other, more complex behaviors can emerge in other computer programs, and even for some form of open-ended scaffolding of emergent complexity to take place in a computer program, just as it has done on our planet.[20] Could a program be written in which truly radical forms of complex behavior simply emerge from the program's interacting components? This is a topic of interest to artificial-life researchers, particularly in light of the view that life on earth and with it the conditions for complexity-increasing evolution have presumably emerged from the interactions of simpler physical components interacting in mechanistic ways. Artificial-life researchers experiment with the idea that closed computational models might produce rich, lifelike emergent behavior; early artificial chemistry projects such as the *Tierra* model[21] provided examples of how small digital ecosystems of interacting agents could develop nontrivial behaviors found in biological systems.

Unsurprisingly, this area has also been fascinating for artists and computational creativity researchers.[22] Even in closed worlds, where the aesthetic expectations of humans are absent, could a program generate interesting complexity, rich structures that we might find compelling and appreciate as being produced by a creative process?

A typical approach to exploring this concept is through agent-ecosystem interaction models, such as the example of Driessens and Verstappen's *E-volver* discussed in chapter 1. As part of a creative artistic practice, these are similar to the kinds of composed processes described above, such as the musical structuring processes in Lewis's Voyager. They exhibit a clear organization imposed by the programmer, such as between different types of agent behavior or between the agent and its environment. In this way, the hope is that the artist can manage the process and ensure that they produce something that they are happy with but that exhibits surprising behavior, diversity, and clearly emergent structures. They illustrate Whitelaw's notion of the "system story,"[23] discussed in chapter 1, the idea that these composed artificial life systems are grounded in a set of narrative concepts such as creature and environment (rather than, say, cell or atom). Such a formula makes for potentially compelling art, as the story that plays out is live and unscripted.

In Jon McCormack's audiovisual installation *Eden*,[24] agents inhabit a simple grid world and operate according to rules borrowed from ecology. A limited resource is needed by the agents to survive and reproduce, and this drives evolutionary competition, possibly stimulating the evolution of new original behaviors (much more about evolution below). Thus it is not only the environment that is modified by the agents: agents are evolvable and adapt to develop new behaviors over time. To make a compelling interactive experience, McCormack sets up this limited resource to be determined by the presence of audience members themselves. If many audience members are present, then there is more food for the agents and they thrive. If few audience members are present, the resource is diminished, and the population is placed under greater pressure. Thus the narrative of the artwork is one in which agents are driven to attract audience members. McCormack observes that over time the agents developed a form of emergent hibernating behavior, conserving energy at night when there are no visitors to the gallery, and jumping into action during the day.[25]

More generally, we can design rich agent behaviors and then put these agents together in virtual worlds to see what transpires in *in silico* experiments. Computer game makers creating worlds of virtual characters have naturally encountered such examples of interesting emergence, but generally computer games are carefully scripted, and a major challenge is to find smart ways to combine open-ended potential with a degree of control over what happens next. The evolutionary artist William Latham attempted several times to create mainstream computer game titles with emergent behaviors but was limited by the need to stick to a more prescribed script that would ensure the gameplay experience. The potential for the bottom-up generation of game narratives, however, has started to have traction. Emily Short's Versu system, for example, creates interactive storytelling experiences by creating a cast of characters and placing them together in a storyworld, allowing the player to influence the game in unpredictable ways, and watching as narratives emerge from the playing out of character interactions.

Again, music often offers a more abstract domain of application. In several examples of complex-system-based musical works, composers have started by observing how certain complex systems produce patterns that resemble musical patterns. For example, Shawn Bell and Liane Gabora[26] use network models found in fields such as social science and brain research, specifically a hierarchical network architecture known as a *scale-free* network, to generate complex patterning that, they argue, is also the kind of patterning that composers actively seek. In another influential series of examples, the composer Agostino di Scipio builds *audible ecosystems* using a cycle of feedback through a series of digital signal processes, an acoustic environment and possibly a human performer. The goal of the digital signal processing stage is to transform the incoming audio (picked up by microphones) and render it (back into the environment, using loudspeakers) in such a way as to drive emergent complexity over time.[27]

Although the Game of Life and these various creative models are very interesting from the point of view of studying emergence, and give us complex behavior emerging naturally out of a simple algorithm, they come at a cost: we cannot control them easily, even less so than simpler rule-based or parametric systems. Without methods to automatically explore the worlds of possibilities they offer, they may be of limited use for creative practitioners; making such works do what you expect may require going deep into the underlying mathematics, without success. Similarly, in complex systems science as a whole, the subject of guided self-organization has become an important topic.[28] We have some understanding of the creative potential of self-organizing processes but little understanding of how we can control them. After all, this is something of a contradiction in terms. Finding ways to combine emergence and control remains a major challenge for the practical application of complex systems.

The closed-world examples discussed above fall into the *generator* category introduced at the beginning of this chapter, again following a *structure-and-generate* creative process, in which the individual user (or distributed team, such as in the case of casual creators) both designs a search space and searches it, or sets into motion the systematic exploration of a creative design space. McCormack's *Eden* example is different in that there is a feedback path from generative system to an evaluating audience. Rule-based evaluators do exist as well, but really only make sense in the context of some sort of search algorithm, and are introduced in the section "Evolving and Searching," later in the chapter.

Learning

Supervised Learning: Classification and Regression The most common and currently the most successful way we have for a system to gain knowledge from the world, without the programmer manually adding it in, is through forms of machine learning, such as neural networks. I will focus exclusively on neural networks in this section, being the area of greatest advancement and activity in recent years, although there are many other forms of machine learning systems. Such systems gain knowledge through being fed training data in some form, which is used to systematically shape the structure of the learning system so that it embodies knowledge of that training data in some way. For example, in a typical classification scenario, a neural network will be trained to recognize objects in images and to return relevant tags related to categories of things. Say an image contains a cat, then the goal might be that the network should output the category for "cat." If an image contains a cat and a dog, a network might report both "cat" and "dog" (more sophisticated text outputs like "a black dog is chasing a ginger cat across the street" are also possible with modern neural networks; these go beyond simple classification). Training such a network, in the paradigm of *supervised learning*, means feeding it one image at a time, along with the expected categories, and comparing what it output to what it *should have* output. The goal of the training algorithm is to minimize the difference (the error) between these two things. One of the most common neural network training algorithms, the *backpropagation* algorithm, for example, adjusts the weights of the network (more about networks and weights below), which affect how a signal is transformed as it passes through the layers of the network. It does this by making small adjustments to each weight such that the combined effect of these changes is to bring the network's last output closer to the target output. The poorer the network's estimate is, the more its structure should be adjusted to correct the error. This process is called error minimization. Much of the challenge of the science of neural networks has been in solving how to take the error in the output, at each training step, and use it to adjust the structure of the network. Doing this means understanding how much each part of the network has contributed to the error in the prediction, and adjusting it accordingly, a problem known as the *credit assignment problem*. For larger networks this assignment of credit or blame becomes increasingly (indeed vanishingly) hard, and special designs are required to make the problem of successfully training large networks more computationally tractable.[29]

If this is done very gradually and very many times, then in principle the neural network is able to gain some generality over the data, which is central to the intelligence of such systems. The aim, of course, is not simply to learn the classifications of the *training* data (the raw information) but to derive a general classification ability that can be applied to unseen data, thus to be able to make inferences about previously unknown inputs, responding appropriately. A system could in principle learn to respond perfectly to the training dataset but still perform very poorly on the test set. This is the problem of *overfitting* to the training data; the system has taken the data too literally, so to speak, and hasn't managed to learn how to generalize the underlying patterns. For example, the network might learn that cats are always either black or white, but then fail to recognize a black and white cat (which, all things considered, is quite forgivable. Many categories have distinct forms: the lowercase and uppercase letter *R* doesn't have an in-between thing that should also be considered an *R*. We often make such mistakes ourselves.) Thus when training machine learning systems, a randomized portion of the training dataset is put aside so that there is also a testing dataset, used to evaluate the performance of the algorithm after it has been trained.

This notion of generalization is key to the science of machine learning. A learning system cannot simply commit to memory the configuration of pixels that make up a cat, because every new picture of a cat will present a different configuration of pixels, never seen before. The point is to develop some sort of *knowledge* about cats, and inevitably a successful machine learning system—one that can successfully generalize—has learned some kind of underlying principles that enable it to do this. Simply committing the pixel configurations to memory makes for a system that is excellent at recognizing things it has already seen and hopeless with anything new. This is trivial; because it has seen this data already, it could simply store it for later recall.

Successful machine learning has always required careful management to handle the fragile balancing act that is avoiding overfitting and learning something meaningful. For a long time, extensive image preprocessing had to be performed on images before they were fed into image classification networks, doing things like enhancing edges and increasing contrast, so that the burden on the network was lessened. Simplified classification task scenarios also significantly increase the chances of successful learning. A system can be trained to recognize the digits 0 through 9, either written by hand or spoken. If this system is deployed in a situation where we know that only digits will be in the input set (for example, a handwritten bank card number, where the numbers are written into boxes on a form, or during a phone call where a customer must speak the number aloud), then we can achieve a much higher performance, thanks to the constrained context.

Neural networks are just one kind of system used in classification, and classification is just one task that machine learning systems can be used to perform. Another common task is regression, where the system is expected to make a continuous-valued prediction, instead of a discrete, categorical distinction. For example, we may wish to find a system that, given a set of factors about a house such as its floor area, number of bedrooms, proximity to the city center, age, and so on will predict its sale price. Besides classification and regression there are other types of activity that machine learning systems can perform. One example is reinforcement learning, where the system must learn to do something not from a dataset of inputs and outputs but from positive or negative feedback (imagine that whenever an autonomous robot crashes into something it gets negative feedback, and whenever it gets nearer to its destination it gets positive feedback).

What Is a Neural Network? Neural networks are currently the dominant solution in many of the key application areas of machine learning. Neural networks (strictly speaking artificial neural networks or ANNs) are inspired by real biological neural systems. These take the form of arrangements of processing nodes connected by a matrix of weightings that are loosely inspired by the synapses in biological brains.[30] Neural networks are typically organized in discrete layers. Each layer can be thought of as a mathematical transformation that applies to a large matrix of data. A digital image, for example, can be fed into a neural network: the first layer of the network would have a node for each data point (for example, one node for each of the pixels) in the image, but successive layers might have different sizes. A typical neural network design is to have increasingly smaller layers in sequence. You could have a neural network that takes a large image as input, with thousands of nodes, and has a single node as output, indicating whether or not the image contains a cat. Such an output node in a classification network outputs an activation strength, so for example a classifier would have one output node for each thing it is trying to classify, each of which is activated ("hot") when the thing it classifies is detected.

It is worth noting that this may sound very processor intensive, compared to writing a few simple if-statements, and indeed it is. Today's best neural networks can require huge amounts of computing power to process rich audiovisual media or large quantities of natural language, involving very large numbers of floating point calculations. But such is the complexity of the task—human brains also have enormous computing resources to devote to audio and visual perception tasks. In both cases, the computation can be performed with an architecture consisting of very many simple processing units rather than one large central processing unit (CPU), hence there is a benefit to running neural networks on graphics processing units (GPUs), originally intended for the parallel computing demands of graphics in video processing and games applications.

In the twenty-first century, the power of neural networks took a leap forward with the development of a generation of networks known as deep learning networks. Deep learning networks are very large, with a large number of layers. They employ the same basic principles as earlier neural networks, but run on high-performance parallel computing architectures with massive datasets, and use a handful of tricks that address the problems of training large networks.[31] Improved performance means that we are now able to perform classification tasks successfully on raw data, such as image pixel data or audio waveforms, without hardwired preprocessing stages. In image processing, where edge detection has been performed previously by hardwired preprocessing, we can now identify stages in the network where the edge detection task has been learned. These networks can also be examined to reveal some of the learning that has taken place. A cat-detecting network has layers that reveal different visual archetypes representing the concept of a cat.

Another part of the puzzle of deep learning architectures is to find network configurations that are suited to learning in a given domain, ensuring that the network architecture is constrained enough that the learning algorithm can operate effectively. Very deep networks suffer from the problem that it becomes increasingly difficult, to the point of being impossible, to assign credit or blame to network weights and thus adjust the network. However, large, multilayered networks can be made that have significantly constrained architectures. An example is the convolutional neural network (CNN), a type of network that is very effective at image processing tasks. CNNs take inspiration from real animal visual cortical neurons, which focus on narrow *receptive fields* of the image, rather than the entire image. Unlike a more generic network architecture, this architecture has many repeated components and a much smaller number of network connections, making learning (knowing which weights to adjust by how much) more tractable.

Embedding Spaces An important idea in machine learning is that of dimensionality reduction—that we can reduce an information rich data source to a smaller space of parameters or concepts that describe the source, an idea that is closely related in some way to the theory of conceptual spaces, as well as the information-based theories of curiosity, interestingness, and beauty discussed in chapter 4. Closely related to this notion of dimensionality reduction is the idea of an *embedding space*, also known as a latent space. An embedding space is a multidimensional space that represents conceptual knowledge about the data, which can offer us an insight into the underlying logic of the space. Embedding spaces can also provide a way to manipulate the output of generative networks, with fascinating potential for computational creativity.[32]

One celebrated example of a system learning apparently sophisticated underlying concepts is the *Word2Vec* system. As the name suggests, this is a mapping from words from natural language to a very high dimensional continuous vector space, such that each word is represented by a vector in that vector space. Once trained, the model can perform operations on words as if they were simple geometric vectors. A vector is a line representing a path between two points in a space, and adding two vectors together means composing a new path, one vector followed by the other. In the vector space of Word2Vec, you can start to do simple arithmetic on the vectors attached to the words in that space, and it turns out that this arithmetic corresponds to some extent to the underlying conceptual logic (or arithmetic) of the language. In a widely used example, if you take the vector for "king," subtract the vector for "man" and then add the vector for "woman," you end up with the vector for "queen."

How does this work? The Word2Vec system is trained based on context. A word is fed into the system along with some number of contextual words: those words found immediately before or after the target word in a block of naturally occurring text. (Such data is plentiful, it is everywhere on the Internet, and it doesn't need to be prepared very carefully for ingestion by the system, so this really is a very friendly learning context when it comes to working with big data.) Now imagine that the system encounters blocks of text such as "the king was a happy man who ruled the land" or "the queen was a happy woman who ruled the land" and many more like this. Such examples provide the necessary context to infer that king and queen are equivalent entities (associated with ruling), but that they also have systematic, consistent differences (king goes with man and queen goes with woman). Similar results have been obtained with other kinds of ontological relationships, such as that between capital cities and countries (*Paris* is to *France* as *Canberra* is to *Australia*). While such a system has therefore acquired some kind of conceptual knowledge, note here that unlike a classifier, this system is not trained on target associations (it is an unsupervised rather than a supervised learning system), only on the context in which words appear. It also does not have a concept of error minimization in the way that classifiers and regression algorithms have; it simply finds patterns in the source data.

The embedding space here can be used in reverse to generate logical and meaningful outputs. Subtract *France* from *Paris* and add *Australia* and if all goes well the word you find at that point in the embedding space will be *Canberra*. Thus, sentences that are not only grammatically but also logically and factually correct can be automatically constructed, seeded with specific bits of content. Here we get a glimpse of the generative power of learning systems. Such embedding spaces, as mentioned, also suggest a bridge to conceptual spaces theory, introduced in chapter 2. One of Gärdenfors's key objectives in the development of conceptual space theory is to ground distinct concepts in continuous real-valued geometries, which is what embedding spaces do very well.[33]

Ian Simon and colleagues[34] demonstrate with a music generation system how latent spaces provide a form of interface to control neural network generation and discuss the affordances of this interface. In their case, this includes the ability to interpolate between different sequences in a "semantically meaningful" way, since in theory there are novel points in the latent space that correspond to unheard-before sequences but still embody the logic of musical structure learned by the system, and the ability to apply specific transformations to sequences such as to increase note density or change the instrumentation, by following known meaningful dimensions in the latent space.

Autoencoders Things begin to get particularly interesting for the possibilities of generative systems when we consider this reversing of the dimensionality reduction process, enabling novel artifacts to be generated from low-dimensional embedding spaces which have been developed by training systems on real-world examples. An autoencoder is a type of neural network designed to learn to reproduce an artifact, typically an image, but doing so via a lower dimensional space. The network has a symmetrical structure of shrinking and then expanding layers, and the goal of the training is simply to reproduce the input data, which is nontrivial because of the dimensionality reduction. As the signal passes through the network, information is necessarily lost as the number of dimensions encoding the image is reduced. Thus a successfully trained autoencoder will take an image as input and output that same image. Once this has been achieved, we can probe the middle layer of the network and begin to play with what the network generates. Each of the original images in the training set is represented by a point in that embedding space. But we can now stimulate the network with new points in the embedding space and see what it generates. When done successfully, new points in the embedding space will generate novel outputs that nevertheless conform in some way to the "logic" of the artifact in question.

An example of this being used in a creative way is the work of Kunwar Singh and colleagues,[35] training an autoencoder on hand-drawn pencil sketches and then developing a co-creative system in which new input sketches are varied as they pass through the embedding space, to produce related results. Autoencoders have also been successful in sound and music applications. The WaveNet system,[36] considered a major breakthrough in neural network approaches to speech synthesis, was trained on raw audio data, but this time being trained to predict the next point in the waveform. As well as the raw audio data, the training also included the encoded text of the words being spoken. The autoencoder was able then to concatenate together new sentences in response to input text (the network feeds back on itself; as it generates new audio it feeds that audio signal back into its input in order to make its next sample prediction). The WaveNet concept was then also applied to piano music, resulting in coherent-sounding concatenations of generated piano sequences. The results sound impressive, but readers may wish to go to the examples[37] and consider what the network is actually modeling. The sequences are musically coherent at a certain level, but over longer timescales are rambling, sounding like a patchwork of concatenated segments.

WaveNet has been used in other Google creative projects, most notably by the Magenta lab,[38] who created a synthesizer that models a training set of other synthesizers, in a similar way to the text-to-speech synthesis example. This enables the creation of new synthesis sounds by exploring the embedding space.

We can see here that unlike simple classifiers and rule-based systems, these examples involve systems that present a more unorthodox convolution of generators and evaluators. Autoencoders can both perceive and generate artifacts, and offer very interesting possibilities for tightly integrated creative processes. This is taken further in the case of generative adversarial networks.

Generative Adversarial Networks (GANs) Just as humans experience optical illusions and misunderstanding, so too even the best machine learning systems make mistakes in their own ways. Even if a classifier performs well, it can be easy to find examples that trick it. This, it turns out, points to a clever way of producing systems that successfully generate novel artifacts that are *typical* of a certain dataset. In *adversarial* approaches, a generative system is coupled with a classifier system. The generative system is given the goal of tricking a classifier into thinking that the outputs it produces are real (the real stuff is stuff it has been shown from a dataset of gathered, non-generated artifacts). The classifier simply has to output a binary decision: does the object it is looking at come from the training set of *real* objects, or is it from the set of outputs generated by the generative network. Meanwhile, the generative network's job is to generate outputs that the classifier mistakenly classifies as real. The classifier is trained on the real data, which it must correctly classify as real, and in addition both the classifier and the generator are trained in tandem, as new outputs from the generator are fed into the classifier. Whenever the classifier outputs a decision, its weights are updated to reduce the error in the decision. Meanwhile, for all stimuli created by the generator, the generator's weights are updated to *increase* the error in the classifier's decision.

This has proven to be very effective at producing original, realistic images, which have sophisticated structure. In one example the system generates numerous original images of what seem to be bedrooms. Each is actually generated by a GAN that has been trained on bedroom images.[39] Alec Radford, Luke Metz and Soumith Chintala also showed in this work that they could identify parameters in the embedding space of their GANs corresponding to specific concepts such as windows.[40] In one compelling demonstration, they show that they can manipulate image generation by smoothly transitioning through a series of different bedroom images, all of which are basically coherent but with a TV gradually transitioning into a window. They could also therefore choose to generate images with specific features (windows or no windows, for example). Jun-Yan Zhu and colleagues[41] provide equally impressive results with images of clothing, bags, and landscapes.

The success of GANs is in some ways surprising and also enlightening. Remember that no *extra* data is provided to the system beyond the original training set, yet GANs are able to *extend* the conceptual space of the training set, in this case producing images that have the coherence of real bedrooms. More clearly than autoencoders, GANs consist of both generative and evaluative components interacting together. In this case, the iteration of new generated images might be considered to resemble some sort of imaginative or ideation process, getting closer to the type of thought that takes place in freeform imagination.

Sequential Learning Most of the examples discussed so far have been image focused, and this has indeed been where a lot of the success in creative applications has taken place. Images are generally treated as instantaneous stimuli (although they are not as far as human perception is concerned; the eye travels around the image). For time-based domains such as music and language we encounter sequential learning, where the system's goal is to predict the next element in a sequence, say of words in language or notes in a piece of music. To do this the network takes as its input one or more of the previous elements in the sequence, and as its target, the next element in the sequence. A Markov model does this simply by building a table of probabilities: given a certain sequence of events, what is the probability of each possible next element in the sequence? A slightly more sophisticated variant called a hidden Markov model makes the additional assumption that there is a hidden process underlying the observed events, and attempts to model *that* process. For example, the number of people coming out of a train station exit (thing you are observing and trying to predict) will be highly dependent on the arrival of trains at the station (hidden process that strongly dictates the observed process).

Recurrent Networks The neural networks described above are called feedforward networks: an input is fed forward through the layers of the network, and the resulting error is then propagated back through the network to adjust the weights to improve the network performance. Other neural network architectures introduce feedback into the system. *Recurrent* neural networks (RNNs) are used to learn patterns in sequences and to model temporal processes. Modeling sequences usually reduces the problem to predicting a plausible next event given the most recent previous events—given the last N elements in the sequence, predict the next element (this is the same task performed by Markov models). Variations of the backpropagation algorithm exist for training recurrent neural networks, propagating the error assignment backward over time.

In RNNs, unlike Markov models, the learned structures are not probabilities but instead *activation* strengths (which relate to prediction confidence) for the predicted next value, given the input sequences. A recurrent neural network architecture called the long short-term memory (LSTM) network deals specifically with relations between elements separated by long time lags, and so is well suited to music, where long-term structure is an important component. LSTMs, for example, are very good at dealing with underlying structural principles in music. Most music is arranged according to an underlying metrical structure (bars divided into beats divided into sub-beat intervals) and also has phrase structure (which may have a complex relationship to metrical structure). Many sequential learning systems are not excellent at maintaining metrical structure naturally and need that to be explicitly defined.

These types of system are naturally generators: if you have a system that predicts the next event in a sequence then you have a system that can generate potentially original sequences. Once again these follow a structure-and-generate paradigm, with structuring taking place through the sequential learning process.

Other Network Architectures Myriad other types of neural networks exist based on different learning strategies. Continuous-time recurrent neural networks (CTRNNs) are fully connected networks, meaning that rather than being arranged in layers, every node has a connection into every other node. Nodes in CTRNNs maintain an activation state over time, meaning that the network has a form of memory. Such networks are commonly used to model locomotive and simple navigation behaviors in robotics. There is no training algorithm that works well for such fully connected networks. Instead artificial evolution (discussed below) is used to discover suitable weights and node parameters in a trial-and-error manner. Echo-state networks are recurrent networks like CTRNNs that serve a simple purpose of creating complex resonances in response to simple stimuli. These networks are not actually trained but can be systematically generated with known dynamic properties. They are usually coupled with a machine learning system that is trained on their output. The NeuroEvolution of Augmenting Topologies (NEAT) algorithm is an approach to evolving networks using a spatial model for how nodes are located and connected, resulting in original architectures that do not necessarily conform to standard models (more about neuroevolution later).

Other network architectures include self-organizing maps and other kinds of *unsupervised* learning algorithms that do not learn specific target outputs but instead discover how the input data is organized, simply through exposure to the data. These can be very useful as an automatic preprocessing stage which learns the structure of the dataset. Self-organizing maps, for example, have been used to model the learning of phonemes in early language acquisition.[42] When we learn our first language, one of the things we need to do is to learn to distinguish between the phonemes, the smallest atoms of the spoken language, that are combined to make words. Computationally, simple exposure to spoken language, without an explicit reward feedback (the "supervised" part of supervised learning) is sufficient to explain how an individual learns to perceptually group phonemes. It is only necessary that the phonemes we hear in everyday speech are sufficiently clustered for this learning to take place.

Style Transfer and Cross-Domain Synthesis Two other general techniques are briefly mentioned here because of their recent success and novel application of generative algorithms, although they are not exclusively associated with machine learning. Style transfer refers to the process of learning the style inherent in a certain dataset and then applying it to novel structures. In a typical scenario, in the painting domain, a photo is adapted so that it appears to have been painted in a distinct painting style such as that of Vincent van Gogh or Edvard Munch. This can be achieved using deep learning networks that learn the low-level properties of the style—how brush strokes look and how the lines of an image might be redrawn as expressive brush strokes—and are then able to apply this style to the content of the source image. In essence, in the visual domain, the goal is to preserve the low-level properties of the style, and the high-level properties of the source image.[43] It is of course not quite so simple to establish what the difference is between style and content in images, so many different mathematical interpretations might pertain with different resulting effects. A striking example of this is the mash-up of dinosaur drawings and plant drawings by Chris Rodley (figure 5.3). There is no obvious sense in which the *style* of one image has been transposed onto the *content* of another. Instead, the source images are merged in such a way that groups of plants are arranged into the shapes of dinosaurs. Style transfer is being developed in music and visual art at various levels. In music, it has a long history in the domains of harmonization and arrangement, applied, for example, to lead sheets. Pachet and Roy[44] look at specific jazz harmonization strategies based on real artists to create an automated system that can harmonize in different styles.

In another visual art example, Eric Chu proposes an "Artistic Influence GAN" or AIGAN,[45] in which the generator of a network trained on a specific style takes as input an additional vector representing influencers, thus producing outputs purporting to be Artist A influenced by Artist B: "What if Banksy had met Jackson Pollock during his formative years, or if David Hockney had missed out on the Tate Gallery's famous 1960 Picasso exhibition? How would their subsequent art differ?"

Jean-Pierre Briot and François Pachet[46] review methods of musical style transfer in musical domains, noting that much of the work in this area focuses on more explicit forms of "structure imposition," where specific structural qualities are applied from one piece to the "musical texture" of another piece. This includes using the longer-term structure of a piece, as determined by the piece's self-similarity (a measure of how similar sections of the piece are to other sections of the same piece).

Cross-domain synthesis deals with situations in which content in one domain is used to generate content in another domain, such as generating

Figure 5.3
A visual relative of style transfer: high-level structures (dinosaurs) are filled out with low-level structures (plants). Image credit: Chris Rodley.

text from images. This can be done using supervised learning. For example, a similar approach to an autoencoder can be used, this time with the stimulus matched with the expected output. One of the more obvious and common areas of application of this is between text descriptions and media. Machine learning systems have long demonstrated success in generating text descriptions from images, but more recently, GANs have been used to generate images from text descriptions. In this case the generator learns a mapping from a description to an image, and the discriminator learns to discriminate between real and generated images, given the text description.[47]

Closely related to such text-to-content generation is the idea of generating content that satisfies specific aesthetic or psychological criteria, such as to make happy or sad music. This can be done in a wide variety of ways (for example, Monteith, Martinez, and Ventura use Markov models.)[48] Alternatively, we might want to create sensible combinations of elements, such as animated images that go with a piece of music or vice versa.

The Creative Capacity of Machine Learning Systems Big data and deep learning have opened up impressive new avenues for the automated generation of content. Large datasets of written language, speech, music, images, and so on can be fed into these systems to train them on specific styles. In music, you might use one of the many research datasets, such as the Luxembourg folksong database, stored in machine-readable MIDI[49] form, commonly used by researchers for experimental purposes. Note that usually the dataset simply dictates what is typical of a given art form, rather than necessarily what is good or bad. We train machine learning systems on Bach or Picasso with the expectation of making things that sound or look like Bach or Picasso. Thus it is perhaps easy to dismiss such systems as merely concerned with imitation and fakery.

What kind of creative potential do we expect machine learning systems to have? Given their strict grounding in a set of training data, systems that can perform tasks such as sequential learning, while impressive in their capability to capture principles of style, would seem unlikely to produce something original, by definition, or to pass the Lovelace test, since the results of the generative process could always be explained with appeal to the dataset and the algorithm's design. Yet they may be perfectly useful at generating outputs typical of some style.

Like a process that only produced random outputs, machine learning systems certainly have the potential, by sheer fluke, to produce a novel output that is engaging and clearly departs from the style of the training corpus. But this is not a given and certainly not something to be relied upon. The groundedness of machine learning in an existing dataset suggests that these systems have limited potential to diverge, because they cannot escape the limited set of data they have experienced. They are mimickers, creators of derivative work.

Compared to the set of evolutionary algorithms we will consider in the next section, which express their creative capacity through a generate-and-test process, performing exploratory search, it may be true that machine learning does not lend itself so readily to the view of creativity defined throughout this book. Most highly successful machine learning results are in narrow domains where teams of engineers revise systems in order to make incremental improvements, so the ability for systems to generalize and learn in novel situations is limited. Sturm, as we saw in chapter 1, likens the potential misrepresentation of the capacity of machine learning-based systems to a trick horse, Clever Hans, who seems to know how to do arithmetic but is actually simply responding to some simpler stimulus from its trainer[50] (we will touch on this issue of evaluation in more detail in chapter 7).

However, while it may be right to point out overzealous attributions of creative autonomy, these arguments remain far from entirely undermining the creative value of such methods. Simply because a system has been trained on a specific corpus of work and has no other input knowledge about the world does not in itself rule out the possibility of the system generating significantly novel and valuable or interesting outcomes. If a system has indeed learned something about the structure of the content in the training set—that is, learned concepts of some form—then it could in theory generate outputs that express those concepts in novel but well-formed ways. Anecdotally, Pierre Barreau describes how the Aiva system was trained on a classical music corpus but generated something that sounded like traditional *Irish* music. There was no traditional Irish music in the training data, so this may sound like nothing more than a surprising coincidence, but in fact it makes good sense that the knowledge contained in a corpus of classical music is sufficient to generate traditional Irish pieces. Any two musical styles are likely to share some common rules; we might systematically get from one style to another, and hence perhaps even innovate novel, nontrivial, coherent musical styles. This is a tenuous claim but not entirely out of the question.

We can do more to encourage this kind of extrapolation, where a system learns not only a new style but the relations between styles and can therefore apply understanding in one area to another area. General principles of Western music apply to a large number of styles, and diverse musical styles appear to have common compositional principles at a suitable level of abstraction (recall from chapter 4 the case of Balzano's group theoretic work, and abstract concepts from the psychology of aesthetics such as the peak-shift principle). A system can be systematically trained on a broad dataset of examples and then on a very specific dataset of an individual style, and plausibly be expected to extrapolate from that style to other styles.

In the preceding discussion we have seen some other approaches to generating novel outputs using such systems. We might manipulate the structure of a trained network (for instance, mutate its network weights),[51] explore the system's embedding spaces, feed the system back on itself,[52] or creatively curate training datasets to produce specific network behaviors, such as combining extreme isolated styles. In essence, though, all of the examples of structure-and-generate systems we have seen above, whether trained or hand-coded, need to be operated by a controller (or other algorithmic system) who might perform evaluation and make high-level decisions about how the generating system behaves.

On the other hand, systems such as autoencoders and GANs seem to be a little different given that they can be seen as combining evaluation *and* generation components, arranged in different configurations, and the generation components can be steered to be more or less convergent or divergent via the generation goals that are set them. GANs in particular are evocative of a more open-ended imaginative process where novel outputs might be generated. Consider the possible relationship between the GAN's architecture and the peak shift principle—for example, a generator that is constantly seeking to "stimulate" an evaluator, which in turn is constantly becoming "bored." This can drive novelty in systematic, structured ways. Ahmed Elgammal and colleagues[53] propose a modified version of a GAN, called a CAN (creative adversarial network), that attempts to increase the arousal potential (a concept discussed in chapter 4) of generated images, driving the network to generate images explicitly *outside* of the training

Creative Algorithms

set while (in principle) maintaining the coherence of images, as in the previous GAN examples. More generally, the imposition of various kinds of constraints on a generation process can steer it away from mere regurgitation of typical styles found in the system's training data. Briot and Pachet[54] discuss a method for steering a Markovian music generation process away from regurgitation by applying constraints on the reproduction of existing sequences but not so far as to output "junk." Although being nowhere near exhibiting the properties of socially grounded human agents with culturally embedded goals, such divergent generation processes may nevertheless arrive at similar places to a generatively creative cultural process.

But even where they clearly do not perform exploratory search in any way, I would claim that it is important to see such generative techniques as valuable and relevant to computational creativity. The distributed view of creativity that I have developed over the previous chapters highlights the potential for certain systems to play important creative roles despite their

Figure 5.4
Example of images generated by Elgammal's Creative Adversarial Network (CAN). These are the images ranked highest (most liked) by human subjects.

incompleteness as fully independent creative systems. In cases like style transfer and content-aware completion tools, we have seen how new techniques are opening up that support individual creativity simply by speeding up and broadening their creative practice, allowing a more rapid and wider reaching search through a space of possibilities. We should therefore see these systems as forming part of the infrastructure that helps pave the way toward powerful computational creativity, despite their limited use value at present.

The creation of an infrastructure for automating creative tasks allows for accelerating returns. As such systems become increasingly used by people, they provide new contexts in which additional computational creativity techniques can be applied. Good classification systems will mean that we can automatically test generative content to see if it suits a certain style or has specific properties. A system that generates output from sequences of keywords can be coupled with another system that creatively generates the keywords. In this case the generator may not be creative per se, but it plays an essential and powerful role in a holistic creative process. As in brainstorming, where one of the goals is to suppress judgment, there is a place for raw, unmediated generation, stimulating ideas.

Also, such systems have started to demonstrate the potential for scalability and the creation of rich modular architectures. Their scalability means that we could in principle build machine learning–based generative systems that have been trained on extraordinary amounts of data, while achieving high accuracy. Before long a system learning style preference could be trained on a person's life experience, building a very detailed model of that person's taste. Their potential to be built into rich modular architectures means that we can start to treat them as the building blocks for functional creative systems. There is nothing to say that given, say, an architecture such as the IDyOT model proposed by Wiggins, such systems wouldn't generate powerful new "ideas." Or two such systems, trained on two different people and interpolating between them, might result in surprising style blends.

Evolving and Searching

Another way a system can obtain knowledge is by discovering it through search, the core theme developed throughout chapters 2 and 3. Evolutionary computing systems and other forms of search and optimization algorithms—a class of algorithms known technically as *metaheuristic search methods*—have the potential to do this and are now widely used in computer science. A compelling example is the design of a new antenna by researchers at NASA in 2006 that used a genetic algorithm to search a space of possible antenna designs,[55] testing each candidate design to understand how well it would perform at its task. The design that resulted from this automated search outperformed any known human design and resembled nothing a human engineer would have thought to build. Indeed the researchers were not immediately able to explain why the winning design performed well, without further investigation, suggesting that this system would seem to have passed some form of the Lovelace test.

This illustrates a key departure from the kinds of algorithm presented so far. In most learning systems, the primary goal of the system is to reproduce some behavior or knowledge captured in a training set. In rule-based systems, this knowledge is explicitly encoded. We expect the system's behavior to resemble or reflect information in the training set in the case of learning systems, or in the case of rule-based systems, simply to encode the rules written into it. In search-based approaches, there is typically no training set; the goal is known but the means of achieving it is not, and may even have no precedent in the natural world. This is the distinction between structure-and-generate approaches and generate-and-test approaches. Search methods by necessity involve both generators (even if they are incredibly simple) and evaluators (even if these might be performing less obvious evaluation tasks, as is the case with the novelty search algorithms I describe below).

In another significant example, in a more artistic vein, Karl Sims's pioneering 1990s work on evolved virtual creatures used genetic algorithms to produce animated virtual creatures that could move about in 3D worlds with basic simulated physics.[56] The resulting creatures' behaviors clearly resembled natural biological organisms. The system could not be said to have brought new knowledge into the world, because we already know about animal locomotion, but it did work out a number of existing locomotion strategies for itself, mimicking natural evolution. It is interesting to consider that Sims's virtual creatures do not pass the Lovelace test for this reason, even though the system is perhaps just as creatively powerful as the evolved antenna.[57]

In an entertaining survey, a large group of experts in creative applications of evolutionary computing discuss a number of known cases where evolution has produced other surprising results. Sometimes these innovations are undesirable but are nevertheless original solutions to a problem.

For example, when evolving creature locomotion in a virtual environment, one study resulted in the creatures learning to exploit the physics engine: "A large time step enabled the creatures to penetrate unrealistically through the ground plane, engaging the collision detection system to create a repelling force, resulting in vibrations that propel the organism across the ground."[58]

In brief, a genetic algorithm (GA) imitates key elements of Darwin's theory of evolution by natural selection. Candidate designs are encoded in some suitable computational representation, known as the genotype, just as biological organisms have genotypes in the form of DNA that are a sort of blueprint for the organism's form and behavior. These genotypes get turned into phenotypes—the actual entity being evaluated (in biology this is the organism itself). A virtual plant might be represented as a series of instructions stating how the plant's stems should branch, what its leaves look like, and so on. The discussion of parametric systems above includes many such examples.

These genetic representations can be mutated, causing variations in the form of the phenotype. They can also typically be crossed over (*recombined*) with other genotypes, just as the genes of biological organisms are combined in sexual reproduction. Finally, and most importantly, a process of selection is applied to a population of candidate genotypes. The phenotypes are evaluated in some way—for example, organisms that can run faster might be considered better ("fitter" in the language of evolutionary biology) than slower organisms. In nature, whichever organisms are better at surviving and reproducing are *naturally selected*; the specific criteria emerge from the set of complex interactions between organism and environment. In genetic algorithms, typically, the programmer or an end-user dictates what constitutes a fitter organism with some kind of fitness test. Iterating this process of selection, as Darwin showed, can have dramatic results: minor, gradual improvements in the short term, radical, creative transformations over longer timescales.

In both examples above, the fitness of candidate genotypes has been encoded as a function (the fitness function) in the genetic algorithm. These are examples of the most common form of artificial evolution, target-based evolution, where an objective goal for the system can be defined and programmed into a comprehensive test for the thing being evolved. In the case of Sims's virtual walking creatures, the test is simply the furthest distance that the creature reaches from its start point in a given amount of time. Since creatures can't teleport and must get from A to B within the constraints of the defined physical environment, they must learn some kind of locomotion strategy.[59]

This artificial evolution has been applied in many ways to different creative tasks. Wiggins and colleagues[60] evolved harmonizations in music using handwritten rule-based selection criteria based on music theory. In their approach, a ranking is generated for each candidate based on a series of explicitly coded criteria derived from common music theory, such as a preference for progression toward the tonic and avoidance of doubling of certain notes. The hope is to find novel, appropriate, and pleasing harmonizations: novel because although we know the criteria for success we don't know what the GA will come up with to satisfy those criteria; appropriate because if successful, the GA will find solutions that satisfy the rules; and pleasing if those rules turn out to be a good description of the music we want to hear. The latter is particularly challenging. It is common to find reasonably good rule sets but nevertheless to find that there are many high-scoring candidates that do not sound good and low-scoring candidates that do. Since music theoretic rules are being used as the selection criteria it is worth noting the difference here with a rule-based approach. In the search-based approach, the system seeks outputs that satisfy the rules. In a rule-based approach, the rules are used to directly generate the outcomes. For example, one could simple choose the next note or chord in a sequence by applying a set of rules either strictly or in terms of the probability of something happening. It is not obvious that one approach is better than the other, and one should never simply assume that a generate-and-test approach is always creatively superior to a structure-and-generate approach. But it should be clear that the two approaches will have different properties.

The success of an evolutionary approach depends a lot on how you go about representing the thing that is being evolved in its genotype form. This needs to support the evolutionary process making minor mutations and recombining different designs in an incremental search for better designs. In the virtual creatures example, each creature consists of a body morphology—a list of various body segments of different shapes and sizes, connected together in a way that is also encoded in the genotype—and some dynamic properties such as oscillatory movement generators. As in our discussion of rule-based systems, such a genotype representation will define an infinite space of possible creatures, but also a constrained one in which certain morphologies are possible and others are not. With a variable-length representation, as in nature, the creature might consist of any number of components (a "mutation" of a genotype might include the addition of a new body segment). Different types of modular representations can also be used that would encourage symmetry and self-similarity. For example, our bodies consist of repeated patterns, such as the common structure of our limbs. These various elements can then be encoded into a linear string just like our DNA, the elements of which can have different states.

Ideally, the evolutionary algorithm can find a smooth and gradual path through genotype space toward fitter and fitter solutions. As long as, once in a while, new random variations result by chance in individuals that are fitter, the evolutionary process gradually works its way toward the best solutions. A common problem, however, is that the process *converges* on a solution that is not the best overall but is better than all of the nearby solutions in the genotype space. This is called a local optimum, and convergence is a term describing the algorithm homing in on what it determines to be the best solution. Because it is the fittest solution in a local region of the search space, an evolutionary algorithm might get locked into it, and thus might fail to incrementally find its way to other parts of the search space where better solutions might exist. This is one of the central problems of evolutionary optimization. One strategy for solving it is to find algorithms that are better at widely exploring the space without getting stuck in these evolutionary dead-ends. For example, a class of algorithms called particle swarm optimizers introduce momentum and memory to the process, so as to better map the space and not get stuck. Another strategy is to find good genetic representations which produce *smooth* spaces without too many local optima. This depends on many factors and is a complex subject, but suffice it to say that some genetic representations are smoother and less bumpy than others. A "fitness landscape" can be smooth like Mount Fuji, with a single peak—wherever you stand there is a clear path to the top, and even on a misty day you know which way to go—or jagged like the Manhattan skyline, with myriad sharp spikes and sudden jumps in fitness.

A more general problem for evolutionary search methods is being able to come up with clear fitness criteria. Many researchers interested in evolving aesthetic artifacts have wondered if simple aesthetic criteria can be captured in algorithms so that artifacts can be evolved that exhibit aesthetically pleasing properties on request. Unsurprisingly this has proven elusive, although partially satisfying solutions have been found. If we refer back to the discussion throughout chapter 4 about the many factors that underlie aesthetic appreciation, we can begin to imagine how aesthetic considerations might be encoded into an aesthetic fitness function. Given the individual and cultural specificity, and the multiple meanings and dimensions that might influence aesthetic appreciation, an exhaustive or accurate model of a person's aesthetic appreciation would seem to have remote potential. There is no fitness function for beauty.

Nevertheless, just as generative neural networks are not accurate models of human creative processes, yet have clear creative potential in the hands of users, naive approaches to target-based aesthetic evolution may still be useful and effective for a number of reasons. We may define naive aesthetic criteria as features that are grounded in some notion of formal aesthetics but that we acknowledge to be incomplete or incapable of accurately describing aesthetic experience. Brian Ross, William Ralph, and Hai Zong[61] used features such as color histograms derived from popular artworks as a fitness target for the generation of new textures that were "harmonious and easy-on-the-eyes." Likewise, in the example of using musical rules above,[62] the rules are clearly insufficient to discriminate good from bad music, yet nevertheless constrain the search space in a way that may be useful. In this target-based, aesthetically evaluated paradigm, we may not be able to say that the fitness function used is sufficient to create outputs that are consistently novel and aesthetically appealing. Rather, they structure the space of possible outcomes in a way that may be of creative value. In Wiggins et al.'s case, the rules constrain the space to pieces of music that conform to certain stylistic requirements, and yet the evolutionary search has the potential to come up with diverse or even surprising (and possibly nasty) results within this rules space. This may be sufficient as a way of batch-generating music that consistently achieves a desired standard, or as an idea generator that does not always produce pleasing outcomes but that does so often enough that the user can easily scan the output for new ideas. Note the potential payoff here: stricter rules might guarantee more consistent results but at the expense of diversity and surprise. It can also be used as more of an intellectual exercise, seeing the how algorithm might fail, exploit the rule set in novel ways, or fixate on certain structures.

Matching Target Artifacts In Ross, Ralph, and Zong's case,[63] the user can potentially choose a source artifact they want to generate something to resemble. Why, though, would someone want to simply match a specific target artifact? Is there any value in a search-based approach if the outcome is a specific target that we already know and have access to? We see a number of target-based evolutionary systems that do aim to match a source artifact in some way, that explore different creative objectives. One benefit that has been investigated in detail is that we can find new encodings for representing that artifact, which can then be affected in some way. A number of people have used evolution to evolve audio synthesis algorithms to match target sounds. Matt Yee-King[64] searched the space of possible FM synthesis parameters to match target sounds. Once the target sound has been matched, the user has a MIDI synthesizer, and multiple controllable parameters with which they can play back that sound and manipulate it. One potential use here is to morph between different sounds using smooth synthesis parameter variation. Similarly, Roger Johansson showed that it was possible to reproduce images to a high degree of accuracy using only a small number of simple polygons. A mere fifty polygons, each with ten vertices and a single ARGB color, could be arranged to produce a highly accurate representation of the Mona Lisa. Lower numbers of polygons make for interesting distortions. Such approaches could be used to make collages from source materials. The artist Petros Vrellis used a related approach to produce a reproduction of an image by weaving a single line of thread around a circular series of hooks.[65] Like style transfer techniques, this provides a way to reconfigure the representation of a given piece of content. The outcome is the product of the target image and the constraints of the process used to create it. Note in the final case, it is hard to think of a non-search-based way to generate this outcome. The way the threads merge to create areas of light and dark in the image would be hard to systematically discover.

Multiobjective Search Evolutionary search aimed at reproducing an existing artifact has limited application, but as we have seen, it can be hard to write more general-purpose fitness functions that successfully stimulate an evolutionary algorithm to generate both desirable and novel outcomes. This approach also lacks potential for control or interaction by the user. A fruitful alternative has been to take a multiobjective approach,[66] where

Figure 5.5
Petros Vrellis's work *Christ Savior by El Greco (as string-art)*. The work is created using a relatively simple optimization algorithm that attempts to approximate a source image using the intersection of straight lines, then rendered using threads wound across pegs. Image credit: Petros Vrellis.

numerous criteria are encoded in fitness functions that then form part of a multiobjective search. For example, in architecture, we can define several desirable properties of a building which can easily be modeled and measured in a 3D simulation of the building, such as sunlight exposure, travel time between rooms, sightlines, insulation efficiency, and airflow. It is very likely that these criteria will conflict; the most well-insulated building is unlikely to have the largest windows. In that case, we can perform multiobjective search to take into account all of the criteria at once. This results in not one solution but an entire space of solutions, each of which is as good as it can be for some combination of criteria. What this means is that for each of these solutions, there is no *other* known solution that is better in *all* criteria. These solutions are therefore known as nondominated solutions. For example, one building design might have the most light of all discovered designs, while another has the best insulation of all discovered designs. These would both be valid candidates. Meanwhile, a third design might have better insulation than the light-maximizing design and better light than the insulation-maximizing design. This design is not best at anything, but equally, it is not dominated by either of the alternatives (other designs out there *will* be dominated if they have mediocre light and insulation). It may turn out to be a winning compromise (after all, we rarely want to maximize one feature at the expense of all of the other features in a given design task). This space of solutions is called a Pareto front or Pareto set, named after the Italian economist Vilfredo Pareto, who pioneered the idea of this optimal set of nondominated solutions in an economic context.

Multiobjective evolution, resulting in a set of solutions, provides alternative forms of interactivity between users and evolved populations. Think of the resulting Pareto set as a reduction of the search space to a new space that might be easier to search manually or using some other, secondary process. This opens up more exploratory potential. It can even be used to create a two-stage search whereby the correct objectives are searched for as well as being used to search the space. The cost is that each of the multiple objectives might take a long time to compute, so the more objectives, the longer it takes the GA to run. Also, for multiple objectives, the Pareto front may be big and complex and require a very large population to span it properly. Throwing more and more objectives at an evolutionary search with the expectation of having more options may therefore backfire.

Novelty Search More recently, and of particular relevance to creativity, researchers have begun to explore evolutionary algorithms that search not for specific solutions but for diversity of solutions. These *novelty search* algorithms[67] aim to find new candidates in the phenotype space that are suitably different to all other candidates found so far. The result is a set of prototypes which, in theory, gives a good representation of the phenotypic diversity of the space. This is quite similar to multiobjective optimization in that it results in a set of options rather than a single optimum solution, except in novelty search there is no sense of good or bad whatsoever, only *different*.

As we saw in chapter 3, the argument has been made by the pioneers of novelty search, Joel Lehman and Ken Stanley, that in certain cases novelty search will actually outperform target-based search in clearly target-oriented tasks.[68] The reasoning follows quite clearly from the issues discussed above to do with evolutionary algorithms getting stuck in local optima, converging on a solution that appears to be optimal but is in fact a dead end. Likewise, the better performance also makes sense given the issues of creative "divergent" thinking and the value of blind search discussed in chapter 2. Lehman and Stanley consider a task in which a robot has to get through a maze as quickly as possible (see figure 3.1). The fitness of the robot is determined by the proximity of its final position, after a given time, to the maze exit. However, in a maze, you can be very close to the exit as the crow flies but very far away as far as following the maze is concerned (you can *know* the former—by analogy, you are "warmer," closer to a source of heat, without knowing the distance of the *actual path* to the exit). An optimization algorithm might get stuck with a result that seems fit (is warmer) but is not *actually* fit. Novelty search, on the other hand, just keeps exploring the maze, and if it is good at finding new undiscovered places, then it is increasingly likely to find the solution. Such an approach can be important for understanding radical creativity. For example, an optimization algorithm designing bridges might do very well at optimizing an arch bridge design but would never make the leap to discover a suspension bridge design given an arch bridge as its starting point. The space between these two designs would consist of many very poor-performing bridges, and so an optimization algorithm may not be able to make that leap. As we saw in chapter 3, Stanley and Lehman[69] develop this into a computational theory of creativity equivalent to the view of Simonton and others: creativity is inherently blind. They illustrate this with formal, anecdotal, and speculative examples. For example, they ask, if you go on a dating site, do you know precisely what kind of person you are looking for when you set out, or does it require an iterative search?

Variations and original applications of novelty search are now a popular area of research in computational creativity. Georgios Yannakakis and Antonios Liapis propose a variant, "surprise search,"[70] which does not just measure novelty but uses a cognitive model of surprise based on previous experience to determine when something new and sufficiently interesting has been found in the search space.

As with multiobjective search, novelty search can provide a very practical way of simplifying a vast search space in a way that makes evolutionary methods more usable for creative practitioners. In one application, Steffan Ianigro[71] has used novelty search to provide a simple way to reduce a vast number of neural-network generated synthesized sounds to a small set of timbral *prototypes* that can be quickly and systematically searched by way of audio descriptors that can be used to plot the sounds in a 2D space on-screen.

Interactive Evolution As the antenna and virtual creatures examples illustrate, evolutionary algorithms have powerful creative potential in that they discover things that may not have been known by the person who wrote the algorithm, a clear challenge to the Lovelace objection (although not necessarily a clear passing of the Lovelace test). But this assumes the careful design of a fitness function and a genetic representation. As with machine learning, this has led to impressive results with a team of engineers working through problems but so far has not lent itself to easy end-user creative outcomes.[72] Inevitably, users must interact with evolutionary algorithms, for example by iterating through different fitness functions or genetic representations in search of solutions that work according to their expert opinions.

The most extreme form of this, and arguably the most successful so far in computational creativity applications, is the interactive evolutionary algorithm. Here there is no fitness function, only one or more human users reviewing all of the evolutionary algorithm's mutated and recombined candidates and manually judging them. The issues of coming up with tools to analyze the outputs are removed; fitness functions are not needed (as with novelty search, but even in novelty search there is a need to decide which distance metric will be used to measure similarity). In its interactive form, the evolutionary algorithm is only half an evolutionary algorithm, which is complete only when coupled with a human user acting as evaluator.

Interactive evolutionary algorithms have been relatively successful as usable creative tools, and enjoyable interactive creative environments. In the accompanying software for the Nord Modular G2 synthesizer, made by Clavia, an interactive evolutionary algorithm, MutaSynth,[73] was provided so that users could search the space of possible synthesizer configurations through interactive evolution rather than by manually designing or tweaking synths. Any given synth architecture (modular synths, as the name suggests, consist of small signal generating or processing components that can be reconfigured into different synth architectures) will have a list of parameters (the settings of the knobs, sliders, and switches) that can be used to define the synth's genotype, with the resulting sonic behavior of the synth being its phenotype. If you've used a complex synthesizer you'll be familiar with the process of tweaking knobs in an exploratory way; sometimes you may know exactly what effect a given knob will have, but sometimes the results are surprising. The evolutionary interface provides a way to explore the space of possible sounds in a different abstracted manner, gently tweaking multiple parameters at once. The MutaSynth interface provided a grid of mutants, represented graphically as abstract shapes (so that users could remember which grid element corresponded to which sound, even if the shapes had no interpretable meaning). The user could select, mutate, and breed different instances and create a pool of preferred sounds. Because the GA operated directly on the synth parameters, the user could also easily revert at any point to manual control. (This is not always the case in evolutionary systems—some generator algorithms, such as Ianigro's neural network generated synth sounds,[74] described above, are too complex for users to meaningfully manipulate directly.)

An interesting outcome from user studies of interactive genetic algorithms is that they are not used quite in the way that one might anticipate. One issue is that they just take a very long time to use; they are hardly a creative panacea, and user fatigue is a significant limiting factor. Evolution depends on very gradual mutations, each one iteratively tested, so this means a lot of work for the user (or for the fitness function). Solutions to this involve combining automated and interactive search. Woolley and Stanley[75] have looked at the combination of novelty search and interactive search, so that users are always being offered solutions that are suitably

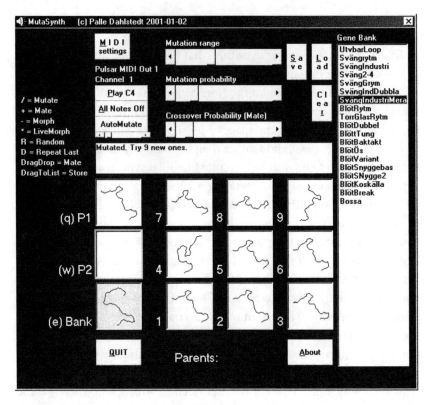

Figure 5.6
Palle Dahlstedt's MutaSynth program, which can be used to evolve the synthesizer sounds on a Nord Modular G2 synthesizer. Image credit: Palle Dahlstedt.

different from instances they've experienced before. Anikó Eckhart, Divya Sharma, and Stayko Chalakov[76] analyzed the results of interactive evolutionary sessions with users and then sought to find aesthetic measures corresponding to those users' preferences for further target-based evolution.

An alternative possible avenue is to develop interactive genetic algorithms that are distributed online among a population of users. If users have common evolutionary goals, then distributing the search process could lead to a greater hit rate for each individual user. Jimmy Secretan and colleagues' Picbreeder project[77] is a pioneering experiment in this area, with users able to evolve images as part of an open collaborative creative project. They can "fork" each other's images or start their own. Distributed evolutionary algorithms can even be passive, meaning that the users are not necessarily aware that they are engaged in evolutionary search. Since the user is only required to give some simple form of rating feedback, to rank the fitness of any given candidate, this can be done simply by asking for a rating, as many pieces of software already ask of us. Even more surreptitiously, the time we spend engaging with the candidate, or the number of downloads, or some other indirect quantity, might be enough to infer a user rating. Indeed, GAs are being used to optimize the design of websites and apps responding directly to user data given different minor alternatives. Online distributed projects such as DarwinTunes for music[78] and Electric Sheep for audiovisual screensavers[79] have employed this strategy in various ways.

Evolutionary algorithms have clear potential to be creative, coming up with completely original forms that may both be surprising and valuable. Several of the evolutionary models we have seen successfully embed one or other form of evaluation, which is combined with a form of exploratory search, meaning that in some ways this approach better corresponds to the properties of creative search examined in previous chapters. However, the existing work in evolutionary computational creativity only goes to illustrate how automating evaluation is not only a very difficult task but also a generally ill-defined one. As producers or consumers of creative artifacts we generally know what we like or what we want, but this does not mean we can easily encode those preferences or desires into meaningful and effective evaluation algorithms. Just like machine learning algorithms, evolutionary approaches offer certain affordances but need to be carefully managed and applied in a way that is fit for purpose to achieve effective results.

Hybrid Systems

It is natural that applied automated creativity systems would combine aspects from these different fields, since our analysis of creative practice in the previous chapters covers all of these bases: learning, concept formation and manipulation, and generate-and-test search for novel outcomes that satisfy given criteria. Human actors engage to some extent in all of these activities, and so can effective creative algorithms. Here, the distributed creativity view of creative processes can influence how we go about conceptualizing the design of such systems. Should they be unified agents, functionally holistic, reflecting an image of an independent human artist, or should they be modular, connectable, *porous* units that resemble societies of agents, or perhaps offer radically different aggregates that perform creative interaction? Since they are ultimately to be embedded in human webs of significance, each of several subcomponents in a hybrid computationally creative system might interact not only with the other parts of the system but act as an independent agent engaged in interactions both within and beyond the system boundaries. These are questions of algorithm design but also of interaction design. The following chapter is dedicated to discussing computational creativity interaction scenarios in depth and working through these problems.

Effective Algorithmic Combinations

Rule-based, learning, and evolutionary approaches describe three broad ways in which intelligence can be embedded into computational systems, with various forms of generative capability. It is also common for computationally creative systems to take the form of hybrid assemblages of these various approaches, which combine different algorithmic techniques to build more holistic creative systems. As an example, consider Joel Lehman, Sebastian Risi, and Jeff Clune's project[80] to evolve novel 3D object designs using novelty search. A deep learning network was trained to classify objects of various types, from a training set of 2D images. Then a 3D form-generating system was used to generate novel shapes, and these 3D images were fed into the network as 2D representations captured from various camera angles. For each form, the network produced a vector indicating the likeness of the form to the set of recognized objects. Then a type of novelty search algorithm that attempts to seek the most different elements within the search space was used to search for forms that best triggered the neural network's various object recognition responses. This is again an example that, on the surface, seems merely to generate forms that resemble those that already exist. But the neural network is in principle capable of generalizing forms in a given category, meaning that the generative system could produce something novel that still possessed the core properties of the object in question. As with other examples discussed above, this basic architecture could be used as a way to explore spaces of forms with given properties. This is one of several examples of using machine learning systems as fitness functions for an evolutionary process. In another example, Peter Mitrano and colleagues[81] used recurrent neural networks trained on a corpus of music as a fitness function for a music-generating program. In an alternative approach, Philip

Bontranger and colleagues[82] demonstrate using a GAN trained to generate images as a genotype-to-phenotype mapping for an interactive evolutionary process. The latent space of the GAN becomes the genotype space of the evolutionary search process.

Another significant area in which neural network and evolutionary approaches are combined is neuroevolution, where neural network architectures and parameters may be evolved rather than (or as well as) being trained by data-driven learning. This is a logical step in the simulation of living systems, which themselves have evolved cognitive architectures, and combine learning and evolution to result in remarkably powerful behaviors.[83] An example of a neuroevolution strategy is the evolution of the parameters of continuous-time recurrent neural networks (CTRNNs) (mentioned above in the case of Steffan Ianigro's work), which are also commonly used for designing robot navigation or movement strategies.[84] These networks have different rules than feed-forward neural networks, with each neuron performing temporal integration of its inputs over time. The networks are also not arranged in layers but are fully connected (every neuron is connected to every other neuron, including a connection back into itself). These factors mean that learning algorithms such as the backpropagation algorithm will not work for training these networks. But even if they did, the tasks that these networks are used to learn are not easily expressed through training data, but are more suited to the reinforcement learning paradigm, where the success of the network at the task is measured and used to seek improved strategies. In the case of CTRNNs, the network architecture is typically fixed, and the evolutionary algorithm simply searches the space of possible parameters, including connection weights and each neuron's temporal dynamics. Another strategy is the NeuroEvolution of Augmenting Topologies (NEAT) system developed by Ken Stanley and Risto Miikkulainen,[85] where the entire architecture of the network is defined by the evolutionary algorithm. This has been used in many creative applications including music, animated dancers, and art. An interesting feature of the NEAT approach is that networks start off simple and become more complex over time. The evolution of the network topology can include the addition or removal of nodes and connections (the evolution naturally tends toward addition of nodes as the networks get better).

Different hybrid approaches can combine evolution and learning: using neuroevolution, a neural network architecture can be evolved to improve learning performance, for example. However, in many cases the learning itself is an outcome of the evolutionary process applied to given problems, and there is no need to implement a separate learning stage. Sebastian Risi and Julian Togelius[86] point out some of the benefits of a neuroevolution approach in the context of games. Such an approach, they show, performs very well in reinforcement learning tasks, those tasks where there is no direct training data to improve performance, only positive or negative feedback. However, depending on the design of the test environment it can be applied to supervised and unsupervised learning tasks, so is broadly applicable. They also argue that methods such as multiobjective and novelty search make it more useful for creative tasks and add that it has more possibilities for open-ended and interactive contexts, such as games, where characters evolve over time.

Myriad other algorithmic combinations exist. We have already seen how constraints are sometimes applied to the generation process to steer output in music. In another musical example by Gabriele Medeot and colleagues,[87] a sequence generating neural network model is steered by another probabilistic model that favors music with richer structure. Here, more structured music is explicitly defined as music that has repeating forms, typically rhythmic or melodic-rhythmic sequences that are repeated but transposed within a scale. Such a model of structuredness could potentially be hand-coded but is in this case created with a second trained network. The structure constraint influences the generation process, and this creates potential competition between the two processes: "The structure network is able to suggest repeats of certain types, but if the melody network assigns very low probability to notes that would form these repeats, it is free to 'override' the structure network's suggestions in a probabilistic and flexible manner."[88] This lends itself to interesting music that doesn't slavishly follow the structuring rule but is also more structured than much music generated by neural networks.

Hybrids Found in Creative Practice
More generally, creative generative artists hand-coding art-making systems of various forms can blend different sources of complex systems behavior. In my interactive music systems,[89] I evolve interactive behaviors in simplified virtual environments, not worrying about the specifics of the musical context in which they will ultimately be used. I seek out behaviors that I think are interesting in an abstract sense, using targeted or multiobjective

evolution. Once I find network behaviors that I like, I manually code interactive musical systems around them. Thus I use trial and error at two stages in the process: when coding fitness functions that dictate the networks' evolved behaviors, and when composing the overall musical nature of the system, in response to the network's behavior. This affords a great deal of creative control but with a core system behavior that acts according to its own generative nature.

Simon Colton[90] has explored complex hybrid approaches in his Painting Fool virtual artist system, particularly in the multimodal nature of the system, not only producing artworks but also textural descriptions that support the work, the process that he describes as "framing." Certain elements of his system involve evolutionary optimization, others involve learning, others still involve handwritten code dictating strategies for producing an artwork. The Painting Fool truly is a hybrid assemblage of techniques, following the philosophy that increasing the creative power of art-generating systems means endowing them with multiple interacting smart components performing different functions and working together to produce more than the sum of their parts. This is a view that is in keeping with the penknife model of the mind and the view that artistic aesthetics emerge through the interaction between different cognitive competencies (both discussed in chapter 4). A cost to this is the difficulty of understanding and communicating what is going on in such complex hybrid systems in such a way as to improve their design.

Multicomponent Cognitive Models

While the above examples of hybrids aim to weave together the available algorithmic methods in pursuit of effective strategies for automating aspects of creativity, other approaches focus more explicitly on constructing multicomponent cognitive models based on human cognition. The two-system, fast/slow model of cognition, as we have seen in chapter 4, has formed the basis for some thinking about creative processes and aesthetic experience, such as Huron's theory[91] that patterns of interaction between surprise and expectation in these two response mechanisms can be pleasing. Agnese Aguello and colleagues[92] have attempted to explicitly build computational creativity-focused architectures, based on this theory, that attempt to model forms of exploratory, reflective, tacit, and analytic cognition. A familiar theme again here is the idea that the two processes might interact with one another with creative effects, possibly dividing along the lines of generators and evaluators, such as the fast thinking process acting as a rapid-production, high-output generator and the slow process performing more formal analysis. This bears some similarity to other previously discussed architectures, such as Wiggins and Forth's IDyOT model,[93] which involves multiple predictive agents that compete for attention in a global workspace.

As well as mimicking nature, other researchers have combined different algorithms in the study of social forms of creative processes. Rob Saunders[94] conducted a series of conceptual experiments into the creative and social properties of an artificial society of artists. Each artificial artist used an evolutionary algorithm to evolve visual images according to its own model of aesthetic preference. The artists' preferences in turn were determined by a type of unsupervised learning algorithm trained on previous experiences. The interaction between the evolving artworks and the learning system in a social population results in interesting self-organizing social dynamics. I will discuss this work in some more detail below under "Social Models."

End-to-End Creative Agents
The bulk of the discussion so far in this chapter covers the algorithmic subsystems that may be used to achieve computationally creative systems, but still does not address the more radical scenario in which the system engages in a complete cycle of production and evaluation resembling what a human creative practitioner does.

Prototypical designs, such as those of Ventura, Gervás, and Colton, have been discussed earlier in which a system provisionally performs this cycle. The basic schematic is the generate-and-test design pattern; a generator produces candidate solutions which are evaluated by an evaluation system. We can think of a nested set of such systems that work to perform complex creative search. Consider the example studied in detail by Simonton of Pablo Picasso exploring representational styles through experimental sketches, leading to his masterpiece *Guernica*. We may identify three layers of iterated evaluation: a cycle of ideation and verification conducted mentally; a series of external experiments in the form of sketches, reflection on these sketches feeds back into the ideation process in the form of new goals and areas of heightened interest; the presentation of work to a public, resulting in a social layer of selection and feedback, also propagating new goals and areas of heightened interest through the layers. By loose comparison, in any self-evaluating computational creativity system, there can be different levels of evaluation and adaptation: external experiments such as actual physical mark-making, may feed back into the systems model of the world. Likewise, situated, sociocultural interaction may give similar feedback.

One obvious direction the research has taken is to consider how a system might *model* the aesthetic orientation and productive capacity of a human individual. If we human beings have consistent taste profiles ourselves, then sufficiently advanced learning systems should be able to model those profiles, given enough information (itself a significant challenge). Just as we have systems that can distinguish cats from dogs, we should be able to make systems that can distinguish between good and bad, given a model upon which to base that distinction (a specific person's taste).

Although this may be conceivable in principle, it may be a remote possibility in practice using current technology, given the complexity of the task. Recall the work of researchers such as Bourdieu, Born, Bloom, and Schubert, Hargreaves, and North in chapter 4, each of which contributes to the social-cultural grounding of aesthetics, particularly in the formation of an identity and set of cultural associations that guide a person's actions. This means that we cannot simply understand their taste from studying a list of things they like and don't like, because the underlying context in which that taste emerged is missing. Needless to say, without the complete data, it is not possible to make a complete model of the system.

Other theoretical concepts discussed in chapter 4, such as the idea of maximizing information compression progress, may also be necessary to correctly establish the learning of aesthetics. This is a different proposition to simply learning structure, as a neural network does. Such considerations present ongoing challenges to the idea of fully modelling human aesthetics, yet despite these obstacles, big data approaches may still be able to go a long way in achieving this aim.

Social Models

Closely related to multicomponent models are social models of creativity: computer models that attempt to create some of the effects of creative processes that occur in the interaction between different individuals. These models also have a close resemblance to artificial life and ecosystemic models, particularly because, unlike models of individual cognitive processes, they are more likely to involve multiple *competing* agents, through which effects might emerge in a self-organized manner, despite the lack of a common objective. More immediately, such models exist in a field of research called computational social science, which looks at collective and emergent phenomena in human social systems.

In a series of studies, Saunders and colleagues[95] set out to study fundamental relationships between individual behavioral characteristics and emergent social phenomena in aesthetic domains. They created simple multi-agent simulations in which populations of virtual agents produce artworks using an evolution-based generation method, and also evaluate each other's productions based on a simple model of individual taste, which adapts based on their life experience. Saunders's agents were designed to be curious, implementing a pleasure response based on the Wundt curve, discussed in chapter 4. Each agent maintains a list of things it has seen before (the agent "sees" with a simple perceptual model that extracts some basic features from the image) and evaluates any new thing it sees by considering how different it is from the things in its memory, much like the novelty search algorithms discussed in the previous section. The Wundt curve dictates that things that are too similar to anything in memory will be deemed boring (score of zero), and anything too radically different will be deemed unpleasant (negative score). Somewhere between these extremes lies a sweet spot of novelty that gives the maximum positive score (thus the Wundt curve does not describe a completely neophile behavior, it requires a balanced amount of novelty).

Saunders's models then define a set of social processes. Agents spend a certain amount of time looking at their own work and a certain amount looking at each other's work, giving scores to others based on how they value the works they see. Another rule describes how much attention agents pay to each other. Agents spend more time interacting with other agents whose work they like.

The resulting simulation shows agents self-organizing into cliques, where the agents in any given clique are highly attuned to each other's work and share a common style. Occasionally a clique might die out, or another might fissure. In other words, the model starts to give some semblance of the kinds of network effects and dynamics discussed toward the end of chapter 4.

It is important to emphasize here what the goals of such models are. Models such as these are necessarily comprised of a number of arbitrary and simplifying design decisions. They cannot possibly claim to be realistic models of the phenomena they are studying. Crude simplifications, such as the idea that an agent has a memory (database) of previously seen artworks and measures perceptual "distance" to new artworks, are clearly far removed from reality. But this is actually considered a necessary step in building a good model; by choosing the most simple parameters to explore, the model is effective because it can be thoroughly understood, and because each assumption can be easily manipulated to understand its effects, just as good thought experiments have the property that they can be *thought through*. In fact, models such as Saunders's push this "keep it simple, stupid" (KISS) principle of simulation modeling: modeling socially creative behaviors in nontrivial ways sets up a tension between the goal of keeping models simple and of getting enough relevant detail and richness of behavior into the model. This has been a challenge for the field; it is looking at one of the most complex aspects of human behavior, aesthetic experience, yet must simplify it radically.

Such models needn't only be valuable for studying socially creative phenomena. They also have the potential to be generative tools. We can imagine more sophisticated variants of Saunders's model whereby a user could run a lab experiment generating a population of producers for art or music of a certain style, seeded from real cultural artifacts, and then running it forward in time to generate variants, perhaps with transformational creative outcomes (new breakaway styles or fusions). A number of researchers have looked at the idea of automated art or music critics that have a taste informed by their individual history (thus distinct from some notion of a generic aesthetic fitness measure). For example, Nick Collins[96] looks at making music critics that have deliberate biases, experimenting how they compare in judging novel music generated by another program.

Conclusion

The vast amount of work and the vast range of algorithmic ideas and methods discussed in this chapter give some illustration of the scale of activity and the potential of the field. However, it should also have indicated how much more vast the possible range of future directions is. Typical of Arthur's law of accelerating returns underlying the social power of creativity itself, every useful algorithmic method forms another unit that can be combined in more complex and sophisticated systems. These algorithms, and the technologies that support them, make up the infrastructure upon which the automation of increasingly effective creative activities can be implemented. The future potential of computational creativity really lies in the novel architectures and holistic multicomponent systems that will effectively exploit the power of these various subsystems. For the time being, the existing work can be seen as a collection of proofs-of-concept and novel algorithmic methods, illustrating what kinds of generative power exist but also acting as cultural probes that begin to help us ask what we want of them in future applications. The discussion in this chapter has focused largely on what is possible and has not given much thought to what we might want to do with such systems, how they might be used (and are being used today), how they fail, and how they might change creative practice. In the following chapter, we begin to look at how such systems are being used creatively.

6 Putting Computational Creativity to Work

Just by rotating this knob, any one of you can produce up to three sonatas per hour. Yet consider how hard it was for your ancestors. They could be creative only be driving themselves into fits of "inspiration"—an unknown form of epilepsy.
—Yevgeny Zamyatin[1]

While there are many algorithmic methods to choose from to create computationally creative systems, they each have specific limitations and affordances that need to be worked with to get anything done. There are no magic bullets or general purpose solutions, no general intelligence systems. For the moment, AI solutions are highly domain-specific tailored tools with quirks and constraints that influence how they might be used. They may be operated by professional programmers who run custom scripts and output the processes of their generation for others to access, or through one-button-interfaces, simple navigation interfaces, or text-based search bars that an unskilled user can explore. Since machine learning is simultaneously so successful and so complicated, some researchers and companies have set out to make general-purpose creative machine learning toolkits that can be more easily used by end-users. The Runway toolkit is described as "an interface and framework that orchestrates the training, use and deployment of artificial intelligence models in design and creative platforms,"[2] taking an ecosystemic approach where different contributors can provide models and templates that can be used by others. Machine learning interaction design poses complex conflicting objectives. In their overview of machine learning approaches to music generation, Briot and Pachet define four key challenges in designing usable generative music tools:

- Control, such as tonality conformance, maximum number of repeated notes, rhythm
- Structure, versus wandering music without a sense of direction
- Creativity, versus imitation and risk of plagiarism
- Interactivity, versus automated single-step generation[3]

This chapter gives an overview of what people are doing with computationally creative systems, how they are being used in creative projects, and how businesses are beginning to apply computational creativity to commercial projects.

Chapter 5 discussed many examples of computational creativity systems, focusing largely on the algorithms themselves. The discussion of these examples inevitably touched on the *use cases* we find emerging around the application of computational creativity to real creative tasks. This chapter turns to this topic proper and accordingly draws in another academic discipline: the study and design of technology use and interaction, which includes the fields of human computer interaction (HCI)[4] and interaction design (often abbreviated IxD).[5]

I will leave a more thorough discussion of the methodologies and theoretical foundations of these subjects and their application to computational creativity to the following chapter, which discusses evaluation. However, it is important to mention that in these fields the subject of distributed agency, discussed in chapter 3, is as important as it is in the social sciences, since questions of where actions originate, how intentions are formed, and what systems or networks can be identified as beneficiaries of various interactions are central to understanding the design of interactions with technology. Lucy Suchman[6] pioneered the application of such thought to design in the 1980s, proposing "situated action" as an alternative to intention, whereby action involves complex and collaborative interplay between people and things, noting that "plans are inherently vague." This work has been developed in the intervening period by many others. Werner Rammert[7] develops the thesis that the role of machines in networks of distributed agency already has tangible effects, and Susanne Bødker[8] identifies a "third wave" of HCI thinking and research, in which greater attention is paid to the emergent nature of interaction.

For now, however, we immediately pick up from the last chapter's survey of computational creativity algorithms to look into how these are being put to work in practice.

Approaching Interaction with Computationally Creative Systems: Interaction Metaphors and the User's Understanding

Interacting with machines and other objects has for a long time been centered largely on acts of direct manipulation. From can openers to cars (older cars, at least), each part of the system has a traceable structure or behavior that you can directly control. Computers, as the logical progression of a shrinking, encapsulation, and complexification of machine behaviors, have brought us to a point where this is no longer true. We have no idea what most machines are doing underneath their shells, and little hope of intuitively working it out by tinkering. Modern machines are becoming in interactive terms closer to biological organisms, which are also doing complex things under the hood that we cannot directly manipulate. The philosopher Dan Dennett[9] has a useful way of talking about such understandings in terms of the different "stances" we take toward different types of object. As far as most of the world goes—that is, the abiotic, non-human-made world—a good understanding of physics, and thus a "physical stance," goes a long way. Humans are good throwers, and dogs are good catchers: both have the cognitive machinery to plan and predict the movement of a ball through the air.

But an understanding of physics does little to help predict the movement of the dog (except when it too is flying through the air). For this we apply a different stance, where animals are understood in terms of goals, perception, and intelligence. We know we can attract the dog with food, and we can train it. We think about whether it is smart enough to open the fridge door or find its way home. With other humans, we are highly adept at modeling the behavior of others, enabling forms of trust and deception not known elsewhere in the animal world. This stance Dennett calls the "intentional stance." The human-made world, according to Dennett, invites a third stance. When wondering what a certain button does on a pocket calculator the logic is to approach it as something that has been designed with a function in mind. We expect its behavior to be predictable and thus usable, and we apply the "design stance." As systems become endowed with increasing levels of computational intelligence, the design stance potentially becomes fragmented and the intentional stance may come into play; confusion or a sense of either the profound or the uncanny may ensue.

This is discussed by authors such as Philip Auslander, and Hollington and Kyprianou (as quoted by Auslander), who remark that an uncanny experience

> occurs when animate and inanimate objects become confused, when objects behave in a way which imitate life, and thus blur the cultural, psychological and material boundaries between life and death, leading to what [Ernst] Jentsch called "Intellectual Uncertainty"—that things appear not to be what they are, and as such our reasoning may need re-structuring to make sense of the phenomenon.[10]

Despite the rapid increase in complexity and opacity in human-made computational systems, we still frequently design systems so that anyone using them has a direct manipulation relationship with the system. I am directly typing characters into a document (although it is occasionally correcting me); a graphic designer drags, drops, and draws onto a virtual canvas; a composer places notes and adjusts intensities on a timeline. Accordingly, good design practice is predicated on the idea that a user must be able to maintain a good understanding of what the system is doing and the system must support them to intuitively achieve goals. If they are ever confused about what is going on or how they can manipulate an object then the system has failed. As we saw in chapter 3, the idea of affordances[11] has been central in helping designers frame both how to integrate heterogeneous components into efficient designs and how to communicate the intended use of something to a user. Designers also talk about constraints and mappings, things that guide the user or reveal intuitive relationships between entities.

In chapter 3, I described the concept of affordances as providing a way for us to think about inanimate objects directing the behavior of smart, intentional users, balancing the asymmetry of agency relations between people and objects, and I considered how material engagement provided a model of co-creative exploration even when the objects involved were wholly passive. The design of such system affordances underlies the notion of usability, which is generally associated with task performance and its measurement. A typical way designers understand usability is through personas and user scenarios. A persona is a portrait of a typical user, detailing their qualities and goals. For example, Instagram users can be classified according to different personas—the professional photographer, the teenager, the amateur artisan. A user scenario describes a specific situation in which the user must interact with an artifact or piece of software, detailing what they are trying to do, what they know, what the particular demands are, such as time constraints, or the potential for distraction.

An example in computational creativity is the work of Aengus Martin[12] examining the use of a system for automating the performance of arrangement-level musical decisions (the arrangement of individual musical elements—drum patterns, chord sequences, bass lines, and so on—into entire compositions). In Martin's case, the system is trained not from a large data set of existing music, as is commonly the case, but from the user's own live arrangements of a musical work. The aim of the system is to accurately model the user's arrangement style so that it can produce new variations of that style, exhibiting an understanding of the structural properties of the user's arrangements. The system is incorporated into the Ableton Live digital audio workstation so that it can be used in a context that is natural to digital musicians. It uses variable order Markov models to record transition probabilities for each individual track, but also a constraint solver system to discover the rules underlying the relationship *between* tracks. The latter system's job is to identify if, for example, certain groupings of tracks always played together or never played together, and override the Markov processes where one of the rules it had learned was being broken.

The important issue with such a system is that it doesn't work perfectly with whatever data it is given to learn. Its learning performance will vary greatly in different musical contexts, and a lot of the work of doing good machine learning, even in the age of sophisticated deep learning algorithms, lies in tweaking the learning system to suit the context. Martin's system's performance depends on a number of parameter settings, and the user is in a position to vastly improve performance by guiding the learning, for example by indicating where the system is likely to find relevant association rules, a process known as feature selection. Thus a machine learning system here is seen like any other piece of software in that it must be operated by a user to work effectively, and the user may need to learn how to use the system effectively; the system isn't necessarily easy to use. Because it is a generative music system, the user must also audition the results, which may take a long time. These considerations begin to paint a picture of user experience and usability in the world of computationally creative systems.

Martin's research then considers what interface is needed for effective user control of feature selection. A default design would involve simply presenting all of the system parameters via various widgets, which the user can manipulate. This could be considered the expert interface. Users would need to invest in reading documentation, following tutorials, and experimenting in order to gain an understanding of what each control does. Alternatively, one could aim to reduce and conceal these issues as best as possible, for example by providing a set of presets with clear user contexts (such as the genre-specific EQ settings found in car radios; rock, pop, classical, etc.). They could provide a wizard-type interface that asked the user a series of questions sequentially. These various interface options offer different levels of detail, rapid access to results, intrusion into the user's workflow, and so on. Examining users working with different prototype manifestations of the interface can reveal which strategies might be best for this particular system. Rather than actually programming all of these candidate interfaces, a Wizard of Oz approach can be used in user studies, where the developers are acting behind the scenes to fill in for the software where it is not fully implemented.

With regard to auditioning the results, Martin found that, predictably, a user would spend less time at the early stages of listening through different candidate agents (an agent is a specific instance of a system for generating the arrangement) and increasingly more time as they narrowed in on agents whose behavior they liked. This can be explained by the fact that it is very quick to pick up when the system is doing things that are clearly wrong, and as the system improves it takes more time to spot issues. However, it could also be that at an early stage the user is in a more exploratory mode, quickly looking through different options, and then later narrowing in on what they think is their preferred behavior. In this latter case, the system needn't get better for this increased attention over time to play out.

Dahlstedt's work on interactive genetic algorithms for sound synthesis,[13] discussed in chapter 5, embodied in the software for the commercial Clavia Nord Modular G2 synthesizer, investigates similar usability issues. In the MutaSynth software, users can interactively evolve synthesizer sounds; given a certain arrangement of oscillators and effects, all of the numerical parameters (the knobs and sliders controlling each component) are compiled into a genotype which can be interactively evolved. Dahlstedt looked at user interface issues such as the ability to remember individual sound configurations or to return to previous configurations. He developed visual icons that represented the genetic code of each synthesizer configuration, so that users had a visual cue to represent the sound. He also provided tools to allow users to easily navigate the search space and store and retrieve synthesizer configurations as they searched. Since this work was deployed in a commercial software tool, Dahlstedt's user research was based largely on responses from users through online feedback, with users identifying the system as effective for rapid undirected search.

These examples continue the paradigm of a user operating a system, albeit a sophisticated system with domain-specific intelligence. A serious goal for computational creativity, and one that is becoming ever present with AI-powered conversational user interfaces, is to reconfigure that interaction into one that better resembles forms of human-to-human interaction. This is a theme that has a lineage in earlier thinking in cybernetics, courtesy of the cybernetician artist Gordon Pask. As documented by Usman Hacque,[14] Pask, in the spirit of the cybernetic revolution, trod a richly multidisciplinary path, creating interactive artworks that communicated and explored. His Musicolor system, for example, was a light artwork that responded to the sound of a live musician, demonstrating a basic understanding of the musical signal and mimicking human traits such as expressing boredom.

More recently, the creativity researcher Todd Lubart[15] proposed four metaphors based on human roles that elaborate on ways in which the computer might act as a collaborator: computer as nanny, computer as pen pal, computer as coach, and computer as colleague. The nanny metaphor uses a slightly odd terminology—I would suggest that "manager" or "facilitator" might be clearer. It refers to the activity of structuring creative processes, such as brainstorming, so that the human can get more out of their creativity, so to speak. The pen pal metaphor refers to something similar in a group setting, with human user and computer iterating through design ideas, with the focus of this interaction being the question of how creative ideas are represented. The coach metaphor refers to the use of the computer supporting an individual to use creativity techniques that stimulate ideas. It is the computer as colleague metaphor, of course, that alludes to a more creatively symmetrical, partnership between user and system, with all of the issues of cognition and communication that this entails. A pertinent question with all of these metaphors is how they might be *partially* realized in computationally creative systems and, if so, to what extent such a metaphor holds. Ultimately, existing metaphors of interaction can be subsumed by new design concepts once the field of practice develops its own directions, and these metaphors can be seen as initial provocations. Other contributors have suggested similar metaphors of human roles. In his work, Lomas[16] refers to the computer as an assistant, which he in fact categorizes as being devoid of any creative autonomy (perhaps akin to Lubart's "nanny"), with the potential through learning and evolution to advance to the status of a collaborator. McCormack refers to the notion of the computer as an equal partner and "first class citizen" in the creative process.

Computational Creativity Activities

A good way to think about the application of computational creativity in the hands of users is to identify the distinct activities that take place during computational creativity algorithm use.[17] I therefore outline nine distinct activities that a person working with a computational creativity system might engage in: selecting algorithms; selecting representations and data formats; manipulating algorithms; generating outputs; reviewing and analyzing outputs; selecting and giving feedback on outputs; feeding source artifacts into a system; specifying goals and constraints; and manipulating outputs.[18] All of these activities can be seen elsewhere besides in computational creativity use cases, but each has a more specific definition and set of design concerns in the computational creativity context.

Note that each of these perspectives conforms to a standard human user perspective, with the human strictly in charge and driving the process. We could consider these interaction scenarios, for example, in terms of Norman's (very much single-user-centric) four stages of interaction: forming an intention, selecting an action, executing the action, and evaluating the outcome.[19]

Selecting Algorithms
Any computationally creative task begins with the selection of algorithms or tools to complete the job. It is worth noting that the selection of the algorithm is itself a task performed by an operator, possibly a creative practitioner, which significantly affects the type of output produced. Whether the practitioner is hand-coding the system themselves or using an out-of-the-box web service, they must make a choice about which tools will best serve their needs. This will depend heavily, perhaps almost exclusively, on what has been demonstrably achieved by others in the past. In this way, algorithm selection is a highly cultural activity, and the concept of a

"community of practice" applies equally well to computational creativity practice as to any other area of creative activity, with its associated schools and genres. Students learning computer music have learned about Markov models for decades and their early application in pioneering works such as the compositions of Iannis Xenakis.[20] They have applied them in their own practice and passed them on to their students. One redefines one's goals based on the observation of others around them, as well as hands-on experience. Competing algorithms may need to signal their value with respect to current knowledge about the state of the art, and in the computational creativity domain this may come about through creative trends as much as scientific evidence. The affordances of such algorithms likewise come to be understood in communities of practice. For example, neural network approaches have proven themselves as effective mash-up tools but are not so well proven as strong ideation tools; but that's not to say a community of practice might not emerge around this use case in the future.

In the increasingly hybrid methods of algorithmic generation, artists may also need to select algorithmic combinations or other ways of constraining generation. We previously saw examples of constraints applied to music sequence generation. Alexandre Papadopoulos, Pierre Roy, and François Pachet[21] explore ways to constrain a Markovian music generation process to avoid plagiarizing content in the original dataset, and in cases such as this the user may be involved in actively configuring algorithmic combinations according to their needs.

It is also possible that the selection of algorithms is itself automated. As we expect the world of computational creativity to be fragmented into many domain-specific tools, meta-tools that help choose between them or that distribute tasks to multiple worker algorithms are likely to be an important part of the mix. Standards that support swappability between algorithms will enhance how easily this can be done (as can be seen in practice in the Runway platform), and mutually add to the ease of adoption for all such algorithms.

Selecting Representations and Data Formats

Machine learning and evolutionary computing researchers put great effort into exploring the ways that the data they are working with are represented. The representation of the data fed into a machine learning model or used as a genotype in an evolutionary search has a significant impact on the outcomes of the generation. Making decisions about data representations is perhaps one of the more obscure ways in which an end-user might interact with a generation process. Largely, the impact of the data representation is hard to predict and requires experimentation. However, there are some relevant general issues. One is the question of the granularity of the data. In music, a successful approach is to sequence together larger readymade units from a database of existing short melodic expressions,[22] rather than trying to create sequences from the ground up from individual notes, and similar representations exist in other domains. This "unit selection" approach has the obvious advantage that the raw ingredients of the generated sequences are themselves quality phrases (e.g., extracted from the original database), and the goal of generation is to sequence them together. While the promise of strong deep learning and related deep algorithms is that they can work from the lowest-level raw ingredients—pixels, waveforms, or individual musical notes—inferring multiple stages of structure generation, such modular methods can lead to practical improvements in output, generation time, and variability. This may be a user's preference, possibly even giving them precise control over the seed set of primitives used in generation (e.g., using their own database of musical licks to mix together). There are many other more nuanced issues of data representation. Some might be reduced to control parameters that a user can manipulate to influence the generation. Largely, however, the best data representations are likely to become common standards and users would become trained in their use, just as musicians are familiar with the MIDI protocol or piano-roll notation.

Manipulating Algorithms

All algorithms have parameters that can be manipulated that alter the way they perform. For example, Markov models have an *order* that indicates how many steps backwards the model looks when making predictions: variable-order Markov models exist, but still have parameters such as *maximum order*. Such parameters may be reduced to a simple GUI of knobs, menus, and sliders that can be tweaked graphically. In the MutaSynth software, discussed in chapter 5,[23] one could directly interact with an interface that controlled the breeding of new synthesizer sounds, specifying algorithmic parameters such as mutation rate. In many of the online examples of work using Google's Magenta machine learning tools,[24] interface elements are offered that control the parameters of sequence generators, such as a neural network's *temperature*, or set model parameters prior to training, such as number of layers. These control points may be more or less intuitive to the user, who may have more or less technical understanding of the system. They will also inevitably be often highly specific to the algorithm in question. In all cases, someone—either the system programmer or a user—will inevitably have to configure the algorithm to work as desired. More powerful algorithms may reduce this need but are far from eradicating it.

Often the manipulation of algorithms needs to be more open-ended than a simple GUI will allow, requiring a programming environment to write scripts or programs that direct the process. For now, therefore, it is still predominantly those who can code who have access to the operation of computational creativity systems. Powerful open-source machine learning and evolutionary computing libraries allow creative practitioners who code to construct arbitrary configurations and variants on existing algorithms. This includes chaining different processes together or nesting one process inside another: for example, a system that uses evolutionary search, with a fitness function defined by a trained neural network that performs object recognition. Configuration of such sorts can also be done using simpler data-flow tools or graphical patching environments. The FloWr framework[25] allows users to plug together small data processing modules to create simple computationally creative algorithms by hand. An important factor here is to find suitable data formats, communication protocols and levels of abstraction that enable a modular approach in which users can easily configure hybrid algorithms.

Again, the manipulation of algorithms can be automated in metaprocesses. In some of the scenarios we've looked at, we have seen layered systems, where one process configures another, as in the use of evolutionary algorithms to optimize neural network configurations.[26]

Generating Outputs

Perhaps the most ubiquitous stage in a computational creativity workflow is the running of a generative algorithm to create outputs. Typically this will be an iterative process involving generating multiple outputs that the user may select from or possibly give feedback on. At one extreme we have the ideal of the casual creator,[27] in which the space of possible outputs is highly constrained and generally benign (a majority of points in the space looks or sounds nice). Here the search of the space itself is of less importance. Anything goes. The most extreme cases are those like MIT Media Lab's generative logo, where any combination is as good as any other—it is the collective effect that is of interest. We also have examples such as the control of a GAN's latent space,[28] where generation of outputs might be directly controlled by some intuitive, smooth user interface; perhaps the user can precisely specify the properties of the thing they want generated, even if they don't know how the outcome will turn out. Memo Akten, Rebecca Fiebrink, and Mick Grierson[29] discuss interface designs that allow a user to design trajectories through an image-generating GAN latent space to produce time-based media. In other cases, such as sequential music or script generation by neural networks, the output would typically be seeded or controlled by some input, possibly a random input, or possibly some source material that should steer the output. Inputs to an algorithm may also be presented in other ways, such as the joke-generating system STANDUP, which allows themes or words to be included in the joke.[30] At the other extreme lies the domain of interactive genetic algorithms; each candidate is a simple mutation or recombination of elements from the previous generation, and the search proceeds in a gradualist manner, the user giving feedback to the system in the form of selections rather than specifying operation parameters.

Important factors in the interaction design experience of generating outputs include: the speed at which the generation can be performed; the speed with which a user can evaluate candidates, or more generally the effort involved in that evaluation; the overall success rate of the algorithm; and how the user can control the generation process or give feedback on the results in further iterations. Different use cases also demand different types of output set. An ideation task may require high diversity, while the production of a final product may require greater convergence on a specific outcome with tighter constraints.

In his own practice-based work, Lomas[31] identifies four modes of exploration: initial exploration, in which the user explores and gains a cursory understanding of the space; secondary exploration, in which the user still engages in a broad search, but better directed by goals derived from an understanding of the space; refined focus, in which the user focuses their search on a narrower space and more specific goals; and looking for novelty, in which the user returns to seeing what novel outcomes lie beyond the spaces they have come to know.

It is also important to note that a user may access generated outputs without having generated them themselves but may still select or give feedback on them (actively or passively). For example, in distributed interactive evolutionary systems like Picbreeder, DarwinTunes[32] and Electric Sheep,[33] the user may or may not be a participant in the generative process but still accesses the outputs of that process. In Steffan Ianigro's distributed genetic algorithm for generating sounds, Plecto,[34] an algorithm pre-generates many prototypes using novelty search, that a user can then search through using a more manual browsing process, sorting the outputs by properties and sifting through them.

Reviewing and Analyzing Outputs

The evaluation of generative outputs often simply means looking at (or listening to or reading) those outputs. Review and analysis factors can be critical in interaction design when, as is likely to be the case, the system does not consistently and immediately produce the desired output. A system's success rate might be relatively low, but it can still be useful if the work involved in identifying good outputs is manageable. Again interactive genetic algorithms are an extreme case where the user's repeated feedback is the means by which the next round of outputs is generated. In all cases, outputs need to be reviewed, but different use cases will demand different approaches to that review, from a rapid skim through results to a more considered analysis.

It is also possible that algorithmic approaches can be used to support the evaluation of outputs, without going so far as actually automating evaluation. Evaluating generative music or other time-based outputs, or long-form literature, can be time consuming, so basic measures and simple visualization techniques can be used to simplify the results. The context of the evaluation or usage of outputs can also be controlled to better fit workflows or to be most convenient or effective. As described above, passive scenarios involving large audiences can be an effective way to trial lots of candidate outputs. Paid "human computing" methods like Amazon's Mechanical Turk[35] can also be used.

Selecting and Giving Feedback on Outputs

Once a generative process has been run and there are candidate outputs that have been reviewed, several things can happen next. The user might simply select one or more final outputs and end the process, or reject all outputs and iterate the process from scratch. They could also interact with the process at this stage by performing more fine-tuned selection or feedback. The most common form of fine-tuned feedback is the rating of some or all elements in the output set, or at least sorting them into good and bad categories or otherwise tagging them. In an ambient interaction paradigm (described below), passive measures might be used instead of active measures, such as how long a person spends interacting with a given output. Furthermore, the evaluation of outputs might go deeper into the specific detail of the output, such as identifying exactly which aspects or regions of the output are good, or giving feedback that indicates overall issues with the set of outputs.

It is important to remember that selection and evaluation are not only about thinking in terms of rating goodness but taking a multifaceted response into account. For example, in a distributed search process, someone might identify an output that is not what they are looking for but that is nevertheless of interest for some reason. To take into account such situations, it is better to think of evaluation as being fluid and having multiple possible manifestations and orderings, resulting from an ongoing interaction between users, systems, and their outputs.

Feeding Source Artifacts or Data into a System

In many computationally creative systems, some form of input data is needed. This may take the form of training data for a machine learning algorithm or target outputs for an evolutionary algorithm to match. In more complex scenarios it might take the form of instances with respect to which a system might aim to demonstrate novelty. Input data may be submitted in order to say "match this" or "avoid this." In style transfer, the user blends different aspects derived from two or more different sources. In various training strategies, we might also combine different datasets together in structured ways, such as training a system on a wide training set first and a more specific set later.

An important factor to consider is where the input data comes from. Does the user create it? Do they have access to various corpuses of data? Is the algorithm capable of trawling the web for publicly accessible resources, or does the data come prepackaged in the system, as in pretrained networks, in which case the user may have limited knowledge about what data the system has been trained on (which is increasingly common)? In some cases, such as in live music performance systems, the data might be input in real time. The system may even explore the world itself, for example in a robotic system that can move around and explore its visual environment, as in the creative robotics work of Petra Gemeinboeck and Rob Saunders, where robots learn patterns in their environment, driving their innate (that is, programmed-in) curiosity. This in turn has significant impacts on the attribution of the output and may constrain what the user can do with the trained system. A trained system might be deemed plagiaristic if it regurgitates outputs from its training set, but that depends on the context. Also important is how easily the data can be organized. How well annotated is it to allow grouping into different categories? Is it in a form that allows different aspects of the data to be presented to the algorithm? Finally, how easy is it to understand how the system has responded to the data? For example, if a machine learning algorithm is failing to reproduce a certain style, is it easy to understand what might be changed in the training set? This impacts how the user can respond and alter the training set or the algorithm itself.

Allowing users to train systems on their own data holds enticing potential. An example of a platform for facilitating this is the Wekinator, created by Rebecca Fiebrink. The Wekinator is named after a machine learning library called Weka, upon which it is built. It allows any user to rapidly associate inputs such as physical gestures with outputs, such as synthesizer parameters. As Fiebrink demonstrates in various studies,[36] "One of the most immediately apparent benefits of using Wekinator to build mappings is the speed and ease with which composers can build a new instrument and modify it." This, importantly, applies to nonprogrammers, expanding access to these tools. She continues with an important observation about how this in turn transforms thinking around music system creation:

> Another critical difference between designing instruments using machine learning and designing instruments by writing code is that composers are able to use their bodies directly in the design process. Instead of reasoning about what sort of movement-sound relationships he might want in an instrument, then deriving a mathematical function that he thinks will facilitate those relationships in a mapping, a composer can simply demonstrate examples of movements and movement-sound pairs that feel and sound right to him.[37]

Specifying Goals and Constraints

With systems that are goal-based or are able to perform some kind of evaluation on their own, it is common that we want to specify goals to the system. In target-based evolutionary search, this means specifying a fitness function or providing example target behavior. I don't include examples such as training neural networks here, because in this case the data is not used to specify a goal but to feed a learning process (although the difference can be minor depending on the circumstances, and reinforcement learning is an exception).

A common way to describe goals is in terms of constraints, such as properties that the output shouldn't contain, or relations that should pertain in the results. An important question is how goals or constraints can be specified in a user-friendly manner. Graphical user interfaces are again possible for this purpose, but also limited in this respect. We can specify constraints in terms of logical relations between elements in some formal language. Example-based approaches are also already very successful since they are intuitive (as in Fiebrink's observation above). We can expect that natural language-based approaches would be very powerful in this regard, since it is natural to specify goals in terms of descriptive language, and we are beginning to see systems that are successful at mapping between natural language descriptions and cultural products. At the same time, we cannot always expect that rules can neatly be derived from data; such processes may not always be successful.

Another question is exactly how the system responds to user-specified goals, such as how it presents or orders the results. A system can spew many results out and leave the user to deal with this mass of options, or be more prescriptive, offering a small number of results (even if they are not evidently better than others). This relates to factors such as how open a user is to alternatives. If the system presents a single output as being preferred, we may be influenced by that analysis, placing trust in the system (and perhaps inadvertently assigning it greater creative authorship). Multi-objective strategies integrate different objectives to come up with a new, narrower search space. The setting of constraints and the sorting of results can be made iterative in various ways, for example by allowing a user to filter results by iteratively adding new constraints, or correcting others. Such technologies that steer or filter generative production without necessarily converging on specific solutions may become critical to good interaction design.

Manipulating Outputs

Lastly, once a system has generated outputs, a user may want to take over and finish the job themselves, which as we have seen is a likely scenario, given the limitations of existing algorithms. This requires simply that outputs are generated in, or easily convertible to some common format that a user can manipulate. This cannot always be guaranteed. For example, if the output being generated is a piece of interactive software, possibly involving a neural network or other complex behavior, then this object may not be represented in a very usable form or be easily manipulable by a user. It may remain opaque to the user, presenting potential situations where the generated artifact is nearly but not quite acceptable, with no easy way to better refine it. For example, the outputs created by Picbreeder are complex neural networks that generate bitmap images. The bitmap images are editable in programs like Adobe Photoshop but only at the pixel level; there are no layers or brushstrokes or other underlying objects that make up the image. Meanwhile, the neural networks that did the image generation are effectively black boxes; there is little hope of an artist manually tweaking their contents in a controlled manner.

In other cases, manipulation may be trivial, for example if a system generates MIDI or vector graphics data, which can be read and manipulated in many different programs. Even then, two other consideration still apply: is the generated data still presented in the most ideal way for manipulation? If it is vector graphics data or 3D point data, is it ordered sensibly? Secondly, if the user manipulates the data, can it then be further manipulated by the algorithm? Is there a two-way exchange between human and machine generated artifacts? For example, if a user edits a Picbreeder-generated image in Photoshop, there is no way for that newly edited image to be fed back into Picbreeder for continued evolution. Picbreeder would first need to find the correct neural network configuration that could generate the new image, which may not be possible.

Computational Creativity Interaction Paradigms

For each of the algorithms discussed in chapter 5, any or all of the above activities may be involved and manifest in very different ways. From this discussion of user interaction activities in computational creativity, we can also identify three broad interaction paradigms.[38]

Operation-based interaction: In some cases, a user operates advanced AI or search algorithms largely as they would any other digitally creative tool—setting parameters, loading training data, running a generator, evaluating the outcomes, iterating, and so on. In music generation, Briot and Pachet[39] discuss the ways in which various algorithms provide "entry points" to their control. For example, "The WaveNet architecture uses conditioning as a way to guide the generation, by adding an additional tag as a conditioning input." Good operation-based interaction requires good design of the interfaces to these algorithmic entry points. Intelligent use of presets and other constraints that simplify the interface may radically improve interface design.

Request-based interaction: In other cases, the system affordances may mark a radical departure from this more typical control-based paradigm, and we may interact with an algorithm via requests for outcomes. This can be described as a service-based or request-based paradigm, which resembles the user experience we find in search engines and natural language interfaces. Direct control of an algorithm is replaced with indirect interaction with the algorithm via the definition of goals and the evaluation of the responses. Consider the Google search bar, or assistants like Siri or Alexa, to be a model for how this might look; the primary interface is a free or constrained text field (or voice equivalent) that spawns a series of results, with which other interface elements can be used to interact (clicking links, setting filters, and so on). By subsuming the direct control of the generative algorithms, a request-based system can potentially be more intuitive and flexible than an operation-based system, but may be harder to understand in terms of potential affordances.

Ambient interaction: In other cases still, the algorithm operates in the background and it is not directly operated or requested by the user. In some of the music performance scenarios we will look at below this is the case: a live musician jamming with a piece of software can take a stance toward that piece of software in which it is human-equivalent (not necessarily humanlike, but performing the same role as a human co-performer). The user does not necessarily control the software or "submit requests" to the software. We could equally describe this as a partner paradigm and see it as an equally radical shift to the request-based paradigm. In other cases, the software may be making suggestions in the background, or filling in or predicting steps in the process, much as a text autocomplete system works.

These concerns lead to other design issues that underlie the usability or user experience for someone operating a computationally creative system: How does the system support playful interaction and divergent goals?

What intuitive interfaces or programming libraries support the programmatic design of behaviors? And how can distributed multiuser creative systems support communication and collaboration between different users? These topics are considered in the following chapter on evaluating computationally creative systems.

Computational Creativity Application Domains

We can also class the application domains of computational creativity into a number of broad categories. In the remainder of this chapter I outline several types of creative use contexts which apply computationally creative systems of varying degrees of sophistication, applying different algorithmic and interaction design paradigms. In one direction, we look at automating relatively routine tasks, such as completing a visual pattern or applying standard audio mix strategies to a piece of music, tasks which are already commonplace. In the other direction, we glance at increasingly anthropomorphic scenarios involving questions around the embedding of systems as participants in cultural contexts, with attributions of creative agency. However, this is far from a smooth, linear spectrum of application domains. For example, performance systems, such as improvising music systems, exist in such a different domain of creative experience and evaluation, focused on real-time collaborative creation, that they shift the type of considerations of agency we take into account. Some application areas, such as distributed evolutionary systems, depend upon, modulate, and will potentially ultimately transform how different creative practitioners collaborate, while for other application areas this is less significant.

Automating Routine Tasks
The most long-standing way in which AI has been applied to digital creative work is in the automation of relatively routine tasks which can empower creative practitioners. These are often not overtly computationally creative, in that they do not directly involve generation of original content, nor evaluation, but they do contribute to a foundational infrastructure that can support the emergence of computationally creative systems. A simple example from music is the ability to perform manipulations on a sound file that require some degree of perceptual intelligence, such as finding event onsets (the moments in an audio recording where a sonic event starts) or

understanding which notes make up a given chord. Imagine a note being struck on the piano in a jazz club, against a backdrop of other instruments, clinking glasses, and chatter. From the sound, you as a human listener are able to identify that a discrete event has taken place. Modern algorithms can do this with relative ease, and variants of this kind of functionality have been in place in commercial computer music production tools for decades. Similarly, in graphic contexts, an equivalent would be the ability to trace the outline of an object in an image.

Music information retrieval—the study of extracting information from musical data such as audio files—offers sophisticated computational methods for extracting events, understanding pitch and harmonic content, separating different sound sources or musical streams, inferring the underlying beat and metrical structure of a piece of rhythmic music, identifying phrase boundaries, recognizing styles and assigning genre classifications, recognizing individual instruments, and building models of the long term structure of music. All of these techniques are in use in some form or other in various creative software products today. Similarly, techniques that allow us to pull apart and manipulate existing audio *as if we were creating it from scratch*—techniques such as additive, granular and concatenative resynthesis—mean that static sound files become dynamic, editable entities. By modeling the underlying components of the sound, we can manipulate the sound in powerful ways. As stated, none of this directly performs the work of computational creativity—most of what I have just described can be characterized as cognitive work that a skilled human could do but that doesn't require creativity—but it provides a set of sophisticated ways in which algorithms are already at work, in use in current creative practice, into which computational creativity methods can tap. The more fluidity that computational intelligence can bring to the digital world, the more easily we can apply computational creativity methods.

Consider as an intermediary example the Sony CRL team's Reflexive Looper,[40] which employs machine intelligence to enhance the usability of the standard looper pedal. The looper pedal is a simple technology in the audio effects domain that is a mainstay for many performing artists, allowing them to create entire tracks by looping and layering elements in real time, particularly by overdubbing loops of themselves playing. The Reflexive Looper applies analysis to work out what parts are being played and when they begin and end. This is a natural extension of the kinds of machine listening applications we've already seen—the ability of music software to understand instrumentation, key, tempo, meter, and distinct events in audio—working toward higher-level music knowledge such as understanding phrase structure, maintaining a statistical model of style, and thus offering new affordances for how the musical content is manipulated by the user.

Meanwhile, the field of creative AI includes a wide array of novel concepts for the application of AI to creative work. As we incorporate new machine perception capabilities and understanding into software as they become available, new system affordances alter how we approach creative work. Smart object or event recognition, or smart modeling of content, has the immediate effect of facilitating new possibilities for creative production, opening up new ways of working and possibly leading to entirely new genres of creative practice.

Creative AI, for example, enables new types of audio or image synthesis. In concatenative synthesis, or audio mosaicing, small grains of audio are gathered into massive databases and then reconfigured to construct new sounds. We can arrange the databases of grains according to each one's low-level acoustic features and then do things like create interfaces that represent these grains in scatter plots, as in Diemo Schwartz's performance system Cat-ART, or use similarity matching to simulate one sound using the grains from another, as in Michael Casey's SoundSpotter software. Techniques such as dynamic time warping, the squashing and stretching of material in time to try to find more appropriate matches of patterns, improve the success of the matching.

Some techniques are pseudogenerative. They do not exactly generate new content but enable the advanced manipulation of existing content because they are capable of accurately modeling that content. Adobe's Content Aware technology in its Photoshop program, for example, fills out backgrounds after an object has been removed, using a model of what the pattern properties of the background are. Similarly, the Melodyne software for audio editing is capable of pulling apart the notes in a chord from an audio recording and tuning individual notes. Depending on the situation, the results in both cases can be very successful, but might still fail if the scenario falls outside a common set of expectations.

In games and virtual environments, the production of scenes has long been a target of procedural content generation. Introducing variation in trees and mountain ranges can be done easily using rule-based generative systems. Increasingly, generative AI tools are continuing this trend. Cityscapes can be filled out autonomously: given a city plan, the height, structure, facade details, and texturing of the city's buildings can be filled out using similar predictive algorithms. Style transfer–like methods can be used to apply transforms to a scene. The structure of one scene can be applied to content from other sources: a car changes make and model, people change clothes, Paris morphs into Phoenix.[41]

Closer to the more lofty end of computational creativity, we are witnessing the automation of tasks such as the mixing and mastering of music, where creative judgment is required. While for many, such as myself, these are tasks for which taste and creative style matter, and significant training makes a difference, they can also be construed as formulaic, scientifically grounded, and objectively good or bad. As discussed extensively in chapter 4, we can avoid the argument about which of these is really the case by recognizing this as a question that has different answers depending on cultural context. In some musical domains, the sonic production of work, including mixing, equalization, and the application of effects such as reverb, is a quintessential zone of creative activity.[42] In other musical domains, this entire process is a more suppressed area of creative focus. For live, unamplified acoustic music there is no mix, and in many amateur subcultures of digital music, tracks are posted to the web straight out of the creator's music workstation. The same analysis can be applied to other dimensions of creativity. Some musical artists might never have considered the question of what tuning system to use, while for others this might be what marks them out as an innovator.[43] Many bands have simple demands, wanting mixing and mastering that make their songs sound clean and loud, which could conceivably be performed by a perfectly formulaic mastering algorithm. Just as some hi-fi amplifiers offer different default EQ settings, such as for rock, pop, or classical, we can accept off-the-shelf mix and master algorithms that offer different styles. These could take the form of different explicitly stated algorithms, just as each individual digital effect has a clear underlying algorithm with various controls and presets, such as an algorithm that tries to maximize the separation of elements or an algorithm that applies a standard techno mix palette. Or they could be based on machine learning—trained on famous studio engineers, for example—or on evolutionary methods, where over time the algorithms are evolved in response to what is most popular. An example in practice is the work of Abreu, Caetano, and Penha,[44] who used a target-based evolutionary search method to find orchestrations of musical works based on target spectral features.

In short, while in some corners of creative practice the mix might be everything, this is a situation where the creative talent of expert human sound engineers may not figure in the bottom-line considerations of many artists. In a *prosumer* culture, where we write music digitally and immediately upload it, the advantage of such tools in achieving rapid turnover may outweigh the existing constraints on their ability.

Generative Art and Casual Creators

Despite the many advanced methods for applying AI to creative tasks, the more naive end of the spectrum, where simple generative processes could be hand-coded very quickly, is also an area of significant transformation and great immediate application. This is lowly, or *merely generative*, computational creativity, and explicitly so. The creative coder whips up an algorithmic process that generates patterns in a short sketch, perhaps only using it to generate a single output. They may do this as a convenient way to try out multiple variations or simply as a form of material engagement, working using code and algorithms in order to discover new structures that they would not have encountered otherwise, and tapping into the long historical lineage of mathematically driven design. Galanter[45] describes a "complexism" turn in digital art that responds to the nature of complex systems as a building material for behaviors, resembling the "truth-to-materials" principle of the brutalist movement. Here the software is enacting minimal agency in the creative process. Students are often taught to code in this way using creative coding environments such as Processing (a programming environment for artists and designers with a shallow learning curve), learning to appreciate how algorithms work and how they can be effective to produce outputs that wouldn't come about by hand.

Nevertheless, these use cases are important as forms of generative design and creation are becoming increasingly practiced across creative spheres. This has been a well-established field of activity for some time in graphic art and music and is becoming increasingly prominent in design and architecture, where advanced computer-aided manufacturing techniques are freeing us from the constraint to create using only a simple palette of shapes. The challenge is putting the act of casual algorithmic creation into the hands of nonprogrammer users. Related to this are questions around the contexts in which casual creation is of interest. Compton and Mateas[46] touch upon the potentially great cultural value of rapid personalized creation using creativity support tools. This has started to become a site of interest for a new generation of creative tools in which the act of creation itself is gamified. Nelson et al., for example, present Gamika, a system for metacreating simple 2D computer games (think Pong, Asteroids, or ball-in-maze games),[47] which they believe will support popular forms of social engagement such as jamming (in the hacker sense, creating new games in a social environment) and sending novel artifacts to friends, possibly with a surprise or challenge involved.

Such casual creation systems are also important because several of the techniques described in chapter 5 still need some kind of content-creating subsystem in order to operate. Evolutionary computing approaches require a genotype-to-phenotype transformation that usually has some degree of complexity. As we saw, it is not normally effective to evolve phenotypes directly (such as mutating individual pixels within an image or individual samples within an audio file). The effectiveness of the content creation system at producing richly varied and complex structures will influence the effectiveness of the overall algorithm. Thus even if generative methods themselves are not particularly powerful in the hands of a programmer, finding effective generative methods underlies many potential advances in computational creativity.

For example, a recent trend has been for conceptual creative works that take as their focus the remixing of large databases of existing content. *Of Oz The Wizard* is a beautiful example, a remix of *The Wizard of Oz* movie with the entire movie rearranged so that the script is in alphabetical order. *Double Oh* is a mash-up of every instance of everyone saying "Double-O" in every James Bond movie ever. Christian Marclay's *The Clock* is a 24-hour video mash-up gallery exhibit made entirely from famous movies, where at each moment there is a clock depicted or a person stating the time, telling the correct time of day as seen by the viewer. Not all of these works were made by particularly advanced means (in Marclay's case, a team was recruited to watch movies and note when such events appeared). Nevertheless, AI techniques such as automatic subtitle generation or event and object detection will advance the kinds of tricks we can use and the speed at which we can work in the creation of such data-driven artworks, leading to new aesthetic concepts.

Likewise, new creative practices, particularly in the area of remix and mash-up, are opened up by commercial software that enables the conversion of a recorded sound or image into a more readily editable model of that sound or image—for example, music software that can convert a recorded piece of music into a series of virtual instruments and score information that recreates the music as well as determining the tempo and meter. Thus a novice musician could produce an accompaniment to a piece of recorded music simply by transforming and filtering the note information that is extracted from it. If such techniques seem too commonplace or mundane to call them AI, remember from chapter 1 that our perception of AI is in a constant state of change, the goalposts forever shifting—AI defined as everything we don't yet know how to do.

Other types of AI systems reveal their own peculiarities that have been the focus of aesthetic exploration. In 2015, a series of images created by "deep dreaming" neural networks went viral on the Internet.[48] These images were derived from a neural network that had been trained to recognize certain things such as dogs. As with the deep learning image processing systems described earlier, these neural networks work directly on image pixel data, meaning that you can feed the pixels of an image file directly into them, from which the object recognition occurs. An interesting feature of such networks, therefore, is that they can be run backward, making alterations to the pixels themselves. For example, you can iteratively make small adjustments to the image pixels that increase the network's perception that there is a dog in the image. By doing so, any minor curve or color gradient that vaguely resembles some part of a dog gets gradually sculpted so as to look more doglike. There's no better word to describe the results than "psychedelic." A regular image becomes peppered with dog hallucinations, seamlessly injected into the surface details. In other cases, clouds become sheep and more abstract effects occur—contours and edges become flowy, almost painterly. Such tools have been made available for public access and use, the result being *lots* of images with trippy dog hallucinations added to them. Importantly, then, these systems are highly narrow in their application: they are powerful tools but still tools, with a characteristically domain-specific nature. AI-powered effects now form part of a growing palette of visual processes used by artists and designers. For example, a recent makeup photo shoot of model Kylie Jenner was adorned with AI-generated "makeup" effects, a custom image transform that mutated the face in curious ways.[49]

Likewise, it may even be the error in the algorithms, their failure to accurately reproduce outputs, that becomes of greater interest, either because the resulting outputs are structurally interesting in their own right or because of the poetic dissonance of such a creative process. There are many examples of creative work that purposefully draws to light the more daft or unnatural outputs of generative algorithms. In a discussion paper on creative music composition using AI by Bob Sturm and a number of collaborators,[50] Sturm says of his own compositional work: "I did not limit myself to 'cherry picking,' but also challenged myself to work with generated material that was not immediately sensible. ... I was specifically looking for failures of the model." Collaborator Oded Ben-Tal says, "Fairly early on in the composition process I realised I was more interested in exploring the edges of the model, and not its more typical results." In both cases, the artists further manipulated the outputs of the system in the production of the final compositions to greater or lesser extents.

Producing Generative Works and Embedding Generative Variation in Interactive Experiences

From Radiohead's pay-what-you-want online record release *In Rainbows* to U2's notorious collaboration with Apple to bundle a copy of their album *Songs of Innocence* free with iTunes, technology now relentlessly insists on shifting the relationship between creative producer and creative consumer. Bjørk's 2011 *Biophilia* album was a high-profile case of using the computational medium, primarily the tablet, as a way to expand the possibilities of music experience into an interactive realm. Years earlier, Brian Eno produced albums based on generative processes and with other artists began to explore the affordances of the CD-ROM, the medium that heralded the mass distribution of software programs as artworks.

Despite the persistence of older formats such as vinyl, we now listen to music primarily through general purpose computational devices such as computers and smartphones, and thus there is in principle no technological barrier to any artist choosing to release music that employs generative or interactive elements (for example, on the iOS platform, it is simply the difference between releasing an album on iTunes and an app on the App Store). There is a usability barrier, as users tend to consume music through preferred and trusted playback apps such as iTunes or Spotify, and of course there is a creativity barrier, as the means to produce generative music are not yet ready to hand for producers. The same applies to video content.

Why would anyone want to produce generative art, and why would anyone want to experience it? Even in domains such as video games, which would seem to establish the perfect context for generative music, there seems only a weak appetite for generativity. Notions of authorship and association play an important role here; while in some commercial or functional contexts, such as relaxation music or logo design, authorship is not an important factor in the consumption of the creative work, in other contexts it is key. A challenge lies in reconciling the lack of control that comes with generative production with the need for authors to stamp a work's identity. The activities described above lead down different avenues with respect to this challenge; an artist may produce a casual creator, which contains a high degree of their own creative autonomy and can then be placed in other people's hands to arrive at the finished product. Here the task of building a generative system remains very much in the artist's control, whereas using an evolutionary or machine learning process might undermine (or appear to undermine) that control, since they more radically disrupt the autonomy of the creator in their generate-and-test process; if the creator is only playing the role of evaluator and not that of generator, building with their own hands, so to speak, this may challenge their authorship, and once again this will correspond with different attitudes to authorship in different domains.

In 2011, I worked on a project in the band Icarus, a duo consisting of myself and Sam Britton, in which we set out to produce "an album in 1,000 variations." We composed an album of electronic music (our seventh album, so we were well practiced at the electronic music production component of this process), and in addition, we created our own software tools to enable systematic variations to be introduced into each track. A simple kick drum pattern, say, could have four or five variations: one completely regular four-to-the-floor pattern, something with a bit more swing, something with a syncopated offbeat on each fourth beat, and so on. Our system would allow us to set up these prototypes and then smoothly interpolate between them in custom ways. At a higher level, we also set up a similar process regarding the progression of the track through its constituent elements. One version of the same track might start with drums and bass, while another version started with horns and guitar, before following some mutable trajectory through the track's components.

The creative challenge was to find a way to make smooth variations where each variation was coherent in its own right. Just because two kick drum patterns are good, it doesn't follow that a kick drum pattern that is half-of-one-half-of-the-other is also good. Creatively then, the project involved composing music and seeking out interpolation strategies that maintained coherence. The result was 1,000 minutely different copies of the album. Such an approach could be used to allow endless variation. It could be used to allow a listener to play a record many times without hearing it sound exactly the same each time—a common ambition for generative music producers. However, our interest was in the opposite direction, that each listener might own their own unique experience of the album that they get to know like any other album, but never quite sharing the experience of other listeners. We sold the records so that each purchase was unique and was not available to anyone else, a sort of limited edition. This also enabled us to explore issues of music ownership, to say that the purchaser of each copy actually *owned* a share of the copyright of that version, meaning not only the listening rights to a copy of a mass produced record, but partial ownership of the recording. This also meant that the record existed in the form of regular digital files, not a generative software system, making it more compatible with existing music distribution infrastructure.

However, it seems plausible that we will shift to a situation in which producing a piece of music or a film for a service like Spotify or Netflix will include the option to compose interactive and generative experiences. This is technologically entirely possible now, even if it is questionable what kind of adoption might take place and where. The web leads the way. The sophistication of HTML's media tools makes it trivial to create custom media players that combine layered video, audio, animation, and interactive elements. Indeed, if we think of the domains of design and layout evolving from the fixed media of magazines and posters, then the browser itself has already been serving this purpose since its inception.

Of interest are the kinds of formats that will emerge to accommodate creative production in a generative world. At one extreme, a player could simply embed a rich media webpage or other plug-in architecture that allows creators to submit programs of any kind; the producer would be entirely in control of the format of their creation, with both the freedom and burden of choice that comes with this. At the other extreme are simple audio formats such as Native Instruments' STEM format, which specifies that a musical track be made up of four remixable elements, such as bass, drums, keys, and vocals. This allows a very crude level of on-the-fly remixability, useful for expanding the boundaries of DJing, but perhaps too limited to be of widespread appeal. Such a proposition also runs up against an acceptance hurdle for artists, who may be reluctant to give access to the constituent components of their work (and if they did want to then they could do this easily using standard audio files and still cater for a large number of uses), and raises quality issues such as how the artist might apply global effects such as compression.[51] Intermediate formats might take the form of simple instruction sets that define the rules for the music's progression, stochastic systems, or controllable parametric systems, and a good general purpose format would cater for all of these scenarios.

In practice, the more features any such format accumulates, the closer it will come to being a general purpose programming environment. It is not too hard for practitioners with basic coding skills to author reasonably advanced generative works in an environment such as HTML5, and generative-focused authoring tools targeting a general purpose platform such as HTML5 can be developed, around which communities of practice and expertise can form. The FLoWr framework is one such example. In the case of the web, where any paradigm is possible, the concept of a *document object model* is extremely helpful in bringing together the most obvious and functional aspects of page layout. It is also apparent in games engines such as Unity and Unreal. These support general purpose software programming manipulation but have common features and file formats that align with expertise and task decomposition, such as the production of 3D models or the scripting of character behaviors.

Extending this idea, generative and interactive systems open up different affordances in different consumption contexts. In a world of ubiquitous or pervasive computing, the technology enabling generativity can be found everywhere. All modern media devices are computers, all computers can be media devices, and all objects can be imbued with computational capabilities and digital interfaces. This expands the purposes for which we might employ generative media. A compelling example is Ben Houge's work on "Food Opera." Houge, an experienced computer game music composer, began to explore where his generative compositions might be applicable outside of the games world. He turned to the dining experience, long associated with music, and asked how the art of a game music composer might be applied to personalized, adaptive composition-for-food. In his resulting operas, collaborated on with world-leading chefs, he places a speaker at each seat in a collective dining experience and composes adaptive music in which each channel is matched to the menu but also coordinated rhythmically and harmonically with the collective.

Games themselves present several application areas for generative content where the generative production of content is not only beneficial but somewhat necessary. A recent, much discussed example is the game *No Man's Sky*, which uses procedural techniques to generate an astronomical number of planets for players to visit. Planet generation is deterministic, not random, meaning that in a sense these planets *actually* exist, so to speak, as points in the game space; their existence and properties are predicated by the algorithm, rather than being created on the fly. This means that any player could decide to visit a previously unexplored planet, for which they have the pleasure to name it forevermore. There they will see configurations of plants and animals and atmospheric content and other game elements that nobody, not even the game creators, has ever seen, although these will certainly be identifiable as simple combinatorial and exploratory

Figure 6.1
Ben Houge's Food Opera is a novel application of generative music in which adaptive compositions are coupled with dishes and coordinated among the diners in a distributed fine dining audio experience. Image credit: Ben Houge.

variations on what has been seen before. This generative capacity affords a certain game experience, that of authentic discovery.

Lastly, the field has possible functional applications beyond entertainment scenarios. Requena et al.[52] discuss the use of generative music produced adaptively to alleviate pain or attention toward pain in a scenario such as receiving an injection. Similarly, Stefan Ehrlich, Kat Agres, and Gordon Cheng showed that participants could control the mood of music played to them via a brain-computer interface, providing "a tool for listeners to mediate their own emotions by interacting with music."[53]

Creative Blends and Mashups

Style transfer, introduced in chapter 5, is the automated application of a style to an artifact. The classic example is the application of a painterly style such as that of Van Gogh or Munch to a photographic image. From photo filters in Instagram to groove quantize features in digital audio workstations which apply specific rhythmic grooves to musical patterns, the idea of sequentially applying transforms to an aesthetic object to give it a certain style is now completely familiar in digital creative practice. The meaning of style is of course highly variable. It may be acceptable to say that an image filter applied to a photograph is a style applied to the photograph's content, but in reality the photograph embodies a multitude of stylistic components—the choice of subject matter, angle, composition, and so on—and our context influences what draws our focus when we talk about style. Once again, while there may be a natural logic to the relationship between style and content, there is a great deal of domain specificity about where a boundary is drawn between such entities. A neural network performing painterly rendering will have been trained on works of art to derive a model of the fine-grained qualities of brush strokes, and so can modify a photographic image by making it better fit what it expects of this fine-grained detail.

Like other examples discussed earlier, style transfer does not in itself provide either processes of generation or evaluation but instead systematically transforms existing work. Used in this way, style transformations are functionally equivalent to photo filters or groove quantizers, but the potential of the underlying technology is qualitatively different. Systems such as neural networks that are trained on raw image data provide an incredibly fluid toolkit for manipulating style. They have inferred the stylistic qualities themselves, and this learning can be adapted to target different levels of content and composition. They can be used to reverse-engineer individual creative stylistic features at different levels and then mix these together generatively. They speed up the rate at which we can generate outcomes in a certain style. They support the generation of multiplicities. For example, an artist might generate a style filter as a creative output, deployed in the context of a real-time experience or an endless body of work applied to existing datasets of images. An example is such work is the creative practice and associated technologies developed by Parag Mital in his PhD thesis.[54]

More generally we can say that style transfer is a form of blending where an artifact is created through the composition of two or more different processes by a user. In the style transfer examples discussed, this process is sequential, with the application of one style to an existing artifact, but in other examples of blending it needn't be. For example, Singh et al.[55] looked at the capacity for variational autoencoders (VAEs) to blend concepts in image sketches.

Style transfer performs a task that a skilled artist might have been needed to perform and also speeds up that task. Style transfer may not be obviously creative in itself—it is systematic, predictable, and does not involve search—but one of its interesting potential applications is in its potential to *force* quality outputs: a make-everything-nice machine that democratizes creative production. If we can apply a formulaic process that "fixes" the stylistic qualities of an artifact, then we can be more free in our use of the source artifacts. A mundane street photograph rendered in Van Gogh's brush strokes may take on new qualities. The potential implications of this are diverse. Reducing the skill required in a production task makes it easier, of course, and is also likely to make each such outcome considered less valuable. Thus the domain itself, including the criteria for judgment in the domain, is likely to be transformed by the available technology.

Co-Creative Generative Ideation

This book has been particularly concerned with creativity as a social process. In many fields, collaboration is key and strategies for successful collaboration are a subject of critical research. An example is in the design research of Cross and Cross.[56] They identify a number of informal roles design collaborators might take, along with their formal roles, such as in problem clarification, timekeeping, or facilitating. In co-creativity, a human and a computational system collaborate in creative production, meaning that the machine is in some way actively involved in the production of creative outputs, interacting during the process with a human co-creator.[57] The human may be in charge and creatively dominant, but they may be steered by the output of the system.

A key application area is generative ideation. This includes any situation where the machine is used to get some ideas on the table, such as to break a writer's block (recall this is the motivation David Cope gave for embarking on work in generative music). The ideas might not be great, but they might be good enough, contain the spark of an idea, or simply trigger the creative practitioner to develop a new direction. The Aiva music composition system, for example, is based on the observation that commercial composers often need to rapidly turn over a rough idea to a client at the first stage of a pitch before developing it further. Flicking through several generative examples for something to get started on can be more effective than a blank slate. I have found this to be the case in my own creative music practice: getting started always means just getting something on the page, anything, and then manipulating and iterating it.

This we may consider the current dominant model of human-computer co-creativity. The human user by one method or other requests suggestions from the system. The system's output does not need to consist of complete works, and the system itself does not need to perform any evaluation of these outputs, but it is capable of producing things in the right ballpark, which the user might be able to iterate. Schematically, the computational system is a generator in a larger, adaptively creative, human-computer generate-and-test complex.

This approach suits a number of the algorithmic methods we have seen so far, and it also fits well with aspects of creative practice that have been discussed previously. Firstly, the user remains in charge of the overall process. Secondly, the system serves a clearly defined part of the creative process, the exploration of a space of possibilities. Here we can see the system both as a material in the hands of a creative individual—like the potter interacting with clay, the user leads the process but is also led by what the system feeds back—and as a cognitive agent collaborating with the user as part of a process of extended cognition, where the tasks of creative ideation and evaluation are split between system and user. As we have seen, distributed evolutionary systems have demonstrated some success as generative ideation tools, as have neural networks and rule-based systems, all of which can mass produce outputs according to targets, feedback, training sets, or defined constraints.

We have also already seen the most elementary form of co-creation in interactive genetic algorithms where the user selects and the algorithm seeks new random or cross-bred variations within the space that the user is searching. Target-based evolution can also provide co-creative support: as the user is creating something, the algorithm is searching the related space of possibilities for outcomes that suit certain criteria. This was applied in a game level-design scenario by Yannakakis, Liapis and Alexopoulos where the user designs a game level map while the system proposes suggestions based on a hardwired model of playability that it used to test levels with and evolve optimum designs.[58]

Machine learning algorithms such as autoencoders and GANs provide interesting variations on the user experience of co-creation. These enable training on an input set as well as interaction via latent or embedding spaces which gives the user some control over the generation process but with a high likelihood of surprising outcomes (whether good or bad). In Singh et al.'s VAE sketch system, discussed above,[59] the authors argue that the potential conceptual blends the system can produce are valuable for ideation, stimulating the user with unimagined outputs.

Co-creativity can also involve co-development of an output in which the user and the system iterate. This might simply mean that the system generates and the user selects, gives feedback, and alters settings, but it could also involve a more symmetrical relationship resembling a negotiation in which the user may adapt their understanding and goals, and the system may give feedback and, so to speak, alter the settings. Anna Kantosalo and Hannu Toivonen[60] propose the concept of alternating co-creation to describe this situation, distinguishing it from task-divided co-creation. They specifically define symmetric co-creation as that in which the system is able to make fundamental transformations to its own rules for generation.

Kaz Grace and colleagues[61] have explored such "conversational" or "dialogic" AI systems in sketching. A trained sketch-generating neural network uses a model of typicality to generate more or less wild suggestions for designs. These were shown to prompt the designer to come up with new ideas in a manner that evokes classic divergent-thinking stimulation.

"Explainable" AI and the theme of framing in computational creativity (discussed in chapter 7) are important here. A good dialogic interface may require the system to provide additional explanatory content for what it created. Wagstaff et al. showed that a scientific discovery engine performed better in collaboration with scientists if it better explained its discoveries.[62]

Through the above examples, such systems can be seen as standard production tools, much as a Google search might be used to request creatively stimulating or appropriate content, but they are of a particularly creatively potent nature by virtue of their ability to mass produce variants. They are generatively creative in a sense; novel artifacts are produced, regardless of whether they are deemed good or not. These candidates might be immediately abandoned, being deemed of no value, but they might also cause the evaluator, the human, to alter their value system.

The coupled human-computer system, meanwhile, is adaptively creative. The user, even if he or she does not have well-formed outcomes in mind and is engaged in open-ended search, is likely to have motivations and longer-term outcomes in mind such as to impact an audience.

Breeding Creatures

Evolutionary computing approaches, as we have seen, are associated with a slight variant of this relationship between a user and a generative process. The three basic ways that I have discussed evolution being used—targeted fitness-based evolution including multiobjective search, interactive evolution including multiuser evolution, and novelty search—offer different use cases with specific affordances. These approaches, as their inspiration in biology suggests, involve a form of interaction that is slightly more involved than running a generator with given settings. Instead we might think of more responsive and experimental forms of interaction—nurturing of a complex system, akin to selective breeding or the gardening of experimental ecosystems.

Targeted search works when it is possible to define a goal for the system in an algorithmic form. This is particularly applicable in those areas where externally imposed demands must be addressed: object design, interaction design, architecture, graphic design, music for film, and so on. Such objectives can be more or less explicitly stated. An object design task may have specific structural stability requirements, whereas a music composition task may have an expected mood which may be open to some interpretation and contextual influence. In architecture it is now normal practice to run building designs through a building analytics system that reports on measurable qualities of the design: how much sunlight an apartment gets at different times of day, how long it takes to get from one part of the building to another, and so on.

Such analytics frameworks, especially as they become standardized, mean that any number of automatically generated designs can be rapidly evaluated in terms of their performance on these various metrics, and practitioners can set acceptance thresholds for designs or seek optimal compromises according to multiobjective criteria. Remember that using multiple criteria typically results in a spectrum of solutions rather than one single solution. Each point on that spectrum represents a solution that is in some sense optimal: there is no other solution that is better according to each and every one of the criteria, although there may be solutions that are better according to *some* criteria. Recall the example in chapter 5, in building design, of a tradeoff between sunlight exposure and insulation. The more area covered by windows, the greater the exposure but the lower the insulation. Of course *where* the windows are placed matter a great deal in each case. There are better or worse solutions, but there is no objectively best solution that maximizes sunlight exposure and insulation. Nevertheless, the solution space can be reduced by removing *any solution for which there is at least one other solution that is better in both sunlight exposure and insulation* (this resulting set of partially optimal solutions is the Pareto front, introduced in chapter 5). The user can then look along that spectrum and decide where the best payoff is between different criteria, perhaps based on further criteria. This could even be a choice that is handed to the customer, buying their apartment off plan with an option to choose specific design details before it is built.

The fact that such analytics systems don't cover every aspect of the design quality, especially aesthetic criteria, does not mean that targeted evolutionary search cannot take into account such factors. For example, a designer might create a parametric system that they consider to produce elegant structures of a certain desired style, and then seek optimal outputs from that system using analytic criteria. The result is heavily constrained by the designer's initial design but is still the most performant it can be given that constraint. And of course it may be that, in the spirit of form following function, the automated adaptation of designs to satisfy explicit performance criteria tends to result in designs that people find pleasing. The trend toward biologically inspired design is indicative of this. A building that optimizes sunlight exposure might end up with pleasing sinusoidal curves, and a building that optimizes travel time between points might end up with a pleasing radial form. Such methods can effortlessly tap the beauty in nature's "algorithmic design."

Evolutionary optimization can be powerful to the point that it can even break the fitness function. In chapter 5, we saw anecdotes of how evolution effectively outwitted the creators' fitness function designs, finding holes that were unintended. In a more sublime case, a researcher was evolving designs for hardware components and wanted to evolve a series of transistors. As they explained, after a successful evolutionary run, they discovered that "some circuits had amplified radio signals present in the air ... to give good fitness scores. These signals were generated by nearby PCs in the laboratory where the experiments took place."[63] The circuit simply didn't work if it wasn't in exactly the environment in which it had been evolved. In my own first ever implementation of genetic algorithms for music, I had endless trouble trying to find fitness functions that did what I meant, not what I said. The algorithm would constantly optimize things that weren't the things I actually wanted to optimize.

Another application of target-based evolution is to match specific targets based on similarity. The utility of this is not immediately obvious, because it is hardly creative to merely recreate something that already exists. As we saw in chapter 5, Yee-King's EvoSynth[64] uses evolution to tweak the parameters of synthesizers to recreate natural sounds. Once this has been achieved, the types of manipulation that can be performed on the synthesizer are very different to the types of manipulation that can be performed on the sound sample itself, so something has been gained. An obvious application is to be able to create smooth, interesting, or perceptually effective interpolations between one sound and another, and the same process could be applied to images. Another application lies in mosaicing (or "musaicing" in the case of sound), where a target output is recreated using components of a specific type. A classic example is the mosaicing of thousands of tiny color photographs to recreate the image of another color image, an effect commonly seen in ads and animated graphics. Each photograph's average color content is used to place it in the larger composite image. In musaicing, small sound fragments are woven together to recreate other sounds. This can be put to conceptual effect or achieve clever perceptual effects, as with the artist Petros Vrellis[65] recreating famous artworks by threading string around a circular configuration of hooks (discussed in chapter 5), establishing a powerful sublime connection between a medium and the image it is used to create.

Interactive evolutionary search introduces a very different form of user interaction. Here the components of the evolutionary algorithm are distributed between software and human user. The human does the selection and the software produces new variants based on heredity, mutation, and genetic crossover. At first glance, interactive evolution is simply a variant of target-based evolution, except that in this case the target is not written in an algorithm but encoded in some human user's taste. In reality, however, there are issues with thinking of interactive evolution in this way. This should be fairly obvious from our discussion of creative processes from chapter 3. It was discussed in depth by Stanley and Lehman, the creators of the distributed interactive evolutionary art system Picbreeder, and authors of the book *Why Greatness Cannot be Planned: The Myth of the Objective*.[66] They observed that users of their Picbreeder system engaged in exactly the kind of open-ended exploration that we have seen elsewhere in creative practice, allowing the material itself to guide their search. They did not set fixed goals for their search but followed its evolutionary pathways by being prompted by things that appeared along the way. They were interested in the journey as much as in the end product.

Nevertheless, this does not by any means rule out the idea that interactive evolutionary search might achieve outcomes that are valuable and could not have been achieved by other means. The electronic media artist Jon McCormack produced his series of 3D generated plant and animal forms through this kind of interactive evolutionary search of L-system structures.[67] Even as the software developer himself, with direct access to the code describing these forms, it was still an effective practice for McCormack to set up an interactive search strategy to help him navigate the vast space of possible designs. The search experience becomes very different from setting up a parametric system and then tweaking each of the parameters in turn, or even tweaking the code by hand. Interactive search is radically different.

From a survey of the uses of interactive evolutionary computation,[68] it seems that evolutionary computation is particularly commonly applied to creative domains that are not already well established as human creative activities. A possible theory, then, is that if we are practiced at creating something, or it is cognitively manageable, then there is no need for evolutionary computing, but if the form is novel or cognitively demanding or cumbersome to produce (such as McCormack's 3D plant forms[69]), then evolutionary computing is useful. Rather than evolving melodies or visual artworks, we find interactive evolutionary computing used for complex 3D structures, obscure electronic sounds, or abstract animations, as in Scott Draves's evolvable screensaver Electric Sheep.[70] This is a speculative observation, but there are clearly some domain specific areas of application that are better suited to this mode of exploration, at least because they are innately computational in their production.

One vision of the application context for interactive evolutionary computation is that it is hidden, embedded in everyday interaction without you knowing it, conforming to the ambient paradigm described above. When you visit a webpage, it is now common that a team of designers, developers, and content creators is busy behind the scenes tracking your experience and making improvements to the site in response to this data. The time you spend looking for a link, whether you choose to purchase the premium product, whether you agree to sign up to the mailing list, or the success with which an ad distracts you, are all factors that can be measured and that the site's creators have some potential control over through their interface design and content. The powerful thing about websites (and any form of cloud-delivered software-as-a-service), though, is that you can serve a slightly different version of the site to each visitor, manipulating any feature you like and see what effect it has on thousands of users, conducting real-time statistically significant user tests. Such methods are now common, although only relatively recently has this intensive real-time adaptation been put into effect. This strategy was most famously popularized during the 2008 US election campaign that brought Barack Obama to the presidency, where different stories, images, messages, and user-interface elements were trialed in front of a live audience from his campaign homepage.[71]

The same ideas can be applied to subtle aesthetic factors like the appeal of the logo, the color scheme, or the font, and attempts have already been made to create real-time evolvable websites. Various forms of implicit positive or negative feedback can be used to determine the evolutionary selection pressures on these components. The results of such a process, if successful, might then be used to personalize your experience or might be tried out on other users. As our environment becomes increasingly hypernetworked, we can see how the same logic is applied easily to many other forms of artifact. Software components, entire computer programs, digital assets, and robotic behaviors can be made mildly adaptive through distributed evolutionary processes. With modern digital fabrication, the physical world becomes subject to the same potential.

Likewise, in the music, film, and television industries, there has always been a demand to speed up as best as possible the response to feedback and to trial variations in order to gain a comparative understanding of what works. DarwinTunes[72] was an intriguing experiment in creating generative music that evolved in real time according to user feedback. The creators of the system set up an online radio station that played loops of simple techno-music in four-bar blocks. At the end of each block, the music would shift to a new candidate—not exactly the most realistic listening experience, but one not entirely dissimilar to some dance music structures. Listeners could then give feedback via a web interface in real time. Over time, the music evolved and according to the system's authors increased in complexity.

Similarly, in Picbreeder,[73] while the evolutionary nature of the system is most explicit for those visiting the website, the option is also there to go onto the site only to browse, to look at one's friends' creations, or see the most rated images. In other words, in the massively distributed online form of interactive evolution, there is a seamless interplay between evolution as a form of interaction and more familiar forms of interaction related to selection, such as choosing from a list of presets, seeing what is popular, or seeking outputs by their properties.

As an electronic musician, my own interest in evolutionary computation has been not in the direct production of music using evolution but in the evolution of complex software objects that can be used to create music in live improvised performance. Evolved neural networks have been used to develop sophisticated and efficient robot behaviors, and by implication can also be used to produce interactive musical software agents that map inputs to outputs in interesting ways. In the case of audio, such agents are simply digital audio effects, and the space of possible audio effect processors is yet another creative space that is clearly defined and clearly constrained, yet full of rich unexplored possibilities. With PhD student Steffan Ianigro this work has developed toward an online distributed evolutionary computing interface and repository for evolved audio effects.[74]

Here again, the evolutionary component of such an interface can be either operation-based—something the user might manipulate, configure, and control—or ambient, in which case users might download and try out different modules, without being necessarily aware that they are feeding back into a distributed, interactive evolutionary algorithm.

Distributed Evolutionary Systems

Further to the algorithmic specifics defined above, there are various ways in which systems can be enhanced by making them distributed. This includes using a distributed user base (as in distributed interactive genetic algorithms) or creating virtual populations of agents that interact with each other. It also includes the development of modular systems that are created by multiple developers, as in the FloWr framework for computational creativity.[75] When considering these systems, we come up against the distributed view of creativity discussed in chapter 3 and find that the generative form of creativity is much more explicitly expressed in these circumstances.

Distributed interactive genetic algorithms are interactive genetic algorithms in which multiple users have access to and influence over the evolving population. The primary aim of adding a multiuser element to such systems, usually stated, is to attempt to solve the problem of user fatigue. Evolution of complex structures requires many generations of mutation, genetic crossover, and selection, and it is too much to expect one person to sit and manage this process for too long, especially if we are expecting this to be an intrinsically motivated experience. Distributed interactive evolution purportedly address this problem by spreading the work across multiple users, lightening each user's workload. However, it remains to be conclusively demonstrated that the fatigue issue really gives an accurate portrayal of the problem with interactive genetic algorithms.

As we saw Lehman and Stanley demonstrating with their system Picbreeder, users don't tend to have clear objectives when evolving images but instead engage with the system through the type of interaction that Malafouris[76] described as material engagement, allowing their search to be directed by what is thrown back at them. The achievement of a concrete objective, then, is replaced by a more fluid notion of creative achievement.

At the extremes either everything or nothing produced by the system is an exciting discovery for a given user. More likely, the user experiences fluctuations in their level of engagement and excitement. The experience might well be an end in itself, of which the resulting images and their artistic merits are not fully representative. In addition, applying notions of perceived originality and identity, users may *wish* to put in effort as a way to carve out something that is uniquely theirs.

Applications like Picbreeder are compelling but are yet to make professional grade tools, although they may not be far off. Many visitors to the site are there out of curiosity rather than with a creative aim in mind. Without a clear model of what users are there for we should be wary of projections such as the assumption that fatigue is holding them back from achieving goals.

There is another reason why distributed interactive genetic algorithms might be more effective than single user algorithms. This is not to do with the efficiency of finding universally agreed "good" outcomes, but the efficiency with which the algorithm is able to match solutions with uses—something the Internet, with its many-to-many structure, is of course excellent at doing. Creative practitioners frequently go online to obtain resources produced by third parties that they can use in their own work, such as clip art, copyright-free audio samples, virtual studio plug-ins, and creative coding libraries. For the most part these resources are produced by people, but it would make little difference if they were produced automatically, as long as they serve the purpose we seek (caveat: again, it is worth noting how the social value of authorship varies from one domain to another). A distributed interactive genetic algorithm not only distributes the selective pressures imposed by different individuals but also distributes the results; all of the outputs generated so far by earlier evolution by users. Someone can go onto a site such as Picbreeder and interact with it not via selective evolution but in the more familiar way of scrolling through a list of objects that have been favorited or otherwise tagged as valuable.

By placing many evolved objects in front of many users, a distributed interactive genetic algorithm completes the Gibsonian (or equally we could say "niche constructionist") vision of ecological complexity accelerating evolutionary discovery. Since affordances describe relationships between pairs of entities, increasing the combinatorial mix increases the discovery of useful interactions. Just as the users may find objects they need, *objects*

Putting Computational Creativity to Work

may find users they need. To state that an evolved aesthetic object is actually in search of a user may be considered a flippant anthropomorphism, but in fact it is perfectly suited to interpretation by way of cultural teleofunction. By displaying the object in front of many users we are increasing the chance that it finds a use, just as Post-It note glue needed to find its use.

Performance and Interaction

Performative domains such as live music or dance can suggest very different algorithmic requirements and somewhat different aims within the space of computational creativity practice and its motivation, particularly when there is a real-time interactive element to the performance. There are several areas where this may be the case: live music performance, in particular improvised music; games and other forms of interactive entertainment such as interactive storytelling or interactive TV; and other forms of dramatic performance including interactive gestural experiences and robotics.

In one respect, the creation of a performance can be considered to have exactly the same expectations and goals associated with it as any other creative production, and in some cases the difference is more of a technicality. For example, a music performance system that interprets a score of solo piano music could plausibly be run offline, resulting in note data that could then be rendered on a digitally controlled piano. The system could run back and forth through its rendered output making modifications or trialing different candidates, just as a system generating a visual artwork might. Both systems may be subject to time constraints, depending on the use context, but not the constraint of real-time performance.

Introducing interaction, however, introduces a strict real-time requirement; events simply can't be mapped out in advance. Consider the same interpretation system with the only difference being that it must follow a conductor. The expressive performance would need to change depending on the input given by the conductor. The system can no longer simply perform its computation up front, because it needs to have knowledge about the changing tempo in order to make decisions about the placement or accentuation of notes.

Now imagine that the system also has to interact with other musicians reading a score, or further still, switch this performance context for one in which the music is improvised around an agreed structure, perhaps without a score at all. There are many forms of improvised performance with varying types of organizing structure. In traditional jazz, one or more prior chord sequences and melodic lines are used, usually with a series of solos over the main chord sequence, topped and tailed by the lead melody. In free improvisation, a common theme is the aspiration toward "non-idiomatic" performance, where stylistic premeditation or organizing structures are eschewed as best as possible. Performers working in this domain inevitably abound with idioms, but they nevertheless often take the approach of minimizing the pre-agreement of elements.

In all of these cases, details aside, the basic constraint is the same, that the creative work unfolds in time rather than being created in what may be thought of as an out-of-time process. The work is live and cannot be started over, events that have occurred cannot be edited in light of what has later transpired, and choices about current actions can only be made in light of uncertain expectations about what is to come later.[77]

The real-time domain may therefore be described as having all of the demands of a non-real-time computational creativity scenario, with the additional demands of having to deal with this irreversibility with respect to past events and uncertainty about future events. In practice, though, there is also a prominent body of work in improvised systems that doesn't burden itself too much with the traditional issues of creative generation and instead focuses on the interaction experience and the potential to stimulate co-creative activity with one or more human partners. One burden, to generate original content, is lightened in place of another, to operate under real-time demands. Thus in a common free improvised music scenario, a solo musician will perform in a duet with a software system and the question is not so much whether the system generates original and pleasing music each time it runs but how it is experienced as an interactive agent expressing forms of musical intelligence and a sense of agency. For researchers such as Pachet (whose experiments with the Continuator[78] are described in chapter 1 and are discussed further below) a core question was how such a system stimulated new creative ideas in the performer and enabled them to reflect on their own performance. That is not to say that the system shouldn't aspire to the wider goal of producing a varied and original output, but that there is an intermediate and distinct area of interest in this particular case. It is also important to note that in the minutiae of the system's output (constrained though it may be), and also in the

Putting Computational Creativity to Work

co-creative interaction between performers, most systems designed to focus on performer engagement do still somehow contribute to the production of original and compelling creative events.

There are several candidate examples of system behaviors that might successfully give the partner musician this experience. Being able to play in the same key as the musician and follow the beat are basic examples, but they don't speak much to the system's ability to engage musically or creatively. A common elementary approach for system developers is to get the system to perform in a copycat manner, such as playing back reinterpreted fragments of the human player's performance (an example is the work on the Omax system[79]). This communicates that the machine is listening and responding, and establishes some connection between the two agents that is not just down to the human's capability. Although this sounds like the kind of thing a human improviser might do, some musicians playing with such systems report finding it disconcerting to have their own musical performance thrown back at them.[80] This depends on how literally the material is treated. More generally, of course, this is an example of a creative musical decision that is very much a matter of taste and compositional intention, as varied as musical styles are across the board.

More impressively, the system might attempt to find "continuations" of what the musician has played. In other words, rather than recycle the material, it might follow what is being played and come up with expectations about what should come next. This means that a flowing call-and-response interaction between a human and machine musician could be set up or the machine could play alongside the human with a sense of appropriate expectation. Couple this with a strong ability to make rhythmic predictions, and a strong sense of interaction can be set up. François Pachet, whose Continuator[81] is an early success story in this field, refers to such novel interaction scenarios as facilitating *flow*—the state of immersion that comes when experiences are suitably stimulating, which we encountered in chapter 2. He also refers to them as *mirroring* systems in that they mirror the performer's style.

Other ways to establish a sense of interaction might be more obscure. When improvisers play they don't necessarily perform continuations of what each other is playing, and in some styles of free improvisation there is little even that the audience might pick up about the interaction. In one experiment by Young et al.,[82] audiences were played improvised recordings where an ensemble of free improvising musicians played with each other but may or may not have been able to hear each other (the performers, in separate rooms, were given headphones playing either a live feed of the other musicians, or white noise intended to block out the other musicians). The results showed that from the audience's perspective it wasn't always easy to tell whether the musicians could hear each other. This is a concept that was further corroborated by a formal study of causality in a standard jazz improvisation session, where musicians were seen not to have as much influence on each other as the score had on the musicians.[83] While the musicians may be responding to what they hear, they are not doing so in explicitly obvious ways like copycat playing or tight synchrony. Of course, in other instances they may be very explicitly doing this, so such results may be interpreted as being highly case specific.

Key concepts here that are closely related to autonomy and agency are *causality* and *coupling*. Causality is the influence one system has on another, and in performative contexts such as those we have just considered above, it is important to ask which systems influence which others. One way we can think of causality (referred to as Granger causality after its creator) is in terms of whether any given system's future state is best predicted by its own recent history or the recent history of things external to it. If the better predictor is the external factor, then there is a causal relationship involved. Autonomy can be thought of as the greater influence of the system's internal state on its future state.[84]

From cybernetic thinking, and commonly used in artificial life, we have the idea of coupling. Coupling is simply the linking of two or more elements in a cycle of cause and effect. Loose coupling refers to the situation in which elements are coupled but also strongly self-determined or influenced by other outside factors. They can be decoupled and carry on largely as usual. Despite the looseness of the coupling, however, loosely coupled systems can have strong interaction effects. Loosely coupled oscillators may, under the right circumstances, synchronize, as is the case when two pendulum clocks are standing on the same surface, such as a mantelpiece, and start to tick in perfect phase. Even though there is only a very weak force transmitted through the surface, it slowly takes effect, and once the oscillators are aligned the force acts to stabilize the synchronization and keep them from drifting. Under other circumstances, however, such as when the natural oscillating frequencies of the coupled systems are different, the result of the interaction might be more unstable and lead to complexity or punctuated moments of stability.

This thinking can be applied to the way that improvising musicians interact, and a number of experimental machine improvisation systems have worked at this level of abstraction and dynamic attention.[85] In general this type of work is less about simulating human musicality and more about the creation of dynamic computer music performances that exhibit simple forms of machine agency. Works of this type have been placed under various banners from algorithmic composition to musical metacreation. The agency may not be focused on explicitly musical objectives such as achieving a harmonic outcome or exhibiting a musical understanding of the fellow performer. It may be responding to simpler conditions imposed by the composer and teased out by evolutionary selection, but in such a way that also drives the sense of flow described by Pachet.

In my own work,[86] I have used types of oscillatory systems that are capable of complex behavior. The actual behavior of the oscillatory system is shaped by an evolutionary algorithm that selects for abstract properties such as complexity, repetition, and responsiveness. These different goals are combined and experimented with manually. The resulting dynamic system can then be used in an interactive composition, responding to input from a live musician in the form of low-level features such as loudness, pitch, and spectral and timbral features, and driving the behavior of a separate digital music system which may itself contain generative elements. This is a naive system from the point of view of what musical AI is capable of but has been proven effective at exactly that issue of engaging musicians and creating a powerful sense of musical interaction and flow.

As with the lofty-versus-lowly computational creativity distinction in offline generative tasks, the pinnacle of such real-time co-creative systems is that the system should have a model of what it is involved in creating and can adapt what it is doing based on that model and the observed outcomes as they unfold. Because this is done in real time and involves other co-creators, this must in some sense take the form of a negotiation. In the lofty form of real-time creativity in improvisation, then, the system is sharing the creative task with other complex creative agents and the target is moving. The system must have an overall expectation of the outcome, an idea of how its output contributes to that outcome, and must also be prepared to adapt both of these based on its experience, else there will be a permanent gap between the system's expectation and the outcome.

As with other art forms, the creation of music is never simply a matter of the production of abstract artifacts but is also guided by factors relating to display, whether competitive or cooperative. In the words of Philip Auslander,[87] "Musical performance is not just about achieving certain sonic ends—it is crucially also about perceptibly overcoming challenges presented by the means used to achieve those ends."

This observation is context for Auslander's discussion of issues of liveness and agency in the presentation of machine generated music. Interviewed by Auslander, Mari Kimura, a violinist who has performed extensively with the robot system, the GuitarBot, reveals a level of implicit misrepresentation in the GuitarBot performances:

> My compensating for the robot's or computer's lack of musical "integrity" as the performance goes along should be hidden from, or unnoticeable to, the audience. In short, my aim is that the performance as a whole come across to the audience as if the robot or computer is thinking, feeling, and being sensitive; that it possesses the "rights and responsibilities" of a true musician.[88]

Yu and Blackwell[89] elaborate on audience perceptions of agency drawing more squarely on psychological principles, namely the apparent mental causation model and the expectancy violation theory. The apparent mental causation model dictates how people identify causal relation; causation of event B by event A is perceived when event A precedes event B, event B occurs as expected, and event A is the only plausible source of the outcome. Expectancy violation theory claims that a person becomes more alert to a system when it violates expectations.

Relatedly, Banerji[90] contends that there are significant issues surrounding expectations; he proposes that technologies such as machine learning can "legitimize agency" in automated music systems, more specifically that "ML constitutes an effective means of encoding the socio-political ideals at the center of this musical practice." Such systems lay claim to a form of autonomy in that the programmer wasn't involved in specifying by hand the system's style, but such systems are not necessarily by virtue of this better creators of interactive experience. Models and studies of audience and performer perception also play a role in building this understanding.

By contrast, tests of agents not based in ML reveal that human beings experience illusions of "adaptation" in interactions with systems which lack any adaptive capacity. Such results suggest that HCI research with artificial social interactants may be used to raise new questions about the nature of human interaction and interpersonal adaptation in the formation of relationships over time.[91]

Perceptions of agency and autonomy also relate to perceptions of humanness or lifelikeness, and this is an area that can be explored to dramatic effect. Several artists have been interested in creating forms of agencies that are original, not imitations of human behavior, as a creative objective in their own right, as sources of contemplation. Simon Penny, a leading figure in cybernetic-inspired interactive art, explains:[92] "An artwork, in my analysis, does not didactically supply information, it invites the public to consider a range of possibilities, it encourages independent thinking. So building an interactive artwork requires more subtle interaction design than does a system whose output is entirely pragmatic, such as a bank automat."

He says of his celebrated interactive robotic artwork *Petit Mal*:

> It was not my intention to build an artificially intelligent device, but to build a device which gave the impression of being sentient, while employing the absolute minimum of mechanical hardware, sensors, code and computational power. The research emerged from artistic practice and was thus concerned with subtle and evocative modes of communication rather than pragmatic goal based functions. My focus was on the robot as an actor in social space ... Every attempt was made to avoid anthropomorphism, zoomorphism or biomorphism. It seemed all too easy to imply sentience by capitalising on the suggestive potential of biomorphic elements.[93]

In the domain of performance and interactivity, perhaps, then, we find the most explicit conceptual studies of the agency of digital systems.

Complete Creative Production Cycles and the Machine-as-Artist

Lastly we come to the lofty computational creativity scenario where a machine is embedded in a recognizable human role: a simulated, virtual, or machine artist. Everything discussed so far in this chapter can easily be understood as a continuation of human machine use in the arts, with new technology applied to existing human goals, realized in the hands of human artists. I have considered how such applications may have radical impacts on the production of creative outputs as well as on the related social configurations and cultures of production and consumption, but none of these scenarios comes with the philosophical baggage that we see in the machine-as-artist scenario. This philosophical bent comes in turn with much confusion about what purpose such a scenario would serve. Indeed, for many the idea of creating a machine artist has little to do with practical use-cases and is instead a matter of philosophical enquiry, a theme explored throughout this book.

Where exactly does the distinction lie with the previously discussed scenarios? In many of those scenarios, machines perform some active role in a creative production task, and I believe they should largely be rightly considered computationally creative systems—that is, systems that in part automate creative production—even if they do so in relatively nonaware and nonautonomous ways such as in a structure-and-generate design pattern or an interactive evolutionary computing scenario. In all of these cases, machines are still active makers of artistic outputs in some capacity.

In a machine-as-artist scenario, the machine is not simply a production tool but an agent that performs a recognizable pattern of art creation that we would associate with a human artist, which may include social and cultural relations with other individuals, such as audiences and co-producers.

Take the full bells-and-whistles version of this scenario. You step into your city's modern art museum, and while browsing the permanent collection, you find an abstract expressionist painting created by a machine artist. The machine has a name and an identity, a recognizable style nurtured over several years of development. It can in some capacity discuss or explain what it is doing and even justify or "sell" the value of what it is doing through channels other than the painting itself. On further investigation, you find a list of programmers and creatives credited for creating and managing this machine artist, but you are nevertheless satisfied by the breadth and sophistication of its output, supported by documentary evidence, that it is a legitimate creative author, not simply a trick or form of industrialized art production.

As early computational creativity figures such as Cohen and Cope presented their work, there was some degree of willingness by audiences and commentators to view their systems in this light, and as we have seen these systems took on the role of philosophical probes, looking into both machine creativity as an abstract phenomenon, and the potential for machines to perform tasks and fulfill roles that humans do.

In fact, we face a more nuanced breakdown of categories that inform the machine-as-artist scenario, as follows:

1. Systems that allow the application of AI algorithms to art generation, typically as mere generators, but potentially including simple forms of evaluation and feedback.
2. Systems that perform generate-and-test cycles, involving various forms of adaptive and reflective behavior.
3. Systems that perform forms of engagement with audiences and/or grounding of their creative output, such as presenting an "identity," reflecting on current affairs, explaining themselves, responding to feedback, and having grounded motivations such as winning prizes.
4. Systems that convincingly replicate human traits and successfully assume human creative roles.

Here, Category 2 systems can be seen as extensions of Category 1 systems that advance the capacity and autonomy of these systems by introducing algorithms that enable the integration of generation and evaluation into a single adaptive system. Consider taking a successful machine-learning-based generative algorithm, having online users rank its outputs, and then feeding those rankings back into the training of the generation system through reinforcement learning.

Note, however, that embedding systems successfully into cycles of feedback as required by Category 2 would be likely to also involve aspects of Category 3: the system gets embedded in a sociocultural creative context, as a byproduct of extending its creative capacity to involve feedback.

At the same time, Category 3 aspects can be explored independently of whether the system exhibits Category 2 generate-and-test capabilities. Some of the most in-depth work in this area is by Colton and his team, working with the Painting Fool system,[94] situated in gallery contexts. One issue Colton has studied is the way in which a system can not only create an aesthetic artifact but also communicate its process and perhaps even convince an audience of the value of the work.[95] Along with each painting, the system generates descriptive text explaining what the motivation of the work was and what mood was applied. This establishes a multifaceted representation of the work, which may achieve some degree of social grounding.

Interest in the fourth category was an original motivator for much work in computational creativity, but this has significantly dwindled as we know more about the technologies and applications of computational creativity. Distributed agency and distributed creativity perspectives have grown sufficiently in the time since Cohen and Cope that we are less inclined to frame computational creativity as a quest to create virtual artists. We are more familiar with AI algorithms that perform sophisticated tasks without being anthropomorphized, instead occupying a more amorphous expanse between designed and intentional stances. Kurzweil's framing, where machine artists overtake human artists, seems no longer to frame the problem in an appropriate way.

IV Impacts

7 Making Creative Systems Effective

We are called to be architects of the future, not its victims.
—Buckminster Fuller

Human nature is not a machine to be built after a model, and set to do exactly the work prescribed for it, but a tree, which requires to grow and develop itself on all sides, according to the tendency of the inward forces which make it a living thing.
—John Stuart Mill[1]

Evaluating the Creativity of Computationally Creative Systems

Empirical Grounding

How do we evaluate whether computational creativity systems are doing creative things, or in the language of distributed creativity, are effective and possibly active contributors in creative production? The radical multidisciplinarity of computational creativity invites a wide range of methods for answering such questions. In engineering and computer science it is often the case that one can specify an objective goal for an AI system. In many creativity-related subtasks this may also be the case. Training a neural network to recognize objects in images requires that we have a dataset of annotated images, meaning that we necessarily have the information required to know exactly how well the system is performing—at least at the given subtask, if not at the wider objective of contributing to a creative task. Meanwhile, human-computer interaction tasks require evaluation of users' responses, and although this is less concrete, data—both qualitative and quantitative—can be gathered about the system's performance. In other cases, practice-based programmer-artists make work and self-evaluate. In the latter, the evidence becomes vaguer still, but the situation is largely similar to the human-computer interaction context. Systems that generate creative outputs can be investigated using all of these evaluation scenarios and others. A scenario that is somewhat more specific to computational creativity is where people are asked to evaluate the aesthetic quality of the system's output or to otherwise evaluate whether they believe the system to be creative or humanlike.

One theme underlying these discussions is how we establish an *empirical grounding* for various forms of evaluation. Empirical grounding is the establishment of a connection between empirical observations of any form, and the results and conclusions we draw about our systems, traversing a mesh of logic, ontology, epistemology, and language. Statements about systems can take more or less empirically well-grounded forms. Statements of self-evaluation by creators of systems, such as that *the resulting music was interesting*, or that *the system exhibited imagination*, for example, are empirically loosely grounded, whereas to say that *audience members reported the resulting music as being interesting* is empirically well-grounded. Other forms of conclusive remark, such as that *the system achieved human-level performance at creative tasks*, or that *the system was successful because it was the first to be exhibited in a public gallery*, can be equally obscuring of empirical issues, depending on the details of how they are reported and the intention behind their use. They may be weakly empirically grounded, with gaps in the connection between the empirical observation and the point being made.

Such evaluation depends on a commitment first and foremost to understanding, resisting the zealous claims of grant-speak, product marketing, or the pressure to report positive results with every study. There is also a difference between evaluation that results in accurate but ineffective analysis, and evaluation that is fine tuned to contribute to improved designs in an iterative process. Simply knowing whether something was liked or not may not get us very far in terms of knowing what to do to improve it. Evaluation must offer clues as to what can be done better, through thoughtful analysis and good experimental design. This often involves setting up some kind of point of comparison or controllable variable that helps us to break systems down into specific parameters, design features, or properties that can be evaluated independently.

From Turing Tests to Rich Descriptions

Computational creativity evaluation would seem to strike at the essence of artistic subjectivity, and the know-it-when-you-see-it attitude toward creativity espoused by some of the field's founders. Surely we just run these systems, and the ones that produce better outcomes are better? Let the market decide. We can get some way to understanding the achievements of computationally creative systems by subjecting these systems to artistic critique or the popular vote, and some researchers have taken this view. It is reasonable, after all, that a general audience or a panel of experts or possibly the system's collaborative partners, such as fellow musicians in the case of a music performance task, would be able to develop a clear consensus. Recall that in her research Amabile showed that panels of experts did indeed come to a clear consensus on evaluations of creativity and also associated creativity with a clear set of related qualities. Studies of computationally creative systems (such as by Collins and Laney[2] and Lamb, Brown, and Clarke[3]) have also shown significant differences between evaluations by experts and nonexperts. Boden also makes the point that novices may generate the same ratings as experts but may be less adept at explaining these evaluations than experts.[4]

In evaluating creativity it is natural to consider doing studies that take the form of a blind test, akin to the Turing test, where machine outputs are considered in terms of their ability to fool judges into thinking they are actually human outputs. Although appealing, and used effectively in some cases, there are some complications with such an approach. Firstly, in these early days many systems frankly often don't produce great outcomes. Asking people whether they like the output or not might not mean much, and indeed many important advances in computational creativity don't actually come hand in hand with immediate improvements in the generative output of systems. If we are interested in the quality of the systems themselves, then it would be a mistake simply to look at what they produce.

Secondly, as we discussed in chapter 2 with respect to Turing-style tests, it is easy to game this mode of evaluation, or at least, there are many types of distortion or obfuscation that affect how we might understand and approach the evaluation process. The most obvious of these is that we must be able to tell apart the role of the human creator (the programmer, co-creator, system trainer, etc.) in establishing the quality of outputs, leaving the system with a smaller, more manageable task, while giving the impression that the quality of the output is thanks to the machine intelligence. Consider again the claim, from chapter 1, that a certain system did 95 to 98 percent of the work in composing an album of original music. Such a claim would not only need to be explained but also backed up. Exactly where are human hands used in the process, and how much weight might we give to various production tasks—choosing instrumentation, making minor (or major) arrangement edits, mixing, performance intonation? It would be flippant to take such a distribution of creative attribution at face value. Society devotes much effort to arguing over the minutiae of such issues in human affairs—we may never solve the timeless debate over how much credit the studio engineer, Alan Parsons, deserves for the creative achievement of Pink Floyd's *Dark Side of the Moon*, one of the bestselling albums of all time (in fact, cases such as this are historically responsible for shifting public perceptions about *who* might be considered a creative agent in a particular domain[5]).

In a demonstration of the ease with which *certain* parts of the creative process can be trivialized, James Humberstone, in a TED talk on music, gets the audience to pick notes at random from the chromatic scale and then produces an electronic dance music track from this selection of notes, unadulterated. One point here is that repetition has a massive impact on how you experience a sequence, and an arbitrary bar of music takes on new meaning when repeated several times, setting up reliable expectation and satisfaction. Add some production techniques, with a booming synth sound, and the randomly composed piece begins to sound like a convincing musical work of some genre. There is a conscious sleight of hand here: the assumption that the choice of notes is really the key to the composition diverts us from recognizing that an arbitrary choice of notes can be a fine starting point for a creative process.

This captures part of the problem with what would generally be called an artistic Turing test approach to computational creativity evaluation. But before we slip into this terminology, is it even fair to call the evaluation of a system's output a Turing test, given that it is certainly not a literal application of the text-based imitation test described in Turing's paper?

Writing about generative music systems, Chris Ariza[6] makes the case that the Turing test concept is misused in creative arts contexts frequently. He distinguishes between several different sorts of Turing-related tests. The John Henry Test (JHT), first of all, is simply a head-to-head human versus computer performance test. In general, the JHT does not require blind judges.

Games like chess or Go are domains in which computers have beaten the best human performers, and these have directly measurable and indisputable outcomes. There could be such tests in creative practice, but they need to have an indisputable objective target. For a banal example, we certainly could compare the *speed* at which a computer and human can compose original musical melodies, and indeed this may be of importance in some use-cases. Ariza then classifies the bulk of existing examples of Turing tests in computer music as being "toy" tests, referring to the fact that they do not fully satisfy the requirements of the original Turing test. This builds on Harnad's hierarchy of Turing tests, which views the original Turing test (TT, or T2) sitting in between a total Turing test (TTT, or T3)—the *Blade Runner* scenario, where physiological features are also part of the imitation, culminating in fully humanlike robots—and lesser Turing tests that fall short of the language-based, interactive, open-ended nature of the TT. Those lesser tests, which do not involve free linguistic conversation, are the "toy" tests. Ariza then distinguishes the Musical Directive Toy Test (MDtT) from the Musical Output Toy Test (MOtT). The latter represents the majority of tests that have been used in musical contexts, where people are asked to look only at a system's or human's creative outputs in a blind discrimination task and determine which are made by machines. The MDtT is somewhat more interesting and closer to the original Turing test, in that there is a stage of interaction:

> The interrogator, using a computer interface, sends a musical directive to two composer-agents. One of the composers is a machine, the other, a human. The musical directive could be style- or genre-dependent, or it could be abstract—something like "write sad music," "write a march," or "compose a musical game." ... An MDtT could take the form of a real-time musical call and response or improvisation between interrogator and composer agents.[7]

Both, Ariza argues, are not *proper* Turing tests, but at least in the MDtT case there is a level of interaction enabling the interrogator to construct a model of what the system is doing by probing it. Related to this, we can also consider replacing the verbal directives with musical call-and-response and consider how the Turing test might apply to musical interaction in an improvisation scenario. While such call-and-response scenarios are relatively common, it is still more difficult to set up blind tests between people and systems than it is with typed text, and blind tests have been uncommon. The scenario Ariza describes in which verbal instructions are issued is also, until recently, uncommon; given the examples he suggests above, such systems would require natural language processing abilities and some level of sophisticated open-endedness. Even if a system was very good at writing sad music or writing a march, it would presumably be easy to propose something the system couldn't do that a human could. The systems we have now work over a range of parameters that are usually heavily constrained to a specific domain. But we can imagine more feasible examples from current research, like a parametric creative system that uses sentiment analysis to create outputs that are happy, energetic, or lighthearted. Such a system might have critics agree that it was very good at modeling these qualities but would still be a nonstarter at the *real* Turing test task of understanding advanced musical concepts.

Most tests we see today are of the MOtT form. They are easy to set up and run, and can be designed to result in hard numerical data, such as statistics indicating how many people classed each output in which way. "You be the judge!" compels a feature on the Red Bull website about artificially generated pop songs.[8]

While the MOtT has its place, it is important to look at the nature of its limitations. The outputs alone hide important information about what the system itself is doing. MOtTs have a tendency to invite seduction, to anthropomorphize and exaggerate the capability of the given algorithms, to frame them as humanlike from the outset and then see how far the likeness can be pushed. There is nothing pure about these systems; there are countless hacks and trickery and bias that influence how they produce output. When a GAN-generated artwork sold for over half a million dollars in 2018,[9] surprising the entire art world and the computational creativity community, the work certainly looked like a recognizable painterly style, with original content, but it also seems odd to value a one-off from a system that should arguably be best judged by its mass output. Artworks reach this kind of value because their makers have amassed reputation over a long period of work. This out-of-the-blue exaltation of a particular work of a particular system is somewhat at odds with this.

The system's output can be a poor indicator of the quality of the system because it conceals much relevant information about what type of creative work the system is doing. It is also, arguably, not a particularly relevant way to think about how we judge creativity in humans. We pay great heed to the context of creation. As humans we have a good idea of the cognitive machinery that other humans have at their disposal—it is not something we have to explicitly question. With humans, also, we can be mistaken in our evaluation; if you discover a new genre of music, then you might consider the first artist you encounter in that genre to be radically original, but you would be acting with limited historical knowledge, not fully aware of the context of creation. Learning about prior influences, for example, might radically alter your view of the originality of a certain artist. Importantly, this is not about whether we like a piece of work, but about how we understand its genesis.

Given the danger of mistaking the generative capability of the system, the situation worsens the more opacity surrounds the information. Thus in the presentation of your computationally creative system you risk entering a *zone of incredulity* when you show only a small number of handpicked outcomes, worse still if they have been tampered with or edited into some more developed work. That's not to say that the outputs of computationally creative systems shouldn't be curated or improved—it depends on the application context. The creators of *Beyond the Fence*, the "world's first computer-generated musical," were well aware that when the first-night curtain opened to a West End crowd they couldn't just serve up the experimental musings of a team of academics and their algorithms; professionals were involved to ensure quality. There is artistic license there, as long as when the behind-the-scenes work is presented it is done honestly.[10] Likewise, I have video examples online of my improvising music system Zamyatin playing live. For the purpose of documenting this work, I choose the best takes, naturally, as I would with any live recorded work. My commitment to academic honesty does not extend to putting the bad takes of my system in my creative show reel (though it does extend to me offering uncurated versions and live demos to fellow researchers, if they are keen to hear them). When computer-generated work is presented to the public it is both a demonstration of a technology and an artistic output in its own right. Thus creators must strike a balance between intellectual honesty and alright-on-the-night production standards. The danger lies in hailing such limited and controlled outputs as a form of evidence, saying, "See for yourself how sophisticated this system is" without being able to back that up with clear information about the role of the system.

That said, MOtTs or their equivalents in other domains can be useful to demonstrate the shortcomings of existing systems. In a National Public Radio listener survey comparing human and machine sonnets, run by Dartmouth's Neukom Institute (discussed below), the listeners' scores showed that machines were completely incapable of fooling them. The more borderline cases, at 65–35, were those where a human-composed sonnet was mistaken to be computer-composed.

But as Ariza argues, even if the system demonstrates some form of interactivity and open-ended capacity that allows one to probe its behavior, this does not necessarily make it a Turing test, hence the descriptor "toy." In the original test, the question is whether a machine possesses intelligence. The method is a blind game of imitation; it is interactive, linguistic, and open-ended. Marvin Minsky asks what it means for a human or computational system to comprehend that "you can't push a car with a piece of string." What intelligence is involved? Language gives us quite open access to the capacity of another mind, but art, although affectionately seen as a window onto the soul, has a transparency issue. In practice, what has tended to happen is that artistic Turing test results have come back affirmative—yes, this does look like human art/poetry/music—yet leaving us none the wiser as to what is going on. The bar is too low, at least in some areas. Once again, any example from the world of found art, field recordings, or some flavors of mash-up, drone, or noise music might serve this point well; these fields make quite a mess of an output-based Turing test concept. If a system was designed to grab found images from webcams on the Internet and frame them as artworks, I do not think there would be any grounds to reject such works. They must pass.

An artistic variant of the Turing test begs the more basic question: can the Turing test even have variants? The answer, I think, should be no. If the goal of the test becomes split into two distinct goals—(a) be convincingly humanlike, and (b) produce good art—then we encounter some conflict between these goals, for which quite different methods come into play. The Turing test was designed to address item (a). For item (b) we should take a more invasive and open approach, and put aside questions of humanlikeness. Ariza summarizes that "the TT is an attractive concept: it is not surprising that it has found its way into discourse on generative music systems. More practical methods of system evaluation, however, may do more to promote innovation."[11]

A more expansive approach would not necessarily reject outright the idea of a blind test. But with the various issues surrounding Turing tests, not least the view that Turing's original use of the tests was as a conceptual thought experiment, not a serious proposal for testing something, the case for blind tests is diminished.

One reason we would perhaps see the need to conduct blind tests, however, is in order to ensure that no bias for or against machine creativity was influencing judgments. Cope was convinced of bias against his machine compositions, and the issue has been raised on other occasions that people judging the work produced by a computer might believe it to be inferior. Taking essentialist views such as Bloom's into account, this is quite plausible. If we care about who made the work, and allow that to influence our view of the work, then of course we may see computer-generated work differently from human creations. This hypothesized bias has been investigated, and the evidence has fallen both for and against its existence in different studies.[12] It remains to be seen if this bias can be definitively shown, but it should be borne in mind that what might seem to be a bias is actually an important part of the puzzle for making good computational creativity systems. Creators do have life stories, personal struggles, relations, cultural and political affiliations that are considered important in the judgment of creative work. It would be wrong to cast off these factors used in judging creative work as mere bias. But as noted by various commentators (such as Colton and Banerji), equally we may be inclined to project these human social properties onto systems even where they don't exist.

A simple solution to the various issues with artistic Turing tests is to expand the approach to data collection and communication. Audience ratings may be important, but they must be augmented with as much relevant information as possible. It may be useful for tests to be blind, but it can also be useful for them not to be. Binary tests (is it or isn't it X?) may be less useful than rich descriptions of both the system itself and people's responses to it. Thus we can think of a rich description approach, which draws on interaction design research methods, may use blind or nonblind tests, qualitative or quantitative methods, objective tests and so on. It transcends the binary simplicity of the Turing test. Social scientific methods based on observation and discourse provide qualitative information to support an understanding of how we perceive systems. Dan Stowell and colleagues[13] explore an array of design research methods that they compare to a Turing test approach in a musical context, with a particular focus on discourse analysis and the identification of actors and relationships between them. Information is gathered in the context of more or less structured tasks that reveal interaction affordances and conceptions.

Stowell et al. conclude that Turing-style tests can be useful in certain contexts, but that a number of constraints regulate when this may be the case:

1. *Is the system primarily designed to emulate the interaction provided by a human, or by some other known system?* If so, the musical Turing test method can be recommended.
2. *Is the performer's perspective sufficient for evaluation?* In many cases, the answer to this is yes, although there may be cases in which it is considered important to design an experiment involving audience evaluation. Many of the same methods (interviews, questionnaires, Turing-test choices) are applicable to audience members—and because audiences can often result in large sample sizes compared against performer populations, survey methods such as Likert scales are more likely to be appropriate.
3. *Is the system designed for complex musical interactions, or for simple/separable musical tasks?* If the latter, then simplified tasks may hold some attraction. If the former, then we recommend a more situated evaluation such as our discourse analysis approach, which avoids the need to reduce the musical interaction down to atomic tasks.
4. *Is the system intended for solo interaction, or is a group interaction a better representation of its expected use pattern?* The experimental design should reflect this, using either solo or group sessions.
5. *How large is the population of participants on which we can draw for evaluation?* Often the population will be fairly small, which raises issues for the statistical power of quantitative approaches. Qualitative approaches should then be considered.

Anna Jordanous, whose PhD thesis[14] was the first to focus specifically on evaluation in computational creativity, similarly develops a multifaceted approach that combines qualitative and quantitative methods, including those derived from design and social sciences. She notes that research in computational creativity tends to shy away from evaluation due to conceptual and practical difficulties. A third of the papers she surveyed did not critically discuss creativity, half had no discussion of evaluation, and only a third attempted to evaluate the creativity of the systems they presented. One issue Jordanous identified was the perception that it was difficult to find grounds for comparative studies between different systems, since different systems are geared toward different aims or contexts. "One researcher noted the difficulty of finding 'even one other system that's doing exactly what you're doing," hence causing practical difficulties in comparing systems like for like."[15] By contrast, in some areas such as narrative story generation systems, there were seen to be enough examples of systems doing similar things, and correspondingly, attempts at comparative research existed in this area.

Jordanous puts forward a flexible approach to evaluation which begins by identifying aspects of creativity that are relevant to the specific domain. From a wide analysis of discourse on creativity, she identifies a global list of fourteen attributes associated with creativity, similar to Amabile's associated criteria (here again, treating the complex concept of creativity from a cluster-concept point of view):

- Social interaction and communication
- Domain competence
- Intention and emotional involvement
- Active involvement and persistence
- Variety, divergence, and experimentation
- Dealing with uncertainty
- Originality
- Spontaneity/subconscious processing
- Independence and freedom
- Progression and development
- Thinking and evaluation
- Value
- Generation of results
- General intellect

Jordanous demonstrates this with a study of four creative music improvisation systems. To do this she recruited participants who had experience of music improvisation as well of computer programming. She asked the participants to discuss the above list of terms associated with creativity and think about the terms in the context of improvisation. From the responses, she ordered the list in terms of those elements most associated with improvisation, giving a domain-specific frame for creativity in that context. The above list is in fact ordered in this way, so the top three elements in the list—social interaction and communication; domain competence; intention and emotional involvement—were identified as being significantly more strongly associated with improvisational creativity than the remainder.

She then asked the participants to rate the four systems on each of the measures, resulting in multidimensional scores, which could also then be weighted according to the respective significance of each of the associated features. Importantly, the participants were not only asked to look at the outputs of the system or interact with the system but also to read about each system and attempt to understand how it worked. The result is a rich engagement with both the system and the nature of the evaluation question being asked. This significantly diminishes the mystique around the evaluation of creativity. Note, for example, that the top three aspects of improvisational creativity identified in the study don't directly engage with the concept of novelty at all.

Looking Under the Hood
The idea of looking under the hood to accurately evaluate computationally creative systems leads to a situation where we may want to more formally break down creative events performed by machines and people into categories. Although creativity theory gives us notions of stages in creative thought such as incubation and illumination, these may be too abstract to associate with specific outputs from a computational process. Forming concepts, developing an idea and implementing that idea are each relevant, semi-independent creative processes, and the evaluation of a system may involve understanding exactly which of these tasks it actually performs. In all creative systems, the system will perform some of these activities independently, but it may also embody its programmers' creative input. It is important to tease apart these factors, but how?

Colton, Pease, and Charnley[16] propose a breakdown into four domains into which creative output might be organized. These are:

- *Framing* Anything that establishes the context for a creative act[17]
- *Aesthetic measure* The measure by which something's aesthetic value is determined
- *Concept* A general schematic for the production of work
- *Example of concept* A specific example of work conforming to a concept

This "FACE" model is then further divided into creative acts that result in actual objects and creative acts that result in processes, which will then be used to create objects. They also propose that along with creative acts, administrative acts need to be considered in the model: those acts that aren't directly creative but that are auxiliary to the creative process.

This breakdown is then applied to the analysis of the creativity of systems, which takes into account both human and nonhuman actors in the attribution of different creative and administrative acts. In conjunction with this, Colton, Pease, and Charnley propose the IDEA model[18] for framing the context of development: "Software is not developed in a vacuum, so we must factor out the input of the programmer/user/audience when we assess the impact of the creative acts performed by software. To do so, we assume an (I)terative (D)evelopment—(E)xecution—(A)ppreciation cycle within which software is engineered and its behavior is exposed to an audience." This allows for situations in which a programmer might change the code of a system (it is therefore properly framed by a distributed creativity point of view). Thus when a programmer writes a generative program, looks at the results, and then modifies their code in order to produce better results—as all practice-based computational creativity artists from Cohen onward have inevitably done—this model has built into it the distinction between what the system does and what the human does, while still seeing the totality as creative.

Instances of creative acts performed by different actors from one of Colton, Pease, and Charnley's analyses include the following:

- The programmer uses their aesthetic to select an image for printing.
- The software generates a new set of functions by crossing over two pairs of functions.
- The programmer takes their aesthetic and turned it into code that can calculate a value for images.
- The software uses machine learning techniques to approximate the programmer's aesthetic.
- The software invents a novel aesthetic function.
- The software applies the new aesthetic to choosing the best image from those produced.
- The software produces a commentary about its process and product.

Although Colton, Pease, and Charnley's FACE and IDEA frameworks offer terminology to aid analysis, it is not universally agreed terminology. The terms *framing, aesthetic measure, concept,* and *example* risk assuming a certain system architecture or set of relations between individual components. As we have seen, aesthetic appreciation can be multifaceted and endowed with meaning that complicates the notion of it being measurable. But a generalized approach in this spirit, which attempts to identify creative events within a wider interaction scenario and attribute authorship to those events, can be effective and helps us get away from a limited black-box perspective.

Putting Numbers on Aspects of Creativity

Given a rich descriptive approach to evaluating computationally creative systems, a common scenario that arises is one in which we look not at specific system outputs but at the distribution of outputs that the system produces. Even if this is not done in an interactive way, we can require that a proper system evaluation means seeing a significant quantity of output that is demonstrative of the system's scope, rather than a single output or curated selection of outputs. Such a corpus can be subject to more formal analysis, including the potential that with large enough numbers we begin to build a more statistically grounded view of the system's behavior. This can also be done in the context of another large dataset: the body of existing work in the world that the system has been exposed to. By taking a statistical view over larger numbers of outputs we can begin to characterize and perhaps quantify what type of creative affordances a system might have, building a profile that can be tailored to specific creative goals. This accords with the view that creativity itself has different manifestations and that there may be different ways for us to recognize creativity, as we saw previously with Jordanous's list of creativity-related terms.

Any computational system may be able to produce infinite outputs and might be interactive or data driven, so it may not be practical or possible to consider the entirety of its output, but we can at least aim to go large, or even interactively probe the system, and see what this tells us. If we do so, it may become immediately clear that the system produces work of a high quality but only within a tightly limited range that appears formulaic after sufficient iterations (this is common for generative systems and can often be desirable), or that the system produces mostly poor work, with the occasional, one-in-a-thousand moment of extraordinary happenstance discovery. An important observation to make is that neither is necessarily a failure. Even some highly esteemed artists might be said to exhibit the first trait, quite consciously. And a system of the latter variety might be effective in a domain like still images—it doesn't take that long to flip through 100 thumbnail images in search of certain desirable properties, so this success rate *might* be considered usable in certain co-creative professional contexts. (As Pierre Barreau from Aiva put it, it's not like a self-driving car where a 99 percent success rate is not good enough. Even a 1 percent success rate can be effective.[19]) It helps to be able to build this kind of profile of our systems, where we attend to different ideas of what creative value a system might have; this is key to understanding what their creative capacity is.

To this end, one of the innovators of the modern field of computational creativity, Graeme Ritchie,[20] set out to formalize the various ways any set of outputs could be described as creative in relation to whatever came before it. In Ritchie's formulation, the stuff that came before is called the "inspiring set." This is stuff the system knows about—in other words, the database of existing artifacts that has been fed as an input to the system.[21] In this formulation it is generally implied, though not essential, that the inspiring set is limited to a single, reasonably well-defined artistic domain, such as jazz music or abstract expressionism. Ritchie then defines intermediary measures for each of the system's outputs. One is *typicality*, which is a measure of how much the output resembles a typical example of the inspiring set. Another is *quality*, a measure of the perceived or otherwise computed quality of the work. The last is *novelty,* which is a measure of how different outputs are from the inspiring set.

It is interesting that Ritchie includes typicality. While on the one hand typicality may be seen as something that is undesirable, being boring or unoriginal, it bears a more complex relationship with value. As we saw in chapter 4, creative works are often created with the aim of having clear membership of an existing domain, thus to be *typical*. This may be as part of an expression of identity and also possibly in order to interact with the perceiver's expectations in managed ways. Something can be typical and novel at the same time. Recall that the shifting nature of conceptual spaces means that any agent within a domain can potentially construct a new set of criteria for understanding the domain, and thus a new dimension along which novelty is introduced, which doesn't upset the parameters of the existing domain. Something that is at once typical and novel clearly displays the traits of a given domain but does something exceptional within those constraints. Typicality is also arguably more easily evaluated than novelty. For example, asking if a piece of music is a typical example of blues can make use of more concrete criteria than asking if it is original, and can also be inferred from indirect data such as annotations.

Having defined these intermediary concepts, Ritchie defines eighteen measurements related to creativity, described as criteria for "attributing creativity to a computer program."[22] Criterion 1 simply states that the average typicality of artifacts should be above a certain threshold. Thus here typicality is viewed as a basic requirement for the system, to satisfy the expectations of the given creative domain. Criterion 2 is a different slant on the same idea, stating that the proportion of artifacts passing a given threshold of typicality should be greater than a given ratio. Criterion 3 and 4 do the same for quality. Later criteria dig into higher-order notions of creativity, blending these lower-order elements. One of the most common conceptions of creativity is about finding outputs that are atypical and yet still high quality, and in Ritchie's formulations there are several ways we can do this. Criterion 5, for example, states that out of the set of the system's atypical outputs, some given proportion must be high quality.

The full list is as follows:

1. On average, the system should produce suitably typical output.
2. A decent proportion of the output should be suitably typical.
3. On average, the system should produce highly valued output.
4. A decent proportion of the output should be highly valued.
5. A decent proportion of the output should be both suitably typical and highly valued.
6. A decent proportion of the output is suitably atypical and highly valued.
7. A decent proportion of the atypical output is highly valued.
8. A decent proportion of the valuable output is suitably atypical.
9. The system can replicate many of the example artifacts that guided construction of the system (the inspiring set).
10. Much of the output of the system is not in the inspiring set, so is novel to the system.
11. Novel output of the system (i.e., not in the inspiring set) should be suitably typical.
12. Novel output of the system (i.e., not in the inspiring set) should be highly valued.
13. A decent proportion of the output should be suitably typical items that are novel.
14. A decent proportion of the output should be highly valued items that are novel.
15. A decent proportion of the novel output of the system should be suitably typical.
16. A decent proportion of the novel output of the system should be highly valued.
17. A decent proportion of the novel output of the system should be suitably typical and highly valued.
18. A decent proportion of the novel output of the system should be suitably atypical and highly valued.[23]

Ritchie's criteria avoid pinning down a single conception of creativity in a single equation, seeking instead a diversity of mathematical formulations of varying ideas about what creativity might mean. As with Jordanous's list, from a family resemblance point of view we can see how all of Ritchie's criteria resemble some sort of typical comment a person might make about someone else's creativity: *he really understood the style and was able to take it further; she didn't do radical work often, but when she did it was brilliant.*

How useful this is in practice depends firstly on how well and how easily we can determine typicality, quality and novelty. The default way is to ask people, perhaps in large numbers via an online survey. In certain circumstances it may also be possible to automate this, although we have seen the problems with the automated measurement of quality. Besides, if the system has access to the same process to evaluate typicality and quality as the automated analysis uses, then the problem can be considered largely circular! It is also challenging to think about applying Ritchie's ideas in a non-domain-specific context, where typicality may be harder to define.

A multiplicity of measures for defining the creativity of systems sits well with the rich description approach to evaluating computational creativity and the family resemblance stance. It also feeds well into applied areas of computational creativity, with the various qualities identified by Ritchie's criteria relating to different use-cases, domains, and stages of the creative processes. Systems made for concept ideation might produce short, rapid-fire, multiplicitous suggestions and might have low typicality requirements, with parameters to control the breadth or level of risk involved in the output generation. Systems made for live musical accompaniment would need to work in real time without feedback or curation and so might have much stricter typicality requirements.

On the typicality front, another important consideration is plagiarism. We want things to be typical of a style or even of a specific artist, but we rarely want them to fall into the plagiarism category. This is a fine legal line. Asked in an interview if Emmy ever plagiarizes, Cope responds: "I'll let the courts decide this. ... Note, however, that most composers plagiarize dozens if not hundreds of works in a single piece of music, and most do this subconsciously."[24] Cope is alluding of course to the fact that copying style is a critical and functional part of creating original music. Yet most creative work, derivative though it may be in various respects, manages to clearly avoid accusations of plagiarism, which in specific creative domains have clear and known parameters. Systems such as Aiva run plagiarism detectors to double check that their output doesn't end up reproducing verbatim sections of the input music, which is perfectly possible in the context of RNNs regurgitating transition expectations. Unlike the measures we've talked about above, plagiarism should be a more hard and fast thing to check for, depending on known and legally argued rules dictating what counts; generative algorithms should be able to easily run their output through plagiarism checkers.

In one final example, Elgammal and Saleh[25] conduct a study to attempt to quantify creativity in human-produced work. They do this using an automated process running over a massive dataset of Western artworks since 1400. What is interesting in this study is that they measure creativity using a standard combination of novelty and value, but they measure value as *influence*, which is measured with hindsight with respect to the works that followed. That is, if one artwork can be shown to have influence on future artworks, its creativity score goes up. This is a fascinating idea, but entirely concordant with an evolutionary, teleofunctional, generative perspective in which the value of works is determined by their ability to stick around and cast influence.

Running Prizes

A number of competitions have been run to try to identify successful systems. I visited the Neukom Institute at Dartmouth College, based in New Hampshire in the US, just as they were judging their Neukom Turing tests for the creative arts in June 2017. The prize was in its second year and had four separate tasks, one in music, one in dance (applied to the animation of 3D figures), and two in literature. The AccompaniX accompaniment task required the system to follow a musical melody, also with a score provided, and come up with a musical accompaniment. The DanceX task required the system to control the limb coordinates of a 3D virtual dancer duetting with the recorded data from a real dancer. The DigiLit task required the system to complete a short story seeded with the first half of the story. And the PoetiX task required the system to generate sonnets based on a single word theme fed to it.

An ambitious thing the Neukom team did was to require that participants submit working programs rather than simply outputs, running those programs using novel inputs to establish a basic degree of interactivity with the systems. The prize committee organized creating the test inputs, running the programs to generate various outputs, and then having a judging team, including the general public, judge those outputs. In this way, they combined a blind MOtT (or equivalent in other domains) with a degree of interactivity in that the systems have to be able to work with unknown inputs. Attempts to look inside the systems or to generate large batches of outputs were beyond the scope of this team's capability; although this is positively argued for in the above work, it is hardly practical to do so with every test.

Similarly, each task was designed so as to have a reasonable level of common interest, to be carefully constrained to a domain-specific area, and to allow interaction. In other words, the tasks had to be widely appealing, manageable, clearly defined and yet still challenging and capable of demonstrating clear creative capability. In areas such as music, being widely appealing, while at the same time being sufficiently domain-specific as to state a clear goal, is a considerable challenge. The team had to avoid highly genre-specific tasks so as to widen the field but also to avoid something so completely genre-ambiguous so as to have clearly defined objectives.

In each case, human responses to the tasks were also gathered, so that a blind user test could take place. Some interesting discussion arose here around the poetry task. For example, use of punctuation and formatting such as italics had to be removed from the human-composed poems because this was a clear giveaway, with the computer-composed poems generally avoiding such elements for simplicity and greater success. This prompted the question of whether dumbing down the human work by constraining it in this way was an acceptable thing to do in order to create a level playing field.

Related to this was the question of whether the poetry should be constrained to a narrative form. Non-narrative poetry is much easier for computers simply because it potentially removes a level of advanced concept manipulation which is harder for existing algorithms to manage. Poems that riff on a series of associations in an impressionist manner without the burden of constructing a meaningful narrative are much easier to get a program to produce. In the world of human poetry, there is nothing invalid about such works, and yet the fact that this makes it easier for computer programs prompted some people to suggest that perhaps the call *should* include the requirement to work in a narrative form.

Practice-Based Artistic Research

Practice-based research is research in which a creative practitioner engages in their practice in a reflective and systematic manner, with a mind to making contributions to knowledge in an academic forum. Knowledge outcomes may take the form of knowledge about the processes of creating work, such as the methods by which a painter chooses a color palette, or knowledge about the materials and products themselves, such as how color exposure achieves persistence effects and complementary colors in, for example, the light works of James Turrell. Linda Candy[26] distinguishes these with the subtly different terms practice-led (about the practice) and practice-based (about the outcomes) research, although it is common to see practice-based research used as a catch-all term for simplicity. As a celebrated example of the power of practice-oriented contributions to knowledge, consider Barbara Bolt's[27] discussion of the artist David Hockney, who researched the use of visual aids in historical drawing practice "in which Hockney literally draws out his emerging understanding through this practice and his long-standing immersion in it."[28] Hockney was able to identify the use of visual aids by historical artists because of his intimate firsthand experience as a drawing artist and was able to experimentally verify these ideas through his own practice. We can see immediate parallels with the story of Harold Cohen and his expert development of AARON's drawing and coloring skill, and the similar stories of David Cope and George Lewis.

Practice-based research is an important dimension in the evaluation of computational creativity systems simply because much of the work in computational creativity has historically been done by practicing artists. More generally, it is an effective and efficient setup: an individual creative practitioner, working with code, incorporates creative autonomy into the software they are making, deploys it in real creative scenarios, and then has the potential to evaluate the system using a variety of means, adding individual reflection to other formal methods such as audience or performer interviews and surveys. As discussed in chapter 1, this works well because they come with both the expert knowledge of their domain that enables them to develop the system and the social connection to the domain that enables them to create the contexts in which the work is situated.

An artist reflecting on their own work risks a lack of objectivity that those working with managed user studies strive to avoid. But it can easily be forgotten that if they apply rigor and a commitment to intellectual honesty, they can achieve much of what might be achieved by a much larger study. Even formal studies that have one or two third-party users can be highly effective at identifying core themes and design issues. In user interface design, Nielsen and Landauer showed that as the number of users tested increases, the number of problems discovered plateaus relatively quickly.[29] In a trial of user tests revealing design problems in a mock system, they found that even a single user test could reveal up to a third of the potential problems. Three users revealed well over half the problems, and adding further user tests resulted in diminishing returns. Above ten users, very little was gained by adding extra users. Much like Knuth's maxim that optimization is often not worth doing ("We should forget about small efficiencies, say about 97% of the time: premature optimization is the root of all evil"),[30] an obsession with formal studies can be a poor use of resources. This is not to say that statistically significant results with larger sample sizes can't be valuable in other circumstances. Thus when it comes to working creatively with autonomous systems, taking a practice-based or autoethnographic approach can simply be a quick way to get meaningful results that inform future design decisions.

In practice-led or process-focused research, evaluation takes the form of knowledge about the individual's creative practice and how the system's creative autonomy can best be put to good use. Cohen, Cope, Lewis, Brown, and other early creative practitioners can be seen to be engaging with this form of knowledge gathering, even if they do not explicitly identify it as such. This includes philosophical reflection on their work, which potentially stimulates new concepts. Cohen's discussion of the creative autonomy of AARON in chapter 1 was of this nature.

A generation of electronic media art researchers now combine computing research with practice-based research, including HCI and interaction design methods where necessary. These practitioners develop original creative works involving innovation in algorithms and methods. This leads to the potential for knowledge outcomes across three levels. Formal studies of the algorithms objectively demonstrate algorithmic properties. For example, a generative system might be formally analyzed using any of Ritchie's criteria. Practice-based studies are subjective and address the artist's workflows and methods. Other HCI-oriented studies address third-party users, including co-creators and audiences.

For example, in studies by Jon McCormack and myself[31] on the use of ecosystem computer models as creative tools, we reported on the formal properties of those ecosystem models, the creative potential of using these models, and we outlined candidate design principles that could be used to create creative tools for third-party users.

In my own work on autonomous music improvisation[32] systems and in related work by Yee-King,[33] Eldridge,[34] Vear,[35] Banerji,[36] Ackermann,[37] Carey,[38] and others, studies have been conducted with very small numbers of musicians (between one and ten, usually around two or three), performing with the systems and engaging in detailed discursive analysis. This has included focus groups, discourse analysis, tests based on dedicated tasks, and so on. In my work with Zamyatin, for example, I found that performers had a greater sense of system autonomy when playing with the system than when watching someone else play with the system.[39] This reinforces the idea that looking at outputs is less informative than an interactive paradigm. I also found that performers were able to use sophisticated language that did not fall into anthropomorphization of the system—they definitely did not view the system as a virtual musician—while being able to discuss and describe the system character. Performers intuitively wanted to prod the system through performance with it, to gain an understanding of the system, whether a formal descriptive understanding or a more intuitive sense of what it would and wouldn't do. Through this process they habituated to the system and quickly became comfortable playing with it. In this sense one could see the system as falling somewhere between performer (albeit minimal in its humanlikeness), instrument, and composition.

Interaction Design for Computational Creativity

I began this chapter discussing empirical grounding. While the empirical grounding of systems producing cultural artifacts in opaque ways is relatively challenging, it is easier to empirically ground the evaluation of systems in operation-based and co-creation contexts where there is a clear human-computer interaction scenario established, and the system can be seen to perform certain functions. Thus we can look at evaluating the success of computational creativity systems from the point of view of an interaction designer, picking up themes from chapter 6 and the various application scenarios considered there.

Supporting Artistic Creativity and Open-Ended Exploration

Creative tasks have formed a distinct strand of focus for interaction designers, creative technologists, and educators for some time.[40] As well as simply getting known tasks done efficiently and accurately, creative spheres must support the conditions for creativity, which may include phenomena such as managing broad searches, a sense of flow, the ability to handle complexity, and the ability to precisely manipulate artifacts in multiple ways. The design of creative software tools has responded to this specific set of needs. Resnick and colleagues[41] describe the most general requirements for creative software systems as having *low floors, wide walls, and high ceilings*. Low floors refers to the barrier for entry. Software should aim to be as learnable as possible, a benefit to its adopters and also clearly quite valuable to the software's creators. Wide walls refers to the breadth of the software's capabilities. It needs to be versatile and allow for a wide diversity of outputs. Individuals should be able to carve out their own unique forms of expression that are facilitated rather than dictated by the software. This requirement is interesting because creatively empowering *constraints*, factors that narrow the space of creative possibilities and intensify focus, can also be something that creative practitioners desire.[42] High ceilings refers to the potential richness or complexity of creative reach made possible by the system. This is particularly relevant in computational media where creators can develop outputs of great cumulative complexity, through programming software behaviors, for example. More generally, this requirement is about being as enabling for professional users as for beginners.

Different design factors can support each of these requirements. Software that instructs you as you work, provides built-in help, enables you to get started by hacking existing examples, or that is designed so that the initial interface is stripped down and focused on more elementary tasks can support the more rapid adoption of the software and the achievement of basic goals (low floors). This supports the constructivist learning principle that you learn best through doing, particularly through exploring and discovering things from your own mistakes. It is also encouraging and thus enjoyable for users, and of course means that the user is being rewarded with creative outputs from the outset, and achieving their objectives in the shortest possible time with the least effort involved in learning. Csikszentmihalyi's principle of *flow* informs how we might think about scaffolding further levels of complexity and learning experience.

Designing for wide walls and high ceilings can be implemented in many ways: providing different tools and perspectives on the same artifacts; enabling a plug-in or library-based community approach that enables the software to be expanded endlessly; providing generalized rather than specific solutions to user needs; enabling different input and output formats and interoperability with other software; and providing professional functions such as unlimited undo and batch processing.

Effectively Communicating with Computers: Language, Code, and Graphical User Interfaces

In imagining how we might support these objectives of creativity support tools, we can take stock of two extremes that stand as alternatives to traditional graphical user interface (GUI) based control of digital systems, one where we talk to machines in much the same way that we communicate with other people, and the other where we use code as the core medium for computational expression. The former is, on the surface, more inclusive and requires little training or expertise, at least in the operation of machines, but remains an emerging technology, and it is not clear what kinds of intermediate forms we will have to work through as we get there. The latter suggests a high barrier to entry, and yet is widely recognized as the best way we currently have to interact with the full scope of computational intelligence available to us. As coding becomes easier and coding education becomes more focused in schools, the maxim that "coding is the new literacy" may play out. We already inhabit a rich ecosystem of programmers, from those making new chip designs and working in assembly languages to creative professionals who occasionally script something or write a macro in Excel.

Although it is not the only way to create complex computational outputs such as generative and interactive works, artists who work with code are more readily able to access the tools needed to achieve these aims; they can either create them themselves or incorporate existing programming libraries into their work in ways that cannot be achieved by nonprogramming end-users. Code is an eminently shareable medium and with the strong culture of open-source software one can access large repositories of existing code that has been made to perform specific functions, including supporting interoperability with external hardware. Thus in terms of wide walls and high ceilings, code is extraordinarily powerful. The problem for creative coding has tended to be the low floors dimension. Code is tricky to learn and can be incredibly taxing and frustrating to use. While many efforts are focused on making code easier, the vast infrastructure of the digital world also involves a certain amount of lock-in, where complexity and opacity protect expert knowledge.

Frameworks exist for helping us formalize these usability issues. Blackwell and Green's[43] cognitive dimensions of notations framework, for example, applies to digital manipulation tasks and is generally useful in identifying bottlenecks in usability "to analyze the interactions between: a) the structure of the information, b) the environment that allowed that structure to be manipulated, and c) the type of activity the user wanted to perform."

They identify the following set of cognitive dimensions affecting how one can go about performing a complex task with a piece of software:

Viscosity Resistance to change.

Visibility Ability to view components easily.

Premature commitment Constraints on the order of doing things.

Hidden dependencies Important links between entities are not visible.

Role-expressiveness The purpose of an entity is readily inferred.

Error-proneness The notation invites mistakes and the system gives little protection.

Abstraction Types and availability of abstraction mechanisms. Systems that allow many abstractions are potentially difficult to learn.

Secondary notation Extra information in means other than formal syntax.

Closeness of mapping Closeness of representation to domain.

Consistency Similar semantics are expressed in similar syntactic forms.

Diffuseness Verbosity of language.

Hard mental operations High demand on cognitive resources.

Provisionality Degree of commitment to actions or marks.

Progressive evaluation Work-to-date can be checked at any time.

With viscosity, for example, the question is how easily one can make changes, including going back to change something they've done. A typewriter is particularly viscous compared to a modern word processor; it is difficult to change text that has been written. With provisionality, the question is how easily someone can play with a set of possibilities without making commitment to those possibilities. Wherever computationally creative systems need interfaces, these kinds of straightforward usability questions come into play.

Natural language-style programming languages have been elusive. Languages like Apple's AppleScript aspired toward natural language-style syntax, but although this might have improved readability it did not make the programming experience any less brittle, requiring a precise and limited use of words and syntax ordering as usual. But the intense demand for natural language processing systems now means that we have far more fluid interfaces that appear poised to enable programming-like actions by non-programmers, as well as programmers operating with objects, behaviors, and data they are not familiar with. This book is written at a possible cusp in this field where submitting requests to a computer via natural language is now relatively normal but has not yet opened up the capacity to operate a machine with the open-endedness of programming via natural language. It may be a short while before it is possible to issue open-ended instructions in the form of requests for content generation to a system that would in turn summon generative functions to satisfy that request. With the convergence of a range of AI-based technologies such on-demand generation could arrive very quickly, transforming the basic nature of the interfaces with which we perform computational creativity, perhaps enabling a far more dynamic and less brittle interaction with computers in general. But the technical challenges of building and integrating systems broad enough to satisfy open-ended requests should not be underestimated, and as ever the question of whether such means of interaction with machines will be embraced by a population of creative users remains dependent not only on the capability of the technology but on the cultures of practice surrounding it.

8 Speculative Futures

"Do you suppose there'll be a Third Industrial Revolution?"

Paul paused in his office doorway, "A third one? What would that be like?"

"I don't know exactly. The first and second ones must have been inconceivable at one time."

"To the people who were going to be replaced by machines, maybe. A third one, eh? In a way, I guess the third one's been going on for some time, if you mean thinking machines. That would be the third revolution, I guess—machines that devaluate human thinking. Some of the big computers like EPICAC do that all right, in specialized fields."

"Uh-huh," said Katharine thoughtfully. She rattled a pencil between her teeth. "First the muscle work, then the routine work, then, maybe, the real brainwork."

—Kurt Vonnegut[1]

So fast moving is this area, and so muddied by various forms of hype and emotional responses, that speculating about where we might end up even in a couple of years, let alone a decade or so, is a risky activity. But speculation is not prediction, and certainly not prophecy. It serves to point to and examine different possible futures, to allow discussion of where we want to go, what might need to be done to get there, and what we might want to look out for. I draw on the topics and examples discussed so far to analyze such possibilities and to frame the most prominent themes appearing in the emerging future of computational creativity. Most of the trends imagined below are already apparent and have already been identified in the preceding chapters, and are merely being extrapolated given what we can see the technology capable of, framed from the perspective of distributed, networked creativity. I divide this concluding chapter into three areas: industry, covering the nature of creative production and the use of commercially developed computationally creative systems; society, covering the impact on cultural production and social behavior; and lastly, the most speculative and philosophical topic, the question of how machine creativity may cause us to reflect on our status as intelligent and creative beings.

In Industry

Speeding Up Creative Practice
AI is just one of a host of technological domains that has the potential to destroy jobs, threatening entire spheres of human work. Autonomous vehicles, if successful, have the potential to remove millions of paid driving tasks, not just professional drivers, but those for whom driving is a *part* of their work, and do so very quickly. Factory jobs are constantly being replaced. Now increasingly cognitive jobs are on the chopping board. A Bank of England report estimates that a full 50 percent of all current jobs could be at risk from automation. Some job losses are heavily resisted, as when the original Luddites went out and sabotaged machinery. But others slip away without much being said about them; photo development shops, once omnipresent, were obliterated by the advent of the digital camera, removing thousands of skilled and unskilled jobs.[2]

In a keynote on the impact of AI on jobs,[3] Toby Walsh argues that every business needs to have an AI plan, embracing AI technologies or mitigating the risks of AI innovation to their business. As a rule of thumb, he says, if you think of any human task that doesn't require much conscious thought, then it is likely that a machine can either do it or can just about do it now. For example, driving on freeways machines can do now, but driving in cities they can't. That might seem like a somewhat strange comment from the point of view of computational creativity; we effortlessly perform certain creative tasks which seem still far removed from machines' capabilities, but it nevertheless seems a reasonable rule of thumb in the majority of cases. Walsh points out that while Moore's law might have leveled off, algorithms continue to exponentially improve in performance, and funding for AI is doubling every two years. The momentum behind this transformation and its potential for exponential change is significant. But, he adds, while machine success in landmark competitive games, like Go and poker, came quicker than expected, the landscape of AI progress is bumpy and highly unpredictable. Other predictions, such as those of Kurzweil[4] in computational creativity, have failed to materialize to plan.

Nevertheless, technology doesn't need to fully automate a task for it to erode jobs. Anything that helps someone do a task more efficiently or effectively—in other words, that increases productivity—will mean that fewer people are needed to get the same thing done. This has been happening in music, design, and media technology for some time through new powerful software tools.

At the same time, the overall social transformations caused by a technological development are harder to understand. Increased productivity doesn't always result in fewer people working in a sector. The reduced cost might mean that increasing demand takes up the slack or even drives up employment in a sector. This is, after all, what happens when a new technology first becomes viable. According to the Jevons paradox[5] in environmental economics, the increase in efficiency with which a resource can be used can lead to greater use of that resource. Consumption of coal increased after the invention of the Watt steam engine, which was a significantly more efficient engine than its predecessors. Wider cultural implications can also shift our approach to work. Judy Wajcman[6] argues that a current paradox of the acceleration of technology is that we have become more competitive and work focused, equating being busy with being successful.

The Stanford University report *Artificial Intelligence and Life in 2030*[7] summarizes the impact of AI on work as follows:

> AI will likely replace tasks rather than jobs in the near term, and will also create new kinds of jobs. But the new jobs that will emerge are harder to imagine in advance than the existing jobs that will likely be lost. Changes in employment usually happen gradually, often without a sharp transition, a trend likely to continue as AI slowly moves into the workplace. A spectrum of effects will emerge, ranging from small amounts of replacement or augmentation to complete replacement. For example, although most of a lawyer's job is not yet automated, AI applied to legal information extraction and topic modeling has automated parts of first-year lawyers' jobs. In the not too distant future, a diverse array of jobholders, from radiologists to truck drivers to gardeners, may be affected.
>
> AI may also influence the size and location of the workforce. Many organizations and institutions are large because they perform functions that can be scaled only by adding human labor, either "horizontally" across geographical areas or "vertically" in management hierarchies. As AI takes over many functions, scalability no longer implies large organizations.

Although the same report has a dedicated section on entertainment, it has little specific to say, except to list some of the applications of AI at present. So are creative jobs at threat from automation, and what changes are they likely to undergo? The above points, along with the themes I have built, frame some of the more convincing possibilities, which follow here. These following points, as I emphasize above, are speculations rather than predictions.

Certain domains of art practice will always place authorship and human connection front and center. In whatever ways these might be altered by automation, they will not take away the central role of the human as artist. A very large part of this domain of activity is amateur art production, where the individual achievement associated with the creation of the work is a critical factor, and the eradication of paid work is not a factor anyway (the economics of art is complicated by this vast reserve of potentially free human labor—people want to make art, with or without money involved). Although automation may transform specific activities it will not change the basic *use* of art as a human social pursuit based around individual authorship. In light of this, it seems unlikely that the machine-as-artist, an anthropomorphic agent with a personality and individual reputation, is likely to materialize outside of specific, highly conceptual instances.

Certain other domains of art practice are more faceless. Elevator music, advertising content, decorative art, building designs (outside of the realm of the superstar architect), and other similar areas all have the potential to be highly automated without disrupting artist-audience relations and other social patterns. What this means in practice, as outlined in the Stanford AI report, is that fewer people are needed to create the same work at the same rate, but there will still be individuals involved in the operation of such generative tools rather than full automation. This may be associated with a shift in skills. One possibility is that practitioners become spread over wider domains, a new generation of generalist creative producers: a single person produces an entire animated commercial including the storyboard, script, character animation, and music. Other more specific AI-related tasks might arise. Technicians specialized in the relevant technologies may emerge, as they have most prominently in the computer-focused creative industries such as animation, games, and areas of music. In architecture, we already have experts in building analytics who collaborate with experts in parametric design and multiobjective optimization. This could be a model for other areas.

Speculative Futures

In the extreme, major industries may rise up around specific areas of automated creativity. Examples include the automated generation of mood music by existing streaming services, content generation for interactive digital contexts such as games, and applications in targeted advertising. Generated or curated playlists on streaming services like Spotify are now a primary means by which people discover music. Some bring together highly author-associated works (like *Hits of the 70s*), whereas others are more faceless; they could already be generative without you knowing it. Context-based playlists on streaming services, such as workout or relaxation music, have become increasingly popular.[8] Tracks on such playlists are not strongly author-associated, yet generate serious income for their composers, and such companies have unprecedented power to control what music gets played on their platform via such suggestions. Elsewhere, large media organizations may create cultural products, such as AI pop stars, just as they already manufacture fictional characters and open-ended story worlds.

Certain production tasks such as audio mixing or mastering in the music domain are becoming automatable to the point that many types of content creators are already opting for automated solutions for cost reasons, even if the quality is diminished, just as we have seen in other areas (the canonical example being the replacement of live musicians with virtual instruments in orchestral screen composition). Other people may choose not to make this trade, and debates may remain unresolved indefinitely over whether human or machine outputs are better, just as questions of digital versus analogue audio production technology remain ongoing. Domains such as this might make interesting case studies for style arms races, where individual professionals attempt to differentiate their style from current machine capabilities. Nevertheless, it is plausible that the automation of tasks such as audio mixing and mastering has the potential to become acceptable and widely adopted very quickly, given that in machine learning terms the task is very clearly defined and exact input/output data is abundant.

In general, digital creative tasks may be sped up, but again due to any number of possible cultural factors this may not mean that creative production itself is sped up. It is possible that individual creators strive for greater quality or quantity given these powerful support tools. This may vary in detail from one domain to another. We may set the bar higher for quantity, or work might involve more background conceptual investment; the time it takes to make a conceptual artwork like Tracey Emin's *My Bed* may not be reflected in the object itself. The conceptual development is invisible labor, often indistinguishable from other life activities. Alternatively, giving artists the potential for mass production through generative means might play out in different ways in different cultural scenarios: imagine an artist producing 7 billion artworks, one for each person on the planet, or composing 1,000 years of generative music (at least the latter, in a very simple sense,[9] and some variants of the former,[10] have already happened).

As well as speeding up creation, automation may shift the skill base. Being an expert in music theory or having the manual skill to draw real images may become increasingly less necessary in the capacity to create sophisticated works of music or art, as has already happened. Such automation may "democratize" creative tasks in a number of ways. As has happened in previous generations, newcomers with a new skill set and aesthetics may define new genres with their own cultural foundations and systems of value. The self-taught will be increasingly empowered with the help of technology, and yet they will seek new skill sets pertaining to the expert use of that technology. Content creation in general may become more of a participatory activity, at least in certain contexts, continuing the shift toward prosumer content creation associated with the widespread adoption of the Internet. In the spirit of Instagram filters, the idea that everyone can create *beautiful* things cheaply and easily can be taken forward in obvious ways by computational creativity technology. At the same time, establishment art forms may continue to uphold longer-standing skills, knowledge, and traditions.

Digital creativity is becoming increasingly networked and complex, associated with a number of transformations both technologically and culturally grounded. Creative practice in some domains may evolve toward richer and more complex ecosystems of practice. For example, forms of practice such as remix and mash-up, where digital artifacts are reconfigured, involve a greater exchange of content between individuals.[11] Creative coding tools such as MaxMSP and Processing emphasize reuse of code and libraries, meaning that creative practice becomes more cumulative, with the authorship of works involving more and more participants and complex chains of attribution. The rise of interactive media involves more numerous and more diverse creative collaborations between technologists and artists. With machine learning comes an additional pathway of attribution: when a neural network produces content we might trace attribution to the programmer, the operator, the system itself, and in addition, the artists sampled in the training set. Here, software embodies aspects of cumulative culture, runaway niche construction[12] and the principle of increasing technological returns.[13] Layers are constantly being added to the ecosystem, and digital creativity can be said to have an incredibly diffuse authorship. As creative software capacities are added to this tapestry, they may perform subliminal roles but ones that only make sense from a distributed creativity perspective.

This final point is a restatement of the theme developed throughout this book that computationally creative technologies are already seeping gradually into creative practice in small niches within each creative domain, not in some explosive, disruptive transformation. The front line of commercialized computational creativity demonstrates this.

Starting in earnest around 2015, a number of startups have emerged in the UK, US, and Europe aiming to provide computer-generated music, and similar trends are seen in graphic design, advertising copy and concept development, design thinking, architecture, and video production. Some aim to sell music for high-budget synchronization to films, TV shows, and advertisements. Others aim to sell music in very low-cost scenarios such as the creation of amateur YouTube videos. Others still aim to sell generative co-creation tools to professionals.

The vast growth of amateur content creation means that millions of prosumers are in need of a jingle to place over their home video, and small companies are always looking for cheap music for product promos. My design students often produce concept videos for their design ideas, and as students, doing so with negligible production costs is critical to them. In all of these cases, the originality of the added music is not high on the list of criteria. Indeed, my students generally want to put their favorite music on their videos, copyright issues notwithstanding. The company JukeDeck is targeting this market, and aiming for a fully automated process. Another company, Landr, is providing automated mastering of tracks, with little in terms of options—simply submit your tracks and get them back mastered. Cultural studies researcher Jonathan Sterne's[14] research into Landr, whose business is now well established, shows that it is already transforming communities of practice. Mastering is a highly skilled process applied at the end of the music production pipeline but also a relatively expendable one. Amateur bands releasing music online might skip this stage altogether, and many people would be hard pressed to tell the difference between a mastered and unmastered track, except that a mastered track will be more functional: it will fit in better on a playlist and sound better across different types of speakers. As Sterne notes, Landr's mastering algorithm may not stack up against a professional standard to the trained ear but is good enough for a large community of amateur producers to choose this much cheaper option, allowing them to rapidly produce and upload tracks that stand out more easily (in large part because the mastering makes the tracks sound louder). Interestingly, this includes musical fragments as well as finished tracks. Hip-hop beat-makers were seen to be using it on beats that they sold to rappers, a partly counterproductive approach, since traditionally the mastering would only apply after the vocals have been added (else there is no "room" in the mix for the vocals). Sterne also notes that a good mastering engineer may do very little to a track, but Landr always appears to be doing something, since doing nothing would appear a poor job (in the case of the real human, this may be a sign of great confidence instead).

Related to this, companies like Viddyoze aim to reduce the effort involved in making animated videos. They are doing this by templatizing animation creation, meaning that a user works from one of a range of templates, manipulating the properties that template provides. This could be seen as a form of casual creator system, packaging skilled creation tasks into a ready-made parametric system that can easily be personalized. The result is very limited in its versatility but nevertheless offers unskilled users the potential to create useful rich assets. Such templating methods are common in creative software, as in the selection of styles in Word or PowerPoint.

The startup Aiva uses a recurrent neural network trained on a classical music corpus to generate new musical scores. The music is generated in the form of a score for piano, which is then developed by the human composer into something for a larger ensemble. They target this use of neural networks at a specific stage in the workflow where they need to rapidly turn over initial proposals for a piece to show to a client, which the composer and client can agree on. Pierre Barreau, Aiva's CEO, says that this is the pain point he has identified in commercial music composition: there may be only a forty-eight-hour window in which to prepare something for a client. While it is possible to work at this speed, it doesn't guarantee the best results under time pressure. The goal of Aiva is not to replace the human with a fully automated system but to support this process. The company is committed to the value of the human composer in the interaction with the client, counseling the client on the value of different approaches. But Barreau also points out the value of initially seeding the process with something automated, in that the composer can be more objective, supporting the client rather than being invested in one or other composition.

Aiva uses an out-of-copyright classical corpus to train its networks, meaning that there is no risk of a copyright issue arising. Nevertheless, they run a plagiarism checker on all output to ensure that no output ends up reproducing large chunks from the original corpus. But Barreau is confident that even such a simple learn-and-reproduce cycle can result in novel, creative outputs from the system. As discussed in chapter 5, he points to an example output from Aiva that sounds like traditional Irish music, despite being trained only on a classical corpus. This anecdotal example suggests that some properties of the music that transcend multiple styles may have been picked up, meaning that a system can generate output in a style despite not having been exposed to that style in the past. This is after all the principle of such a learning system—train it on ninety-nine works of a composer and it will in principle have the requisite musical structural knowledge to be able to produce an imaginary hundredth work.

The film and advertising sync world is an interesting target for an AI music business model; individual composers may be awarded highly lucrative royalty payments for very short pieces of content. It is a natural market to try to get into with computer-generated music. And yet, for the same reason it is already a market saturated by competition. Studios compete fiercely for those high-budget jobs, and every piece of music ever composed is a potential candidate for being picked up, with artists happy to get any such revenue for their music. Can there be a cost saving at the top end by automating this, as opposed to coming up with a simpler means by which existing music could be "rented" at low cost? This remains to be seen. But what is interesting in Aiva's case is that the focus is not merely on the cost of production but also on the specifics of the client experience. While we may not need more music, produced more quickly and at lower cost, we can still solve problems of how to help a client find the music they want more quickly. This is part of the business model for another company, Ecrett Music,[15] targeting the speed, accuracy, and satisfaction of discovery (not necessarily of production), *using* generative production.

As far as bringing automation to the world of commercial composition goes, then, a number of confounding factors distinguish this market from others. The most prominent is that, as already raised, creative music production is a desirable job. People have high intrinsic motivation to do it and a huge amount of amateur art-based work goes unpaid. It is hard even for a zero marginal-cost system to compete with that.[16] Also as already mentioned, while sync music is often faceless, there are times when the association with the artist matters; the musical meaning derives from the social connections that are involved in its production or dissemination.[17]

Copyright

Following such considerations, one pressing practical question surrounding the automation of creative production is the attribution of rights and the management of royalties covered by copyright law. The headline-grabbing question here is whether a machine might ever be granted rights that would otherwise be attributable to a human. If machines can be creative in the way that humans can, then do they deserve to be credited and rewarded? Hopefully the arguments in this book have already done enough to drive home the position that the capacity for the production of artifacts is one thing, but it is far from the total human experience, the holistic situatedness of people in the production of cultural artifacts. A system's ability to generate novel and valuable outputs is far from the only factor involved in considering rights attribution. Short of a *Blade Runner*-like future where robot replicants are agitating for recognition as people, validated as *total Turing test* winners (Hanard's T3, discussed in chapter 7), there is little sense in giving creative attribution to machines. Largely, existing copyright law already establishes this same position; in US copyright law, for example, a "human authorship requirement" is explicitly outlined, which rejects the possibility of attribution of copyright to machines and other nonhuman processes, including nature, animals, or plants.[18] This was recently upheld in the widely debated rejection of a copyright claim raised by activists on behalf of a monkey who took a selfie with a photographer's unattended camera.

The human authorship requirement still leaves open a number of possible outcomes for different human stakeholders. A content-generating AI system has associated with it various programmers and data operators, owners, and other individuals who contributed the content in the training data, all potentially laying claim to royalties and attributions from the systems output. But this is not necessarily new; we already inhabit complex ecosystems of production. It is my view that introducing computationally creative systems, while certainly adding greater complexity and very likely introducing novel conventions of rights attribution, will not radically transform rights attribution as we known it and not diminish the logic of the human authorship requirement. Novel conventions of attribution are likely to arise as they do under any new mode of production. On a modern album, we may credit the mastering engineer for the album's sound but not the maker of the synthesizers or guitar amps, yet in some cases instrument-building might be more bespoke and warrant credit. Likewise, the programmer of a machine learning AI music system may be unlikely to warrant royalties for the generated music, but a creative user of the system is more likely to. Eric Drott[19] makes the case that copyright law is not well equipped to deal with the complexity (and ambiguity) of chains of attribution of machine-generated work, because it has so far been predicated on the idea that creation occurs, roughly, in individual brains, whereas AI systems are complex proxies for large groups of engineers and artists (through training data). McCormack, Gifford, and Hutchings[20] note that the disclosure of what data a system was trained on is a legal and moral gray area, but they contend that creators using machine learning–based systems have a responsibility to disclose what they trained those systems on.

A tantalizing argument is also emerging that machine-generated creative outputs should be placed in the public domain and not be copyrightable at all. If there is no immediate human author, only various stakeholders in the creation and operation of the algorithm, yet the algorithm is responsible for the creative innovation, then arguably its output would not (and should not) be covered by existing copyright law. In Japan this is being investigated with the question of whether such systems enable unfair competition.[21] If a machine is capable of bulk generation of cultural artifacts in a given style, then it could certainly have the potential to eclipse human creation in a disruptive and uncompetitive way. Does this matter? Do artists need protecting if their work in cultural production is being done for them? Such a debate will cut deep into the question of the social value of artistic creation and its cultural grounding. Bruce Gain draws attention to the way in which such machines are more like processors of existing cultural heritage than artists. "Copyright law is meant to protect people, not machines, and things created by machines should not be copyrightable by anybody.

They should be in the public domain," attorney Ray Beckerman says in an interview with Gain.²² "There is already an excess of property right promotion in the US copyright world now, and not enough promotion of the public's rights in the public domain."

A counterargument is that AI generation is considered of positive cultural value and must be supported as an extension of human creative production. According to Andres Guadamuz, in an article for *The Conversation*:

> The most sensible move seems to follow those countries that grant copyright to the person who made the AI's operation possible, with the UK's model looking like the most efficient. This will ensure companies keep investing in the technology, safe in the knowledge they will reap the benefits. What happens when we start seriously debating whether computers should be given the status and rights of people is a whole other story.²³

This is an interesting point because it highlights how at this intersection of art and technology we encounter an equivalent intersection between the respective logics of patent systems and creative copyright systems, which are quite different.

In another *Conversation* article, going further, Paresh Kathrani does actually make the case in favor of granting copyright to machines *themselves* on the basis that rights law should uphold intelligence in its own right, and not discriminate what the source of that intelligence is: "While machines may not be able to enforce intellectual property rights (yet), anything less might potentially amount to a violation of the value we place on intelligence in and of itself."²⁴

This sits at odd with the primacy of copyright laws existing to protect people. If there is no apparent social need that is served by machines generating art and music, then why incentivize companies to create business models that do this? Whether artists need to be protected even when art gets made without their protection is a separate, long-standing argument that is itself politically charged, and is certainly beyond the scope of this book. The debates around computational creativity and copyright may only serve to reframe and perhaps even clarify such long-standing social issues.

However, note that removing protections for machine-generated creative works does not necessarily remove the power of commercial entities to disrupt and undermine existing forms of creative production. Drott reminds us that contemporary tech giants are successful because they are platforms—they create environments in which they can control and draw rent from access or mine user data. Content and services may become free, but access to high-tech data services, such as of generation, becomes something that can be profited from. In other words, companies can make money even when they do not own the output of the work; indeed, making content free has been the path to great success.

As with all rules and norms, the shifting ground of copyright law is a product of struggles between different interest groups, which includes but is by no means exclusively limited to what objective observers would consider fair and socially beneficial. It is also enmeshed in society through feedback: if the rewards for creative production are greater, this may attract more people into creative areas, who then join the campaign to protect these rights.

Client-Producer Scenarios

Perhaps the most ready-to-hand metaphor of what interaction with future computational creativity systems might look like is a client-producer model, the seeds of which can be seen in the example of Aiva. According to this model, a creative practitioner requests a creative system to produce candidate outputs satisfying certain requirements. They may do this in any number of ways, using the paradigms discussed in chapter 6: direct manipulation of a neural network's training data and parameters; hand-coding a casual creator system; setting goals for a target-based evolutionary process; or having a system ambiently suggesting completions to what the user has started. The creative practitioner temporarily becomes client to the system-as-producer, expressing executive control, but not doing the work or necessarily exerting creative authority, since to do so means finer-grained control over the output—doing it oneself.

The client-producer model in its fullest manifestation involves a complete shift from users using software to build outputs to users requesting outputs from software (the request-based paradigm presented in chapter 6). Target-based and interactive evolutionary systems are a successful existing manifestation of this request-led approach, but their user scenarios still remain very limited for nonprogrammers and casual use.

One of the more tantalizing scenarios suggested in the previous chapter was an open-ended, service-based approach to computational creativity grounded in a natural language interface. It is easy to imagine a generative version of a search engine interface or language-based assistant. Just as you type requests into the Google search bar or speak commands to an assistant such as Siri or Alexa, such a system would respond to natural language requests by parsing the request into a machine readable form and determining what actions to take to service the result. Rather than take the form of some general intelligence, it may be more plausible to envisage such a system resembling a generative web of subservices. Such a system might take a request and farm it out to a network of services: services for generating subcomponents such as melodies and rhythms; services for putting together higher-level structures such as verse-chorus arrangements; services for writing lyrics; style filter services; services for evaluating outputs to check for certain properties or to give a quality score; and services for setting up iterative processes bringing together generation and testing.

Furthermore, the possibility for such collaborations to be mutually adaptive exists through the potential to build systems that are tweaked and trained to work in the context of a specific user, like a personal assistant. The Stanford AI100 report says that "over the next fifteen years, the Study Panel expects an increasing focus on developing systems that are human-aware, meaning that they specifically model, and are specifically designed for, the characteristics of the people with whom they are meant to interact."

The suggestion of nonexperts becoming creatively empowered through computational tools is possibly a galling one for many creative professionals. As well as lacking the skills to create the content themselves, nonexpert clients may also lack an appreciation of the nuances, tropes, and stereotypes that distinguish the great from the feeble, the kitsch from cutting edge, the underlying mechanisms that make one font or color scheme more appropriate than another. Thus, automated processes may take hold for better or worse, eroding quality for convenience, just as virtual orchestral instruments have won over expensive orchestras in the production of most film music. But it is also possible that the affordances of such technologies instead improve and enhance creative output. Just as architects apply automated analytics to buildings, a client commissioning music could be given detailed analytics relating to their choices, just as music knowledge services have begun to provide tune analytics such as "danceability" and "hotness." Constraint solvers could ensure that generated outputs always achieve a set of requirements, such as legibility in print or audibility across a range of formats (sadly, in the world of music, this may include an even greater escalation of the *radio wars* battle to produce ever louder mixes of tracks).

Imagining a nonexpert user being both client and director, with a computational system supplying the domain-specific expertise, it is interesting to reflect on the agency relations here, the nature of the distributed agency, and the functional relationships between the various entities. Can such content-generation services act as instances of lofty computational creativity, and do they need to do so in order to fulfill their function? On the one hand, the director can assume the role of autonomous primary agent, controlling and directing the process, but as we have seen, a good service-provider system might be called upon to exhibit creative authority *over* the client. The musician Frank Zappa quipped that in the old days A&R people just wanted to know if the kids liked a band, whereas today they want to stamp their mark and make a legacy for themselves as curators. In this sense, we can imagine many different approaches taken by clients in relation to how much creative autonomy they allow computational systems, depending on the creative context.

New Domains of Interactive Creation

As well as ways of providing the automated generation of media, digital technology has created completely new forms of media experience that feed into a vision of how creative domains might evolve given computationally creative technologies. Digital environments are demanding increasing amounts of content that are generated on the fly, adaptive to context, or personalized. Computer games are leading this charge and, described as the "killer app" for computational creativity,[25] have drawn on all of the diverse generative creation scenarios we have considered in previous chapters. Yet generativity is emerging only slowly as a mainstream way to produce content. Good games are carefully designed to look and feel right. Generative algorithms are only trusted with certain tasks within narrow constraints, even if sometimes the lack of adaptive content creation can be jarring, as is the case with the predominant use of simple loops and switches in game music.

Meanwhile, games are really just the most obvious incarnation of a larger domain of interactive content, which is vast if you consider that it includes every piece of web design, the layout of every mobile app, every sound effect and transition animation. Any piece of media that is served digitally may not be interactive but has the potential to be, by virtue of the fact that it runs on a computational device in an interactive context.

Our daily experience is becoming increasingly augmented by digital media, with augmented reality at its frontier, which requires the production of media that is inherently adaptive, needing to adjust according to the context in which we are viewing it.

Another music-generation company, Melodrive, is interested in serving professional composers for games and other interactive experiences. Composing interactive music means creating systems rather than compositions. According to Anders-Petter Andersson, Birgitta Cappelen, and Fredrik Olofsson,[26] this can be thought of as designing strategies for decomposing and recomposing musical material: working out its composite elements and developing rules for how these elements can come together. As discussed in chapter 6, a major problem is that the various algorithms that have proven success in music generation in one area or another have not proven sufficiently generalizable in a use-case scenario. Currently the best ways to make generative music for interactive experiences in a way that enables the composer to have control over what they are doing are either very bland—the typical strategy is to cross-fade between different loops of music as required—or involve the composer to code their own systems. The latter is not unreasonable with the rise of the competent coder musician/artist, but even so, those practitioners benefit from any strategies and support tools that simplify or speed up the generative music creation process. Melodrive's approach is developer-focused, providing creative generative music algorithms accessible through programming libraries but also providing simpler workstation-based templates around specific themes. This assumes the rise of music developers to whom such services will be useful. These may be music-savvy developers or code-savvy musicians: new breeds of professional filling new technologically mediated niches.

In Society

Any impact on professional creative production will be paralleled by impacts on the experience of audiences (or "end-users," in the context of interaction design). What is computational creativity going to mean for consumers of art and music, as well as for those amateur producers who enjoy making it, outside of professional concerns?

The ability for people to generate astronomic amounts of creative content may seem an intimidating prospect, but really, we have lived for a long time in a world where no one person can experience even a small fraction of all human-produced content. Even without automated means, merely through more routine developments that facilitate production (such as everyone having a video camera in their pocket), the quantity of creative content that exists is already incomprehensibly large.

Casual everyday creativity is as likely a target of generative technologies as any professional domain, given its immense scale.[27] The prosumer revolution has accentuated this great amassing of cultural products. It has arisen out of the basic conditions of the Internet and World Wide Web, that anything we create can be rapidly deployed to a public space where it can be consumed instantly by the rest of the world. We also interact digitally via private forums such as group and one-to-one chats, producing and consuming additional content in smaller communities. Most of this interaction is rapid and expressive, and the value of any technology that supports more expressive communication through these networked channels can be immense. One of music-culture theorist Jaques Attali's predictions[28] is that the world of music becomes increasingly many-to-many in nature, a more rapid-fire, fluid everyday process of creation. Although the prosumer revolution, where everyone with a smartphone becomes a public creator of literary and photographic aesthetic material, has partially driven such a scenario, we are still far from a situation in which creative art forms become casual media for everyday communication. Everyday language, photography, and video are probably the leading media for fluid communication but are generally distinguished from professionally produced movies, images, music, and text. Graphical art, music, animation, and more complex "professional" movie sequences are not commonly produced in daily interaction. Would generative creative tools, with their capacity to speed up creative production, change this? With the ability to employ machine tools to generate artworks and music, would these become increasingly used to play a role in everyday communication?

In one possible scenario, our daily, digitally mediated communication begins to take on richer and richer media forms, in much the same way that companies and entertainment producers use rich media to communicate to the public through video, audio, and increasingly interactive experiences. If it became trivially easy, and possibly also entertaining in its own right, to produce such content, then it is a relatively uncontroversial suggestion that we would do so daily for small audiences or even individuals. A party invite or a message to say "I love you" could take the form of a unique, for-the-moment audiovisual spectacle. The use of looped GIFs, emojis, stickers, and memes in digital communication is the bedrock for this context. Messenger apps such as Snapchat and WhatsApp are increasingly facilitating the layering of media with such interactive and generative elements. Although these are relatively out-of-the-box functions, a shift toward increasing personalization would be a compelling development that could be served by generative tools. I think this domain of everyday communicative aesthetic interaction is where generative technologies will drive the most innovative developments of creative forms. Within this environment, artists and companies may find new participatory ways to interact with their audiences and customers, mediated by the support for creative expression enabled by generative technologies.

In this scenario, control-based, service-based, and ambient interaction paradigms are all plausible directions. For example, predictive text sets the scene for an ambient mode of generative interaction where suggestions for media are offered by the system according to what is being written. The user may be clearly active in the creation of the content (e.g., drawing shapes on a screen, or submitting source material to a style transfer algorithm) or may simply be selecting from suggestions proposed for the occasion (as we select animated GIFs, stickers, emojis, and meme imagery today). In turn, those suggestions may be generated by a system or may be more of a remixed or reappropriated nature, being drawn from a database of existing artifacts.

This obscures the creative autonomy not only of the system but of the user. The need for originality or virtuosity might be very low in such scenarios, and personal and group identity dynamics could dictate much of how creative roles are distributed. It is also plausible that we would produce such media for ourselves in an entertainment-on-demand scenario, playful interaction with a creative system as a means to an end, although it is hard to imagine people *not* sharing things—it is increasingly natural to casually drop one's creations on social media, even if they are produced in the course of casual entertainment.

Another dimension to this discussion is the rise of new aesthetic cultures that are, loosely put, characterized by "big data." Mash-ups and remixes are forms of cultural production that are premised on the iterative reworking of existing content. They are not necessarily original forms in this sense, and many art forms have rich histories of reuse, reference, and parody of existing content, but the evolution of mash-up and remix methods is underpinned in part by new technological capabilities, beginning most notably with the audio sampler in music and Photoshop-like programs in visual domains. The sampler heralded the application of sampling techniques in hip-hop, other forms of urban music, and strands of art music in the late twentieth century. Now advanced information processing methods are continuing to drive new capabilities for mash-up and remix, as evidenced in the examples in chapters 5 and 6. Remix and mash-up practices are in turn related to the cultural shift from narrow cultural niches of taste toward a more "omnivore" approach to diverse aesthetic forms.[29]

Given that cultural production is laden with issues of situatedness, technologies like the sampler can be put to powerful use, as well as being tools of enhanced efficiency in their own right. Arguably, in addition, the digital audio sampler not only satisfied a need but also spurred on new creative forms through sheer experimentation and discovery that placed reference and reuse front and center. We could expect the same kinds of innovative use, adaptation, and application of emerging AI, evolutionary, and machine learning technologies, particularly in their application to big data.

Nefarious Uses

The election of the populist Donald Trump in the US was the culmination of a number of forces, one of which was the growth of social networks and their various risks and affordances. Analysis, including the claims of the campaign team technologists themselves, suggested that targeted memes of believable misinformation and emotionally salient materials were effective at mass manipulation, and that the dynamics of social networks provided new affordances by which social groups could form, consolidate, and potentially be controlled.

Social manipulation is, on this basis, a serious threat to society posed by AI. Cambridge Analytica, the company that performed data analytics via Facebook to support individually targeted campaigns for the Trump election and Brexit referendum, claimed to be able to produce detailed models of electorates.[30] Replacing statistical analysis based on focus groups and postcodes with the aggressive mining of online data using automated techniques leads to a completely different relationship between the public and those groups that wish to influence them. The entire population can be modeled and studied, and real-time trial and error of different strategies can be used to find election-winning formulae, resembling a highly effective and creative evolutionary search process. The same techniques are available to companies, political parties, religious groups, and others whose intention is to influence and convert.

If the technologies of big data, social network analysis, psychological profiling and so on are proving effective at social manipulation, then the successful implementation of the technologies of computational creativity could add further capability to such efforts. Human art engages with such phenomena as the manipulation of emotion, the suggestion of meaning, the suspension of disbelief, the experience of the sublime, the attraction of attention, the creation of distraction, the creation of objects of desire, the stimulation of ecstatic and spiritual experiences, marking personal and group identity, and in the world of Internet epidemiology, the creation of highly shareable artifacts. Of particular relevance to this argument for the nefarious power of generative technologies is a body of research showing how the use of emotional, nonrational materials is at least as—if not significantly more— effective than rational argument, statistics, and appeals to expertise in effective social influence, in both product marketing and political persuasion.[31] But equally relevant are the themes developed in chapter 4 of art and music's potential function in social group formation and identity.

It is not inconceivable, then, that computational creativity researchers may find their research being used in scenarios removed from the playful creation of autonomous robot artists that help us reflect on human nature, and nearer to industrial-scale social manipulation.

One way that computational creativity could be used for nefarious use is in the creation of addictive activities like gambling that can be exploited for profit and can also be used to instill passivity in a population, limiting group coordination and political engagement. If cultural production supports culturally engaged individuals, then there is the potential that highly personalized automated cultural production creates feedback cycles that render individuals culturally detached. Another application could be in personalized emotional manipulation. This includes recruitment to a cause, inciting positive or negative emotions toward specific groups, manipulation of memory and associations, or tainting of experiences in real time. The creative generation of plausible misinformation, smears, and conspiracy theories is a well-established tool in political manipulation. We may imagine autonomous algorithms generating and testing possibilities directly on a population, without human evaluation or filtering. If one meme reaches a million people, it hardly matters that 10,000 memes fail to go viral. Such techniques could be employed in the management of social groups. If we understand the dynamics of social groups and the role cultural production plays in their structure, stability, and evolution, then it may be possible to better force fission or fusion, enforce or erode cohesion and morale, stimulate in-fighting and so on.

Although some of these scenarios may sound farfetched, the concept that aesthetic objects influence people and may therefore steer them toward certain social affiliations is broadly supported by some of the work discussed in chapter 4. A danger lies in the potential of organizations to apply cultural influence on very large scales and over very long periods where tangible effects may be seen but are not obvious to those subject to them. Historically, attempts have been made to use music to motivate people in simpler ways. An example is the Muzak company, which experimented with the use of music in factories to stimulate greater work productivity. Their method was based on the concept of *stimulus progression*, where music is organized into blocks of time during which it gradually intensifies in tempo, loudness, and brightness. Although Muzak might have been claimed to have measurable effects, it was not a popular idea, and whatever benefits it might have offered were outweighed by competing factors. Musak lived on in the creation of "elevator music," with the company name becoming a generic term for bland mood music, which was considered functional in environments such as shopping malls where a mood was needed but an unobtrusive sonic profile was also considered desirable.

With linguistic creativity, the potential effects are more evident. Making up fake news stories that have meme-potential—plausibility and high salience—as well as being geared toward a certain political goal, can be put to powerful use. The extraction of highly salient details and biased, leading angles on otherwise factually accurate information, can also be applied to real news stories.

Even if not used in such purposefully nefarious ways, the rapid rise of industrial-scale AI applications has been highlighted as problematic in other ways, as in the analysis of AI and society researcher Kate Crawford.[32] Crawford notes how AI is often very dysfunctional in practice, even if it performs well in standardized metrics. This can be because the data used to train it is poor or simply highly ambiguous, especially when it lacks any depth of context. A significant problem arises when large complex sociotechnical systems start to rely on such technology and to trust it when its trust hasn't been earned and without the necessary human support to fix resulting errors. In creative domains, poor training data—simple untagged corpuses of images and notes, for example—has the potential to misrepresent and dumb-down the complexity of cultural phenomena. Crawford also points to the power such industrial-scale AI systems concentrates in the hands of large corporations and their owners when they are provided as platform services.[33]

I have purposefully chosen to draw attention to some potentially very dark scenarios in the long-term application potential of creative technologies because, traditionally in computational creativity, the focus on social impact has largely been around how we would feel if machines created beautiful paintings and symphonies (see the following section), not how sociocultural dynamics will be impacted. This view stands in contrast to Smith and Leymarie's[34] optimistic vision of the impact of the machine as artist, and I feel it is an underrepresented position that needs to be considered more thoroughly. AI researchers and commentators have recently begun to mobilize around the dangers of AI, from the more obvious areas of automated weapons to nefarious uses in the financial industries. But given the great social importance of independent voices being politically and culturally autonomous, free of explicit or implicit influence, it is not too early to take a very serious look at the kinds of nefarious uses of creative technologies outlined in incredibly skeletal form here.

Beyond the Creative Species

Science writers have noted the historical "humiliations" that have come along with progress in the scientific understanding of the world. The earth is not at the center of the universe, or even of our own solar system, and humans are merely animals, evolved from a common ancestor with other life on this planet. We are neither central nor possessing of essential irreproducible qualities. This trend continues with the revelations of research in psychology, neuroscience, and evolutionary biology that reveals our biases, gene-driven motivations, failures of rationality and fast-brain (animal) responses. While psychology and neuroscience reduce the brain to something predictable, so AI threatens to demonstrate that machines can indeed do anything that we can, and in many cases already do so faster and better.

For as long as humans have existed we have been the most creative force we know of in the universe, but this seems soon to be placed into question.

Artistic creativity and artistic appreciation are, for some, central to this potential new phase of humility. David Cope, not confronted himself by such concerns, complains that for many people "it's all about machines versus humans, and 'aren't you taking away the last little thing we have left that we can call unique to human beings—creativity?'"—to which his response is "I just find this so laborious and uncreative." But how would people respond to evidence, not so much that *machines can be creative*—a question that, as I have discussed, invites enough ambiguity that we should just move past it—but that artistic behaviors can be modeled and predicted, that human aesthetic responses can be manipulated, and that creative production can be industrialized? What impact might we expect on the politics and social dynamics of identity, on cohesion and competition, on individual social relations and the socialization and enculturation of young people, and on the sense of satisfaction, enjoyment, and mutual appreciation that the creation of art and music provides for us, if we knew that all of these phenomena were modelable and predictable? Does computational creativity promise a new era of creative development and empowerment or will it herald, as the comment-stream contributor quoted at the very beginning of this book suggests, cultural redundancy and the loss of *everyone's souls*? This is a broad cluster of questions, and in this conclusion I will break the discussion down into two topics.

Machines, Souls, Authenticity, and Culture

A common complaint about machines making art is that they are merely *simulating* but are not *experiencing* as we do the aesthetic pleasure of art. They do not feel emotion and without this they cannot be legitimate creators of art. For some this failure may be manifest in poorer quality output; the simulation will always be incomplete and substandard. Machines will make refined rip-offs but will never produce sublime masterpieces or "truly original" work because to do so would require them to truly experience the emotion that we experience when presented with great art. For others, it may be that AI will be perfectly able to fake great creative work, but even if the work is in every way indistinguishable from human works of beauty, there would remain the conceptual issue that the machine is faking its experience.

With respect to the latter, the logic of the Turing test holds that we cannot pass judgment on what we cannot distinguish. Smith and Leymarie's optimistic appraisal is that we will, through developments in computational creativity, enter an era where machines understand the greatness of artworks as well as we do, an era of "humane machine intelligence," with "empathy and responsibility."[35] True to the spirit of Turing's test, if it *seems* empathetic and appreciative, then we must accept it as so.

The social perspective taken in this book skips this dilemma of true or simulated feeling, instead looking at what it means to be an art producer or consumer embedded in a cultural system, which I believe is what is really at issue when we consider what is the hard problem for efforts in lofty machine creativity. The algorithms used in computational creativity are largely derived from tools used to predict and to optimize, and insofar as there is data to predict or objective criteria to optimize, I believe that machines will be used to create amazing works of cultural production, following radically original paradigms. They will do so operating across the full spectrum from lowly generative machines, through complex collaborative co-creative interfaces, to lofty end-to-end creative agents that learn aesthetic principles, form their own conceptual spaces, perform search, and apply rules of novelty seeking and stylistic innovation. This is within the grasp of computational creativity, and systems that simulate or predict humans' emotional responses to aesthetic stimuli are also plausible.

Even if these systems perform beyond all expectations, the question of authenticity remains. From the social perspective this is not a matter of genuine feeling but of real situatedness. Just as with the philosophical question of authenticity of feeling, this is a question that lives outside of the technical, engineering domain, yet the social starting point is more tractable and empirically grounded than the philosophical one. As elaborated upon throughout chapters 3 and 4, humans apparently do not engage in art and music and other forms of cultural production merely as seekers of aesthetic enjoyment but as participants in processes of cohesion, competition, identity formation, and other social struggles. And there is evidence that the role of music and art in this effort is enmeshed not just in recent cultural history but in deep evolutionary history. For all their technical capacity, it will remain a social challenge to forcibly or otherwise embed an art- or music-generating algorithm into the role of either producer or consumer of art or music in ways that resemble our own cultural and biological situatedness.

This, for me, is a clear basis for rejecting the simple idea that through efforts in computational creativity we arrive at the creation of a "genuine machine artist," no matter what feats of creation that machine is capable of, not because it will never feel but because it will never sit in the situation of a person laden with a cultural history and life-determining choices about what creative actions to pursue. This is to take the view of "artist" as a social role. But the view of machine creativity presented in this book is one that is enacted through complex human machine networks. Within those networks, machines might fill many different roles and in their own way be culturally embedded systems. As their impact is felt and concepts of creative production are transformed, we may find new ways to think about what it means to be an artist, including extending the term to machines and transforming it as we do.

The social case against AI artists has been made by numerous commentators, but there is some difference in the detail. Sean Dorrance Kelly, a philosopher, argues that "human creative achievement, because of the way it is socially embedded, will not succumb to advances in artificial intelligence. To say otherwise is to misunderstand both what human beings are and what our creativity amounts to." While I agree broadly, I don't agree with the basis for this. He opines as I do that humans create artworks that reflect their situatedness in society, but for him it is insofar as this allows them to project a worldview:

> We count Schoenberg as a creative innovator not just because he managed to create a new way of composing music but because people could see in it a vision of what the world should be. Schoenberg's vision involved the spare, clean, efficient minimalism of modernity. His innovation was not just to find a new algorithm for composing music; it was to find a way of thinking about what music is that allows it to speak to what is needed now.
>
> … we must be able to interpret the work as responding that way. It would be a mistake to interpret a machine's composition as part of such a vision of the world.[36]

I see no reason why machines couldn't become adept independent social commentators, purveyors of visions and catchy or sociopolitically-relevant concepts, but the issue instead is where and why and with or for whom they perform such tasks; what is their grounding, and what skin do they have in the game of human social interaction?

New Creative Frontiers

Ahmed Elgammal, a key figure whose pioneering work on creative adversarial networks (CANs) we saw in chapter 5, navigates, as many commentators have done, between a vision of AI radically influencing the creation of art and of it having a comparable impact in many ways to previous transformations in the technology of art production. With Taishi Fukuyama he writes:

> Society is having an eerily similar debate to the one we had about photography and recorded or electronic sound back in the day. And the artists whose perspectives triumphed in those debates long ago because of the profound expressiveness of their art can speak to our concerns about AI. Machine learning systems and algorithms may prove not to disinherit us, but to become a new medium for human expression.[37]

But elsewhere Elgammal is keen to stress that AI systems are not simply tools, largely on the basis that they can be adaptive. Thus for him as with many creators of machine-generated works, it is important whether people accept the work "as art," asking if it is "able to qualify or count as art, and if it exhibits qualities that make it desirable or pleasurable to look at. In other words, could [CAN-generated] artifacts be recognized as quality aesthetic objects by human beings?"[38] This is a confounding issue: if the AI system is considered a mere tool, operated by an artist, then there should be little issue as to whether the output is art or not. So why should this be thrown into question? It arise as an issue only if the human operators were to attempt to render themselves invisible in the process. To recap, Gaut claims that art may be considered art for any of these reasons:

1. Possessing positive aesthetic properties
2. Being expressive of emotion
3. Being intellectually challenging
4. Being formally complex and coherent
5. Having the capacity to convey complex meanings
6. Exhibiting an individual point of view
7. Being original
8. Being an artifact or performance which is the product of a high degree of skill
9. Belonging to an established artistic form
10. Being the product of an intention to make a work of art[39]

The concern relates most clearly to item 10. In AI-generated artwork there is some intention to produce art, possessed not by the machine but by the operator. For a machine intention to have any meaning, the operator (and their intention to make art) must be removed, *and* the machine must develop that intention independently; it can't be programmed to have the intention to make art! But since so many of Gaut's other criteria are trivially achieved, this is hardly a problem. The work can still be seen as art. The machine may be designed to predict human aesthetic responses, model cultural progressions, and optimize novelty within stylistic spaces, and perform very well at such tasks, producing legitimate art autonomously, as an author, but not an intentional one, not a being motivated as we are.

Thus while machine capabilities may cause us to take stock of our place in the universe, their application in the arts may do little to transform what role art plays in society, and will instead be adapted to those existing human motivations as technologies have already. AI may radically change how we *make* art, without necessarily replacing the primacy of the human artist. Whereas machines may drive cars and rockets and diagnose illnesses far beyond the limits of our intelligence and speed, the creation of art is measured as much by where humans are situated in social contexts as by the qualities of the content produced. Yet machines *may still* produce visual and sonic artifacts of great beauty and complexity, perhaps even finding stimuli that trigger emotional responses, awe, enchantment, and amazement beyond that previously known.

In conclusion, I return to the theme of function. In the view I have painted in this book, art and music are involved in the fluid social dynamics of cohesion and competition, with taste, style, and the desire for novelty acting as forces that shape this landscape. In some cultural contexts the production of art is widely dispersed and democratic, in others it is highly concentrated and stars are thrust to prominence through a winner-takes-all dynamic. In these various contexts the creation and exaltation of art can serve different individuals' goals. It may evolve in a way that is far beyond any one person's or group's conscious control, generative rather than adaptive in its nature, spawning new forms that do not exist for any particular purpose, which nobody could have predicted or even known they wanted. Increasingly, especially in music, this production has become more industrialized, serving corporate functions over social ones. Thus again I believe the greater risks associated with the automation of creative production are those associated with the way they might impact the overall shape and dynamic of cultural production rather than the simple replacement of human activities. Such effects may take hold not only due to how good the algorithms are at generation but also how bad they are at fulfilling social roles in their entirety, a problem we see repeated elsewhere in the emergence of AI. We should enter this new world with enthusiasm for what may be possible but with eyes wide open to these broader potential impacts.

Notes

Chapter 1

1. John Brockman, ed., *What to Think About Machines That Think: Today's Leading Thinkers on the Age of Machine Intelligence* (Harper Perennial, 2015).

2. Comment in an email discussion forum, archived at https://www.southampton.ac.uk/~harnad/Hypermail/Explaining.Mind96/0069.html.

3. Make no mistake, today's machines don't dream, but it is certainly a compelling idea that a machine could dream.

4. Dubbed "Bot Dylan" by the newspaper (without approval from the system's creator).

5. Bob L. Sturm, "The 'Horse' Inside: Seeking Causes Behind the Behaviors of Music Content Analysis Systems," *Computers in Entertainment (CIE)* 14, no. 2 (2016).

6. Ray Kurzweil, *The Age of Spiritual Machines: How We Will Live, Work, and Think in the New Age of Intelligent Machines* (Orion, 1999).

7. Brian Eno, *Generative Music 1*, sleeve notes, 1996.

8. Jay Barmann, "Bay Area Billionaire Vinod Khosla Believes that AI Will Replace Musicians and Songwriters in 10 Years," *SFist*, June 14, 2019, https://sfist.com/2019/06/14/bay-area-billionaire-vinod-khosla/.

9. Glenn W. Smith and Frederic Fol Leymarie, "The Machine as Artist: An Introduction," *Arts* 6, no. 1 (2017).

10. To be fair, it should be read as more of a provocation than a prediction. Eno has written widely on generative music and is not as inclined toward predictions as Kurzweil. Eno, *Generative Music 1*.

11. Toivonen and Gross have perhaps the simplest definition of computational creativity: "The goal of computational creativity research is to model, simulate, or enhance creativity by computational means." Yet "enhancing" creativity might be considered too inclusive an activity, admitting all kinds of software that might

speed up or transform a creative process. Hannu Toivonen and Oskar Gross, "Data Mining and Machine Learning in Computational Creativity," *Wiley Interdisciplinary Reviews: Data Mining and Knowledge Discovery* 5, no. 6 (2015).

12. It has been hard to precisely define the scope of this book. My focus is on creative tasks in art and music. Sometimes, for convenience, I will use "art" as a loose catchall term (in the sense of "the creative arts") that includes music, as well as many other things. Another useful catchall term favored by some anthropologists and sociologists is "cultural production," which I introduce in chapter 4. I also occasionally refer to "creative domains," with a similar scope in mind. Lastly, although I include literary work and computer games in my list, this book is primarily about visual art and music. There are many other great texts in these specific subfields.

13. Amílcar Cardoso, Tony Veale, and Geraint A. Wiggins, "Converging on the Divergent: The History (and Future) of the International Joint Workshops in Computational Creativity," *AI Magazine* 30, no. 3 (2009).

14. Cardoso, Veale, and Wiggins, "Converging on the Divergent."

15. We could also describe his work as Inman Harvey has described the field of cognitive robotics research: "philosophy of mind with a screwdriver." Inman Harvey, "Robotics: Philosophy of Mind Using a Screwdriver," *Evolutionary Robotics: From Intelligent Robots to Artificial Life* 3 (2000).

16. Paul Brown, personal communication.

17. Harold Cohen, "Parallel to Perception: Some Notes on the Problem of Machine-Generated Art," *Computer Studies* 4, no. 3/4 (1973).

18. I recommend listening to the more timeless Disklavier piano versions rather than the earlier recordings that used the more of-their-time 1980s MIDI sounds. The use of an acoustic piano helps draw attention away from the computational origin of the performance.

19. David Cope, "An Expert System for Computer-Assisted Composition," *Computer Music Journal* 11, no. 4 (1987); David Cope, "Computational Creativity and Music," in *Computational Creativity Research: Towards Creative Machines*, ed. Tarek R. Besold, Marco Schorlemmer, and Alan Smaill (Atlantis, 2015).

20. David Cope, *Virtual Music: Computer Synthesis of Musical Style* (MIT Press, 2004).

21. Ryan Blitstein, "Triumph of the Cyborg Composer," *Pacific Standard*, February 2010, https://psmag.com/social-justice/triumph-of-the-cyborg-composer-8507.

22. Cope, *Virtual Music*.

23. Cope, *Virtual Music*.

Notes to Chapter 1

24. Cope, *Virtual Music*.

25. It is also worth noting that these pioneers are all male, reflecting the gender inequality in opportunities and role models of that time, which persists to a somewhat lesser extent today.

26. Pamela McCorduck, *Machines Who Think* (Peters, 2004).

27. Toby Walsh, "What AI Can (and Can't) Do," 2017, https://www.youtube.com/watch?v=79O903oGmmU.

28. For example, see this discussion of shifting nomenclature around the terms machine learning (ML) and AI, http://approximatelycorrect.com/2018/06/05/ai-ml-ai-swirling-nomenclature-slurried-thought/.

29. Peter Stone et al., "Artificial Intelligence and Life in 2030," *One Hundred Year Study on Artificial Intelligence: Report of the 2015–2016 Study Panel*, Stanford University, 2016.

30. Stone et al., "Artificial Intelligence and Life in 2030."

31. In 1951, a piece of music was played on a computer, the CSIRAC in Melbourne, Australia, for the first time. This was a rendering of precomposed music, not generative in any way, but this in itself would have presumably drawn attention from different communities to join the frenzy of activity that was about to take place in the space of computer-generated music. Paul Doornbusch, "The Music of CSIRAC, Some Untold Stories," in *Proceedings of the 19th International Symposium of Electronic Art*, ed. K. Cleland, L. Fisher, and R. Harley, ISEA2013, Sydney, 2013.

32. Lejaren A. Hiller Jr. and Leonard M. Isaacson, "Musical Composition with a High Speed Digital Computer," *Audio Engineering Society Convention 9, 1957*.

33. Cope, "An Expert System for Computer-Assisted Composition."

34. Tina Hesman Saey, "Computers Compose Personalized Music," *PopMatters*, June 2007, http://www.popmatters.com/article/computers-compose-personalized-music/.

35. Hesman Saey, "Computers Compose Personalized Music." What calculation and confidence was involved in coming up with this figure is worthy of some cynical scrutiny. If, by this measure, Marcel Duchamp would score 1 percent for his creative contribution to the work *Fountain*, then where does this leave us? I hope not to have to answer this question.

36. Philip Ball, "Iamus, Classical Music's Computer Composer, Live from Malaga," *Guardian*, July 1, 2012, https://www.theguardian.com/music/2012/jul/01/iamus-computer-composes-classical-music.

37. Olivia Goldhill, "The First Pop Song Ever Written by Artificial Intelligence Is Pretty Good, Actually," *Quartz*, September 24, 2016, https://qz.com/790523/daddys-car-the-first-song-ever-written-by-artificial-intelligence-is-actually-pretty-good/.

38. Alex Marshall, "Is This the World's First Good Robot Album?," BBC, January 2018, https://www.bbc.com/culture/article/20180112-is-this-the-worlds-first-good-robot-album.

39. Simon Colton et al., "The *Beyond the Fence* Musical and *Computer Says Show* Documentary," *Proceedings of the International Conference on Computational Creativity, 2016*.

40. Guardian Music, "Warner Music Signs First Ever Record Deal with an Algorithm," *Guardian*, March 2019, https://www.theguardian.com/music/2019/mar/22/algorithm-endel-signs-warner-music-first-ever-record-deal.

41. Joel Lehman et al., "The Surprising Creativity of Digital Evolution: A Collection of Anecdotes from the Evolutionary Computation and Artificial Life Research Communities," *arXiv:1803.03453* (2018).

42. https://www.nextrembrandt.com/.

43. Lara O'Reilly, "A Japanese Ad Agency Invented an AI Creative Director—and Ad Execs Preferred Its Ad to a Human's," *Business Insider*, March 2017, http://www.businessinsider.com/mccann-japans-ai-creative-director-creates-better-ads-than-a-human-2017-3.

44. Henry Bruce-Jones, "Holly Herndon on AI: Technology 'Should Allow Us to Be More Human,'" *FACT Magazine*, November 2019, https://www.factmag.com/2019/11/27/holly-herndon-grimes-zola-jesus-artificial-intelligence-interdependent-music/.

45. Hesman Saey, "Computers Compose Personalized Music."

46. Blitstein, "Triumph of the Cyborg Composer."

47. Ball, "Iamus, Classical Music's Computer Composer, Live from Malaga."

48. More ambiguously, researchers themselves may also appeal to indirect markers of success. When a Japanese data company purchased a work by the AI painting system the Painting Fool to hang in its office, this was presented by its authors as "one of the first instances in Computational Creativity research where creative software has been commissioned directly." Simon Colton et al., "The Painting Fool Sees! New Projects with the Automated Painter," *Proceedings of the International Conference on Computational Creativity, 2015*. Likewise some researchers contributing to the *Beyond the Fence* musical used audience numbers as a proxy for the success of their generative systems.

49. Ball, "Iamus, Classical Music's Computer Composer, Live from Malaga."

50. Smith and Leymarie, "The Machine as Artist."

51. Smith and Leymarie, "The Machine as Artist."

52. François Pachet, "Beyond the Cybernetic Jam Fantasy: The Continuator," *IEEE Computer Graphics and Applications* 24, no. 1 (2004).

Notes to Chapter 1

53. Christine McLeavey Payne, "Musenet," *OpenAI*, April 2019, https://openai.com/blog/musenet/.

54. Sturm, "The 'Horse' Inside."

55. Alexandre Papadopoulos, Pierre Roy, and François Pachet, "Avoiding Plagiarism in Markov Sequence Generation," *Twenty-Eighth AAAI Conference on Artificial Intelligence, 2014*.

56. McLeavey Payne, "Musenet."

57. Aaron Hertzmann, "Can Computers Create Art?," *Arts* 7, no. 2 (2018).

58. Hertzmann, "Can Computers Create Art?"

59. P. M. Todd and G. Werner, "Frankensteinian Methods for Evolutionary Music Composition," in *Musical Networks: Parallel Distributed Perception and Performance*, ed. Niall Griffith and Peter M. Todd (MIT Press/Bradford Books, 1999).

60. More generally, evolutionary computing methods are part of a family of population-based metaheuristic search methods.

61. Gregory S. Hornby, Al Globus, Derek S. Linden, and Jason D. Lohn, "Automated Antenna Design with Evolutionary Algorithms," *Space 2006*, September 19, 2006, https://ti.arc.nasa.gov/m/pub-archive/1244h/1244%20(Hornby).pdf.

62. Philip Galanter, "What Is Generative Art? Complexity Theory as a Context for Art Theory," *GA2003—6th Generative Art Conference, 2003*.

63. Kate Compton and Michael Mateas, "Casual Creators," *Proceedings of the International Conference on Computational Creativity, 2015*.

64. Kate Compton, GalaxyKate, http://www.galaxykate.com/.

65. Andy Lomas, "On Hybrid Creativity," *Arts* 7, no. 3 (2018).

66. Mitchell Whitelaw, "System Stories and Model Worlds: A Critical Approach to Generative Art," February 2006, http://mtchl.net/system-stories-model-worlds/. Whitelaw is also known for the term "metacreation," from his book of that name, which is used prominently in discussions of generative art, particularly that inspired by artificial life. Mitchell Whitelaw, *Metacreation: Art and Artificial Life* (MIT Press, 2004).

67. For a very thorough discussion of current issues relating to the embrace of creative AI, see Blaise Agüera y Arcas, "Art in the Age of Machine Intelligence," *Arts* 6, no. 4 (2017).

68. Karen Hao, "These Awful AI Song Lyrics Show Us How Hard Language Is for Machines," *MIT Technology Review*, November 13, 2018, https://www.technologyreview.com/f/612412/these-awful-ai-song-lyrics-show-us-how-hard-language-is-for-machines/. Curiously, the article claims this is evidence of how far we have to go,

but it makes no sense to cherry-pick one example of bad AI output to use as evidence that all AI output is bad. There are some very good language models out there.

69. Cardoso, Veale, and Wiggins, "Converging on the Divergent."

70. Cardoso, Veale, and Wiggins, "Converging on the Divergent."

71. The focus on crockpot recipes was in order to limit the search to ingredient combinations, the broad assumption being that for all such recipes, the instructions are to mix the ingredients together in a pot. This is a nice example of simplifying a problem space in computational creativity. It will no doubt offend some crockpot connoisseurs, but as ever, we have to start somewhere. Dan Ventura, "The Computational Creativity Complex," in *Computational Creativity Research: Towards Creative Machines*, ed. Tarek R. Besold, Marco Schorlemmer, and Alan Smaill (Atlantis, 2015).

72. Ventura, "The Computational Creativity Complex."

73. Pablo Gervás, "A Personal Perspective into the Future for Computational Creativity," in *Computational Creativity Research: Towards Creative Machines*, ed. Tarek R. Besold, Marco Schorlemmer, and Alan Smaill (Atlantis, 2015).

74. M. T. Pearce, D. Meredith, and G. A. Wiggins, "Motivations and Methodologies for Automation of the Compositional Process," *Musicae Scientiae* 6, no. 2 (2002).

Chapter 2

1. Quoted in George B. Dyson, *Darwin Among the Machines: The Evolution of Global Intelligence* (Basic Books, 2012).

2. Herman Hesse, *Siddartha* (New Direction, 1951).

3. Mel Rhodes, "An Analysis of Creativity," *Phi Delta Kappan* 42, no. 7 (1961).

4. Raymond Williams, *Keywords*, rev. ed. (Fontana Press, 1983).

5. Williams, *Keywords*.

6. Arthur Still and Mark d'Inverno, "A History of Creativity for Future AI Research," *Proceedings of the 7th Computational Creativity Conference (ICCC 2016)*, Universite Pierre et Marie Curie, 2016.

7. Still and d'Inverno, "A History of Creativity for Future AI Research."

8. Richard Florida, *The Rise of the Creative Class—Revisited* (Basic Books, 2014).

9. Amílcar Cardoso, Tony Veale, and Geraint A. Wiggins, "Converging on the Divergent: The History (and Future) of the International Joint Workshops in Computational Creativity," *AI Magazine* 30, no. 3 (2009): 15.

Notes to Chapter 2

10. Geraint A. Wiggins, "A Preliminary Framework for Description, Analysis and Comparison of Creative Systems," *Knowledge-Based Systems* 19, no. 7 (2006).

11. G. Murphy, "Typicality and the Classical View of Categories," *The Big Book of Concepts* (Bradford, 2004).

12. This approach to concepts, also referred to as a cluster concept approach, has roots in the philosophy of Wittgenstein, who argued that there is nothing that unambiguously defines the category of games. Ludwig Wittgenstein, *Philosophical Investigations* (Wiley, 2010).

13. Murphy, "Typicality and the Classical View of Categories."

14. Walter Bryce Gallie, "Essentially Contested Concepts," *Proceedings of the Aristotelian Society, 1955*; Anna Jordanous, "Evaluating Computational Creativity: A Standardised Procedure for Evaluating Creative Systems and its Application" (DPhil thesis, University of Sussex, 2012), http://sro.sussex.ac.uk/id/eprint/44741/1/Jordanous,_Anna_Katerina.pdf.

15. Wiggins, "A Preliminary Framework."

16. Teresa Amabile, *Creativity in Context* (Westview, 1996).

17. One possible hitch here is that if family resemblance is used to identify creativity, then computational creativity that is not very familiar, either in the output itself or the performance of the creative task, might not trigger that association. Indeed, some researchers have seriously examined the possibility of a hypothesized bias against computers as creative producers, as David Cope claimed. This will be discussed in chapter 7.

18. Jared Diamond, "Soft Sciences Are Often Harder than Hard Sciences," *Discover* 8, no. 8 (1987).

19. Rhodes, "An Analysis of Creativity."

20. For most readers it will be an easy sell that the requirement for novelty is also a strict condition of any artistic activity. However, it will be important to take pause to consider the issues with such an assumption when looking cross-culturally, as well as all of the modern Western guises of art making, such as repeat performances. More on this in chapter 4.

21. Amabile, *Creativity in Context*.

22. Dean Keith Simonton, "Creativity and Discovery as Blind Variation: Campbell's (1960) BVSR Model after the Half-Century Mark," *Review of General Psychology* 15, no. 2 (2011).

23. Margaret A. Boden, "Creativity and Artificial Intelligence," *Artificial Intelligence* 103, no. 1 (1998).

24. James C. Kaufman and Robert J. Sternberg, *The International Handbook of Creativity* (Cambridge University Press, 2006).

25. Henri Poincaré, *The Foundations of Science: Science and Hypothesis, the Value of Science, Science and Method*, trans. George Bruce Halstead (Science Press, 1913).

26. Albert Rothenberg and Carl R. Hausman, *The Creativity Question* (Duke University Press, 1976).

27. Margaret Boden, *The Creative Mind* (Weidenfeld and Nicholson, 1990); Simon Schaffer, "Making Up Discovery," in *Dimensions of Creativity*, ed. Margaret Boden (MIT Press, 1994).

28. The historian of science Simon Schaffer (Schaffer, "Making Up Discovery") offers an alternative analysis of the social context of such reveries and why they should not be taken too literally. I come to this in chapter 3.

29. Poincaré, *The Foundations of Science*.

30. A. Koestler, *The Ghost in the Machine* (Hutchinson, 1967).

31. Gilles Fauconnier and Mark Turner, *The Way We Think: Conceptual Blending and the Mind's Hidden Complexities* (Basic Books, 2008). Conceptual blending has become a major theme in computational creativity; see, for example, Francisco Câmara Pereira and Amílcar Cardoso, "Conceptual Blending and the Quest for the Holy Creative Process," *Proceedings of the Symposium for Creativity in Arts and Science of AISB 2002*.

32. Gilles Fauconnier and Mark Turner, "Conceptual Blending, Form and Meaning," *Recherches en communication* 19, no. 19 (2003): 57–86, http://sites.uclouvain.be/rec/index.php/rec/article/viewfile/5191/4921. An example is the counterfactual. Fauconnier observes that a statement such as "In France, Watergate would not have hurt Nixon" is easy for most humans to process and understand, yet provides quite a remarkable and powerful thinking mechanism, in this case comparing US and French political systems.

33. Silvano Arieti, *Creativity: The Magic Synthesis* (Basic Books, 1976).

34. Amabile, *Creativity in Context*.

35. Sam Glucksberg, "The Influence of Strength of Drive on Functional Fixedness and Perceptual Recognition," *Journal of Experimental Psychology* 63, no. 1 (1962).

36. E. Paul Torrance, "The Nature of Creativity as Manifest in Its Testing," in *The Nature of Creativity: Contemporary Psychological Perspectives*, ed. R. J. Sternberg (Cambridge University Press, 1988).

37. G. Polya, *How to Solve It* (Princeton University Press, 1957).

38. Alex F. Osborn, *Applied Imagination* (Charles Scribner, 1953).

Notes to Chapter 2

39. Simonton, "Creativity and Discovery as Blind Variation."

40. In an article on improvisation in the creative process, Keith Sawyer elaborates on one of Picasso's creative sessions, as seen in Henri Georges Clouzot's film *The Mystery of Picasso*. The description supports Simonton's position: "In his studio, Picasso is painting free-form, without preconceived image or composition; he is experimenting with colors, forms, and moods. He starts with a figure of a reclining nude—but then loses interest, and the curve of the woman's leg reminds him of a matador's leg as he flies through the air after being gored by a bull—so he paints over the nude and creates an image of a bull and matador. But this leads him to yet another idea; he paints over the bullfight image and begins work on a Mediterranean harbor. ... Five hours later, Picasso stops and declares that he will have to discard the canvas. ... But the time was not wasted—he has discovered some new ideas that he can use in his next painting." R. Keith Sawyer, "Improvisation and the Creative Process: Dewey, Collingwood, and the Aesthetics of Spontaneity," *Journal of Aesthetics and Art Criticism* 58, no. 2 (2000).

41. Robert J. Sternberg, "The Nature of Creativity," *Creativity Research Journal* 18, no. 1 (2006).

42. Jacob W. Getzels and Mihaly Csikszentmihalyi, *The Creative Vision: A Longitudinal Study of Problem Finding in Art* (Wiley, 1976).

43. Simonton, "Creativity and Discovery as Blind Variation."

44. Boden, *The Creative Mind*.

45. G. A. Wiggins, "Towards a More Precise Characterisation of Creativity in AI," *Case-Based Reasoning: Papers from the Workshop Program at ICCBR'01*, Washington, DC, Naval Research Laboratory, Navy Center for Applied Research in Artificial Intelligence, 2001.

46. Geraint A. Wiggins, "Searching for Computational Creativity," *New Generation Computing* 24, no. 3 (2006).

47. Peter Gärdenfors, *Conceptual Spaces: The Geometry of Thought* (MIT Press, 2004).

48. Patricia D. Stokes and Danielle Fisher, "Selection, Constraints, and Creativity Case Studies: Max Beckmann and Philip Guston," *Creativity Research Journal* 17, nos. 2–3 (2005).

49. Stokes and Fisher, "Selection, Constraints, and Creativity Case Studies."

50. Stokes and Fisher, "Selection, Constraints, and Creativity Case Studies."

51. W. Ross Ashby Digital Archive, http://www.rossashby.info/aphorisms.html.

52. Emile Durkheim, *Selected Writings*, ed. Anthony Giddens (Cambridge University Press, 1972).

53. Dyson, *Darwin among the Machines*.

54. Alan M. Turing, "Computing Machinery and Intelligence," *Mind* 59, no. 236 (1950).

55. Turing, "Computing Machinery and Intelligence."

56. Turing, "Computing Machinery and Intelligence."

57. Norbert Wiener, *Cybernetics or Control and Communication in the Animal and the Machine*, vol. 25 (MIT Press, 1961).

58. Charles Darwin, *On the Origin of Species by Means of Natural Selection, or the Preservation of Favoured Races in the Struggle for Life* (John Murray, 1859).

59. Robert Epstein, Gary Roberts, and Grace Beber, eds., *Parsing the Turing Test* (Springer, 2009).

60. Comment in an email discussion forum, archived at https://www.southampton.ac.uk/~harnad/Hypermail/Explaining.Mind96/0069.html.

61. Selmer Bringsjord, Paul Bello, and David Ferrucci, "Creativity, the Turing Test, and the (Better) Lovelace Test," in *The Turing Test: The Elusive Standard of Artificial Intelligence*, ed. James H. Moor (Springer, 2003).

62. Martin Mumford and Dan Ventura, "The Man Behind the Curtain: Overcoming Skepticism About Creative Computing," *Proceedings of the Sixth International Conference on Computational Creativity, June 2015*.

63. Mumford and Ventura, "The Man Behind the Curtain."

64. This is not exactly how Turing described the test, but it is well known as a simpler but equivalent version.

65. Robert M. French, "The Turing Test: The First 50 Years," *Trends in Cognitive Sciences* 4, no. 3 (2000).

66. Blay Whitby, "The Turing Test: AI's Biggest Blind Alley?," in *Machines and Thought: The Legacy of Alan Turing*, ed. Peter Millican and Andy Clark (Oxford University Press, 1996).

67. Whitby, "The Turing Test: AI's Biggest Blind Alley?"

68. Coventry University, "Turing Test Transcript Reveal How Chatbot 'Eugene' Duped the Judges," June 2015, https://www.coventry.ac.uk/primary-news/turing-test-transcripts-reveal-how-chatbot-eugene-duped-the-judges/.

69. Ian Sample and Alex Hern, "Scientists Dispute Whether Computer 'Eugene Goostman' Passed Turing Test," *Guardian*, June 2014, https://www.theguardian.com/technology/2014/jun/09/scientists-disagree-over-whether-turing-test-has-been-passed.

70. Alec Radford et al., "Language models are unsupervised multitask learners," *OpenAI Blog* 1, no. 8 (2019), citing B. McCann, N. S. Keskar, C. Xiong, and R. Socher, "The Natural Language Decathlon: Multitask Learning as Question Answering," *arXiv preprint arXiv:1806.08730* (2018).

71. Auerbach, David, "A Computer Program Finally Passed the Turing Test? Not So Fast," *Slate Magazine*, June 2014, https://slate.com/technology/2014/06/turing-test-reading-university-did-eugene-goostman-finally-make-the-grade.html.

72. French, "The Turing Test: The First 50 Years."

73. Oliver Bown, "Generative and Adaptive Creativity: A Unified Approach to Creativity in Nature, Humans and Machines," in *Computers and Creativity*, pp. 361–381 (Springer, 2012).

Chapter 3

1. W. Ross Ashby Digital Archive, http://www.rossashby.info/aphorisms.html.

2. This saying is widely credited to Thompson, for example by Daniel Dennett in an Edge.org article (https://www.edge.org/conversation/the-evolution-of-culture), but without citation.

3. John Steinbeck, *East of Eden* (Viking, 1952).

4. Sami Abuhamdeh and Mihaly Csikszentmihalyi, "The Artistic Personality: A Systems Perspective," in Csikszentmihalyi, *The Systems Model of Creativity* (Springer, 2015).

5. Mihaly Csikszentmihalyi, *The Systems Model of Creativity: The Collected Works of Mihaly Csikszentmihalyi* (Springer, 2015).

6. Andrew Pickering, "The Politics of Theory: Producing Another World, with Some Thoughts on Latour," *Journal of Cultural Economy* 2, nos. 1–2 (2009).

7. Pickering, "The Politics of Theory."

8. Alfred Gell, *Art and Agency: An Anthropological Theory* (Clarendon, 1998).

9. Mihaly Csikszentmihalyi, "Society, Culture, and Person: A Systems View of Creativity," in Csikszentmihalyi, *The Systems Model of Creativity* (Springer, 2015).

10. Dean Keith Simonton, "Scientific Creativity as Constrained Stochastic Behavior: The Integration of Product, Person, and Process Perspectives," *Psychological Bulletin* 129, no. 4 (2003).

11. That said, Simonton later accepts that the equal-odds rule applies less in the arts, where there is more potential for manipulating the reception of the work.

12. Thomas S. Kuhn, *The Structure of Scientific Revolutions*, 3rd ed. (University of Chicago Press, 1996).

13. Csikszentmihalyi, "Society, Culture, and Person."

14. Csikszentmihalyi, "Society, Culture, and Person."

15. Robert J. Sternberg and Todd I. Lubart, "An investment theory of creativity and its development," *Human development* 34, no. 1 (1991).

16. Malcolm Gladwell, "Blowing Up," *New Yorker*, April 22, 2002.

17. David N. Perkins, "Creativity: Beyond the Darwinian Paradigm," in *Dimensions of Creativity*, ed. Margaret Boden (MIT Press, 1996).

18. Keynote, *Proceedings of the International Conference on Computational Creativity, 2016*.

19. Kenneth O. Stanley and Joel Lehman, *Why Greatness Cannot Be Planned: The Myth of the Objective* (Springer, 2015).

20. Dava Sobel, *Longitude: The True Story of a Lone Genius Who Solved the Greatest Scientific Problem of His Time* (Penguin, 1996).

21. Sobel's book lists a number of wonderfully crackpot proposals.

22. Charles Landry, *The Creative City: A Toolkit for Urban Innovators* (Earthscan, 2012).

23. Ilkka Kakko and Sam Inkinen, "*Homo Creativus*: Creativity and Serendipity Management in Third Generation Science and Technology Parks," *Science and Public Policy* 36, no. 7 (2009).

24. Richard Florida, *The Rise of the Creative Class—Revisited* (Basic Books, 2012).

25. Csikszentmihalyi, "Society, Culture, and Person."

26. Harold Cohen was also enthusiastic about making this point: "To what extent could we reasonably maintain that the human mind initiates? Concepts are formed on the basis of prior concepts, decisions are made on the basis of feedback from the environment and from the results of previous decisions. The probability is that, if one could identify the starting point for an artist's whole life's work, one would find a set of concepts completely formulated if not completely digested, given to him and not initiated by him." Cohen, "Parallel to Perception: Some Notes on the Problem of Machine-Generated Art," *Computer Studies* 4, no. 3/4 (1973).

27. Csikszentmihalyi, *The Systems Model of Creativity*.

28. Simon Schaffer, "Making Up Discovery," in *Dimensions of Creativity*, ed. Margaret Boden (MIT Press, 1996).

29. Simon Schaffer, "Making Up Discovery," quoting Paul David, "The Hero and the Herd in Technological History: Reflections on Thomas Edison and the Battle of

the Systems," in *Favorites to Fortune*, ed. L. R. Patrice, David S. Higonnet, and Henry Rosovsky Landes (Harvard University Press, 1991), 72–119.

30. Ernst Kris and Otto Kurz, *Legend, Myth, and Magic in the Image of the Artist: A Historical Experiment* (Yale University Press, 1981).

31. Margot F. Brereton, David M. Cannon, Ade Mabogunje, and Larry J. Leifer, "Collaboration in Design Teams: How Social Interaction Shapes the Product," in *Analysing Design Activity*, ed. Nigel Cross, Kees Dorst, and Henri Christiaans (Wiley, 1996), 319–341.

32. Bruno Latour, "On Technical Mediation Philosophy, Sociology, Genealogy," *Common Knowledge* 3, no. 2 (1994).

33. Bruno Latour, *We Have Never Been Modern* (Harvard University Press, 2012).

34. Would Turing have been an actor-network theorist?

35. Lambros Malafouris, "At the Potter's Wheel: An Argument for Material Agency," in *Material Agency: Towards a Non- Anthropocentric Approach*, ed. C. Knappett and L. Malafouris (Springer, 2008), http://cogprints.org/6402/.

36. A. Clark, *Natural-Born Cyborgs: Minds, Technologies, and the Future of Human Intelligence* (Oxford University Press, 2003).

37. Susanne Bødker, "When Second Wave HCI Meets Third Wave Challenges," *Proceedings of the 4th Nordic Conference on Human-Computer Interaction: Changing Roles, 2006*.

38. Paul Dourish, *Where the Action Is: The Foundations of Embodied Interaction* (MIT Press, 2004). It should also be noted, however, that another way of looking at agency for user-centered designers is to focus on a user's sense of agency, in which case the issue of where agency actually lies becomes less important. "A person will have a sense of agency when they consider themselves to have the ownership of, and be responsible for, the consequences that their actions have in the external world." Guo Yu and Alan Blackwell, "Effects of Timing on Users' Agency During Mixed-Initiative Interaction," *Proceedings of the 31st British Computer Society Human Computer Interaction Conference, 2017*.

39. You may object that quantum phenomena are different, but unless you believe them to have decision-making powers, they don't alter this basic indifference to causality that these low-level entities have, they simply follow stochastic rather than deterministic rules.

40. Paul Bello Bringsjord and David Ferrucci, "Creativity, the Turing Test, and the (Better) Lovelace Test," in *The Turing Test: The Elusive Standard of Artificial Intelligence*, ed. James H. Moor (Springer, 2003), 215–239.

41. Richard Dawkins, *The Selfish Gene* (Oxford University Press, 1976).

42. Dan Sperber, "Seedless Grapes: Nature and Culture," in *Creations of the Mind: Theories of Artifacts and Their Representation*, ed. Eric Margolis and Stephen Laurence (Oxford University Press, 2007).

43. James J. Gibson, "The Theory of Affordances," in *Perceiving, Acting, and Knowing*, ed. Robert Shaw and John Bransford (Lawrence Erlbaum, 1977).

44. Gibson, "The Theory of Affordances."

45. Donald Norman, *The Psychology of Everyday Things* (Basic Books, 1988).

46. Extensive discussion of how *exactly* the term should be used in design can be found throughout the design literature. A decent summary of some issues can be found in Leonardo Burlamaqui and Andy Dong, "The Use and Misuse of the Concept of Affordance," in *Design Computing and Cognition '14* (Springer, 2015).

47. Vlad Petre Glăveanu, "On Units of Analysis and Creativity Theory: Towards a 'Molecular' Perspective," *Journal for the Theory of Social Behaviour* 45, no. 3 (2015).

48. Bruno Latour, "What's the Story? Organizing as a Mode of Existence," in *Agency without Actors?*, ed. Jan-Hendrik Passoth, Birgit Peuker, and Michael Schillmeier (Routledge, 2011).

49. Gell, *Art and Agency: An Anthropological Theory*.

50. "Self-sufficiency" is an interesting way to establish this definition. Ultimately, it succumbs to the same criticism as does intentionality—Post-It notes seem perfectly self-sufficient, having established the means to exploit humans to keep them in production.

51. Georgina Born, "Making Time: Temporality, History, and the Cultural Object," *New Literary History* 46, no. 3 (2015).

52. This echoes Robert Plotkin's analysis in his book *The Genie in the Machine*, a book also about machine creativity but more explicitly focused on the field of design. Plotkin portrays computers as genies that realize our wishes as long as we have a suitable interface with which to express those wishes. The history of computational technologies tells a story of improved forms of wish-stating, from the earliest programming language compilers to natural language processing and objective search algorithms. Robert Plotkin, *The Genie in the Machine: How Computer-Automated Inventing Is Revolutionizing Law and Business* (Stanford University Press, 2009).).

53. Although they relate, Simonton is at pains to point out that BVSR is not a Darwinian evolutionary model of creativity, it just shares some underlying features. Dean Keith Simonton, "Creativity and Discovery as Blind Variation: Campbell's (1960) BVSR Model after the Half-Century Mark," *Review of General Psychology* 15, no. 2 (2011): 158.

54. In spite of Shaffer's work on science mythologizing, I am knowingly committing the common crime of ignoring Wallace, the theory's co-inventor, for the sake of brevity.

55. Source unknown, this may be falsely attributed to D'Arcy Thompson, but several online sources cite him as saying this.

56. Charles Lyell, *Principles of Geology: Being an Inquiry How Far the Former Changes of the Earth's Surface Are Referable to Causes Now in Operation*, vol. 1 (J. Kay, 1837).

57. John Maynard Smith and Eörs Szathmáry, *The Major Transitions in Evolution* (Oxford University Press, 1995).

58. Stuart A. Kauffman, *The Origins of Order: Self-Organization and Selection in Evolution* (Oxford University Press, 1993).

59. Humbert R. Maturana and Francisco J. Varela, *Autopoiesis and Cognition: The Realization of the Living* (Reidel, 1980).

60. Niklas Luhmann, *Art as a Social System* (Stanford University Press, 2000).

61. Eva Jablonka and Marion J. Lamb, *Epigenetic Inheritance and Evolution: The Lamarckian Dimension* (Oxford University Press, 1995).

62. R. Boyd and Peter J. Richerson, *Culture and the Evolutionary Process* (University of Chicago Press, 1985).

63. Michael Tomasello et al., "Understanding and Sharing Intentions: The Origins of Cultural Cognition," *Behavioral and Brain Sciences* 28, no. 5 (2005).

64. Dawkins, *The Selfish Gene*.

65. Kevin Kelly, *What Technology Wants* (Penguin, 2010).

66. W. Brian Arthur, *The Nature of Technology: What It Is and How It Evolves* (Penguin, 2009).

67. Arthur, *The Nature of Technology*.

68. Kelly, *What Technology Wants*.

69. Arthur, *The Nature of Technology*.

70. Peter J. Richerson and Robert Boyd, *Not by Genes Alone: How Culture Transformed Human Evolution* (University of Chicago Press, 2005).

71. F. John Odling-Smee, Kevin N. Laland, and Marcus W. Feldman, *Niche Construction: The Neglected Process in Evolution*, Monographs in Population Biology (Princeton University Press, 2003).

72. Although they weren't the first. Such ideas were latent in evolutionary theory. Darwin, and others such as Dawkins, with his extended phenotype theory, have taken into account abiotic elements in various ways in evolutionary theories. Richard Dawkins, *The Extended Phenotype: The Long Reach of the Gene* (Oxford University Press, 2016). The daisyworld hypothesis is another early proof of concept of ideas underlying niche construction theory. Andrew J. Watson and James E. Lovelock,

"Biological Homeostasis of the Global Environment: The Parable of Daisyworld," *Tellus B: Chemical and Physical Meteorology* 35, no. 4 (1983).

Chapter 4

1. Theodor W. Adorno, *Aesthetic Theory* (A & C Black, 1997).

2. Oscar Wilde, letter to a reader, Bernulf Clegg, 1891, Manuscripts and Letters of Oscar Wilde, The Morgan Library and Museum, New York, https://www.themorgan.org/collection/Oscar-Wilde.

3. *Life Is Beautiful* (1997), screenplay by Vincenzo Cerami and Roberto Benigni, director.

4. Berys Gaut, "The Cluster Account of Art," in *Theories of Art Today*, ed. Noël Carroll (University of Wisconsin Press, 2000).

5. There are competing lists. For example, Dutton's list of twelve elements has differences and overlaps. He includes a "special focus" of art, making it stand apart from the normal world (e.g., with curtains, plinths, and white walls). But these differences of opinion in the details generally support the main argument of a cluster approach. Denis Dutton, "A Naturalist Definition of Art," *Journal of Aesthetics and Art Criticism* 64, no. 3 (2006).

6. Gaut's approach is not without critics and controversy, and this point can be contested.

7. Alfred Gell, *Art and Agency: An Anthropological Theory* (Clarendon, 1998).

8. Wilde to Clegg, 1891.

9. Denis Dutton, *The Art Instinct: Beauty, Pleasure, and Human Evolution* (Bloomsbury Press, 2010).

10. Steven Pinker, *The Language Instinct: The New Science of Language and Mind* (Penguin UK, 1995).

11. Jerome H. Barkow, Leda Cosmides, and John Tooby, *The Adapted Mind: Evolutionary Psychology and the Generation of Culture* (Oxford University Press, 1992).

12. Ian Cross, "Music, Cognition, Culture and Evolution," *Annals of the New York Academy of Sciences* 930 (2001).

13. Steven Brown, "Contagious Heterophony: A New Theory about the Origins of Music," *Musicae Scientiae* 11, no. 1 (Spring 2007).

14. W. H. McNeill, *Keeping Together in Time: Dance and Drill in Human History* (Harvard University Press, 1995).

15. Richard Dawkins, *The Selfish Gene* (Oxford University Press, 1976).

16. R. Boyd and Peter J. Richerson, *Culture and the Evolutionary Process* (University of Chicago Press, 1985).

17. F. John Odling-Smee, Kevin N. Laland, and Marcus W. Feldman, *Niche Construction: The Neglected Process in Evolution* (Princeton University Press, 2003).

18. W. D. Hamilton, "The Evolution of Altruistic Behavior," *American Naturalist* 97 (1963).

19. Robert M. Axelrod, *The Evolution of Cooperation*, rev. ed. (Basic Books, 2006).

20. Ellen Dissanayake, "Antecedents of the Temporal Arts in Early Mother-Infant Interaction," in *The Origins of Music*, ed. Nils L. Wallin, Björn Merker, and Steven Brown (MIT Press, 2000).

21. Amotz Zahavi and Avishag Zahavi, *The Handicap Principle: A Missing Piece of Darwin's Puzzle* (Oxford University Press, 1997).

22. Geoffrey Miller, *The Mating Mind* (Random House, 2000).

23. Paul Bloom, *How Pleasure Works: The New Science of Why We Like What We Like* (Random House, 2010).

24. A. Whiten and R. W. Byrne, *Machiavellian Intelligence II: Extensions and Evaluations* (Cambridge University Press, 1997); R. Dunbar, "The Social Brain Hypothesis," *Evolutionary Anthropology* 6 (1998).

25. Niklas Luhmann, *Art as a Social System* (Stanford University Press, 2000).

26. Daniel Kahneman, *Thinking, Fast and Slow* (Macmillan, 2011).

27. Kahneman, *Thinking, Fast and Slow*.

28. George David Birkhoff, *Aesthetic Measure*, vol. 9 (Harvard University Press, 1933), 9.

29. Alex Forsythe et al., "Predicting Beauty: Fractal Dimension and Visual Complexity in Art," *British Journal of Psychology* 102, no. 1 (2011).

30. D. E. Berlyne, *Aesthetics and Psychobiology* (Appleton-Century-Crofts, 1971).

31. Richard F. Voss and John Clarke, "'1/f Noise' in Music: Music from 1/f Noise," *Journal of the Acoustical Society of America* 63, no. 1 (1978).

32. Bill Manaris et al., "Zipf's Law, Music Classification, and Aesthetics," *Computer Music Journal* 29, no. 1 (2005).

33. David I. Perrett et al., "Symmetry and Human Facial Attractiveness," *Evolution and Human Behavior* 20, no. 5 (1999); M. J. Tovée, K. Tasker, and P. J. Benson, "Is Symmetry a Visual Cue to Attractiveness in the Human Female Body?," *Evolution and Human Behavior* 21, no. 3 (2000); Kathrine Shepherd and Moshe Bar, "Preference for Symmetry: Only on Mars?," *Perception* 40, no. 10 (2011).

34. William M. Brown et al., "Dance Reveals Symmetry Especially in Young Men," *Nature* 438, no. 7071 (2005).

35. Studies have found confusing results in this regard. For example, one study found that men preferred symmetry whatever the context, whereas female symmetry preference was limited to faces. Shepherd and Bar, "Preference for Symmetry."

36. Gordan H. Orians and Judith H. Heerwagen, "Evolved Responses to Landscapes," in *The Adapted Mind: Evolutionary Psychology and the Generation of Culture*, ed. Jerome H. Barkow, John Tooby, and Leda Cosmides (Oxford University Press, 1992), 555–579.

37. Dutton, *The Art Instinct*.

38. Orians and Heerwagen, "Evolved Responses to Landscapes."

39. John Tooby and Leda Cosmides, "Does Beauty Build Adapted Minds? Toward an Evolutionary Theory of Aesthetics, Fiction, and the Arts," *SubStance* 30, no. 1 (2001).

40. Tooby and Cosmides, "Does Beauty Build Adapted Minds?"

41. Tooby and Cosmides, "Does Beauty Build Adapted Minds?"

42. S. J. Gould and R. C. Lewontin, "The Spandrels of San Marco and the Panglossian Paradigm: A Critique of the Adaptationist Programme," *Proceedings of the Royal Society of London, 1979*.

43. This refers to the Spandrels of San Marco. Gould and Lewontin use the analogy of spandrels, an architectural structural feature, which are commonly decorated, as a way to discuss evolutionary explanation. The decoration is of course designed to fit the spandrels perfectly, but an observer might mistake the purpose of the spandrels as being to host the decorative art, rather than to support the weight of the roof above. Gould and Lewontin, "The Spandrels of San Marco."

44. Barkow, Cosmides, and Tooby are keen to point out that we should always be thinking of the environment of evolutionary adaptation, not our own environment and context. This is a fair point, but still the landscape hypothesis seems too complex an encoding. Barkow, Cosmides, and Tooby, *The Adapted Mind*.

45. A. S. Bregman, *Auditory Scene Analysis* (MIT Press, 1990).

46. E. W. Large and M. R. Jones, "The Dynamics of Attending: How People Track Time-Varying Events," *Psychological Review* 10, no. 1 (1999).

47. Justin London, *Hearing in Time* (Oxford University Press, 2004).

48. Ian Cross, "Music and Meaning, Ambiguity and Evolution," in *Musical Communication*, ed. Dorothy Miell, Raymond MacDonald, and David Hargreaves (Oxford University Press, 2005), 27–43.

49. Dissanayake, "Antecedents of the Temporal Arts in Early Mother-Infant Interaction."

50. McNeill, *Keeping Together in Time: Dance and Drill in Human History*.

51. G. J. Balzano, "The Group-Theoretic Description of 12-Fold and Microtonal Pitch Systems," *Computer Music Journal* 4, no. 4 (1980).

52. Claude Lévi-Strauss, *The Raw and the Cooked: Introduction to a Science of Mythology* (University of Chicago Press, 1966).

53. Jeffrey Elman et al., eds., *Rethinking Innateness* (MIT Press, 1996).

54. Vilayanur S. Ramachandran and William Hirstein, "The Science of Art: A Neurological Theory of Aesthetic Experience," *Journal of Consciousness Studies* 6, no. 6-7 (1999).

55. Ramachandran and Hirstein, "The Science of Art."

56. Ramachandran and Hirstein, "The Science of Art."

57. Mihaly Csikszentmihalyi, *Flow: The Psychology of Optimal Experience* (Harper and Row, 1990).

58. Daniel E. Berlyne, "Novelty, Complexity, and Hedonic Value," *Attention, Perception, and Psychophysics* 8, no. 5 (1970).

59. Daniel Ellis Berlyne, "A Theory of Human Curiosity," *British Journal of Psychology* 45, no. 3 (1954).

60. Berlyne, "Novelty, Complexity, and Hedonic Value."

61. Jürgen Schmidhuber, "Formal Theory of Creativity, Fun, and Intrinsic Motivation (1990–2010)," *IEEE Transactions on Autonomous Mental Development* 2, no. 3 (2010).

62. We may also include Liane Gabora's honing theory in this cluster of views. Honing theory is similarly focused on the idea that individuals strive to build compressed models of cultural material, and that hard-to-compress material is stimulating for this reason. Gabora further develops a cultural-evolutionary model, however, where cultural dynamics emerge from individuals striving to produce stimulating material. Liane Gabora, "Honing Theory: A Complex Systems Framework for Creativity," *Nonlinear Dynamics Psychology and Life Sciences* 21, no. 1 (October 2016).

63. David Huron, *Sweet Anticipation: Music and the Psychology of Expectation* (MIT Press, 2006).

64. Geraint A. Wiggins and Jamie Forth, "IDyOT: A Computational Theory of Creativity as Everyday Reasoning from Learned Information," in *Computational Creativity Research: Towards Creative Machines*, ed. Tarek R. Besold, Marco Schorlemmer, and Alan Smaill (Atlantis, 2015).

65. Large and Jones, "The Dynamics of Attending."

66. Clifford Geertz, *The Interpretation of Cultures* (Basic Books, 1973).

67. Peter L. Berger and Thomas Luckmann, *The Social Construction of Reality: A Treatise in the Sociology of Knowledge* (Penguin UK, 1991).

68. Pierre Bourdieu, *Distinction: A Social Critique of the Judgment of Taste* (Harvard University Press, 1984).

69. Bourdieu, *Distinction*.

70. Bourdieu, *Distinction*.

71. Pierre Bourdieu, "The Forms of Capital (1986)," *Cultural Theory: An Anthology* 1 (2011).

72. Georgina Born, "The Social and the Aesthetic: For a Post-Bourdieuian Theory of Cultural Production," *Cultural Sociology* 4, no. 2 (2010).

73. Born, "The Social and the Aesthetic."

74. Born also points out a potential rivalry between the sociological study of art and the humanities.

75. Antoine Hennion, "Pragmatics of Taste," in *The Blackwell Companion to the Sociology of Culture*, ed. Mark D. Jacob and Nancy Weiss Hanrahan (Blackwell, 2005), 131–144.

76. Hennion, "Pragmatics of Taste."

77. Philip Auslander, "Lucille Meets GuitarBot: Instrumentality, Agency, and Technology in Musical Performance," in *Musical Instruments in the 21st Century*, ed. Till Bovermann, Alberto de Campo, Hauke Egermann, Sarah Hardjowirogo, and Stefan Weinzierl (Springer, 2017), 297–314.

78. I am not suggesting that Bourdieu saw an evolutionary explanation, but even in a limited short-term historical context the implication is that taste *functions* to serve class divisions, inviting an evolutionary perspective.

79. Bourdieu, *Distinction*.

80. With reference back to Merriam's (1964) ten functions of music: human expression; aesthetic enjoyment; entertainment; communication; symbolic representation; physical response; enforcing conformity to social norms; validation of social institutions and religious rituals; contribution to the continuity and stability of culture; contribution to the integration of society. David J. Hargreaves and Adrian C. North, "The Functions of Music in Everyday Life: Redefining the Social in Music Psychology," *Psychology of Music* 27, no. 1 (1999).

81. Adrian C. North and David J. Hargreaves, "Music and Adolescent Identity," *Music Education Research* 1, no. 1 (1999).

82. North and Hargreaves, "Music and Adolescent Identity."

83. Adrian C. North, David J. Hargreaves, and Susan A. O'Neill, "The Importance of Music to Adolescents," *British Journal of Educational Psychology* 70, no. 2 (2000).

84. Kelly D. Schwartz and Gregory T. Fouts, "Music Preferences, Personality Style, and Developmental Issues of Adolescents," *Journal of Youth and Adolescence* 32, no. 3 (2003).

85. Emery Schubert, David J. Hargreaves, and Adrian C. North, "A Dynamically Minimalist Cognitive Explanation of Musical Preference: Is Familiarity Everything?," *Frontiers in Psychology* 5 (2014).

86. Schubert, Hargreaves, and North, "A Dynamically Minimalist Cognitive Explanation."

87. Kathryn Coe, *The Ancestress Hypothesis: Visual Art as Adaptation* (Rutgers University Press, 2003).

88. Coe, *The Ancestress Hypothesis*.

89. Matthew J. Salganik, Peter Sheridan Dodds, and Duncan J. Watts, "Experimental Study of Inequality and Unpredictability in an Artificial Cultural Market," *Science* 311, no. 5762 (2006).

90. Bloom, *How Pleasure Works*.

91. Bloom, *How Pleasure Works*.

92. As an aside, note the relation to a family-resemblance approach to defining terms like "creativity" and "art."

93. Bloom, *How Pleasure Works*.

94. Cross, "Music and Meaning, Ambiguity and Evolution."

95. I propose this could be called the "Phil Collins effect."

96. Colin Martindale, "Aesthetic Evolution," *Poetics* 15, nos. 4–6 (1986).

97. Martindale, "Aesthetic Evolution."

98. Martindale, "Aesthetic Evolution."

99. Martindale, "Aesthetic Evolution."

100. Colin Martindale et al., "Creativity, Oversensitivity, and Rate of Habituation," *Personality and Individual Differences* 20, no. 4 (1996).

101. Hadi T. Nia et al., "The Evolution of Air Resonance Power Efficiency in the Violin and Its Ancestors," *Proceedings of the Royal Society of London A: Mathematical, Physical and Engineering Sciences* 471, no. 2175 (2015).

102. Gino Cattani and Simone Ferriani, "A Core/Periphery Perspective on Individual Creative Performance: Social Networks and Cinematic Achievements in the Hollywood Film Industry," *Organization Science* 19, no. 6 (2008).

103. Cattani and Ferriani, "A Core/Periphery Perspective."

104. Gino Cattani, Simone Ferriani, and Paul D. Allison, "Insiders, Outsiders, and the Struggle for Consecration in Cultural Fields: A Core-Periphery Perspective," *American Sociological Review* 79, no. 2 (2014).

105. Cattani, Ferriani, and Allison, "Insiders, Outsiders," with reference to Bourdieu.

106. Noah Askin and Michael Mauskapf, "What Makes Popular Culture Popular? Product Features and Optimal Differentiation in Music," *American Sociological Review* 82, no. 5 (2017).

107. Askin and Mauskapf, "What Makes Popular Culture Popular?"

108. Howard Saul Becker, *Art Worlds* (University of California Press, 1982).

Chapter 5

1. Sol LeWitt, "Paragraphs on Conceptual Art," *Artforum* 5, no. 10 (1967).

2. Herbert A. Simon, *The Sciences of the Artificial* (MIT Press, 1996).

3. Hannu Toivonen and Oskar Gross, "Data Mining and Machine Learning in Computational Creativity," *Wiley Interdisciplinary Reviews: Data Mining and Knowledge Discovery* 5, no. 6 (2015).

4. A number of excellent, more technical references are provided throughout which readers can follow if they are interested in more detailed technical discussion.

5. Dan Ventura, "The Computational Creativity Complex," in *Computational Creativity Research: Towards Creative Machines*, ed. Tarek R. Besold, Marco Schorlemmer, and Alan Smaill (Atlantics, 2015), 65.

6. Ventura, "The Computational Creativity Complex," 81.

7. Geraint A. Wiggins and Jamie Forth, "IDyOT: A Computational Theory of Creativity as Everyday Reasoning from Learned Information," in *Computational Creativity Research: Towards Creative Machines*, ed. Tarek R. Besold, Marco Schorlemmer, and Alan Smaill (Atlantis, 2015), 127–148.

8. Christopher Alexander, *A Pattern Language: Towns, Buildings, Construction* (Oxford University Press, 1977).

9. Erich Gamma, *Design Patterns: Elements of Reusable Object-Oriented Software* (Pearson Education India, 1995).

10. Simon Colton et al., "The *Beyond the Fence* Musical and *Computer Says Show* Documentary," *Proceedings of the International Conference on Computational Creativity, 2016*.

11. Toivonen and Gross, "Data Mining," 3.

12. Rodney A. Brooks, "Elephants Don't Play Chess," *Robotics and Autonomous Systems* 6 (1990).

13. Javier Monedero, "Parametric Design: A Review and Some Experiences," *Automation in Construction* 9, no. 4 (2000).

14. Monedero, "Parametric Design."

15. Kate Compton and Michael Mateas, "Casual Creators," *Proceedings of the International Conference on Computational Creativity, 2015*.

16. Robert Aish and Robert Woodbury, "Multi-level Interaction in Parametric Design," in *Smart Graphics: 5th International Symposium, SG 2005, Frauenworth Cloister, Germany, August 22-24, 2005 Proceedings*, ed. A. Butz, B. Fisher, A. Krüger, and P. Olivier P., Lecture Notes in Computer Science 3638 (Springer, 2005), 151–162.

17. Örjan Sandred, "Approaches to Using Rules as a Composition Method," *Contemporary Music Review* 28, no. 2 (2009).

18. Daniel D. Johnson, Robert M. Keller, and Nicholas Weintraut, "Learning to Create Jazz Melodies Using a Product of Experts," *Proceedings of the International Conference on Computational Creativity, 2017*.

19. Man-Kwan Shan and Shih-Chuan Chiu, "Algorithmic Compositions Based on Discovered Musical Patterns," *Multimedia Tools and Applications* 46, no. 1 (2010).

20. For an overview of this topic, see Mark A. Bedau, "Artificial Life," in *The Blackwell Guide to the Philosophy of Computing and Information*, ed. Luciano Floridi (Blackwell, 2003).

21. Thomas S. Ray and Joseph Hart, "Evolution of Differentiated Multi-threaded Digital Organisms," *Proceedings of the IEEE/RSJ International Conference on Intelligent Robots and Systems, 1999*.

22. A survey of ecosystem models in media art can be found in Rui Filipe Antunes, "On Computational Ecosystems in Media Arts," *Leonardo* 49, no. 5 (2016).

23. Mitchell Whitelaw, "System Stories and Model Worlds: A Critical Approach to Generative Art," *Readme* 100 (2005).

24. Jon McCormack, "Eden: An Evolutionary Sonic Ecosystem," *Advances in Artificial Life, Proceedings of the Sixth European Conference, ECAL* LNCS 2159 (2001).

25. Personal communication.

26. Shawn Bell and Liane Gabora, "A Music-Generating System Inspired by the Science of Complex Adaptive Systems," *arXiv preprint arXiv:1610.02475* (2016).

27. Agostino di Scipio, "Sound Is the Interface: From Interactive to Ecosystemic Signal Processing," *Organized Sound* 8, no. 3 (2003).

28. Mikhail Prokopenko, ed., *Guided Self-Organization: Inception*, vol. 9 (Springer Science & Business Media, 2013).

29. Jürgen Schmidhuber, "Deep Learning in Neural Networks: An Overview," *Neural networks* 61 (2015).

30. In brains, electrical pulses or spikes are generated by neurons and pass down synapses to other neurons, which may in turn fire. In most ANNs, by contrast, the synapse is modeled by a single number that is used to multiply the output, or activation, of one node before adding it to the input of another node. Thus literally an ANN is at its heart just a set of matrix multiplications, with some other operations thrown in. Complex aspects of real neurons and synapses that are not typically modeled in ANNs include the role of timing in the electrical spikes, the mathematics involved in calculating when a neuron should fire, and the influence of various chemicals on the neurons' behavior.

31. For a detailed but rapid overview of these innovations see Schmidhuber, "Deep Learning in Neural Networks."

32. A discussion of the concepts found embedded in different layers can be found in the excellent and stunning visual explanations of "The Building Blocks of Interpretability," https://distill.pub/2018/building-blocks/.

33. Peter Gärdenfors, *Conceptual Spaces: The Geometry of Thought* (MIT Press, 2004). There is also a tantalizing familiarity here for followers of structuralist thinking, such as the work of anthropologist Claude Lévi-Strauss, who devised systems of binary logic that were seen to apply to cultural systems of mythology, religion, marriage, totemism, and so on.

34. Ian Simon et al., "Learning a Latent Space of Multitrack Measures," *arXiv preprint arXiv:1806.00195* (2018).

35. Kunwar Yashraj Singh, Nicholas M. Davis, Chih-Pin Hsiao, Ricardo Macias, Brenda Lin, and Brian Magerko, "Unified Classification and Generation Networks for Co-Creative Systems," in *Proceedings of the International Conference on Computational Creativity, 2017*, 237–244.

36. Aaron van den Oord et al., "WaveNet: A Generative Model for Raw Audio," *arXiv preprint arXiv:1609.03499* (2016).

37. Deep Mind, "WaveNet: A Generative Model for Raw Audio," *Deep Mind Blog*, https://deepmind.com/blog/wavenet-generative-model-raw-audio/ (2016).

38. Jesse Engel et al., "Neural Audio Synthesis of Musical Notes with WaveNet Autoencoders," *arXiv preprint arXiv:1704.01279* (2017).

39. Alec Radford, Luke Metz, and Soumith Chintala, "Unsupervised Representation Learning with Deep Convolutional Generative Adversarial Networks," *arXiv preprint arXiv:1511.06434* (2015).

40. Radford, Alec, Luke Metz, and Soumith Chintala, "Unsupervised Representation Learning with Deep Convolutional Generative Adversarial Networks," *arXiv preprint arXiv:1511.06434* (2015).

41. Jun-Yan Zhu et al., "Generative Visual Manipulation on the Natural Image Manifold," *European Conference on Computer Vision, 2016*.

42. Teuvo Kohonen et al., "Phonetic Typewriter for Finnish and Japanese," ICASSP-88, *International Conference on Acoustics, Speech, and Signal Processing, 1988*.

43. Walid Ahmad, "Making AI Art with Style Transfer Using Keras," *ML Review*, 2017, https://medium.com/mlreview/making-ai-art-with-style-transfer-using-keras-8bb5fa44b216.

44. François Pachet and Pierre Roy, "Non-Conformant Harmonization: The Real Book in the Style of Take 6," *Proceedings of the International Conference on Computational Creativity, 2014*.

45. Eric Chu, "Artistic Influence GAN," *32nd Conference on Neural Information Processing Systems, 2018*.

46. Jean-Pierre Briot and François Pachet, "Music Generation by Deep Learning: Challenges and Cirections," *arXiv preprint arXiv:1712.04371* (2017).

47. Scott Reed et al., "Generative Adversarial Text to Image Synthesis," *Proceedings of the 33rd International Conference on Machine Learning, 2016*.

48. Kristine Monteith, Tony R. Martinez, and Dan Ventura, "Automatic Generation of Music for Inducing Emotive Response," *Proceedings of the International Conference on Computational Creativity, 2010*.

49. MIDI: Musical Instrument Digital Interface. This is a format that stores musical information such as notes and gestures—anything that a performer might do with their hands.

50. Bob L. Sturm, "The 'Horse' Inside: Seeking Causes behind the Behaviors of Music Content Analysis Systems," *Computers in Entertainment (CIE)* 14, no. 2 (2016).

51. Stephen Thaler, "Neural Nets That Create and Discover," *PC AI Intelligent Solutions for Today's Computers* 10, no. 3 (1996).

52. Akin Kazakçi, Cherti Mehdi, and Balázs Kégl, "Digits That Are Not: Generating New Types through Deep Neural Nets," *International Conference on Computational Creativity, 2016*.

53. Ahmed Elgammal, Bingchen Liu, Mohamed Elhoseiny, and Marian Mazzone, "CAN: Creative Adversarial Networks, Generating 'Art' by Learning about Styles and Deviating from Style Norms," *arXiv preprint arXiv:1706.07068* (2017).

54. Briot and Pachet, "Music Generation by Deep Learning."

55. Gregory Hornby, Al Globus, Derek Linden, and Jason Lohn, "Automated Antenna Design with Evolutionary Algorithms," *Space 2006*, September 19, 2006, https://ti.arc.nasa.gov/m/pub-archive/1244h/1244%20(Hornby).pdf.

56. Karl Sims, "Evolving 3D Morphology and Behavior by Competition," in *Artificial Life IV Proceedings*, ed. R. Brooks and P. Maes (MIT Press, 1994).

57. Discovering something that is new to you but not new to the world is what Margaret Boden has dubbed psychological creativity, or P-creativity, as opposed to historical creativity, or H-creativity. Boden, *The Creative Mind* (Weidenfeld and Nicholson, 1990).

58. Joel Lehman et al., "The Surprising Creativity of Digital Evolution: A Collection of Anecdotes from the Evolutionary Computation and Artificial Life Research Communities," *arXiv preprint arXiv:1803.03453* (2018).

59. Such evolutionary approaches rely on good models of the world. Bugs or poor logic in the setup of the environment or the fitness measure might result in inappropriate solutions. In an anecdotal example, a team of engineers was trying to evolve an efficient engine by modeling a plane's flight and trying to minimize the fuel consumption of the engine for a given target speed and distance. However, the model they built allowed the engine to run in reverse, and in so doing, to *generate* fuel (while still traveling the required distance at the required speed, just in reverse). Naturally, the evolutionary algorithm considered this magic design to be the winner.

60. Geraint Wiggins et al., "Evolutionary Methods for Musical Composition," School of Artificial Intelligence, Division of Informatics, University of Edinburgh, 1998, http://www.doc.gold.ac.uk/~mas02gw/papers/CASYS98a.pdf.

61. Brian J. Ross, William Ralph, and Hai Zong, "Evolutionary Image Synthesis Using a Model of Aesthetics," *IEEE Congress on Evolutionary Computation, 2006*.

62. Wiggins et al., "Evolutionary Methods for Musical Composition."

63. Ross, Ralph, and Zong, "Evolutionary Image Synthesis."

64. Matthew Yee-King, "The Use of Interactive Genetic Algorithms in Sound Design: A Comparison Study," *Computers in Entertainment: Special Issue on Musical Metacreation*, 2016.

65. In fact, Vrellis used a simpler "hill-climbing" technique, which is surprisingly effective. (Personal communication, April 13, 2018.)

66. Carlos M. Fonseca and Peter J. Fleming, "Multiobjective Genetic Algorithms," *IEE Colloquium on Genetic Algorithms for Control Systems Engineering, 1993*.

67. Joel Lehman and Kenneth O. Stanley, "Exploiting Open-Endedness to Solve Problems through the Search for Novelty," *Proceedings of the Eleventh International Conference on Artificial Life (ALIFE XI), 2008*.

68. Lehman and Stanley, "Exploiting Open-Endedness."

69. Stanley and Lehman, *Why Greatness Cannot Be Planned: The Myth of the Objective* (Springer, 2015).

70. Georgios N. Yannakakis and Antonios Liapis, "Searching for Surprise," *Proceedings of the International Conference on Computational Creativity, 2016*.

71. S. C. Ianigro and Oliver Bown, "Exploring Continuous Time Recurrent Neural Networks through Novelty Search," *Proceedings of the International Conference on New Interfaces for Musical Expression, 2018*.

72. Although end-user tools in architectural design are getting very effective at using evolutionary search.

73. Palle Dahlstedt, "A MutaSynth in Parameter Space: Interactive Composition through Evolution," *Organized Sound* 6, no. 2 (2006).

74. Steffan Ianigro and Oliver Bown, "Plecto: A Low-Level Interactive Genetic Algorithm for the Evolution of Audio," *International Conference on Evolutionary and Biologically Inspired Music and Art, 2016*.

75. Brian G. Woolley and Kenneth O. Stanley, "A Novel Human-Computer Collaboration: Combining Novelty Search with Interactive Evolution," *Proceedings of the 2014 Annual Conference on Genetic and Evolutionary Computation, 2014*.

76. Anikó Ekárt, Divya Sharma, and Stayko Chalakov, "Modelling Human Preference in Evolutionary Art," *European Conference on the Applications of Evolutionary Computation, 2011*.

77. Jimmy Secretan et al., "Picbreeder: Evolving Pictures Collaboratively Online," *Proceedings of the Computer Human Interaction Conference (CHI 2008)*.

78. Robert M. MacCallum et al., "Evolution of Music by Public Choice," *Proceedings of the National Academy of Sciences* 109, no. 30 (2012).

79. Scott Draves, Electric Sheep, software and information available at https://electricsheep.org/ (accessed May 1, 2020).

80. Joel Lehman, Sebastian Risi, and Jeff Clune, "Creative Generation of 3D Objects with Deep Learning and Innovation Engines," *Proceedings of the 7th International Conference on Computational Creativity, 2016*.

81. Peter Mitrano, Arthur Lockman, James Honicker, and Scott Barton, "Using Recurrent Neural Networks to Judge Fitness in Musical Genetic Algorithms," in *Proceedings of the 5th International Workshop on Musical Metacreation (MUME) at the 8th International Conference on Computational Creativity (ICCC)*, 2017.

82. Philip Bontrager et al., "Deep Interactive Evolution," *International Conference on Computational Intelligence in Music, Sound, Art and Design*, 2018.

83. Indeed, learning and evolution are understood to interact in nontrivial ways. Consider the Baldwin effect, a process whereby a creature learns something about its environment, thereby altering its relationship with that environment, thereby shifting the evolutionary pressures that apply to it. The Baldwin effect predicts that under the right circumstances this means that something that was once learned later evolves to become innate. The Baldwin effect has been used to explain the form of various creatures and has been demonstrated to work experimentally.

84. R. D. Beer, "On the Dynamics of Small Continuous Recurrent Neural Networks," *Adaptive Behavior* 3, no. 4 (1995); R. D. Beer, "Toward the Evolution of Dynamical Neural Networks for Minimally Cognitive Behavior," *From Animals to Animats 4: Proceedings of the Fourth International Conference on Simulation of Adaptive Behavior*, ed. Pattie Maes et al. (MIT Press, 1996); R. D. Beer, "The Dynamics of Active Categorical Perception in an Evolved Model Agent," *Adaptive Behavior* 11, no. 4 (2003).

85. Kenneth O. Stanley and Risto Miikkulainen, "Evolving Neural Networks through Augmenting Topologies," *Evolutionary Computation* 10, no. 2 (2002).

86. Sebastian Risi and Julian Togelius, "Neuroevolution in Games: State of the Art and Open Challenges," *IEEE Transactions on Computational Intelligence and AI in Games* 9, no. 1 (2017).

87. Gabriele Medeot et al., "StructureNet: Inducing Structure in Generated Melodies," *Proceedings of the 19th International Society for Music Information Retrieval Conference, ISMIR 2018*.

88. Medeot et al., "StructureNet."

89. Oliver Bown, "Experiments in Modular Design for the Creative Composition of Live Algorithms," *Computer Music Journal* 35, no. 3 (2011); Bown, "Player Responses to a Live Algorithm: Conceptualising Computational Creativity without Recourse to

Human Comparisons?," *Proceedings of the International Conference on Computational Creativity, 2015.*

90. See, for example, Colton, "The Painting Fool"; Colton et al., "The Painting Fool Sees!"

91. David Huron, *Sweet Anticipation* (MIT Press, 2006).

92. Agnese Augello et al., "Artwork Creation by a Cognitive Architecture Integrating Computational Creativity and Dual Process Approaches," *Biologically Inspired Cognitive Architectures* 15 (2016).

93. Wiggins and Forth, "IDyOT: A Computational Theory of Creativity."

94. R. Saunders, "Curious Design Agents and Artificial Creativity" (PhD thesis, Faculty of Architecture, University of Sydney, 2001).

95. Saunders, "Curious Design Agents and Artificial Creativity"; Rob Saunders and J. S. Gero, "The Digital Clockwork Muse: A Computational Model of Aesthetic Evolution," *Proceedings of the AISB'01 Symposium on AI and Creativity in Arts and Science, 2001*; Rob Saunders and J. S. Gero, "Artificial Creativity: Emergent Notions of Creativity in Artificial Societies of Curious Agents," *Proceedings of the Second Iteration Conference, Melbourne, Australia, 2001.*

96. Nick Collins, "Towards Machine Musicians Who Have Listened to More Music Than Us: Audio Database-Led Algorithmic Criticism for Automatic Composition and Live Concert Systems," *Computers in Entertainment (CIE)* 14, no. 3 (2016).

Chapter 6

1. Yevgeny Zamyatin, *We* (Penguin, 1993).

2. Cristóbal Valenzuela, Alejandro Matamala, and Anastasis Germanidis, "Runway: Adding Artificial Intelligence Capabilities to Design and Creative Platforms," *Proceedings of the NeurIPS 2018 Workshop on Machine Learning for Creativity and Design,* Montreal, Canada, 2018.

3. Jean-Pierre Briot and François Pachet, "Music Generation by Deep Learning: Challenges and Directions," *arXiv preprint arXiv:1712.04371* (2017).

4. Ben Shneiderman, *Designing the User Interface: Strategies for Effective Human-Computer Interaction* (Pearson Education India, 2010).

5. Yvonne Rogers, Jenny Preece, and Helen Sharp, *Interaction Design: Beyond Human Computer Interaction*, 3rd ed. (John Wiley & Sons, 2011).

6. Lucy A. Suchman, *Plans and Situated Actions: The Problem of Human-Machine Communication* (Cambridge University Press, 1987).

7. Werner Rammert, "Where the Action Is: Distributed Agency Between Humans, Machines, and Programs," in *Paradoxes of Interactivity: Perspectives for Media Theory, Human-Computer Interaction, and Artistic Investigations*, ed. Uwe Seifert, Jin Hyun Kim, and Anthony Moore (De Gruyter, 2008).

8. Susanne Bødker, "Third-Wave HCI, 10 Years Later—Participation and Sharing," *Interactions* 22, no. 5 (2015).

9. Daniel Clement Dennett, *The Intentional Stance* (MIT Press, 1989).

10. Simon Hollington and Kypros Kyprianou, "Technology and the Uncanny" (paper presented at the EVA London Conference, July 2007), http://www.eva-conferences.com/eva_london/2007/papers (accessed May 4, 2009), quoted in Philip Auslander, "Lucille Meets GuitarBot: Instrumentality, Agency, and Technology in Musical Performance," in *Musical Instruments in the 21st Century*, ed. Till Bovermann, Alberto de Campo, Hauke Egermann, Sarah Hardjowirogo, and Stefan Weinzierl (Springer, 2017), 297–314.

11. James J. Gibson, "The Theory of Affordances," in *Perceiving, Acting, and Knowing*, ed. Robert Shaw and John Bransford (Lawrence Erlbaum, 1977).

12. I was Aengus's PhD co-supervisor with Craig Jin at Sydney University. A. Martin C. Jin, B. Carey, and O. Bown, "Creative Experiments Using a System for Learning High-Level Performance Structure in Ableton Live," *Proceedings of the Sound and Music Computing Conference, Copenhagen, Denmark, 2012*; Aengus Martin, Craig T. Jin, and Oliver Bown, "Implementation of a Real-Time Musical Decision-Maker," *Proceedings of the Australasian Computer Music Conference, Brisbane, Australia, July 2012*; Aengus Martin, Craig T. Jin, and Oliver Bown, "Design and Evaluation of Agents That Sequence and Juxtapose Short Musical Patterns in Real Time," *Computer Music Journal* 41, no. 4 (2018).

13. Palle Dahlstedt, "A MutaSynth in Parameter Space: Interactive Composition through Evolution," *Organised Sound* 6, no. 2 (2006).

14. Usman Haque, "The Architectural Relevance of Gordon Pask," *Architectural Design* 77, no. 4 (2007).

15. Todd Lubart, "How Can Computers Be Partners in the Creative Process: Classification and Commentary on the Special Issue," *International Journal of Human-Computer Studies* 63, no. 4 (2005).

16. Andy Lomas, "On Hybrid Creativity," *Arts* 7, no. 3 (2018).

17. Bonnie A. Nardi, *Context and Consciousness: Activity Theory and Human-Computer Interaction* (MIT Press, 1996).

18. Having discussed at length the potential fluidity of agency, this user-focused approach seems to fall back into a dualist framework with its human-user orientation.

We *could* look at software activities as well as human activities, and indeed these are covered during the discussion. But despite the ways in which we have identified software systems as playing a role in creativity, the human remains the primary instigator and operator of any human-computer interaction today, the "pukka" agent. That said, in many cases we can consider how each of the activities might be pushed into the automated realm, "climbing the meta-mountain" in Colton's terms. Simon Colton and Geraint A. Wiggins, "Computational Creativity: The Final Frontier?," *Proceedings of the 20th European Conference on Artificial Intelligence, 2012.*

19. Donald A. Norman, "Stages and Levels in Human-Machine Interaction," *International Journal of Man-Machine Studies* 21, no. 4 (1984).

20. Iannis Xenakis, *Formalized Music* (Indiana University Press, 1971).

21. Alexandre Papadopoulos, Pierre Roy, and François Pachet, "Avoiding Plagiarism in Markov Sequence Generation," *Twenty-Eighth AAAI Conference on Artificial Intelligence, 2014.*

22. Briot and Pachet, "Music Generation by Deep Learning."

23. Dahlstedt, "A MutaSynth in Parameter Space."

24. See https://magenta.tensorflow.org/demos/ for examples.

25. John William Charnley, Simon Colton, and Maria Teresa Llano, "The FloWr Framework: Automated Flowchart Construction, Optimisation and Alteration for Creative Systems," *Proceedings of the International Conference on Computational Creativity, 2014.*

26. Karl Mason, Jim Duggan, and Enda Howley, "Neural Network Topology and Weight Optimization Through Neuro Differential Evolution," *Proceedings of the Genetic and Evolutionary Computation Conference Companion, 2017.*

27. Kate Compton and Michael Mateas, "Casual Creators," *Proceedings of the International Conference on Computational Creativity, 2015.*

28. As in Jun-Yan Zhu, Philipp Krähenbühl, Eli Shechtman, and Alexei A Efros, "Generative Visual Manipulation on the Natural Image Manifold," *European Conference on Computer Vision, 2016.*

29. Memo Akten, Rebecca Fiebrink, and Mick Grierson, "Deep Meditations: Controlled Navigation of Latent Space," *arXiv preprint arXiv:2003.00910* (2018).

30. Anna Kantosalo et al., "From Isolation to Involvement: Adapting Machine Creativity Software to Support Human-Computer Co-creation," *Proceedings of the Fifth International Conference on Computational Creativity, 2014.*

31. Lomas, "On Hybrid Creativity."

32. Robert M. MacCallum, Matthias Mauch, Austin Burt, and Armand M. Leroi, "Evolution of Music by Public Choice," *Proceedings of the National Academy of Sciences* 109, no. 30 (2012).

33. Scott Draves, "Electric Sheep," Software and information available from http://electricsheep.org/ (accessed May 2, 2020).

34. Steffan Ianigro and Oliver Bown, "Plecto: A Low-Level Interactive Genetic Algorithm for the Evolution of Audio," *International Conference on Evolutionary and Biologically Inspired Music and Art, 2016*.

35. Amazon's service for sourcing human microtasks. See https://www.mturk.com/.

36. Rebecca Fiebrink, "Machine Learning as Meta-Instrument: Human-Machine Partnerships Shaping Expressive Instrumental Creation," in *Musical Instruments in the 21st Century*, ed. Till Bovermann et al. (Springer, 2017).

37. Fiebrink, "Machine Learning as Meta-Instrument."

38. Introduced in O. Bown and A. R. Brown, "Interaction Design for Metacreative Systems," in *New Directions in Third Wave Human-Computer Interaction: Volume 1—Technologies* (Springer, 2018).

39. Briot and Pachet, "Music Generation by Deep Learning."

40. Marco Marchini, François Pachet, and Benoît Carré, "Rethinking Reflexive Looper for Structured Pop Music," *Proceedings of the International Conference on New Interfaces for Musical Expression, 2017*.

41. Michael Irving, "AI Neural Network Builds New Virtual Cities by Studying Real Ones," New Atlas, 2018, https://newatlas.com/nvidia-deep-learning-3d-environment/57502/.

42. Howard Saul Becker, *Art Worlds* (University of California Press, 1982).

43. Note here, many music analysis algorithms, for efficiency, might assume the music they analyze to be created using instruments that are tuned using Western, equal-tempered tuning, and tuned to A440 (middle A is 440Hz). If this is hardwired into the music-analytic system, then music not conforming to this tuning might contain *machine invisible* innovation—that is, the analysis tools are completely incapable of handling the creative innovation, being incapable of even perceiving the sound in a meaningful way.

44. José Abreu, Marcelo Caetano, and Rui Penha, "Computer-Aided Musical Orchestration Using an Artificial Immune System," *International Conference on Evolutionary and Biologically Inspired Music and Art, 2016*.

45. Philip Galanter, "Complexism and the Role of Evolutionary Art," in *The Art of Artificial Evolution: A Handbook on Evolutionary Art and Music*, ed. Juan Romero and Penousal Machado (Springer-Verlag, 2008).

46. Compton and Mateas, "Casual Creators.."

47. Mark J. Nelson, Swen E. Gaudl, Simon Colton, Edward J. Powley, Blanca Pérez Ferrer, Rob Saunders, Peter Ivey, and Michael Cook, "Fluidic Games in Cultural Contexts," *Proceedings of the International Conference on Computational Creativity*, Atlanta, GA, 2017.

48. A great overview of deep dream approaches can be found here: Alexander Mordvintsev, Christopher Olah and Mike Tyka, "Inceptionism: Going Deeper into Neural Networks," *Google AI Blog*, 2015, https://ai.googleblog.com/2015/06/inceptionism-going-deeper-into-neural.html.

49. Amelia Abraham, "What Happens When a Beauty AI Does Kylie Jenner's Make-Up," *Dazed Digital*, 2019, https://www.dazeddigital.com/beauty/head/article/43138/1/beauty-gan-kylie-jenner.

50. Bob L. Sturm et al., "Machine Learning Research That Matters for Music Creation: A Case Study," *Journal of New Music Research* 48, no. 1 (2019).

51. Here again, Becker provides an even-handed discussion of the cultural diversity of domains, including how attitudes toward the role of creative agency and identity in different activities can vary. Becker, *Art Worlds*.

52. Gloria Requena et al., "Melomics Music Medicine (M3) to Lessen Pain Perception during Pediatric Prick Test Procedure," *Pediatric Allergy and Immunology* 25, no. 7 (2014).

53. Stefan K. Ehrlich et al., "A Closed-Loop, Music-Based Brain-Computer Interface for Emotion Mediation," *PLOS ONE* 14, no. 3 (2019).

54. Parag Kumar Mital, "Audiovisual Scene Synthesis" (DPhil thesis, Goldsmiths, University of London, 2014).

55. Kunwar Yashraj Singh, Nicholas Davis, Chih-Pin Hsiao, Ricardo Macias, Brenda Lin, and Brian Magerko, "Unified Classification and Generation Networks for Co-Creative Systems," *Proceedings of the International Conference on Computational Creativity*, 2017, 237–244.

56. Nigel Cross and Anita Clayburn Cross, "Observations of Teamwork and Social Processes in Design," *Design Studies* 16, no. 2 (1995).

57. Another commonly used alternative term for co-creation is "mixed initiative methods," referring to the sharing of the initiative between human and computer.

58. G. N. Yannakakis, A. Liapis, A., and C. Alexopoulos, "Mixed-Initiative Co-creativity," 9th International Conference on the Foundations of Digital Games, Fort Lauderdale, 2014, https://www.um.edu.mt/library/oar/bitstream/123456789/29459/1/Mixed-initiative_co-creativity.pdf.

59. Singh et al., "Unified Classification and Generation Networks."

60. Anna Kantosalo and Hannu Toivonen, "Modes for Creative Human-Computer Collaboration: Alternating and Task-Divided Co-Creativity," *Proceedings of the Seventh International Conference on Computational Creativity, 2016*.

61. See, for example, Pegah Karimi et al., "Deep Learning in a Computational Model for Conceptual Shifts in a Co-Creative Design System," *arXiv preprint arXiv:1906.10188* (2019).

62. Kiri L. Wagstaff et al., "Guiding Scientific Discovery with Explanations Using DEMUD," *Proceedings of the Twenty-Seventh AAAI Conference on Artificial Intelligence, 2013*.

63. Jon Bird and Paul Layzell, "The Evolved Radio and Its Implications for Modelling the Evolution of Novel Sensors," *Proceedings of the 2002 Congress on Evolutionary Computation*.

64. Matthew Yee-King, "The Use of Interactive Genetic Algorithms in Sound Design: A Comparison Study," *Computers in Entertainment: Special Issue on Musical Metacreation* (2016).

65. Video documentation of the work can be seen here: https://vimeo.com/175653201/description.

66. Kenneth O. Stanley and Joel Lehman, *Why Greatness Cannot Be Planned: The Myth of the Objective* (Springer, 2015).

67. Jon McCormack, "Aesthetic Evolution of L-Systems Revisited," in *Applications of Evolutionary Computing*, Vol. 3005, ed. G. R. Raidl (Springer, 2004).

68. Hideyuki Takagi, "Interactive Evolutionary Computation: Fusion of the Capabilities of EC Optimization and Human Evaluation," *Proceedings of the IEEE* 89, no. 9 (2001).

69. McCormack, "Aesthetic Evolution of L-Systems Revisited."

70. Draves, "Electric Sheep."

71. Dan Siroker, "How Obama Raised $60 Million by Running a Simple Experiment," *Optimizely Blog*, 2010, https://blog.optimizely.com/2010/11/29/how-obama-raised-60-million-by-running-a-simple-experiment/.

72. MacCallum et al., "Evolution of Music by Public Choice."

73. Jimmy Secretan, Nicholas Beato, David B. D Ambrosio, Adelein Rodriguez, Adam Campbell, and Kenneth O. Stanley, "Picbreeder: Evolving Pictures Collaboratively Online," *Proceedings of the SIGCHI Conference on Human Factors in Computing Systems*, 2008, 1759–1768.

74. Ianigro and Bown, "Plecto: A Low-Level Interactive Genetic Algorithm."

75. Charnley, Colton, and Llano, "The FloWr Framework."

76. Lambros Malafouris, "At the Potter's Wheel: An Argument for Material Agency," in *Material Agency: Towards a Non-anthropocentric Approach*, ed. C. Knappett and L. Malafouris (Springer, 2008), http://cogprints.org/6402/.

77. Note that looking at it this way many art forms have performative aspects. A sculptor chipping at rock or a painter making marks on a canvas may not be under the pressure of the gaze of an audience, they can throw away what they have done and start again, but they are still faced with various constraints in terms of what they can undo and what they can correctly anticipate.

78. Pachet, "Beyond the Cybernetic Jam Fantasy: The Continuator,"" *IEEE Computer Graphics and Applications* 24, no. 1 (2004).

79. Gérard Assayag and Shlomo Dubnov, "Using Factor Oracles for Machine Improvisation," *Soft Computing—A Fusion of Foundations, Methodologies and Applications* 8, no. 9 (2004).

80. I have found this through personal communication with musicians reporting on performing with such systems.

81. Pachet, "Beyond the Cybernetic Jam Fantasy."

82. Personal communication with Michael Young. This was an informal study conducted during a meeting of the Live Algorithms for Music research network at Goldsmiths College in 2006.

83. François Pachet, Pierre Roy, and Raphaël Foulon. "Do Jazz Improvisers Really Interact? The Score Effect in Collective Jazz Improvisation," in *Routledge Companion to Embodied Music Interaction*, ed. Micheline Lesaffre, Pieter-Jan Maes, and Marc Leman (Routledge, 2017).

84. A. Seth, "Measuring Autonomy and Emergence via Granger Causality," *Artificial Life* 16 (2010).

85. David Borgo, *Sync or Swarm: Improvising Music in a Complex Age* (A & C Black, 2005); Tim Blackwell and Michael Young, "Self-Organised Music," *Organised Sound* 9, no. 2 (2004).

86. Oliver Bown, "Experiments in Modular Design for the Creative Composition of Live Algorithms," *Computer Music Journal* 35, no. 3 (2011); Bown, "Player Responses to a Live Algorithm: Conceptualising Computational Creativity without Recourse to Human Comparisons?," *Proceedings of the International Conference on Computational Creativity, 2015.*

87. Auslander, "Lucille Meets GuitarBot."

88. Quoted in Auslander, "Lucille Meets GuitarBot," 114.

89. Guo Yu and Alan Blackwell, "Effects of Timing on Users' Agency during Mixed-Initiative Interaction," *Proceedings of the 31st British Computer Society Human Computer Interaction Conference, 2017*.

90. Ritwik Banerji, "De-instrumentalizing HCI: Social Psychology, Rapport Formation, and Interactions with Artificial Social Agents," in *New Directions in Third Wave Human-Computer Interaction: Volume 1—Technologies*, ed. Michael Filimowicz and Veronika Tzankova (Springer, 2018).

91. Banerji, "De-instrumentalizing HCI."

92. Simon Penny, "Agents as Artworks and Agent Design as Artistic Practice," in *Human Cognition and Social Agent Technology*, ed. Kerstin Dautenhahn (John Benjamins, 2000).

93. Penny, "Agents as Artworks."

94. Simon Colton, "The Painting Fool: Stories from Building an Automated Painter," in *Computers and Creativity*, ed. Jon McCormack and Mark d'Inverno (Springer, 2012), 3–38.

95. Simon Colton, Jakob Halskov, Dan Ventura, Ian Gouldstone, Michael Cook, and Blanca Pérez Ferrer, "The Painting Fool Sees! New Projects with the Automated Painter," *Proceedings of the International Conference on Computational Creativity, 2015*.

Chapter 7

1. John Stuart Mill, *On Liberty* (John Parker and Sons, 1859).

2. Tom Collins and Robin Laney, "Computer-Generated Stylistic Compositions with Long-Term Repetitive and Phrasal Structure," *Journal of Creative Music Systems* 1, no. 2 (2017).

3. Carolyn Lamb, Daniel G. Brown, and C. L. Clarke, "Human Competence in Creativity Evaluation," *Proceedings of the Sixth International Conference on Computational Creativity, 2015*.

4. Anna Jordanous, "Evaluating Computational Creativity: A Standardised Procedure for Evaluating Creative Systems and its Application" (DPhil thesis, University of Sussex, 2012).

5. Howard Saul Becker, *Art Worlds* (University of California Press, 1982).

6. Christopher Ariza, "The Interrogator as Critic: The Turing Test and the Evaluation of Generative Music Systems," *Computer Music Journal* 33, no. 2 (2009).

7. Ariza, "The Interrogator as Critic."

Notes to Chapter 7

8. Phillip Williams, "Can Artificial Intelligence Write a Great Pop Song?," *Red Bull Music* (blog), 2018, https://www.redbull.com/gb-en/SKYGGE-artificial-intelligence-making-pop-songs.

9. *Portrait of Edmund Belamy*, a GAN-generated artwork produced by arts collective Obvious, based on a system developed by Robbie Barrat.

10. At the 2016 International Conference on Computational Creativity in Paris, a panel discussion was held on the *Beyond the Fence* project, and a handful of papers have been written on the work. The authors provide all the necessary detail and frankly discuss the sometimes difficult working relationship with the professional team and directors, who had less commitment to the computer-generated material than the authors had hoped. Two relevant issues in the discussion were (a) the advertisement of the work as a computer-generated musical (it was a musical that used certain computer-generated elements), and (b) any evaluation of the systems based on the success of the musical in terms of ticket sales, critical reviews, or audience feedback.

11. Ariza, "The Interrogator as Critic."

12. David C. Moffat and Martin Kelly, "An Investigation into People's Bias Against Computational Creativity in Music Composition," *Assessment* 13 (2006); Philippe Pasquier et al., "Investigating Listener Bias Against Musical Metacreativity," *Proceedings of the Seventh International Conference on Computational Creativity, 2016*.

13. Dan Stowell et al., "Evaluation of Live Human-Computer Music-Making: Quantitative and Qualitative Approaches," *International Journal of Human-Computer Studies* 67, no. 11 (2009).

14. Jordanous, "Evaluating Computational Creativity."

15. Anna Jordanous, "A Standardised Procedure for Evaluating Creative Systems: Computational Creativity Evaluation Based on What It Is to Be Creative," *Cognitive Computation* 4, no. 3 (2012).

16. Simon Colton, A. Pease, and J. Charnley, "Computational Creativity Theory: The FACE and IDEA Descriptive Models," *Proceedings of the Second International Conference on Computational Creativity, 2011*.

17. A new term for an idea that has appeared in various guises in this book, as in Auslander's and Becker's discussions. See Philip Auslander, "Lucille Meets GuitarBot: Instrumentality, Agency, and Technology in Musical Performance," in *Musical Instruments in the 21st Century*, ed. Till Bovermann, Alberto de Campo, Hauke Egermann, Sarah Hardjowirogo, and Stefan Weinzierl (Springer, 2017), 297–314; and Howard Saul Becker, *Art Worlds* (University of California Press, 1982).

18. Colton, Pease, and Charnley, "Computational Creativity Theory."

19. Personal communication.

20. Graeme Ritchie, "Assessing Creativity," *Proceedings of AISB'01 Symposium, 2001;* Graeme Ritchie, "Some Empirical Criteria for Attributing Creativity to a Computer Program," *Minds and Machines* 17, no. 1 (2007).

21. Once again, with online systems it is not always feasible to determine what this set is, but we can safely ignore that issue. This also overlooks the broader issue that in human life there is no boundary between art and non-art—a painter's inspiring set is not simply the set of all artworks she has seen but the set of all visual experiences she has had, including her dreams, as well as the set of all narratives, relationships, symbolic associations, emotions, and so on. Engineers may take positivist license to ignore this inconvenience in the first instance.

22. Ritchie, "Some Empirical Criteria."

23. Ritchie, "Some Empirical Criteria."

24. Patricio da Silva, "Interview with Composer David Cope—Part III," *The Sound Stew* (blog), 2010, http://www.thesoundstew.com/2010/07/interview-with-composer-david-cope-part_23.html.

25. Ahmed Elgammal and Babak Saleh, "Quantifying Creativity in Art Networks," *arXiv preprint arXiv:1506.00711* (2015).

26. Linda Candy, "Practice Based Research: A Guide," *CCS Report* 1 (2006).

27. Estelle Barrett and Barbara Bolt, *Practice as Research: Approaches to Creative Arts Enquiry* (I. B. Tauris, 2014).

28. C. Gray and G. Burnett, "Making Sense: 'Material' Thinking and 'Materializing Pedagogies,'" *Interactive Discourse: International Online Journal of Learning and Teaching in Higher Education* 1, no. 1 (2007).

29. Jakob Nielsen and Thomas K. Landauer, "A Mathematical Model of the Finding of Usability Problems," *Proceedings of the INTERACT '93 and CHI '93 Conference on Human Factors in Computing Systems, 1993.*

30. Donald Knuth attributed the observation to Sir Charles Anthony Richard Hoare, http://wiki.c2.com/?RulesOfOptimization.

31. Oliver Bown and Jon McCormack, "Taming Nature: Tapping the Creative Potential of Ecosystem Models in the Arts," *Digital Creativity* 21, no. 4 (2010).

32. Bown, "Experiments in Modular Design for the Creative Composition of Live Algorithms," *Computer Music Journal* 35, no. 3 (2011); Bown, "Player Responses to a Live Algorithm: Conceptualising Computational Creativity Without Recourse to Human Comparisons?," *Proceedings of the International Conference on Computational Creativity, 2015.*

33. Matthew John Yee-King, "An Automated Music Improviser Using a Genetic Algorithm Driven Synthesis Engine" (Workshops on Applications of Evolutionary Computation, 2007).

34. Alice Eldridge, "Collaborating with the Behaving Machine: Simple Adaptive Dynamical Systems for Generative and Interactive Music" (DPhil thesis, University of Sussex, 2007).

35. Craig Vear, "Music, Dimensions and Play: Composing for Autonomous Laptop Musicians and Improvising Humans," *Digital Creativity* 25, no. 4 (2014).

36. Ritwik Banerji, "Maxine's Turing Test—A Player-Program as Co-Ethnographer of Socio-Aesthetic Interaction in Improvised Music," *Proceedings of the Artificial Intelligence and Interactive Digital Entertainment (AIIDE'12) Conference, 2012.*

37. Margareta Ackerman and David Loker, "Algorithmic Songwriting with Alysia," *International Conference on Evolutionary and Biologically Inspired Music and Art, 2017.*

38. Benjamin Leigh Carey, "_derivations and the Performer-Developer: Co-evolving Digital Artefacts and Human-Machine Performance Practices" (DPhil thesis, University of Technology, Sydney, 2016).

39. Bown, "Player Responses to a Live Algorithm."

40. Ben Shneiderman et al., "Creativity Support Tools: Report from a US National Science Foundation Sponsored Workshop," *International Journal of Human-Computer Interaction* 20, no. 2 (2006).

41. Mitchel Resnick, Brad Myers, Kumiyo Nakakoji, Ben Shneiderman, Randy Pausch, Ted Selker, and Mike Eisenberg, "Design Principles for Tools to Support Creative Thinking," 2015, https://www.cs.umd.edu/hcil/CST/Papers/designprinciples.pdf.

42. Peter Dalsgaard and Kim Halskov, "Designing Urban Media Façades: Cases and Challenges," *Proceedings of the SIGCHI Conference on Human Factors in Computing Systems, 2010.*

43. Alan Blackwell and Thomas Green, "Notational Systems—The Cognitive Dimensions of Notations Framework," in *HCI Models, Theories, and Frameworks: Toward an Interdisciplinary Science*, ed. John M. Carroll (Morgan Kaufmann, 2003).

Chapter 8

1. Kurt Vonnegut, *Player Piano* (Dial Press, 1952).

2. This example comes from a speaker on an ABC radio podcast, who unfortunately I have been unable to track down.

3. Toby Walsh, "What AI Can (and Can't) Do," 2017, https://www.youtube.com/watch?v=79O903oGmmU.

4. Ray Kurzweil, *The Age of Spiritual Machines: How We Will Live, Work and Think in the New Age of Intelligent Machines* (Orion, 1999).

5. Blake Alcott, "Jevons' Paradox," *Ecological Economics* 54, no. 1 (2005).

6. Judy Wajcman, *Pressed for Time: The Acceleration of Life in Digital Capitalism* (University of Chicago Press, 2015).

7. Stone et al., "Artificial Intelligence and Life in 2030," *One Hundred Year Study on Artificial Intelligence: Report of the 2015-2016 Study Panel, Stanford University*, September 2016.

8. Hypebot, "Context, Not Genre Drives Playlist Popularity," http://www.hypebot.com/hypebot/2018/03/context-not-genre-drives-playlist-popularity-analysis.html (accessed June 19, 2020).

9. Jem Finer, Longplayer, https://www.longplayer.org

10. As mentioned in chapter 6, my band Icarus made an album in 1,000 variations. Brian Eno has produced an album with generative artworks. In general it is trivial for a generative artist to produce a trillion variations on an image.

11. Oliver Bown, Alice Eldridge, and Jon McCormack, "Understanding Interaction in Contemporary Digital Music: From Instruments to Behavioural Objects," *Organised Sound* 14, no. 2 (2009).

12. Kevin N. Laland, John Odling-Smee, and Marcus W. Feldman, "Niche Construction, Biological Evolution and Cultural Change," *Behavioral and Brain Sciences* 21, no. 1 (1999).

13. W. Brian Arthur, *Increasing Returns and Path Dependence in the Economy* (University of Michigan Press, 1994).

14. Jonathan Sterne and Elena Razlogova, "Machine Learning in Context, or Learning from LANDR: Artificial Intelligence and the Platformization of Music Mastering," *Social Media+ Society* 5, no. 2 (2019). Also with notes from work presented at an Aarhus symposium on sociological approaches to music and AI hosted by Georgina Born.

15. Cat Ellis, "AI-Powered Music Generator Ecrett Builds Complex Compositions for Your Videos," *Tech Radar News*, February 10, 2019, https://www.techradar.com/news/ai-powered-music-generator-ecrett-builds-complex-compositions-for-your-videos.

16. Zero-marginal cost refers to the situation in which the cost of production for a product becomes negligible at the scale it is being produced. Digital goods have

led the way due to their effectively free cost of reproduction, with a single app potentially having a vanishingly small cost of development in relation to its reach. Many commentators, notably Rifkin, have argued that advanced manufacturing and automation are bringing both physical production and increasingly sophisticated knowledge work into the zero marginal cost realm, with radical implications for capitalism. Jeremy Rifkin, *The Zero Marginal Cost Society: The Internet of Things, the Collaborative Commons, and the Eclipse of Capitalism* (St. Martin's Press, 2014).

17. Georgina Born, Eric Lewis, and Will Straw, *Improvisation and Social Aesthetics* (Duke University Press, 2017).

18. Yasser M. El-Gamal and Ehab Samuel, "Copyright Protection for AI Machine Created Works?," *Manatt Blog*, 2017, https://www.manatt.com/insights/articles/2017/copyright-protection-for-ai-machine-created-works.

19. Aarhus symposium on Music and AI, organized by Georgina Born, May 2019.

20. Jon McCormack, Toby Gifford, and Patrick Hutchings, "Autonomy, Authenticity, Authorship and Intention in Computer Generated Art," *arXiv preprint arXiv:1903.02166* (2019).

21. Bruce Gain, "When Machines Create Intellectual Property, Who Owns What?," *Intellectual Property Watch* (February 2017), http://www.ip-watch.org/2017/02/16/machines-create-intellectual-property-owns/.

22. Gain, "When Machines Create Intellectual Property, Who Owns What?"

23. Andres Guadamuz, "Should Robots Be Given Copyright Protection," *The Conversation*, June 26, 2017, https://theconversation.com/should-robot-artists-be-given-copyright-protection-79449.

24. Paresh Kathrani, "Could Intelligent Machines of the Future Own the Rights of Their Own Creations," *The Conversation*, December 1, 2017, https://theconversation.com/could-intelligent-machines-of-the-future-own-the-rights-to-their-own-creations-86005. The full paragraph from which this quote comes: "Let's not forget that machines are already becoming more human-like, including the humanoid Sophia, who, after being made a citizen of Saudi Arabia, says she wants to have a baby. It seems clear that, while machines may not be able to enforce intellectual property rights (yet), anything less might potentially amount to a violation of the value we place on intelligence in and of itself." I find the idea of making a robot a citizen of a country truly terrifying, inappropriate, and distasteful, given how limited some people's basic rights are. It is quite clear that the granting of citizenship to Sophia has nothing to do with how impressive her AI is.

25. Antonios Liapis, Georgios N. Yannakakis, and Julian Togelius, "Computational Game Creativity," *Proceedings of the International Conference on Computational Creativity, 2014*.

26. Anders-Petter Andersson, Birgitta Cappelen, and Fredrik Olofsson, "Designing Sound for Recreation and Well-Being," *Proceedings of the 2014 New Interfaces for Musical Expression Conference, Goldsmiths, London, July 2014*.

27. The theorist of the political economy of music, Jacques Attali describes this accumulating mass of creation, in the case of music, as stockpiling time. Jacques Attali, *Noise: The Political Economy of Music* (University of Minnesota Press, 1977).

28. Attali, *Noise: The Political Economy of Music*.

29. Born, Lewis, and Straw, *Improvisation and Social Aesthetics*.

30. Paul Lewis and Paul Hilder, "Leaked: Cambridge Analytica's Blueprint for Trump Victory," *Guardian*, March 23, 2018, https://www.theguardian.com/uk-news/2018/mar/23/leaked-cambridge-analyticas-blueprint-for-trump-victory.

31. William Davies, *Nervous States: How Feeling Took Over the World* (Random House, 2018).

32. Notes from a guest lecture at University of New South Wales, December 2019.

33. Currently the debate about how much regulation should be applied to AI systems' use is raging. For example, in Australia at the time of writing there is debate about the use of AI in sending out debt notices to benefits recipients, which went badly wrong and aggressively chased many innocent people for debts they didn't owe. Josh Taylor, "People Should Be Held Accountable for AI and Algorithm Errors, Rights Commissioner Says," *Guardian*, December 16, 2019, https://www.theguardian.com/law/2019/dec/17/people-should-be-held-accountable-for-ai-and-algorithm-errors-rights-commissioner-says.

34. Glenn W. Smith and Frederic Fol Leymarie, "The Machine as Artist: An Introduction," *Arts* 6, no. 1 (2017).

35. Smith and Leymarie, "The Machine as Artist."

36. Sean Dorrance Kelly, "A Philosopher Argues that an AI Can't Be an Artist," *MIT Technology Review*, February 21, 2019.

37. Ahmed Elgammal and Taishi Fukuyama, "We Need to Embrace AI's Humanity to Unlock Its Creative Promise," *VentureBeat*, May 18, 2019.

38. Marian Mazzone and Ahmed Elgammal, "Art, Creativity, and the Potential of Artificial Intelligence," *Arts* 8, no. 1 (2019).

39. Berys Gaut, "The Cluster Account of Art," in *Theories of Art Today*, ed. Noël Carroll (University of Wisconsin Press, 2000), 25–45.

References

Abreu, José, Marcelo Caetano, and Rui Penha. "Computer-Aided Musical Orchestration Using an Artificial Immune System." *International Conference on Evolutionary and Biologically Inspired Music and Art, 2016*.

Abuhamdeh, Sami, and Mihaly Csikszentmihalyi. "The Artistic Personality: A Systems Perspective." In Csikszentmihalyi, *The Systems Model of Creativity*, 227–237. Springer, 2015.

Ackerman, Margareta, and David Loker. "Algorithmic Songwriting with Alysia." *International Conference on Evolutionary and Biologically Inspired Music and Art, 2017*.

Adorno, Theodor W. *Aesthetic Theory*. A & C Black, 1997.

Agüera y Arcas, Blaise. "Art in the Age of Machine Intelligence." *Arts* 6, no. 4 (2017).

Ahmad, Walid. "Making AI Art with Style Transfer Using Keras." *ML Review*, November 24, 2017. https://medium.com/mlreview/making-ai-art-with-style-transfer-using-keras-8bb5fa44b216.

Aish, Robert, and Robert Woodbury. "Multi-level Interaction in Parametric Design." In *Smart Graphics: 5th International Symposium, SG 2005, Frauenworth Cloister, Germany, August 22-24, 2005 Proceedings*, edited by A. Butz, B. Fisher, A. Krüger, and P. Olivier P., Lecture Notes in Computer Science 3638, 151–162. Springer, 2005.

Akten, Memo, Rebecca Fiebrink, and Mick Grierson. "Deep Meditations: Controlled Navigation of Latent Space." *arXiv preprint arXiv:2003.00910* (2018).

Alcott, Blake. "Jevons' Paradox." *Ecological Economics* 54, no. 1 (2005).

Alexander, Christopher. *A Pattern Language: Towns, Buildings, Construction*. Oxford University Press, 1977.

Amabile, Teresa. *Creativity in Context*. Westview Press, 1996.

Andersson, Anders-Petter, Birgitta Cappelen, and Fredrik Olofsson. "Designing Sound for Recreation and Well-Being." *Proceedings of the 2014 New Interfaces for Musical Expression Conference, 2014*.

Antunes, Rui Filipe. "On Computational Ecosystems in Media Arts." *Leonardo* 49, no. 5 (2016).

Arieti, Silvano. *Creativity: The Magic Synthesis*. Basic Books, 1976.

Ariza, Christopher. "The Interrogator as Critic: The Turing Test and the Evaluation of Generative Music Systems." *Computer Music Journal* 33, no. 2 (2009).

Arthur, W. Brian. *Increasing Returns and Path Dependence in the Economy*. University of Michigan Press, 1994.

Arthur, W. Brian. *The Nature of Technology: What It Is and How It Evolves*. Penguin, 2009.

Askin, Noah, and Michael Mauskapf. "What Makes Popular Culture Popular? Product Features and Optimal Differentiation in Music." *American Sociological Review* 82, no. 5 (2017).

Assayag, Gérard, and Shlomo Dubnov. "Using Factor Oracles for Machine Improvisation." *Soft Computing: A Fusion of Foundations, Methodologies and Applications* 8, no. 9 (2004).

Attali, Jacques. *Noise: The Political Economy of Music*. University of Minnesota Press, 1977.

Augello, Agnese, Ignazio Infantino, Antonio Lieto, Giovanni Pilato, Riccardo Rizzo, and Filippo Vella. "Artwork Creation by a Cognitive Architecture Integrating Computational Creativity and Dual Process Approaches." *Biologically Inspired Cognitive Architectures* 15 (2016).

Auslander, Philip. "Lucille Meets GuitarBot: Instrumentality, Agency, and Technology in Musical Performance." In *Musical Instruments in the 21st Century*, edited by Till Bovermann, Alberto de Campo, Hauke Egermann, Sarah Hardjowirogo, and Stefan Weinzierl, 297–314. Springer, 2017.

Axelrod, Robert M. *The Evolution of Cooperation: Revised Edition*. Basic Books, 2006.

Ball, Philip. "Iamus, Classical Music's Computer Composer, Live from Malaga." *The Guardian*, July 1, 2012. https://www.theguardian.com/music/2012/jul/01/iamus-computer-composes-classical-music.

Balzano, G. J. "The Group-Theoretic Description of 12-Fold and Microtonal Pitch Systems." *Computer Music Journal* 4, no. 4 (1980).

Banerji, Ritwik. "De-Instrumentalizing HCI: Social Psychology, Rapport Formation, and Interactions with Artificial Social Agents." In *New Directions in Third Wave Human-Computer Interaction: Volume 1-Technologies*, edited by Michael Filimowicz and Veronika Tzankova, 43–66. Springer, 2018.

Banerji, Ritwik. "Maxine's Turing Test—A Player-Program as Co-Ethnographer of Socio-Aesthetic Interaction in Improvised Music." *Proceedings of the Artificial Intelligence and Interactive Digital Entertainment (AIIDE'12) Conference, 2012*.

References

Barkow, Jerome H., Leda Cosmides, and John Tooby. *The Adapted Mind: Evolutionary Psychology and the Generation of Culture*. Oxford University Press, 1992.

Barrett, Estelle, and Barbara Bolt. *Practice as Research: Approaches to Creative Arts Enquiry*. I. B. Tauris, 2014.

Becker, Howard Saul. *Art Worlds*. University of California Press, 1982.

Bedau, Mark A. "Artificial Life." In *The Blackwell Guide to the Philosophy of Computing and Information*, edited by Luciano Floridi, 197–214. Blackwell Publishing, 2003.

Beer, R. D. "The Dynamics of Active Categorical Perception in an Evolved Model Agent." *Adaptive Behavior* 11, no. 4 (2003).

Beer, R. D. "On the Dynamics of Small Continuous Recurrent Neural Networks." *Adaptive Behavior* 3, no. 4 (1995).

Beer, R. D. "Toward the Evolution of Dynamical Neural Networks for Minimally Cognitive Behavior." *From Animals to Animats 4: Proceedings of the Fourth International Conference on Simulation of Adaptive Behavior*. MIT Press, 1996.

Bell, Shawn, and Liane Gabora. "A Music-Generating System Inspired by the Science of Complex Adaptive Systems." *arXiv preprint arXiv:1610.02475* (2016).

Berger, Peter L., and Thomas Luckmann. *The Social Construction of Reality: A Treatise in the Sociology of Knowledge*. Penguin UK, 1991.

Berlyne, Daniel Ellis. *Aesthetics and Psychobiology*. Appleton-Century-Crofts, 1971.

Berlyne, Daniel Ellis. "Novelty, Complexity, and Hedonic Value." *Attention, Perception, and Psychophysics* 8, no. 5 (1970): 279–286.

Berlyne, Daniel Ellis. "A Theory of Human Curiosity." *British Journal of Psychology* 45, no. 3 (1954).

Bird, Jon, and Paul Layzell. "The Evolved Radio and Its Implications for Modelling the Evolution of Novel Sensors." *Proceedings of the 2002 Congress on Evolutionary Computation, 2002*.

Birkhoff, George David. *Aesthetic Measure*. Vol. 9. Harvard University Press, 1933.

Blackwell, Alan, and Thomas Green. "Notational Systems—The Cognitive Dimensions of Notations Framework." In HCI Models, Theories, and Frameworks: Toward an Interdisciplinary Science, edited by John M. Carroll. Morgan Kaufmann, 2003.

Blackwell, Tim, and Michael Young. "Self-Organised Music." *Organised Sound* 9, no. 2 (2004).

Blitstein, Ryan. "Triumph of the Cyborg Composer." *Pacific Standard*, February 22, 2010. https://psmag.com/social-justice/triumph-of-the-cyborg-composer-8507.

Bloom, Paul. *How Pleasure Works: The New Science of Why We Like What We Like*. Random House, 2010.

Boden, Margaret. *The Creative Mind.* Weidenfeld and Nicholson, 1990.

Boden, Margaret A. "Creativity and Artificial Intelligence." *Artificial Intelligence* 103, no. 1 (1998).

Bødker, Susanne. "Third-Wave HCI, 10 Years Later—Participation and Sharing." *Interactions* 22, no. 5 (2015).

Bødker, Susanne. "When Second Wave HCI Meets Third Wave Challenges." *Proceedings of the 4th Nordic Conference on Human-Computer Interaction: Changing Roles, 2006.*

Bontrager, Philip, Wending Lin, Julian Togelius, and Sebastian Risi. "Deep Interactive Evolution." *International Conference on Computational Intelligence in Music, Sound, Art and Design, 2018.*

Borgo, David. *Sync or Swarm: Improvising Music in a Complex Age.* A & C Black, 2005.

Born, Georgina. "Making Time: Temporality, History, and the Cultural Object." *New Literary History* 46, no. 3 (2015).

Born, Georgina. "The Social and the Aesthetic: For a Post-Bourdieuian Theory of Cultural Production." *Cultural Sociology* 4, no. 2 (2010).

Born, Georgina, and Kyle Devine. "Music Technology, Gender, and Class: Digitization, Educational and Social Change in Britain." *Twentieth-Century Music* 12, no. 2 (2015).

Born, Georgina, Eric Lewis, and Will Straw. *Improvisation and Social Aesthetics.* Duke University Press, 2017.

Bourdieu, Pierre. *Distinction: A Social Critique of the Judgement of Taste.* Harvard University Press, 1984.

Bourdieu, Pierre. "The Forms of Capital (1986)." *Cultural Theory: An Anthology* 1 (2011).

Bown, Oliver. "Experiments in Modular Design for the Creative Composition of Live Algorithms." *Computer Music Journal* 35, no. 3 (2011).

Bown, Oliver. "Generative and Adaptive Creativity: A Unified Approach to Creativity in Nature, Humans and Machines." In Computers and Creativity, 361–381. Springer, 2012.

Bown, Oliver. "Player Responses to a Live Algorithm: Conceptualising Computational Creativity without Recourse to Human Comparisons?" *Proceedings of the International Conference on Computational Creativity, 2015.*

Bown, Oliver, and Andrew R. Brown. "Interaction Design for Metacreative Systems." In *New Directions in Third Wave Human-Computer Interaction: Volume 1—Technologies*, edited by Michael Filimowicz and Veronika Tzankova, 43–66. Springer, 2018.

Bown, Oliver, Alice Eldridge, and Jon McCormack. "Understanding Interaction in Contemporary Digital Music: From Instruments to Behavioural Objects." *Organised Sound* 14, no. 02 (2009).

Bown, Oliver, and Jon McCormack. "Taming Nature: Tapping the Creative Potential of Ecosystem Models in the Arts." *Digital Creativity* 21, no. 4 (2010).

Boyd, Robert, and Peter J. Richerson. *Culture and the Evolutionary Process*. University of Chicago Press, 1985.

Bregman, A. S. *Auditory Scene Analysis*. MIT Press, 1990.

Brereton, Margot F., David M. Cannon, Ade Mabogunje, and Larry J. Leifer. "Collaboration in Design Teams: How Social Interaction Shapes the Product." In *Analysing Design Activity*, edited by Nigel Cross, Kees Dorst, and Henri Christiaans, 319–341. Wiley, 1996.

Bringsjord, Selmer, Paul Bello, and David Ferrucci. "Creativity, the Turing Test, and the (Better) Lovelace Test." In *The Turing Test: The Elusive Standard of Artificial Intelligence*, edited by James H. Moor, 215–239. Springer, 2003.

Briot, Jean-Pierre, and François Pachet. "Music Generation by Deep Learning: Challenges and Directions." *arXiv preprint arXiv:1712.04371* (2017).

Brockman, John, ed. *What to Think About Machines That Think: Today's Leading Thinkers on the Age of Machine Intelligence*. Harper Perennial, 2015.

Brooks, Rodney A. "Elephants Don't Play Chess." *Robotics and Autonomous Systems* 6 (1990).

Brown, Steven. "Contagious Heterophony: A New Theory About the Origins of Music." *Musicae Scientiae* 11, no. 1 (Spring 2007).

Brown, William M., Lee Cronk, Keith Grochow, Amy Jacobson, C. Karen Liu, Zoran Popović, and Robert Trivers. "Dance Reveals Symmetry Especially in Young Men." *Nature* 438, no. 7071 (2005).

Burlamaqui, Leonardo, and Andy Dong. "The Use and Misuse of the Concept of Affordance." In *Design Computing and Cognition '14*, edited by John S. Gero and Sean Hanna, 295–311. Springer, 2015.

Candy, Linda. "Practice Based Research: A Guide." *CCS Report* 1 (2006).

Cardoso, Amílcar, Tony Veale, and Geraint A. Wiggins. "Converging on the Divergent: The History (and Future) of the International Joint Workshops in Computational Creativity." *AI Magazine* 30, no. 3 (2009).

Carey, Benjamin Leigh. "_derivations and the Performer-Developer: Co-Evolving Digital Artefacts and Human-Machine Performance Practices." DPhil thesis, University of Technology, Sydney, 2016.

Cattani, Gino, and Simone Ferriani. "A Core/Periphery Perspective on Individual Creative Performance: Social Networks and Cinematic Achievements in the Hollywood Film Industry." *Organization Science* 19, no. 6 (2008).

Cattani, Gino, Simone Ferriani, and Paul D. Allison. "Insiders, Outsiders, and the Struggle for Consecration in Cultural Fields: A Core-Periphery Perspective." *American Sociological Review* 79, no. 2 (2014).

Charnley, John William, Simon Colton, and Maria Teresa Llano. "The FloWr Framework: Automated Flowchart Construction, Optimisation and Alteration for Creative Systems." *Proceedings of the International Conference on Computational Creativity, 2014.*

Chu, Eric. "Artistic Influence GAN." *32nd Conference on Neural Information Processing Systems, 2018.*

Clark, Andy. *Natural-Born Cyborgs: Minds, Technologies, and the Future of Human Intelligence.* Oxford University Press, 2003.

Coe, Kathryn. *The Ancestress Hypothesis: Visual Art as Adaptation.* Rutgers University Press, 2003.

Cohen, Harold. "Parallel to Perception: Some Notes on the Problem of Machine-Generated Art." *Computer Studies* 4, no. 3/4 (1973).

Collins, Nick. "Towards Machine Musicians Who Have Listened to More Music Than Us: Audio Database-Led Algorithmic Criticism for Automatic Composition and Live Concert Systems." *Computers in Entertainment (CIE)* 14, no. 3 (2016).

Collins, Tom, and Robin Laney. "Computer-Generated Stylistic Compositions with Long-Term Repetitive and Phrasal Structure." *Journal of Creative Music Systems* 1, no. 2 (2017).

Colton, Simon. "The Painting Fool: Stories from Building an Automated Painter." In *Computers and Creativity*, edited by Jon McCormack and Mark d'Inverno, 3–38. Springer, 2012.

Colton, Simon, Jakob Halskov, Dan Ventura, Ian Gouldstone, Michael Cook, and Blanca Pérez Ferrer. "The Painting Fool Sees! New Projects with the Automated Painter." *Proceedings of the International Conference on Computational Creativity, 2015.*

Colton, Simon, Maria Teresa Llano, Rose Hepworth, John Charnley, Catherine V. Gale, Archie Baron, François Pachet, Pierre Roy, Pablo Gervás, Nick Collins, Bob L. Sturm, Tillman Weyde, Daniel Wolff, and James Robert Lloyd. "The *Beyond the Fence* Musical and *Computer Says Show* Documentary." *Proceedings of the International Conference on Computational Creativity, 2016.*

Colton, Simon, A. Pease, and J. Charnley. "Computational Creativity Theory: The Face and Idea Descriptive Models." *Proceedings of the Second International Conference on Computational Creativity, 2011.*

References

Colton, Simon, and Geraint A. Wiggins. "Computational Creativity: The Final Frontier?" *Proceedings of the 20th European Conference on Artificial Intelligence, 2012.*

Compton, Kate, and Michael Mateas. "Casual Creators." *Proceedings of the International Conference on Computational Creativity, 2015.*

Cook, Michael, and Simon Colton. "Generating Code for Expressing Simple Preferences: Moving on from Hardcoding and Randomness." *Proceedings of the International Conference on Computational Creativity, 2015.*

Cope, David. "Computational Creativity and Music." In *Computational Creativity Research: Towards Creative Machines*, edited by Tarek R. Besold, Marco Schorlemmer, and Alan Smahill, 309–326. Atlantis, 2015.

Cope, David. "An Expert System for Computer-Assisted Composition." *Computer Music Journal* 11, no. 4 (1987).

Cope, David. *Virtual Music: Computer Synthesis of Musical Style.* MIT Press, 2004.

Cross, Ian. "Music, Cognition, Culture and Evolution." *Annals of the New York Academy of Sciences* 930 (2001).

Cross, Ian. "Music and Meaning, Ambiguity and Evolution." In *Musical Communication*, edited by Dorothy Miell, Raymond MacDonald, and David Hargreaves, 27–43. Oxford University Press, 2005.

Cross, Nigel, and Anita Clayburn Cross. "Observations of Teamwork and Social Processes in Design." *Design Studies* 16, no. 2 (1995).

Csikszentmihalyi, Mihaly. *Flow: The Psychology of Optimal Experience.* Harper and Row, 1990.

Csikszentmihalyi, Mihaly. *The Systems Model of Creativity: The Collected Works of Mihaly Csikszentmihalyi.* Springer, 2015.

Dahlstedt, Palle. "A MutaSynth in Parameter Space: Interactive Composition through Evolution." *Organised Sound* 6, no. 2 (2006).

Dalsgaard, Peter, and Kim Halskov. "Designing Urban Media Façades: Cases and Challenges." *Proceedings of the SIGCHI Conference on Human Factors in Computing Systems, 2010.*

Darwin, Charles. *On the Origin of Species by Means of Natural Selection, or the Preservation of Favoured Races in the Struggle for Life.* John Murray, 1859.

David, Paul. "The Hero and the Herd in Technological History: Reflections on Thomas Edison and the Battle of the Systems." In *Favorites to Fortune*, ed. Patrice L. R. Higonnet, David S. Landes, and Henry Rosovskym, 72–119. Harvard University Press, 1991.

Davies, William. *Nervous States: How Feeling Took Over the World.* Random House, 2018.

Dawkins, Richard. *The Extended Phenotype: The Long Reach of the Gene.* Oxford University Press, 2016.

Dawkins, Richard. *The Selfish Gene.* Oxford University Press, 1976.

Dennett, Daniel Clement. *The Intentional Stance.* MIT Press, 1989.

Diamond, Jared. "Soft Sciences Are Often Harder Than Hard Sciences." *Discover* 8, no. 8 (1987).

di Scipio, Agostino. "Sound Is the Interface: From Interactive to Ecosystemic Signal Processing." *Organised Sound* 8, no. 3 (2003).

Dissanayake, Ellen. "Antecedents of the Temporal Arts in Early Mother-Infant Interaction." In *The Origins of Music*, edited by Nils L. Wallin, Björn Merker, and Steven Brown. MIT Press, 2000.

Dixon, Simon. "A Lightweight Multi-Agent Musical Beat Tracking System." *Pacific Rim International Conference on Artificial Intelligence, 2000.*

Doornbusch, Paul. "The Music of CSIRAC, Some Untold Stories." *Proceedings of the 19th International Symposium on Electronic Art, ISEA2013*, Sydney (2013).

Dourish, Paul. *Where the Action Is: The Foundations of Embodied Interaction.* MIT Press, 2004.

Draves, Scott. "Electric Sheep." Software and information available from http://electricsheep.org/ (accessed May 2, 2020).

Dunbar, R. "The Social Brain Hypothesis." *Evolutionary Anthropology* 6 (1998).

Durkheim, Emile. *Selected Writings.* Edited by Anthony Giddens. Cambridge University Press, 1972.

Dutton, Denis. *The Art Instinct: Beauty, Pleasure, and Human Evolution.* Bloomsbury Press, 2010.

Dutton, Denis. "A Naturalist Definition of Art." *Journal of Aesthetics and Art Criticism* 64, no. 3 (2006).

Dyson, George B. *Darwin among the Machines: The Evolution of Global Intelligence.* Basic Books, 2012.

Ehrlich, Stefan K., Kat R. Agres, Cuntai Guan, and Gordon Cheng. "A Closed-Loop, Music-Based Brain-Computer Interface for Emotion Mediation." *PLOS ONE* 14, no. 3 (2019).

Ekárt, Anikó, Divya Sharma, and Stayko Chalakov. "Modelling Human Preference in Evolutionary Art." *European Conference on the Applications of Evolutionary Computation, 2011.*

Eldridge, Alice. "Collaborating with the Behaving Machine: Simple Adaptive Dynamical Systems for Generative and Interactive Music." DPhil thesis, University of Sussex, 2007.

El-Gamal, Yasser M., and Ehab Samuel, "Copyright Protection for AI Machine Created Works?" *Manatt Blog*, September 28, 2017. https://www.manatt.com/insights/articles/2017/copyright-protection-for-ai-machine-created-works.

Elgammal, Ahmed, and Taishi Fukuyama. "We Need to Embrace AI's Humanity to Unlock Its Creative Promise." *VentureBeat*, May 18, 2019.

Elgammal, Ahmed, Bingchen Liu, Mohamed Elhoseiny, and Marian Mazzone. "CAN: Creative Adversarial Networks, Generating 'Art' by Learning about Styles and Deviating from Style Norms." *arXiv preprint arXiv:1706.07068* (2017).

Elgammal, Ahmed, and Babak Saleh. "Quantifying Creativity in Art Networks." *arXiv preprint arXiv:1506.00711* (2015).

Elman, Jeffrey, Elizabeth Bates, Mark H. Johnson, Annette Karmiloff-Smith, Domenico Parisi, and Kim Plunkett, eds. *Rethinking Innateness*. MIT Press, 1996.

Engel, Jesse, Cinjon Resnick, Adam Roberts, Sander Dieleman, Douglas Eck, Karen Simonyan, and Mohammad Norouzi. "Neural Audio Synthesis of Musical Notes with Wavenet Autoencoders." *arXiv preprint arXiv:1704.01279* (2017).

Eno, Brian. "Generative Music 1." Sleeve notes, 1996.

Epstein, Robert, Gary Roberts, and Grace Beber. *Parsing the Turing Test*. Springer, 2009.

Fauconnier, Gilles, and Mark Turner. "Conceptual Blending, Form and Meaning." *Recherches en communication* 19, no. 19 (2003).

Fauconnier, Gilles, and Mark Turner. *The Way We Think: Conceptual Blending and the Mind's Hidden Complexities*. Basic Books, 2008.

Fiebrink, Rebecca. "Machine Learning as Meta-Instrument: Human-Machine Partnerships Shaping Expressive Instrumental Creation." In *Musical Instruments in the 21st Century*, edited by Till Bovermann, Alberto de Campo, Hauke Egermann, Sarah Hardjowirogo, and Stefan Weinzierl, 137–151. Springer, 2017.

Florida, Richard. *The Rise of the Creative Class—Revisited: Revised and Expanded*. Basic Books, 2014.

Fonseca, Carlos M., and Peter J. Fleming. "Multiobjective Genetic Algorithms." *IEE Colloquium on Genetic Algorithms for Control Systems Engineering, 1993*.

Forsythe, Alex, Marcos Nadal, Noel Sheehy, Camilo J. Cela-Conde, and Martin Sawey. "Predicting Beauty: Fractal Dimension and Visual Complexity in Art." *British Journal of Psychology* 102, no. 1 (2011).

French, Robert M. "The Turing Test: The First 50 Years." *Trends in Cognitive Sciences* 4, no. 3 (2000).

Gabora, Liane. "Honing Theory: A Complex Systems Framework for Creativity." *Nonlinear Dynamics Psychology and Life Sciences* 21, no. 1 (October 2016).

Gain, Bruce. "When Machines Create Intellectual Property, Who Owns What?" *Intellectual Property Watch*, February 16, 2017. http://www.ip-watch.org/2017/02/16/machines-create-intellectual-property-owns/.

Galanter, Philip. "Complexism and the Role of Evolutionary Art." In *The Art of Artificial Evolution: A Handbook on Evolutionary Art and Music*, edited by Juan Romero and Penousal Machado, 311–332. Springer-Verlag, 2008.

Galanter, Philip. "What Is Generative Art? Complexity Theory as a Context for Art Theory." *GA2003—6th Generative Art Conference, 2003*.

Gallie, Walter Bryce. "Essentially Contested Concepts." *Proceedings of the Aristotelian society, 1955*.

Gamma, Erich. *Design Patterns: Elements of Reusable Object-Oriented Software*. Pearson Education India, 1995.

Gärdenfors, Peter. *Conceptual Spaces: The Geometry of Thought*. MIT Press, 2004.

Gaut, Berys. "The Cluster Account of Art." In *Theories of Art Today*, edited by Noël Carroll, 25–45. University of Wisconsin Press, 2000.

Geertz, C. *The Interpretation of Cultures*. Basic Books, 1973.

Gell, Alfred. *Art and Agency: An Anthropological Theory*. Clarendon, 1998.

Gervás, Pablo. "A Personal Perspective into the Future for Computational Creativity." In *Computational Creativity Research: Towards Creative Machines*, edited by Tarek R. Besold, Marco Schorlemmer, and Alan Smaill, 393–406. Atlantis, 2015.

Getzels, Jacob W., and Mihaly Csikszentmihalyi. *The Creative Vision: A Longitudinal Study of Problem Finding in Art*. Wiley, 1976.

Gibson, James J. "The Theory of Affordances." In *Perceiving, Acting, and Knowing*, edited by Robert Shaw and John Bransford. Lawrence Erlbaum, 1977.

Glăveanu, Vlad Petre. "On Units of Analysis and Creativity Theory: Towards a 'Molecular' Perspective." *Journal for the Theory of Social Behaviour* 45, no. 3 (2015).

Glucksberg, Sam. "The Influence of Strength of Drive on Functional Fixedness and Perceptual Recognition." *Journal of Experimental Psychology* 63, no. 1 (1962).

Goldhill, Olivia. "The First Pop Song Ever Written by Artificial Intelligence Is Pretty Good, Actually." *Quartz*, September 24, 2016. https://qz.com/790523/daddys-car-the-first-song-ever-written-by-artificial-intelligence-is-actually-pretty-good/.

Gould, S. J., and R. C. Lewontin. "The Spandrels of San Marco and the Panglossian Paradigm: A Critique of the Adaptationist Programme." *Proceedings of the Royal Society of London, 1979.*

Gray, C., and G. Burnett. "Making Sense: 'Material' Thinking and 'Materializing Pedagogies.'" *Interactive Discourse* 1, no. 1 (2007).

Guadamuz, Andres. "Should Robots Be Given Copyright Protection?" *The Conversation*, June 26, 2017. https://theconversation.com/should-robot-artists-be-given-copyright-protection-79449.

Hamilton, W. D. "The Evolution of Altruistic Behavior." *American Naturalist* 97 (1963).

Haque, Usman. "The Architectural Relevance of Gordon Pask." *Architectural Design* 77, no. 4 (2007).

Hargreaves, David J., and Adrian C. North. "The Functions of Music in Everyday Life: Redefining the Social in Music Psychology." *Psychology of Music* 27, no. 1 (1999).

Harvey, Inman. "Robotics: Philosophy of Mind Using a Screwdriver." *Evolutionary Robotics: From Intelligent Robots to Artificial Life* 3 (2000).

Hennion, Antoine. "Pragmatics of Taste." In *The Blackwell Companion to the Sociology of Culture*, edited by Mark D. Jacob and Nancy Weiss Hanrahan, 131–144. Blackwell Publishing, 2005.

Hertzmann, Aaron. "Can Computers Create Art?" *Arts* 7, no. 2 (2018).

Hesman Saey, Tina. "Computers Compose Personalized Music." *PopMatters*, June 24, 2007. http://www.popmatters.com/article/computers-compose-personalized-music/.

Hesse, Herman. *Siddartha*. New Direction, 1951.

Hiller, Lejaren A., Jr., and Leonard M. Isaacson. "Musical Composition with a High Speed Digital Computer." *Audio Engineering Society Convention 9, 1957.*

Hornby, Gregory S., Al Globus, Derek S. Linden, and Jason D. Lohn, "Automated Antenna Design with Evolutionary Algorithms." *Space 2006*, September 19, 2006. https://ti.arc.nasa.gov/m/pub-archive/1244h/1244%20(Hornby).pdf.

Huron, David. *Sweet Anticipation*. MIT Press, 2006.

Ianigro, Steffan, and Oliver Bown. "Exploring Continuous Time Recurrent Neural Networks through Novelty Search." *Proceedings of the International Conference on New Interfaces for Musical Expression, 2018.*

Ianigro, Steffan, and Oliver Bown. "Plecto: A Low-Level Interactive Genetic Algorithm for the Evolution of Audio." *International Conference on Evolutionary and Biologically Inspired Music and Art, 2016.*

Jablonka, Eva, and Marion J. Lamb. *Epigenetic Inheritance and Evolution: The Lamarckian Dimension.* Oxford University Press, 1995.

Johnson, Daniel D., Robert M. Keller, and Nicholas Weintraut. "Learning to Create Jazz Melodies Using a Product of Experts." *Proceedings of the International Conference on Computational Creativity, 2017.*

Jordanous, Anna. "Evaluating Computational Creativity: A Standardised Procedure for Evaluating Creative Systems and Its Application." DPhil thesis, University of Sussex, 2012.

Jordanous, Anna. "A Standardised Procedure for Evaluating Creative Systems: Computational Creativity Evaluation Based on What It Is to Be Creative." *Cognitive Computation* 4, no. 3 (2012).

Kahneman, Daniel. *Thinking, Fast and Slow.* Macmillan, 2011.

Kakko, Ilkka, and Sam Inkinen. "Homo Creativus: Creativity and Serendipity Management in Third Generation Science and Technology Parks." *Science and Public Policy* 36, no. 7 (2009).

Kantosalo, Anna, Jukka M. Toivanen, Ping Xiao, and Hannu Toivonen. "From Isolation to Involvement: Adapting Machine Creativity Software to Support Human-Computer Co-Creation." *Proceedings of the Fifth International Conference on Computational Creativity, 2014.*

Kantosalo, Anna, and Hannu Toivonen. "Modes for Creative Human-Computer Collaboration: Alternating and Task-Divided Co-Creativity." *Proceedings of the Seventh International Conference on Computational Creativity, 2016.*

Karimi, Pegah, Mary Lou Maher, Nicholas Davis, and Kazjon Grace. "Deep Learning in a Computational Model for Conceptual Shifts in a Co-Creative Design System." *arXiv preprint arXiv:1906.10188* (2019).

Kathrani, Paresh. "Could Intelligent Machines of the Future Own the Rights of Their Own Creations." *The Conversation*, December 1, 2017. https://theconversation.com/could-intelligent-machines-of-the-future-own-the-rights-to-their-own-creations-86005.

Kauffman, S. *The Origins of Order: Self-Organization and Selection in Evolution.* Oxford University Press, 1993.

Kaufman, James C., and Robert J. Sternberg. *The International Handbook of Creativity.* Cambridge University Press, 2006.

Kazakçi, Akin, Cherti Mehdi, and Balázs Kégl. "Digits That Are Not: Generating New Types through Deep Neural Nets." *International Conference on Computational Creativity, 2016.*

Kelly, Kevin. *What Technology Wants*. Penguin, 2010.

Kelly, Sean Dorrance. "A Philosopher Argues That an AI Can't Be an Artist." *MIT Technology Review*, February 21, 2019.

Koestler, A. *The Ghost in the Machine*. Hutchinson, 1967.

Kohonen, Teuvo, Kari Torkkola, Makoto Shozakai, Jari Kangas, and Olli Venta. "Phonetic Typewriter for Finnish and Japanese." *International Conference on Acoustics, Speech, and Signal Processing, 1988*.

Kris, Ernst, and Otto Kurz. *Legend, Myth, and Magic in the Image of the Artist: A Historical Experiment*. Yale University Press, 1981.

Kuhn, Thomas S. *The Structure of Scientific Revolutions*. 3rd ed. University of Chicago Press, 1996.

Kurzweil, Ray. *The Age of Spiritual Machines: How We Will Live, Work and Think in the New Age of Intelligent Machines*. Orion, 1999.

Laland, Kevin N., John Odling-Smee, and Marcus W. Feldman. "Niche Construction, Biological Evolution and Cultural Change." *Behavioral and Brain Sciences* 21, no. 1 (1999).

Lamb, Carolyn, Daniel G. Brown, and C. L. Clarke. "Human Competence in Creativity Evaluation." *Proceedings of the Sixth International Conference on Computational Creativity June, 2015*.

Landry, Charles. *The Creative City: A Toolkit for Urban Innovators*. Earthscan, 2012.

Large, E. W., and M. R. Jones. "The Dynamics of Attending: How People Track Time-Varying Events." *Psychological Review* 10, no. 1 (1999).

Latour, Bruno. "On Technical Mediation Philosophy, Sociology, Genealogy." *Common Knowledge* 3, no. 2 (1994).

Latour, Bruno. *We Have Never Been Modern*. Harvard University Press, 2012.

Latour, Bruno. "What's the Story? Organizing as a Mode of Existence." In *Agency without Actors*, edited by Jan-Hendrik Passoth, Birgit Peuker, and Michael Schillmeier. Routledge, 2011.

Lehman, Joel, Jeff Clune, Dusan Misevic, Christoph Adami, Lee Altenberg, Julie Beaulieu, Peter J. Bentley, et al. "The Surprising Creativity of Digital Evolution: A Collection of Anecdotes from the Evolutionary Computation and Artificial Life Research Communities." *arXiv preprint arXiv:1803.03453* (2018).

Lehman, Joel, Sebastian Risi, and Jeff Clune. "Creative Generation of 3D Objects with Deep Learning and Innovation Engines." *Proceedings of the Seventh International Conference on Computational Creativity, 2016*.

Lehman, Joel, and Kenneth O. Stanley. "Exploiting Open-Endedness to Solve Problems through the Search for Novelty." *Proceedings of the Eleventh International Conference on Artificial Life (ALIFE XI), 2008.*

Lévi-Strauss, Claude, *The Raw and the Cooked: Introduction to a Science of Mythology.* University of Chicago Press, 1966.

Lewis, Paul, and Paul Hilder. "Leaked: Cambridge Analytica's Blueprint for Trump Victory." *The Guardian*, March 23, 2018. https://www.theguardian.com/uk-news/2018/mar/23/leaked-cambridge-analyticas-blueprint-for-trump-victory.

LeWitt, Sol. "Paragraphs on Conceptual Art." *Artforum* 5, no. 10 (1967).

Liapis, Antonios, Georgios N. Yannakakis, and Julian Togelius. "Computational Game Creativity." *Proceedings of the International Conference on Computational Creativity, 2014.*

Lindauer, Marius, Jan N. van Rijn, and Lars Kotthoff. "The Algorithm Selection Competition Series 2015–17." *ArXiv abs/1805.01214* (2018).

Lomas, Andy. "On Hybrid Creativity." *Arts* 7, no. 3 (2018).

London, Justin. *Hearing in Time.* Oxford University Press, 2004.

Lubart, Todd. "How Can Computers Be Partners in the Creative Process: Classification and Commentary on the Special Issue." *International Journal of Human-Computer Studies* 63, no. 4 (2005).

Luhmann, Niklas. *Art as a Social System.* Stanford University Press, 2000.

Lyell, Charles. *Principles of Geology: Being an Inquiry How Far the Former Changes of the Earth's Surface Are Referable to Causes Now in Operation.* Vol. 1. J. Kay, 1837.

MacCallum, Robert M., Matthias Mauch, Austin Burt, and Armand M. Leroi. "Evolution of Music by Public Choice." *Proceedings of the National Academy of Sciences* 109, no. 30 (2012).

Malafouris, Lambros. "At the Potter's Wheel: An Argument for Material Agency." In *Material Agency: Towards a Non- anthropocentric Approach*, edited by C. Knappett and L. Malafouris. Springer, 2008. http://cogprints.org/6402/.

Manaris, Bill, Juan Romero, Penousal Machado, Dwight Krehbiel, Timothy Hirzel, Walter Pharr, and Robert B. Davis. "Zipf's Law, Music Classification, and Aesthetics." *Computer Music Journal* 29, no. 1 (2005).

Marchini, Marco, François Pachet, and Benoît Carré. "Rethinking Reflexive Looper for Structured Pop Music." NIME, 2017.

Marshall, Alex. "Is This the World's First Good Robot Album?" BBC, January 2018. https://www.bbc.com/culture/article/20180112-is-this-the-worlds-first-good-robot-album.

Martin, A., C. Jin, B. Carey, and O. Bown. "Creative Experiments Using a System for Learning High-Level Performance Structure in Ableton Live." *Proceedings of the Sound and Music Computing Conference, Copenhagen, Denmark, 2012.*

Martin, Aengus, Craig T. Jin, and Oliver Bown. "Design and Evaluation of Agents That Sequence and Juxtapose Short Musical Patterns in Real Time." *Computer Music Journal* 41, no. 4 (2018).

Martin, Aengus, Craig T. Jin, and Oliver Bown. "Implementation of a Real-Time Musical Decision-Maker." *Proceedings of the Australasian Computer Music Conference, Brisbane, Australia, July 2012.*

Martindale, Colin. "Aesthetic Evolution." *Poetics* 15, nos. 4–6 (1986).

Martindale, Colin, Karen Anderson, Kathleen Moore, and Alan N. West. "Creativity, Oversensitivity, and Rate of Habituation." *Personality and Individual Differences* 20, no. 4 (1996).

Mason, Karl, Jim Duggan, and Enda Howley. "Neural Network Topology and Weight Optimization through Neuro Differential Evolution." *Proceedings of the Genetic and Evolutionary Computation Conference Companion, 2017.*

Maturana, H., and F. Varela. *Autopoiesis and Cognition: The Realization of the Living.* Reidel, 1980.

Maynard Smith, John, and Eörs Szathmáry. *The Major Transitions in Evolution.* Oxford University Press, 1995.

Mazzone, Marian, and Ahmed Elgammal. "Art, Creativity, and the Potential of Artificial Intelligence." *Arts* 8, no. 1 (2019).

McCann, B., N. S. Keskar, C. Xiong, and R. Socher. "The Natural Language Decathlon: Multitask Learning as Question Answering." *arXiv preprint arXiv:1806.08730* (2018).

McCorduck, Pamela. *Machines Who Think.* Peters, 2004.

McCormack, Jon. "Aesthetic Evolution of L-Systems Revisited." In *Applications of Evolutionary Computing*, Vol. 3005, edited by G. R. Raidl. Springer, 2004.

McCormack, Jon. "Eden: An Evolutionary Sonic Ecosystem." *Advances in Artificial Life, Proceedings of the Sixth European Conference, ECAL* LNCS 2159 (2001).

McCormack, Jon, Toby Gifford, and Patrick Hutchings. "Autonomy, Authenticity, Authorship and Intention in Computer Generated Art." *arXiv preprint arXiv:1903.02166* (2019).

McNeill, W. H. *Keeping Together in Time: Dance and Drill in Human History.* Harvard University Press, 1995.

Medeot, Gabriele, Srikanth Cherla, Katerina Kosta, Matt McVicar, Samer Abdallah, Marco Selvi, Ed Newton-Rex, and Kevin Webster. "StructureNet: Inducing Structure in Generated Melodies." *ISMIR*. 2018.

Mill, John Stuart. *On Liberty*. John Parker and Sons, 1859.

Miller, Geoffrey. *The Mating Mind*. Random House, 2000.

Mital, Parag Kumar. "Audiovisual Scene Synthesis." DPhil thesis, Goldsmiths, University of London, 2014.

Mitrano, Peter, Arthur Lockman, James Honicker, and Scott Barton. "Using Recurrent Neural Networks to Judge Fitness in Musical Genetic Algorithms." In *Proceedings of the 5th International Workshop on Musical Metacreation (MUME) at the 8th International Conference on Computational Creativity (ICCC)*. 2017.

Moffat, David C., and Martin Kelly. "An Investigation into People's Bias against Computational Creativity in Music Composition." *Assessment* 13 (2006).

Monedero, Javier. "Parametric Design: A Review and Some Experiences." *Automation in Construction* 9, no. 4 (2000).

Monteith, Kristine, Tony R Martinez, and Dan Ventura. "Automatic Generation of Music for Inducing Emotive Response." *Proceedings of the International Conference on Computational Creativity*, 2010.

Mumford, Martin, and Dan Ventura. "The Man Behind the Curtain: Overcoming Skepticism About Creative Computing." *Proceedings of the Sixth International Conference on Computational Creativity*, 2015.

Murphy, Gregory L. *The Big Book of Concepts*. Bradford, 2004.

Nardi, Bonnie A. *Context and Consciousness: Activity Theory and Human-Computer Interaction*. MIT Press, 1996.

Nelson, Mark J., Swen E. Gaudl, Simon Colton, Edward J. Powley, Blanca Pérez Ferrer, Rob Saunders, Peter Ivey, and Michael Cook. "Fluidic Games in Cultural Contexts." *Proceedings of the International Conference on Computational Creativity*, Atlanta, GA, 2017.

Nia, Hadi T., Ankita D. Jain, Yuming Liu, Mohammad-Reza Alam, Roman Barnas, and Nicholas C. Makris. "The Evolution of Air Resonance Power Efficiency in the Violin and Its Ancestors." *Proceedings of the Royal Society of London A: Mathematical, Physical and Engineering Sciences* 471, no. 2175 (2015).

Nielsen, Jakob, and Thomas K. Landauer. "A Mathematical Model of the Finding of Usability Problems." *Proceedings of the INTERACT '93 and CHI '93 Conference on Human Factors in Computing Systems, 1993*.

Norman, Donald. *The Psychology of Everyday Things*. Basic Books, 1988.

Norman, Donald A. "Stages and Levels in Human-Machine Interaction." *International Journal of Man-Machine Studies* 21, no. 4 (1984).

North, Adrian C., and David J. Hargreaves. "Music and Adolescent Identity." *Music Education Research* 1, no. 1 (1999).

North, Adrian C., David J. Hargreaves, and Susan A. O'Neill. "The Importance of Music to Adolescents." *British Journal of Educational Psychology* 70, no. 2 (2000).

Odling-Smee, F. John, Kevin N. Laland, and Marcus W. Feldman. *Niche Construction: The Neglected Process in Evolution*. Princeton University Press, 2003.

O'Reilly, Lara. "A Japanese Ad Agency Invented an AI Creative Director—and Ad Execs Preferred Its Ad to a Human's." *Business Insider*, March 12, 2017. http://www.businessinsider.com/mccann-japans-ai-creative-director-creates-better-ads-than-a-human-2017-3.

Orians, Gordan H., and Judith H Heerwagen. "Evolved Responses to Landscapes." In *The Adapted Mind: Evolutionary Psychology and the Generation of Culture*, edited by Jerome H. Barkow, John Tooby, and Leda Cosmides, 555–579. Oxford University Press, 1992.

Osborn, Alex F. *Applied Imagination*, Charles Scribner, 1953.

Pachet, François. "Beyond the Cybernetic Jam Fantasy: The Continuator." *IEEE Computer Graphics and Applications* 24, no. 1 (2004).

Pachet, François, and Pierre Roy. "Non-Conformant Harmonization: The Real Book in the Style of Take 6." *Proceedings of the International Conference on Computational Creativity, 2014*.

Pachet, François, Pierre Roy, and Raphaël Foulon. "Do Jazz Improvisers Really Interact? The Score Effect in Collective Jazz Improvisation." In *Routledge Companion to Embodied Music Interaction*, edited by Micheline Lesaffre, Pieter-Jan Maes, and Marc Leman. Routledge, 2017.

Papadopoulos, Alexandre, Pierre Roy, and François Pachet. "Avoiding Plagiarism in Markov Sequence Generation." *Twenty-Eighth AAAI Conference on Artificial Intelligence, 2014*.

Pasquier, Philippe, Adam Burnett, Nicolas Gonzalez Thomas, James B. Maxwell, Arne Eigenfeldt, and Tom Loughin. "Investigating Listener Bias against Musical Metacreativity." *Proceedings of the Seventh International Conference on Computational Creativity, 2016*.

Pearce, M. T., D. Meredith, and G. A. Wiggins. "Motivations and Methodologies for Automation of the Compositional Process." *Musicae Scientiae* 6, no. 2 (2002).

Penny, Simon. "Agents as Artworks and Agent Design as Artistic Practice." In *Human Cognition and Social Agent Technology*, edited by Kerstin Dautenhahn, 395–414. John Benjamins, 2000.

Pereira, Francisco Câmara, and Amílcar Cardoso. "Conceptual Blending and the Quest for the Holy Creative Process." *Proceedings of the Symposium for Creativity in Arts and Science of AISB 2002*.

Perkins, David N. "Creativity: Beyond the Darwinian Paradigm." In *Dimensions of Creativity*, edited by Margaret Boden, 119–142. MIT Press, 1996.

Perrett, David I., D. Michael Burt, Ian S. Penton-Voak, Kieran J. Lee, Duncan A. Rowland, and Rachel Edwards. "Symmetry and Human Facial Attractiveness." *Evolution and Human Behavior* 20, no. 5 (1999).

Pickering, Andrew. "The Politics of Theory: Producing Another World, with Some Thoughts on Latour." *Journal of Cultural Economy* 2, nos. 1–2 (2009).

Pinker, Steven. *The Language Instinct: The New Science of Language and Mind*. Vol. 7529. Penguin UK, 1995.

Plotkin, Robert. *The Genie in the Machine: How Computer-Automated Inventing Is Revolutionizing Law and Business*. Stanford University Press, 2009.

Poincaré, Henri. *The Foundations of Science: Science and Hypothesis, the Value of Science, Science and Method*. Translated by George Bruce Halstead. Science Press, 1913.

Polya, G. *How to Solve It*. Princeton University Press, 1957.

Prokopenko, Mikhail. "Guided Self-Organization." *HSFP Journal* 3, no. 5 (2009).

Radford, Alec, Luke Metz, and Soumith Chintala. "Unsupervised Representation Learning with Deep Convolutional Generative Adversarial Networks." *arXiv preprint arXiv:1511.06434* (2015).

Radford, Alec, Jeffrey Wu, Rewon Child, David Luan, Dario Amodei, and Ilya Sutskever. "Language Models Are Unsupervised Multitask Learners." *OpenAI Blog* 1, no. 8 (2019).

Ramachandran, Vilayanur S., and William Hirstein. "The Science of Art: A Neurological Theory of Aesthetic Experience." *Journal of consciousness Studies* 6, nos. 6–7 (1999).

Rammert, Werner. "Where the Action Is: Distributed Agency between Humans, Machines, and Programs." In *Paradoxes of Interactivity: Perspectives for Media Theory, Human-Computer Interaction, and Artistic Investigations*, edited by Uwe Seifert, Jin Hyun Kim, and Anthony Moore. De Gruyter, 2008.

Ray, Thomas S., and Joseph Hart. "Evolution of Differentiated Multi-Threaded Digital Organisms." *Proceedings of the IEEE/RSJ International Conference on Intelligent Robots and Systems, 1999*.

Reed, Scott, Zeynep Akata, Xinchen Yan, Lajanugen Logeswaran, Bernt Schiele, and Honglak Lee. "Generative Adversarial Text to Image Synthesis." *Proceedings of the 33rd International Conference on Machine Learning, 2016*.

Requena, Gloria, Carlos Sánchez, José Luis Corzo-Higueras, Sirenia Reyes-Alvarado, Francisco Rivas-Ruiz, Francisco Vico, and Alfredo Raglio. "Melomics Music Medicine (M3) to Lessen Pain Perception During Pediatric Prick Test Procedure." *Pediatric Allergy and Immunology* 25, no. 7 (2014).

Resnick, Mitchel, Brad Myers, Kumiyo Nakakoji, Ben Shneiderman, Randy Pausch, Ted Selker, and Mike Eisenberg. "Design Principles for Tools to Support Creative Thinking." https://www.cs.umd.edu/hcil/CST/Papers/designprinciples.pdf. (revised October 30, 2005).

Rhodes, Mel. "An Analysis of Creativity." *Phi Delta Kappan* 42, no. 7 (1961).

Richerson, Peter J., and Robert Boyd. *Not by Genes Alone: How Culture Transformed Human Evolution*. University of Chicago Press, 2005.

Rifkin, Jeremy. *The Zero Marginal Cost Society: The Internet of Things, the Collaborative Commons, and the Eclipse of Capitalism*. St. Martin's Press, 2014.

Risi, Sebastian, and Julian Togelius. "Neuroevolution in Games: State of the Art and Open Challenges." *IEEE Transactions on Computational Intelligence and AI in Games* 9, no. 1 (2017).

Ritchie, Graeme. "Assessing Creativity." *Proceedings of AISB'01 Symposium, 2001*.

Ritchie, Graeme. "Some Empirical Criteria for Attributing Creativity to a Computer Program." *Minds and Machines* 17, no. 1 (2007).

Rogers, Yvonne, Jenny Preece, and Helen Sharp. *Interaction Design: Beyond Human Computer Interaction*. 3rd ed. John Wiley & Sons, 2011.

Ross, Brian J., William Ralph, and Hai Zong. "Evolutionary Image Synthesis Using a Model of Aesthetics." *IEEE Congress on Evolutionary Computation, 2006*.

Rothenberg, Albert, and Carl R. Hausman. *The Creativity Question*. Duke University Press, 1976.

Salganik, Matthew J., Peter Sheridan Dodds, and Duncan J. Watts. "Experimental Study of Inequality and Unpredictability in an Artificial Cultural Market." *Science* 311, no. 5762 (2006): 854–856.

Sandred, Örjan. "Approaches to Using Rules as a Composition Method." *Contemporary Music Review* 28, no. 2 (2009).

Saunders, Rob. "Curious Design Agents and Artificial Creativity." PhD thesis, Faculty of Architecture, University of Sydney, 2001.

Saunders, Rob, and J. S. Gero. "Artificial Creativity: Emergent Notions of Creativity in Artificial Societies of Curious Agents." *Proceedings of the Second Iteration Conference, Melbourne, Australia, 2001*.

Saunders, Rob, and J. S. Gero. "The Digital Clockwork Muse: A Computational Model of Aesthetic Evolution." *Proceedings of the AISB'01 Symposium on AI and Creativity in Arts and Science, 2001.*

Sawyer, R. Keith. "Improvisation and the Creative Process: Dewey, Collingwood, and the Aesthetics of Spontaneity." *Journal of Aesthetics and Art Criticism* 58, no. 2 (2000).

Schaffer, Simon. "Making Up Discovery." In *Dimensions of Creativity*, edited by M. A. Boden, 13–51. MIT Press, 1994.

Schmidhuber, Jürgen. "Deep Learning in Neural Networks: An Overview." *Neural Networks* 61 (2015).

Schmidhuber, Jürgen. "Formal Theory of Creativity, Fun, and Intrinsic Motivation (1990–2010)." *IEEE Transactions on Autonomous Mental Development* 2, no. 3 (2010).

Schubert, Emery, David J. Hargreaves, and Adrian C. North. "A Dynamically Minimalist Cognitive Explanation of Musical Preference: Is Familiarity Everything?" *Frontiers in Psychology* 5 (2014).

Schwartz, Kelly D., and Gregory T. Fouts. "Music Preferences, Personality Style, and Developmental Issues of Adolescents." *Journal of Youth and Adolescence* 32, no. 3 (2003).

Secretan, Jimmy, Nicholas Beato, David B. D'Ambrosio, Adelein Rodriguez, Adam Campbell, and Kenneth O. Stanley. "Picbreeder: Evolving Pictures Collaboratively Online." *Proceedings of the Computer Human Interaction Conference (CHI 2008), 2008.*

Seth, A. "Measuring Autonomy and Emergence via Granger Causality." *Artificial Life* 16 (2010).

Shan, Man-Kwan, and Shih-Chuan Chiu. "Algorithmic Compositions Based on Discovered Musical Patterns." *Multimedia Tools and Applications* 46, no. 1 (2010).

Shepherd, Kathrine, and Moshe Bar. "Preference for Symmetry: Only on Mars?" *Perception* 40, no. 10 (2011).

Shneiderman, Ben. *Designing the User Interface: Strategies for Effective Human-Computer Interaction.* Pearson Education India, 2010.

Shneiderman, Ben, Gerhard Fischer, Mary Czerwinski, Mitch Resnick, Brad Myers, Linda Candy, et al. "Creativity Support Tools: Report from a Us National Science Foundation Sponsored Workshop." *International Journal of Human-Computer Interaction* 20, no. 2 (2006).

Simon, Herbert A. *The Sciences of the Artificial.* MIT Press, 1996.

Simon, Ian, Adam Roberts, Colin Raffel, Jesse Engel, Curtis Hawthorne, and Douglas Eck. "Learning a Latent Space of Multitrack Measures." *arXiv preprint arXiv:1806.00195* (2018).

Simonton, Dean Keith. "Creativity and Discovery as Blind Variation: Campbell's (1960) BVSR Model after the Half-Century Mark." *Review of General Psychology* 15, no. 2 (2011).

Simonton, Dean Keith. "Scientific Creativity as Constrained Stochastic Behavior: The Integration of Product, Person, and Process Perspectives." *Psychological Bulletin* 129, no. 4 (2003).

Sims, Kim. "Evolving 3D Morphology and Behavior by Competition." *Artificial Life IV Proceedings*. MIT Press, 1994.

Singh, Kunwar Yashraj, Nicholas M. Davis, Chih-Pin Hsiao, Ricardo Macias, Brenda Lin, and Brian Magerko. "Unified Classification and Generation Networks for Co-Creative Systems." In *Proceedings of the International Conference on Computational Creativity, 2017*, 237–244.

Smith, Glenn W., and Frederic Fol Leymarie. "The Machine as Artist: An Introduction." *Arts* 6, no. 1 (2017).

Sobel, Dava. *Longitude: The True Story of a Lone Genius Who Solved the Greatest Scientific Problem of His Time*. Penguin, 1996.

Sperber, Dan. "Seedless Grapes: Nature and Culture." In *Creations of the Mind: Theories of Artefacts and Their Representation*, edited by Eric Margolis and Stephen Laurence. Oxford University Press, 2007.

Stanley, Kenneth O., and Joel Lehman. *Why Greatness Cannot Be Planned: The Myth of the Objective*. Springer, 2015.

Stanley, Kenneth O., and Risto Miikkulainen. "Evolving Neural Networks through Augmenting Topologies." *Evolutionary Computation* 10, no. 2 (2002).

Steinbeck, John. *East of Eden*. Viking, 1952.

Sternberg, Robert J. "The Nature of Creativity." *Creativity Research Journal* 18, no. 1 (2006).

Sternberg, Robert J., and Todd I. Lubart. "An Investment Theory of Creativity and Its Development." *Human Development* 34, no. 1 (1991).

Sterne, Jonathan, and Elena Razlogova. "Machine Learning in Context, or Learning from LANDR: Artificial Intelligence and the Platformization of Music Mastering." *Social Media+ Society* 5, no. 2 (2019).

Still, Arthur, and Mark d'Inverno. "A History of Creativity for Future AI Research." *Proceedings of the International Conference on Computational Creativity, 2016*.

Stokes, Patricia D., and Danielle Fisher. "Selection, Constraints, and Creativity Case Studies: Max Beckmann and Philip Guston." *Creativity Research Journal* 17, nos. 2–3 (2005).

Stone, Peter, Rodney Brooks, Erik Brynjolfsson, Ryan Calo, Oren Etzioni, Greg Hager, Julia Hirschberg, et al. "Artificial Intelligence and Life in 2030." *One Hundred Year Study on Artificial Intelligence: Report of the 2015–2016 Study Panel*, Stanford University. September 2016.

Stowell, Dan, Andrew Robertson, Nick Bryan-Kinns, and Mark D. Plumbley. "Evaluation of Live Human-Computer Music-Making: Quantitative and Qualitative Approaches." *International Journal of Human-Computer Studies* 67, no. 11 (2009).

Sturm, Bob L. "The 'Horse' Inside: Seeking Causes Behind the Behaviors of Music Content Analysis Systems." *Computers in Entertainment (CIE)* 14, no. 2 (2016).

Sturm, Bob L., Oded Ben-Tal, Una Monaghan, Nick Collins, Dorien Herremans, Elaine Chew, Gaëtan Hadjeres, Emmanuel Deruty, and François Pachet. "Machine Learning Research That Matters for Music Creation: A Case Study." *Journal of New Music Research* 48, no. 1 (2019).

Suchman, Lucy A. *Plans and Situated Actions: The Problem of Human-Machine Communication*. Cambridge University Press, 1987.

Takagi, Hideyuki. "Interactive Evolutionary Computation: Fusion of the Capabilities of EC Optimization and Human Evaluation." *Proceedings of the IEEE* 89, no. 9 (2001).

Taylor, Josh. "People Should Be Held Accountable for AI and Algorithm Errors, Rights Commissioner Says." *The Guardian*, December 16, 2019. https://www.theguardian.com/law/2019/dec/17/people-should-be-held-accountable-for-ai-and-algorithm-errors-rights-commissioner-says.

Thaler, Stephen. "Neural Nets That Create and Discover." *PC AI* 10, no. 3 (1996).

Todd, P. M., and G. Werner. "Frankensteinian Methods for Evolutionary Music Composition." In *Musical Networks: Parallel Distributed Perception and Performance*, edited by Niall Griffith and Peter M. Todd, 313–339. MIT Press, 1999.

Toivonen, Hannu, and Oskar Gross. "Data Mining and Machine Learning in Computational Creativity." *Wiley Interdisciplinary Reviews: Data Mining and Knowledge Discovery* 5, no. 6 (2015).

Tomasello, Michael, Malinda Carpenter, Josep Call, Tanya Behne, and Henrike Moll. "Understanding and Sharing Intentions: The Origins of Cultural Cognition." *Behavioral and Brain Sciences* 28, no. 5 (2005).

Tooby, John, and Leda Cosmides. "Does Beauty Build Adapted Minds? Toward an Evolutionary Theory of Aesthetics, Fiction, and the Arts." *SubStance* 30, no. 1 (2001).

Torrance, E. Paul. "The Nature of Creativity as Manifest in Its Testing." In *The Nature of Creativity: Contemporary Psychological Perspectives*, edited by R. J. Sternberg, 43–75. Cambridge University Press, 1988.

Tovée, M. J., K. Tasker, and P. J. Benson. "Is Symmetry a Visual Cue to Attractiveness in the Human Female Body?" *Evolution and Human Behavior* 21, no. 3 (2000).

Turing, Alan M. "Computing Machinery and Intelligence." *Mind* 59, no. 236 (1950).

Turkle, Sherry. *Alone Together: Why We Expect More from Technology and Less from Each Other*. Hachette UK, 2017.

Valenzuela, Cristóbal, Alejandro Matamala, and Anastasis Germanidis. "Runway: Adding Artificial Intelligence Capabilities to Design and Creative Platforms." *Proceedings of the NeurIPS 2018 Workshop on Machine Learning for Creativity and Design*, Montreal, Canada, 2018.

van den Oord, Aaron, Sander Dieleman, Heiga Zen, Karen Simonyan, Oriol Vinyals, Alex Graves, Nal Kalchbrenner, Andrew Senior, and Koray Kavukcuoglu. "WaveNet: A Generative Model for Raw Audio." *arXiv preprint arXiv:1609.03499* (2016).

Vear, Craig. "Music, Dimensions and Play: Composing for Autonomous Laptop Musicians and Improvising Humans." *Digital Creativity* 25, no. 4 (2014).

Ventura, Dan. "The Computational Creativity Complex." In *Computational Creativity Research: Towards Creative Machines*, edited by Tarek R. Besold, Marco Schorlemmer, and Alan Smaill, 65–92. Atlantis, 2015.

Vonnegut, Kurt. *Player Piano*. Dial Press, 1952.

Voss, Richard F., and John Clarke. "'1/F Noise' in Music: Music from 1/F Noise." *Journal of the Acoustical Society of America* 63, no. 1 (1978).

Wagstaff, Kiri L., Nina L. Lanza, David R. Thompson, Thomas G. Dietterich, and Martha S. Gilmore. "Guiding Scientific Discovery with Explanations Using DEMUD." *Twenty-Seventh AAAI Conference on Artificial Intelligence, 2013*.

Wajcman, Judy. *Pressed for Time: The Acceleration of Life in Digital Capitalism*. University of Chicago Press, 2015.

Walsh, Toby. "What AI Can (and Can't) Do." 2017. https://www.youtube.com/watch?v=79O903oGmmU.

Watson, Andrew J., and James E. Lovelock. "Biological Homeostasis of the Global Environment: The Parable of Daisyworld." *Tellus B: Chemical and Physical Meteorology* 35, no. 4 (1983).

Whitby, Blay. "The Turing Test: AI's Biggest Blind Alley?" In *Machines and Thought: The Legacy of Alan Turing*, edited by Peter Millican and Andy Clark, 519–539. Oxford University Press, 1996.

Whitelaw, Mitchell. *Metacreation: Art and Artificial Life*. MIT Press, 2004.

Whitelaw, Mitchell. "System Stories and Model Worlds: A Critical Approach to Generative Art." February 2006. http://mtchl.net/assets/system_stories.pdf.

Whiten, A., and R. W. Byrne. *Machiavellian Intelligence II: Extensions and Evaluations.* Cambridge University Press, 1997.

Wiener, Norbert. *Cybernetics or Control and Communication in the Animal and the Machine.* Vol. 25. MIT Press, 1961.

Wiggins, Geraint A. "A Preliminary Framework for Description, Analysis and Comparison of Creative Systems." *Knowledge-Based Systems* 19, no. 7 (2006).

Wiggins, Geraint A. "Searching for Computational Creativity." *New Generation Computing* 24, no. 3 (2006).

Wiggins, Geraint A. "Towards a More Precise Characterisation of Creativity in AI." *Case-Based Reasoning: Papers from the Workshop Program at ICCBR'01.* Washington, DC, Naval Research Laboratory, Navy Center for Applied Research in Artificial Intelligence, 2001.

Wiggins, Geraint A., and Jamie Forth. "IdYot: A Computational Theory of Creativity as Everyday Reasoning from Learned Information." In *Computational Creativity Research: Towards Creative Machines,* edited by Tarek R. Besold, Marco Schorlemmer, and Alan Smaill, 127–148. Atlantis, 2015.

Wiggins, Geraint, George Papadopoulos, Somnuk Phon-Amnuaisuk, and Andrew Tuson. "Evolutionary Methods for Musical Composition." 1998. http://www.doc.gold.ac.uk/~mas02gw/papers/CASYS98a.pdf.

Williams, Raymond. *Keywords.* Rev. ed. Fontana Press, 1983.

Wittgenstein, Ludwig. *Philosophical Investigations.* 4th ed., edited by P. M. S. Hacker and Joachim Schulte. Wiley, 2009.

Woolley, Brian G., and Kenneth O. Stanley. "A Novel Human-Computer Collaboration: Combining Novelty Search with Interactive Evolution." *Proceedings of the 2014 Annual Conference on Genetic and Evolutionary Computation, 2014.*

Xenakis, I. *Formalized Music.* Indiana University Press, 1971.

Yannakakis, Georgios N., and Antonios Liapis. "Searching for Surprise." *Proceedings of the International Conference on Computational Creativity, 2016.*

Yannakakis, G. N., A. Liapis, and C. Alexopoulos. Mixed-initiative Co-creativity. 9th International Conference on the Foundations of Digital Games, Fort Lauderdale. 2014.

Yee-King, Matthew John. "An Automated Music Improviser Using a Genetic Algorithm Driven Synthesis Engine." *Workshops on Applications of Evolutionary Computation,* 2007.

Yee-King, Matthew John. "The Use of Interactive Genetic Algorithms in Sound Design: A Comparison Study." *Computers in Entertainment: Special Issue on Musical Metacreation* (2016).

Yu, Guo, and Alan Blackwell. "Effects of Timing on Users' Agency during Mixed-Initiative Interaction." *Proceedings of the 31st British Computer Society Human Computer Interaction Conference, 2017.*

Zahavi, Amotz, and Avishag Zahavi. *The Handicap Principle: A Missing Piece of Darwin's Puzzle.* Oxford University Press, 1997.

Zamyatin, Yevgeny. *We.* Penguin, 1993.

Zhu, Jun-Yan, Philipp Krähenbühl, Eli Shechtman, and Alexei A Efros. "Generative Visual Manipulation on the Natural Image Manifold." *European Conference on Computer Vision, 2016.*

Index

Note: Page numbers in *italics* refer to Illustrations.

$1/f^2$ distribution (brown noise), 121
AARON (system), 10–11, 20, 24, 28, 97, 164, 288
Ableton Live digital audio workstation, 219–220
adaptive creativity, 68, 70, 97
Adorno, Theodor, 111
aesthetic perception, 118–120, 190, 209, 211
   adaptive perspectives, 126–132
   auditory perception, 123–125
   and complexity, 120–121
   of the human brain, 118–119
   imagination-tension prediction-reaction-appraisal (ITPRA) model, 131
   pitch perception, 130–131
   and symmetry, 121
affordances, 23, 91, 93–96, 181, 218, 223, 232, 235, 256, 282, 315
agency, 33, 74, 81–82, 85, 86–87, 89, 90, 92, 95–97, 98, 104, 105, 108, 151, 212, 216, 261, 262, 263, 266
Aguello, Agnese, 209
Aish, Robert, 168
Aiva (system), 17, 25, 189, 247, 286, 304–305, 309
Akten, Memo, 226

Alexander, Christopher, design patterns, 160
algorithmic methods, 24–27, 163–175
   evolutionary strategies, 26, 163–164
   learning, 163–164
   machine learning (ML), 25
   rule-based systems, 24
algorithms
   domain-specific, 159
   generators versus evaluators, 158
   historic development, 162
Amabile, Teresa, 46, 53, 241, 271, 279
ancestress hypothesis, 141
apparent mental causation model, 262
Arieti, Silvano, 50
Aristotle, 92
Ariza, Chris, 272, 273, 276
art
   as conspicuous consumption, 114
   family-resemblance features (Gaut), 112–114, 322
Arthur, Brian, 104–105, 108
artificial intelligence (AI), 3–6, 18, 20, 23, 24, 25, 60, 64–65, 74, 75, 161–164
   creative AI, 33, 35, 235
   history of, 15–16
   social impact, 298–301
   startups, 303–304

artificial life, 31, 61, 100, 172, 173, 211, 260
artistic behavior, 23
  and creative domains, 151–154
artistic creativity, 9, 23, 57, 109, 111, 291–292
Ashby, William Ross, 59, 73
asymmetrical dualism, 74, 85, 96
Attali, Jacques, 313
audible ecosystems, 174
Auerbach, David, 67
Auslander, Philip, 137, 174, 218, 262
authorship, 241, 256, 282, 300, 302, 306, 307. *See also* intellectual property
autoencoders, 181–182, 184, 188, 190, 246, 248
autopoietic system, 100–101, 118

Babbage, Charles, 60
Baldwin, James, 118
Baldwin effect, 118
Balzano, Gerald, 126, 127, 128, 190
Banerji, Ritwik, 262, 277, 290
Barreau, Pierre, 189, 282, 304–305
Becker, Howard, 153–154
Bell, Shawn, 174
Ben-Tal, Oded, 240
Berlyne, Daniel, 128, 129
Beyond the Fence (musical), 17, 275
Bezier curves, 167
Birckhoff, George, 120
Blackwell, Alan, 262
Blade Runner (movie), 3, 5
blind variation and selective retention (BVSR), 52, 53, 69, 75, 76, 91, 98
Bloom, Paul, 117, 152, 211, 277
  essentialism, 142–145
Boden, Margaret, 10, 48, 56, 57, 271
  Creative Mind, The, 54–55
Bødker, Susanne, 88, 216
Bolt, Barbara, 288

Born, Georgina, 96, 136, 211
Bourdieu, Pierre, 135–138, 141, 150, 153, 211
Boyd, Robert, 103
Bringsjord, Selmer, 63, 69, 90, 171
Briot, Jean-Pierre, 187, 191, 215–216, 232
Britton, Sam, 241
Brooks, Rodney,
Brooks, Rodney, "Elephants Don't Play Chess," 163
Brown, Paul, 17, 30, *165*, 168, 289
building design, 200, 250–251
Butler, Samuel, 43, 59

Cage, John, 19
Campbell. Donald, 52
Cardoso, Amilcar, 8
Casey, Michael, 235
casual creators, 30–31, 168
Cat-ART (system), 235
Clarke, John, 120
Clavia Nord Modular G2 synthesizer, 203, 220
Clever Hans, 4, 21, 189
client-producer model, 308–310
Clock, The (artwork), 238
co-creativity, human-computer, 246–249
coding, 292–293
Coe, Kathryn, 141, 150
Cohen, Harold, 10, 11, 12, 14, 17, 20, 29, 33, 43, 85, 96, 171, 176, 288, 289
Colton, Simon, 210, 277, 280–281
complexity theory, 59, 61, 100, 120, 128, 170, 172, 175
Compton, Kate, casual creators, 30–31, *31*, 168
computational creativity
  definition of, 325n
  lofty-versus-lowly, 236, 261, 263
  understanding of, 8–9

computational creativity, evaluation of, 269–280
  combined methods, 289–290
  by competition, 286–287
  by experts, 271
  FACE model, 280–281
  IDEA model, 281
  by output, 282–283
  plagiarism, 285–286
  by practice-based research, 288–289
  Ritchie's criteria, 283–285
computational creativity systems, 23, 38, 40, 67, 96, 158–159, 210, 215, 216, 233, 264, 269, 271, 275, 280, 282, 293, 298, 307. *See also* evolutionary computing; user interaction activities
  communication with, 292–294
  current usage, 237–249
  current usage for live performances, 257–263
  general requirements for, 291–292
  motivations for usage, 38–40
  nonexpert users, 310–311
  scheme for creation of (Gervás), 38
computational social science, 212
concatenative synthesis, 235
conceptual blending, 50, 159, 161, 162
conceptual spaces, 54–55, 56, 78, 131, 179, 181
Continuator (system), 20–23, 25, 258, 259
continuous-time recurrent neural network (CTRNN), 185, 207
Cope, David, 12–14, 17, 19, 29, 43, 85, 264, 266, 277, 285, 288, 289, 319
copyright. *See* intellectual property
Cosmides, Leda, 122
coupling, 260
Crawford, Kate, 317, 318
creative adversarial network (CAN), 190, *191*, 322
creative domains, 116, 150, 285
  future developments, 312–315
  social dynamics of, 151–154
  social manipulation, 315–318
creativity, 68–70. *See also* artistic creativity; generative creativity
  bisociation, 50
  candle problem, 51, 53
  and chance, 76–81
  dimensions, 47
  as group process, 9, 75–81
  history of meaning, 43–45
  investment theory, 53, 77
  novelty in, 47
  psychological research, 48–54
  and scientists, 49–50
  social models of, 211–213
  stages of creativity (Wallas), 49
  surprise in, 48
  Torrance test, 51–52
  understanding of, 45–47
  value in, 48
Cross, Ian, 145, 246
cross-domain synthesis, 187–188
Csikszentmihalyi, Mihaly, 73, 75, 77, 83, 85, 91, 128
  concept of flow, 53, 128
  Domain Individual Field Interaction (DIFI), 83–84
cultural capital, 135–137
cultural production, 45, 111, 136, 145, 298, 307
curiosity, 128, 129, 130, 179, 229, 256
cybernetics, 60, 221

Dahlstedt, Palle, 204, 220–221
DarwinTunes (system), 205, 227, 254
Dawkins, Richard, 104
Dennett, Dan, 217
Derman, Emanuel, 3
Di Scipio, Agostino, 174
Diamond, Jared, 46
Dissanayake, Ellen, 116
distributed creative systems, 74, 91, 96, 106, 145

Domain Individual Field Interaction
  (DIFI), 83–84
Double Oh (video artwork), 238
Dourish, Paul, 88
Draves, Scott, 18, 253
Driessens, Erwin, 31, 34, 173
Drott, Eric, 307
Durkheim, Emile, 59
Dutton, Denis, 114
Dyson George, *Darwin among the
  Machines*, 59

Ecrett Music, 305
Eden (artwork), 173, 175
Edmonds, Ernest, 17
Ehrlich, Stefan, 245
Eldridge, Alice, 290
Electric Sheep (system), 205, 227
Elgammal, Ahmed, 190, *191*, 286, 322
Eluvium (artist), *Shuffle Drones*, 6
emergence, 61, 100
Emmy (system), 13, 14, 17, 22, 285
Endel (system), 17
Eno, Brian, 6–7, 240
entrainment, 125
essentialism hypothesis, 143
Eugene Goostman (chatbot), 64–65, 67
evolutionary computing, 193. *See also*
  computational creativity systems
  current usage, 249–257
  distributed interactive genetic algorithms, 255
  fitness function, 194, 196–197, 202, 251
  genetic algorithm (GA), 82, 161, 193, 194, 203, 204, 220, 226, 227
  hybrid systems, 206–209
  interactive evolutionary algorithm, 202–204, 249, 252–253
  multiobjective search, 198–200, 206
  multiuser evolution, 233, 249, 255
  novelty search, 80, 162, 193, 200–202, 203, 206, 208, 212, 227, 249
  optimization, 196, 251
  particle swarm optimizers, 196
  target-based, 80, 194, 197, 198, 201, 204, 229, 237, 248, 251, 252, 309
  user interaction activities, 249
evolutionary psychology, 50, 122, 137
  cognitivist theories, 115–116
  cohesionist theories, 116–117
  competitivist theories, 117–118
  consequentialist theories, 115
  emergentist theories, 118
  of music, 130–131
evolutionary theory, 97–102, 116
  adaptationism, 122
  natural selection, 58, 194
  neural Darwinism, 130, 132
E-volver (artwork), 31–32, 33, *34–35*, 173
EvoSynth (system), 251
Ex Machina (movie), 74
exocept, 50

fast and slow thinking systems, 119, 131, 132, 145, 209, 210
Fauconnier, Gilles, 50
Ferriani, Gino, 149–151
Fiebrink, Rebecca, 229
FloWr framework, 243, 255
Fol Leymarie, Frederic, 20
Food Opera (artwork series), 243, *244*
Forth, Jamie, 131, 132, 160, 210
frequency bias, 103, 106, 182
Fuller, Buckminster, 269
function, 91–92, 323

Gabora, Liane, 174
Galanter, Philip, 28, 29, 237
Game of Life (system), 171, 172, 174
games, 18, 29, 168, 174, 178, 208, 235, 311, 312
Gamika (system), 238
Gärdenfors, Peter, 56, 181
Gaut, Berys, 322
Geertz, Clifford, 134

Index

Gell, Alfred, 74, 85, 96, 113
Gemeinböck, Petra, 229
generative adversarial network (GAN), 183–184, 190
generative art, 33
    definition of, 28
generative creativity, 68, 70, 92, 97
    and authorship, 240–243
    usage by artists, 237–240
generative systems, 28–36, 181–188
Gervás, Pablo, 38, 159, 210
Gibson, James, 93–94
Glaveanu, Vlad, 95–96
global workspace theory, 131
Gould, Stephen, 122
Grace, Kaz, 248
graphical user interface (GUI), 292
Guadamuz, Andreas, 308
Guernica (artwork), 210
GuitarBot (system), 262

Hacque, Usman, 221
Hargreaves, David, 138–140, 146
Harnad, Stevan, 3, 61, 273
Harrison, John, 81–82
Hebbian learning, 126
Hennion, Antoine, 136–137
Herndon, Holly, 18
Hertzmann, Aaron, 23
Hesse, Hermann, 43
Hiller, Lejaren, 17
Hirstein, William, 127
Hitchhiker's Guide to the Galaxy, A (book), 3
Hockney, David, 288
Hofstadter, Douglas, 14
Houge, Ben, 243, 244
human-computer interaction (HCI), 7, 88, 216, 289
Humberstone, James, 272
Huron, David, 130, 131, 143, 145, 209

Iamus (system), 17, 19, 67
Ianigro, Steffan, 202, 203, 207, 227
Icarus (band), 241–242
Illiac Suite (composition), 17
imagination-tension prediction-reaction-appraisal (ITPRA) model, 131
information compression, 129, 130, 211
Information Dynamics of Thinking (IDyOT), 132, 160, 192, 210
intellectual property, 240–243, 303, 306–309
interaction design (IxD), 7, 216
interactive evolutionary search, 249, 252–253
Issacson, Leonard, 17

J13 Records (label), 17
Jevons paradox, 299
Johansson, Roger, 198
John Henry Test (JHT), 272
Jordanous, Anna, 278–280

Kantosalo, Anna, 248
Kathrani, Paresh, 308
Kauffman, Stuart, 100
Kekulé, August, 49
Kelly, Kevin, *What Technology Wants*, 104
Kelly, Sean Dorrance, 321
Khosla, Vinod, 6
Klondike spaces, 77–78
Koestler, Arthur, 50
Kubrick, Stanley, 37
Kuhn, Thomas, 76
Kurzweil, Ray, 5–7, 10, 14, 59, 266, 299

Lamarck, Jean-Baptiste, 102–103
Landr (firm), 303–304
Landry, Charles, 81–82, 145
    The Creative City, 83
Latham, William, 17, 174
Latour, Bruno, 86–87, 89
Lehman, Joel, *80*, 201, 206, 252, 255

Lévi-Strauss, Claude, 126
Lewis, George, 12, 173, 288
LeWit, Sol, 157
Liapis, Antonios, 202
LIFT Architects (firm), *167*
Lomas, Andy, 222, 226
  3D morphologies, 31, *32*
Lovelace objection, 61, 62, 68, 87, 90, 171–172, 188, 193, 202
Lubart, Todd, 79, 221, 222
Luhmann, Lutz, 100, 118
Luxembourg folksong database, 188
Lyell, Charles, 99

machine learning (ML). *See also* neural networks
  autoencoders, 181–182, 184, 188, 190, 246, 248
  creative potential, 188–192
  embedding space, 179–181
  expert system, 12, 25, 164
  reinforcement learning, 25, 177, 208, 230, 265
  rule-based systems, 207
  supervised learning, 25, 175–178, 180, 186, 188, 208
  unsupervised learning, 25, 129, 180, 186, 208, 210
  variational autoencoders (VAEs), 246
  Word2Vec, 180–181
machine-as-artist, 263–266
machines as creative producers, 264, 277, 298. *See also* computational creativity
  future scenarios, 321–324
  history, 10–24, 58–67
  impact of, 40
  modeling human aesthetics, 211
  nature of, 20, 23–24
  problem of authenticity, 319–320
  public perception, 62–63
Magenta lab, 182, 224
Malafouris, Lambros, 87, 88, 90, 171

Marclay, Christian, 238
Markov modeling, *22*, 26, 184, 224
Martin, Aengus, 219–220
Martindale, Colin, 147, 151
  habituation theory, 146
Maturana, Humberto, 100
Maynard Smith, John, 100
McCann Japan (firm), TV commercials, 18
McCormack, Jon, 18, 174, 252, 253, 290, 307
  Eden (artwork), 173, 175
Mechanical Turk, 227
Melodyne (software), 235
meme, 93, 104
Mercedes-Benz, 30
mere generation, 36
Meredith, David, 39
Miikkulainen, Risto, 207
Mill, John Stuart, 269
Miller, Geoffrey, 117
Minsky, Marvin, 65, 276
MIT Media Lab, 30
Mital, Parag, 246
Mitrano, Peter, 206
modulation, 169
Monedero, Javier, 167–168
multicomponent cognitive models, 209
Mumford, Martin, 62
Murphy, Gregory, 45
musaicing, 251–252
MuseNet (system), 21, 23
music
  evolutionary psychology, 130–131
  live performance issues, 257–263
  social psychology of, 138–145
music, machine-generated
  early systems, 17
  in medicine, 245
  views on, 5–7
Musical Directive Toy Test (MDtT), 273
Musical Output Toy Test (MOtT), 273, 274, 275, 287

Index

Musicolor (system), 221
MutaSynth (system), 203, *204*, 220, 224

Nake, Freider, 17
Nancarrow, Conlon, 19
NASA, evolutionary designed radio antenna, 26, *27*, 193
network analysis, 149–151
Neukom Turing tests for the creative arts, 275, 286–287
neural networks, 26, 178–179, 185–186
 continuous-time recurrent neural network (CTRNN), 185, 207
 convolutional neural network (CNN), 179
 creative adversarial network (CAN), 190, *191*
 deep learning networks, 179
 generative adversarial network (GAN), 183–184, 190, 248
 NeuroEvolution of Augmenting Topologies (NEAT), 185, 207
 recurrent neural network (RNN), 184–185
NeuroEvolution of Augmenting Topologies (NEAT), 185, 207
Next Rembrandt (project), 18
niche construction, 98, 105, 106–107, 118, 119, 138, 153, 256, 303
No Man's Sky (computer game), 244
Norman, Donald, 94, 222
North, Adrian, 138–140, 146

Occam's razor, 115, 122
Omax (system), 259

Pachet, François, 17, 20, 22, 187, 215, 258, 259, 261
Painting Fool (system), 209, 265
pandemonium model, 119
parametric design, 166–170, *167*
parametric systems, 29–30
Pareto set, 200, 250

Pask, Gordon, 221
Pearce, Marcus, 39
Penny, Simon, 263
Perkins, David, Klondike spaces, 77–78
Petit Mal (artwork), 263
Picbreeder (system), 204, 227
Pickering, Andrew, 74, 85
PIERRE (system), 37–38
Pinker, Steven, 115, 117, 127, 144–145
plagiarism, 223, 285–286, 305. *See also* intellectual property
Plecto (system), 227
Poincaré, Henry, 49, 50
Post-it note, 81, 257
procedural content generation (PCG), 29, 33, 182
Processing (coding environment), 237
prosumer revolution, 313

Radford, Alec, 65
Ramachandran, Vilayanur, 60, 127
Rammert, Werner, 216
ratchet effect, 103, 104
recurrent neural network (RNN), 184–185
 long short-term memory (LSTM) network, 185
Reflexive Looper (system), 234
remix and mash-up, 238–239
Requena, Gloria, 245
Rhodes, Mel, 43, 47, 95
Richerson, Peter, 103, 106, 116, 142
Risi, Sebastian, 208
Ritchie, Graeme, 283–285
Rodley, Chris, 186, *187*

Salganik, Matthew, 141–142
Saunders, Rob, 210, 212, 213, 229
scale-free network, 174
Schaffer, Simon, 84
Schmidhuber, Juergen, 143
 information compression, 129–130
Schubert, Emery, 139–140
Schwartz, Diemo, 235

script (concept), 96
Secretan, Jimmy, 204
self-organization, 59, 61, 175
sequential learning, 184
Short, Emily, *Versu* (system), 174
Silver, Spencer, 81
Simonton, Dean, 48, 52, 53, 54, 69, 75–76, 77, 90, 181, 201, 210
Sims, Karl, 17, 193
Smith, Glenn W., 20
social issues of machine creativity, 313–324
social learning, 101–105, 145
 frequency bias, 106
Sony CSL, 234
SoundSpotter (software), 235
Sperber, Dan, 92–93
spirograph, 29–30, 169
STANDUP (system), 226
Stanford AI report, 299–300, 310
Stanley, Ken, 79, *80*, 201, 207, 252, 255
Star Trek (movie), 3
Steinbeck, John, 73
Sternberg, Robert, 53, 77, 79
Stokes, Patricia, hierarchy of constraints, 57–58
Stowell, Dan, 277–278
structuralism, 126
Sturm, Bob, 4, 21, 189, 240
style transfer, 186–190, *187*, 192, 198, 228, 236, 245–246
Szathmáry, Eörs, 100

teleofunction, 92–93, 98, 256
Thaler, Stephen, 19
 Creativity Machine, 17
theory of mind (ToM), 102
Thompson, D'Arcy, 73, 98
Tierra (artificial life model), 172
Tooby, John, 122
Turing, Alan, 60, 61, 62, 68, 87, 89
Turing test, 63–64, 67, 98, 271, 273–274, 276–278

Turner, Mark, 50
2001 (movie), 3

user experience (UX) design, 7, 15
user interaction activities, 218–231
 automating routine tasks, 233–237
 feeding source artifacts and data, 222, 228–229
 generating outputs, 222, 225–227
 manipulating algorithms, 222, 224–225
 manipulating outputs, 222, 230–231
 reviewing and analyzing outputs, 222, 227
 selecting algorithms, 222–223
 selecting and giving feedback on outputs, 222, 227–228
 selecting representations and data formats, 222, 223–224
 specifying goals and constraints, 222, 229–230
user interaction paradigms
 ambient interaction, 232
 operation-based interaction, 231–232
 request-based interaction, 232

Varela, Francisco, 100
variational autoencoders (VAEs), 246
Veale, Tony, 8
Vear, Craig, 290
Ventura, Dan, 37, 62, 63, 159–160, 188, 210
Verstappen, Maria, 31, 34, 173
Versu (system), 174
Viddyoze, 304
visual arts, machine-generated, early systems, 17–18
Vonnegut, Kurt, 297
Voss, Richard, 120
Voyager (system), 12, 22, 24, 25, 169, 173
Vrellis, Petros, 198, *199*, 252

Index

Wagstaff, Kiri, 249
Wallas, Graham, stages of creativity, 49
Walsh, Toby, 298
WaveNet (system), 182, 232
web pages, adaptive design, 253
Wekinator (system), 229
Whitby, Blay, 64
Whitelaw, Mitchell, 32, 173
Wiener, Norbert, 60
Wiggins, Gerraint, 8, 39, 45, 46, 57, 131, 132, 160, 192, 195
Williams, Raymond, 44
Woodbury, Robert, 168
Wundt curve, 128, 132, 149–150, 212

Xenakis, Iannis, 223

Yannakakis, Georgios, 202
Yee-King, Matt, 198
Yu, Guo, 262